DIY
ALL-IN-ONE
FOR
DUMMIES®
2ND EDITION

**by Roy Barnhart, James Carey, Morris Carey,
Gene Hamilton, Katie Hamilton,
Don R. Prestly and Jeff Strong**

Edited by Jeff Howell

A John Wiley and Sons, Ltd, Publication

DIY All-in-One For Dummies,® 2nd Edition

Published by
John Wiley & Sons, Ltd
The Atrium
Southern Gate
Chichester
West Sussex
PO19 8SQ
England

E-mail (for orders and customer service enquires): cs-books@wiley.co.uk

Visit our Home Page on www.wiley.com

For general information on our other products and services, please contact our Customer Care Department within the U.S. at 877-762-2974, outside the U.S. at 317-572-3993, or fax 317-572-4002.

For technical support, please visit www.wiley.com/techsupport.

Wiley also publishes its books in a variety of electronic formats. Some content that appears in print may not be available in electronic books.

British Library Cataloguing in Publication Data: A catalogue record for this book is available from the British Library

ISBN-13: 978-0-470-97450-6

Printed and bound in China by RR Donnelley

10 9 8 7 6 5 4 3 2 1

WILEY

About the Authors

Jeff Howell is a qualified bricklayer, university construction lecturer and chartered surveyor with more than 30 years' experience in the building industry. He writes about building and DIY for a variety of British newspapers, magazines and construction trade journals, and appears regularly as a guest expert on TV and radio. His website is www.ask-jeff.co.uk.

Roy Barnhart is a lifelong do-it-yourselfer and former professional building and remodelling contractor. He enjoyed eight years as Senior Building and Remodelling Editor for two national home improvement magazines in the USA. As a freelance writer, editor, and consultant, Roy has contributed articles to more than a dozen home improvement magazines, including *Family Handyman* and *House Beautiful*. He has also contributed to four books.

James and Morris Carey, known as the Carey Brothers, are experts on home building and renovation. They share their 20-plus years of experience as award-winning, licensed contractors with millions nationwide through a weekly radio programme in America, daily radio vignette, syndicated newspaper column, and comprehensive Web site (www.onthehouse.com), all titled 'On the House'. Morris and James continue to own and operate a successful home remodelling and construction firm, Carey Bros., and have been named to *Remodeling* magazine's Hall of Fame Big 50, which recognises top achievers in the industry. They've also been honoured as one of the nation's top 500 companies by *Qualified Remodeler* magazine.

Gene and Katie Hamilton have been working on houses and writing about home improvements for over 30 years. They've remodelled 14 houses and write a weekly newspaper column entitled "Do It Yourself . . . Or Not?" which appears in newspapers across America and on Web sites. The Hamiltons are authors of 16 home improvement books, including *Home Improvement For Dummies*, *Carpentry For Dummies*, *Painting and Wallpapering For Dummies*, and *Plumbing For Dummies*. They're the founders of www.HouseNet.com.

Don R. Prestly is a former senior editor for HANDY Magazine for The Handyman Club of America, as well as a former associate editor for *Family Handyman* magazine. In addition to his nearly 20 years of writing and doing home improvement projects, he spent several years as a manager for one of the Midwest's largest home centres.

Jeff Strong began creating sawdust at a very young age while helping his father, a master craftsman, build fine furniture. An accomplished woodworker, Jeff has designed and built countless pieces of furniture. He is the author of *Woodworking For Dummies*.

Publisher's Acknowledgments

We're proud of this book; please send us your comments through our Dummies online registration form located at www.dummies.com/register/.

Some of the people who helped bring this book to market include the following:

Commissioning, Editorial, and Media Development

Project Editor: Simon Bell

    (Previous Edition: Rachael Chilvers)

Commissioning Editor: Nicole Hermitage

    (Previous Edition: Alison Yates)

Assistant Editor: Ben Kemble

Copy Editor: Kate O'Leary

Proofreader: Sally Lansdell

Technical Editor: Andrew Leech

Publisher: David Palmer

Production Manager: Daniel Mersey

Cover Photos: © Robert Cocquyt

Cartoons: Ed McLachlan

Composition Services

Project Coordinator: Lynsey Stanford

Layout and Graphics: Carl Byers, Erin Zeltner

Indexer: Cheryl Duksta

Contents at a Glance

Table of Contents

Introduction

Welcome to DIY and Home Improvement All-in-One For Dummies, the only repair manual you'll ever need. One glance through this book and you quickly see that it's not overloaded with technical details and obscure advice that you'll never want or need to know. Our goal was to compile a book that explains, in a fun and easy-to-understand style, how to complete a wide range of projects. This anybody-can-do-it approach appeals to fledging do-it-yourselfers and seasoned handymen and -women. We encourage you to dust off your toolbox and tackle simple repairs and improvements using our idiot-proof instructions.

Basic steps and illustrations throughout the book walk you through the key points of maintaining and improving your home. These are tried-and-tested solutions to everyday home repair and improvement questions.

Foolish Assumptions

In this book, we make a few assumptions about who you are. We assume that you care about the appearance and condition of your home. We don't think that you're a home improvement fanatic or that you're a DIY expert – you don't need to be. All you need is this book, the right tools, and a desire to see your home be safe, functional, and attractive both inside and out.

How to Use This Book

You can use this book in two ways:

- If you want information about a specific topic, such as stopping cold draughts with weather-stripping or cleaning out gutters, skip to that section using the index or table of contents and get your answer pronto.

- If you want to be a home improvement guru, read the whole book from cover to cover. You'll end up knowing so much that Handy Andy will be calling you for advice.

How This Book Is Organised

This book is actually five books in one. The chapters within each of those books cover specific topics in detail. You can read each chapter or book without reading what came before, so you don't have to waste time reading what doesn't apply to your situation. Occasionally, we refer you to another area in the book where you find more details on a particular subject.

Book I: Planning Your Home Improvement Projects

Undertaking a home improvement project without planning is a recipe for disaster. This book walks you through the decision of whether to take on a task yourself or hire a professional, helps you gather the tools you need to do most home improvement projects, and gives you important tips for staying safe.

Book II: Basic Home Maintenance and Improvement

This book takes you through the various parts of a home, from the foundation to the roof, and tells you how to make common repairs. Included are chapters on window and door maintenance.

Book III: Painting and Wallpapering

A simple coat of paint or layer of wallpaper can have an amazing impact on how a home looks. This book helps you choose the best materials for your situation and get them up onto your walls like a pro. The chapters on painting cover both the interior and the exterior of a house.

Book IV: Carpentry, Woodworking, and Flooring

Working with wood really isn't too difficult, we promise. This book talks about the basics of carpentry and woodworking, from fixing pieces together to sanding and finishing wood projects. You'll find chapters covering the processes of repairing and installing new flooring.

Book V: Plumbing

Plumbing may be an area that you've always found a little bit intimidating – many homeowners do. But when you understand how everything fits together, plumbing repairs aren't any more difficult than other home maintenance projects. In this book, you find information about two major, vexing plumbing problems: Leaks and blockages. Before you call a plumber in a panic, check these chapters – you may be able to fix the problem yourself and save a packet.

Icons Used in This Book

We use the familiar For Dummies icons to help guide you through the material in this book.

Get on target with these great time-saving, money-saving, and sanity-saving tips.

Commit to memory these key titbits of information that come into play in various aspects of your home improvement adventures.

We don't want to scare you off, but DIY is not for the accident-prone. This icon alerts you to potential hazards and how to steer clear of them. We also use this symbol to mark advice for making your home a safer place.

Let this icon serve as a warning that you're treading in trouble-prone waters. Why should you have to learn from your own mistakes when you can learn just as well from others'?

Some projects and repairs require the skills, experience, and know-how that only a professional can offer. Novices and weekend DIYers take note. This icon reminds you not to bite off more than you can chew.

Most people want their toilets to flush, but some aren't happy until they know *how* the toilet flushes. This book doesn't bombard you with loads of technical trivia, but some background titbits can be useful. If you crave obscure details that most normal people don't care about, seek out these icons. If you'd rather live in ignorant bliss, by all means skip these little diversions.

Where to Go from Here

We don't care whether you start with the Table of Contents, the Index, Book V, or even Chapter 1 (what a novel idea). What's important is that you get going. A better home is just around the corner!

Book I
Planning Your Home Improvement Projects

"George installed the fridge, the freezer,
the washing machine, the cooker, the hob
oven, the built-in oven, the dishwasher,
and I installed the chef."

In this book . . .

*W*here do you start? Can you do it yourself? What materials, tools, and knowledge do you need? How much will it cost, and how do you keep from going mad in the process? Dig into these chapters that frame answers to these knotty questions.

Collecting basic household tools and the right stuff for specific jobs doesn't have to be a struggle. Venturing into the local hardware store or home improvement centre need not be a struggle – although with the size of today's DIY superstores, you may need to pack a picnic.

Whether you want to estimate the time and cost involved in a job, or check out the possibility of adding more hands-on adventures to your to-do list, you can build comfort and confidence with a cruise through this book.

Here are the contents of Book I at a glance.

Chapter 1

Gearing Up for Your DIY Adventures

*Y*ou can expect to save at least 20 per cent and sometimes 100 per cent of the cost of any job by doing the work yourself. What's more, you can enjoy the sense of pride and accomplishment that comes with a job well done. That said, you must remember that most people are hard-pressed for time and energy, and some projects require special skills and tools that you may not possess.

We're not suggesting that you tackle really advanced jobs. But countless other projects, such as removing wallpaper or sanding wood, require little in the way of tools and talent. By beginning with unglamorous repairs, such as fixing a broken window catch or tightening a loose hinge, you can quickly build your do-it-yourself skills and confidence.

Just how do you know your limitations? That's the $64,000 question. We know that a handy homeowner can do an awful lot, but when it comes to massive projects, such as replacing all the walls in a house or building a large extension, you have other factors to consider such as your time and your money. This chapter is all about weighing up the pros and cons of doing it yourself versus getting in the professionals.

Taking Everything into Account

Three factors go into the decisions of whether and how to do a job yourself: time, money, and skills. If you have plenty of time, you can tackle almost any project, using only some basic tools and gaining the skills you need as you go. If you have lots of dosh, you can purchase plenty of timesaving tools and gear, or even hire someone else to do the job for you. And if you already have a treasure trove of home improvement skills, you can do the job yourself quickly and for a moderate cost.

But for most mere mortals, the question of to do or not to do the work all by yourself involves finding a balance of all three factors and then doing some soul-searching for a reasonable response.

Calculating the cost

First up, consider the cost of materials. Don't become another statistic of the do-it-yourself damage factor. If the materials are expensive, you're taking a big risk by doing the job yourself. If, for example, you're laying $40-a-metre wool carpet, you're gambling with expensive dice. Make one miscut, and you suddenly find yourself in the carpet remnant business. You have to replace the damaged material, and you'll probably end up calling in a carpet fitter to finish the job after all. Not much saving; plus, you wasted time in the process.

If you're considering a project and want to get a rough idea of the labour costs involved, go to a DIY centre and ask whether an installation service is available. Many DIY shops farm the work out to contractors. These stores often display materials, such as doors, windows, and kitchen units, with two costs: A do-it-yourself price and an installed price. The difference between the two figures is the cost of the labour.

Don't forget the other part of the equation – the cost of tools that you may need. Look at tools as a long-term investment: If you're a budding do-it-your-selfer, you want to add to your stash so that you have a complete workshop that can last a lifetime. However, if a project requires an expensive tool that you may only need once in your life, consider other options, such as hiring or borrowing. See 'Totting Up the Top Tools' later in this chapter.

Tallying the time

Time is a real consideration when you're deciding whether to tackle home repairs and improvements yourself. Estimating the time to complete a job isn't an exact science. Write down the processes involved in a job in step-by-step fashion, and include the shopping time, working time, and clean-up time. Translate the work into numbers of hours . . . and then triple it. The result that you get is liable to be pretty close.

Many novice do-it-yourselfers make the tragic mistake of underestimating the time commitment and then box themselves into an unrealistic deadline, such as painting the living room before Christmas or building a patio for the Bank Holiday family reunion – both noble ideas, but they warrant considerably more time than initially imagined. The work usually takes much longer than you antici-pate. Setting an inflexible deadline only adds more pressure to the project.

Scrutinising your skills

Now for a touchy subject: Recognising your talent. This topic is sensitive because some people are born naturally handy; others are mechanically challenged.

Remember that practice makes perfect. You may not have been born with a hammer in your hand, but you can develop the skills of a confident do-it-yourselfer and go on to hone the skills of a handy homeowner. It's true; as you get older, you get better. After you figure out how to install a dimmer switch, it's like riding a bicycle; you never forget.

Even if you aren't a do-it-yourselfer and you have no desire to become one, you can participate in projects and save money by doing the donkey work. We're talking about simple jobs, such as removing wallpaper, ripping up old floors, scraping paint, and many other tasks that require more time and enthusiasm than talent.

Hiring Help the Smart Way

If a project is simple, such as repairing a faulty boiler, the plan is pretty straightforward. Get a couple of estimates and compare them, making sure to specify the full scope of the job and the quality of materials.

This advice becomes dicey when the project is more complex – say, bath-room refurbishing that involves moving a wall, replacing the fixtures and floor – all subject to surprises, hidden costs, and unexpected complications. Professionals have difficulty quoting for a job without knowing what they may find when the wall comes down or the old floor comes up. An accurate quote is based on complete and accurate information and the cost of fix-tures, which can range from low-end to luxury. As a consumer, you have to spell out exact styles, models, and colours for a precise estimate.

Finding a good builder

Shop 'til you drop . . . for the right builder, that is. Spend as much time choosing a builder as you do choosing a doctor. Start in your local neighbourhood and ask friends and acquaintances for recommendations. The Yellow Pages lists builders, but builders rely on their reputations for new customers.

Check out the builders' vans that you see working in your neighbourhood; the most familiar one probably has good repeat business there. Call in on the neighbour having work done (go on, you can be bold!) and explain that you're looking for a builder. Is your neighbour pleased with the builder's work?

This screening process is the best way that we know to find competent builders – it's direct, immediate, and tells you what you want to know from a reliable source: Another homeowner just like you.

Know what you want before talking to a builder. No, you don't have to know the serial number of the new mixer tap, but you do need to have an idea of the type, style, and features you want. First of all, a contractor can't quote for a job without knowing what you expect to have installed, repaired, or built. Second, the only accurate way to compare quotes from different contractors is to be sure that the work is based on the same specifications.

Some people may tell you to get three quotes from different contractors and choose the middle one – easier said than done. If you do your homework and are satisfied with the references and professional manner of a builder, you may be hard-pressed or time-restricted to dig up two more. The bottom line is to use your best judgement and common sense, and don't let a schedule force you into making a decision. If you interview a builder and are thrilled with what you find, don't baulk at having to wait until he or she is available. Never rush a job and settle for someone you're not completely satisfied with. After all, you only build an extension or refurbish your kitchen once – that is, if you get the job done right the first time.

When you meet with a builder, ask for customer references of work similar to your project, and then check them out. This task takes time, but you can benefit greatly by listening to someone with firsthand experience. Many people consult Trade Associations as a resource or contact a local council for a list of referrals. Even if you find a builder through one of these sources, you should still ask the builder for a list of satisfied customers in your area whom you can call for recommendations.

Covering all your bases

After narrowing your search for the perfect builder, you're ready to get down to business. At this point, it's critical to get everything in writing:

- **Liability:** Ask for a certificate of insurance and make sure that the contractor is insured to cover any injuries that may occur on the job. Reputable builders carry employer's liability insurance and public liability insurance that covers them in the event of third-party injury or property damage. Checking out a builder's insurance is very important, because you may be held liable if the builder or one of his workers is injured while working on your home. You may also be held liable if the builder or one of his employees injures someone else.

  Tell your insurer about the nature of the proposed work, as it will probably increase the value of your property, and you don't want to end up under-insured in the event of making a claim. Take into consideration the increased security risks while the building work is taking place (such as scaffolding against your house, and temporary door and window openings to tempt burglars) – your insurers are unlikely to raise your premiums for this, but you could experience problems if you make a claim and you hadn't told them about the work.

- **Contract:** A complete contract includes a detailed description of the project with a listing of specific materials and products to be used. For a job that involves various stages of completion, a payment schedule itemises when money is to be paid. A procedure for handling any disputes between you and the contractor is also important, along with directions for handling changes in plan due to an unforeseen need for additional work or materials.

  If the project involves removing debris or if it's intrinsically messy (plastering, for example), make sure that the contract has a clean-up clause that clearly defines the builder's responsibility to leave the work site clean and tidy. Also make sure that the contract spells out who's expected to apply and pay for planning permission and building control approval and what's necessary to meet those requirements (see below).

- **Warranty:** If the contractor offers a warranty, make sure that the provisions include the name and address of the person or institution offering the warranty and the duration of the coverage. A full warranty covers the repair or replacement of the product or a refund of your money within a certain period. If the warranty is limited, find out what those limitations are.

- **Planning permission:** Planning rules govern the overall development of land and buildings in an area. They are used to determine such things as density of population, position of buildings in relation to roads and other amenities, and the visual appearance of homes and neighbourhoods. Planning rules are not concerned with how the building work is done (Building Control decides that), but with how it may change the look of the house or the whole neighbourhood. Repairs, maintenance, refurbishment, and most other building work on existing homes do not need planning permission unless your home is a listed building or in a conservation area.

- **Building Control:** The local council Building Control department is responsible for making sure that work conforms with the Building Regulations. Building Regulations apply to all new construction work, including permitted developments, and cover such things as fire safety, structural stability, ventilation, drainage, thermal insulation, and electrical safety. You should check with your Building Control department whether your proposed work needs approval. If it does, then either you or your builder has to pay a fee to have the progress of the work inspected and approved, either by the local authority, or by a licensed private Building Inspector. Don't be afraid of this – these inspections are your best assurance that the work is done correctly, or at least meets minimum Government standards.

Special rules for special buildings

A *listed* building is a building placed on a special list by English Heritage (a Government body) because of its architectural or historical importance. The UK has nearly half a million listed buildings, and whilst castles and palaces are obvious candidates, some fairly ordinary-looking houses can find their way onto the list as well. Grade I is the top listing, and it means you can't change anything, inside or out, without listed building consent. Grade II* is the second listing. Ordinary houses are more likely to be Grade II listed, which just covers the outside.

It is not impossible to make alterations to listed buildings, but any changes have to be in character, and approved first (English Heritage 020 7973 3000, `www.english-heritage.org.uk`).

Conservation areas are historic areas – usually old town centres or medieval villages – where the whole area is protected from unfavourable development. This includes not just the houses, but the streets, trees, gardens, and phone boxes as well. Decisions over any proposed changes are made by the Conservation Department of the local council. If you live in a conservation area, then rejoice – it means your house is worth more than those in surrounding areas, and your neighbours can never bring down the neighbourhood by fitting replacement plastic windows.

Gearing Up for DIY Adventures

Can you expect to create miracles without a magic wand? Of course you can't. And by the same token, you can't expect to do projects around the house without reliable tools.

If you think of every tool you buy as a long-term investment, you'll gradually acquire a reliable stash that can get you through most home repairs and improvements. In this chapter, we walk you through the basic tools that are essential to any toolbox, but we can't resist also tempting you with some of our favourite gadgets and gizmos designed to delight any do-it-yourselfer.

Most people are hard-pressed to find space for a workshop but at a bare minimum, find room for a workbench somewhere in your house, garage, cellar, or shed. Designate this space as a work area, where you can take a door lock apart or stir a tin of paint, lay out a window frame that needs repairing, or stow your tool kit and rechargeable power tools (and read the paper with no interruptions). Your workspace doesn't have to be fancy; anywhere with good lighting and electrical power will do. Lay a length of kitchen worktop across two sawhorses or, if space is at a premium, get a portable bench that you can fold up and store out of the way.

Totting Up the Top Tools

Shop for the tools you need in builders' merchants, hardware shops, or any large DIY warehouse. Don't try to buy all the tools that you'll ever need at one time; instead, buy tools as you need them. Focus on quality rather than quantity and buy the best-quality tool you can afford.

So here it is, our list of the basic tools you need to get on the road to home improvement adventures:

- **13 mm variable-speed reversible drill:** This tool, available as a plug-in or cordless, uses steel blades called bits to drive in or remove screws, drill holes, mix piña coladas, and do other important home improvement tasks. See Figure 1-1.

- **Claw hammer:** We recommend a 16-ounce hammer with a fibreglass handle to cushion the blow to your hand. Watch out for carpal tunnel syndrome, an injury that can occur from repetitive motions, such as constantly hitting your thumb and then hopping around the room.

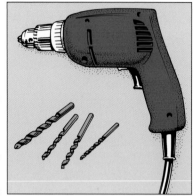

Figure 1-1:
An electric drill with a variety of bits.

- **Pliers:** Vice-grip pliers, or *mole grips*, have toothed jaws that enable you to grip various-sized objects, such as a water pipe, the stuck-on top of a container of PVA adhesive, or the tape measure that you accidentally dropped into the toilet. Because the jaws are adjustable, pliers give you leverage to open and firmly grip an object.

- **Tenon saw:** A small, easy-to-use handsaw is useful for cutting such materials as panelling or shelving.

- **Assorted pack of screwdrivers:** Be sure that you have both slotted (flat-head) and Phillips and Posidrive (cross-head) screwdrivers in a variety of sizes. The slotted type has a straight, flat blade; the cross-head blade has a cross or plus-sign that fits into the grooves of Phillips-head or Posidrive screws.

- **Trimming knife:** Also called a *Stanley knife* or *craft knife.* Choose a compact knife with replaceable blades that's strong enough to open heavy cardboard boxes and precise enough for trimming wallpaper.

  Buy the type with a retractable blade; you'll appreciate it the first time that you squat down with the knife in your pocket. (Ouch!)

- **Staple gun:** You can use this tool for a variety of jobs, like securing insulation, carpet underlay, plastic sheeting, and fabrics.

- **Spirit level:** A straightedge tool that has a series of glass tubes containing liquid with a bubble of air. When the bubble in a single tube is framed between marks on the glass, it shows that the surface is level (horizontal) or plumb (vertical). See Figure 1-2.

- **Metal file:** Filing tools, such as those shown in Figure 1-3, are flat metal bars with shallow grooves that form teeth. Metal files are useful for sharpening the edges of scrapers, putty knives, and even shovels and garden trowels.

Figure 1-2:
A standard spirit level for finding level and plumb lines.

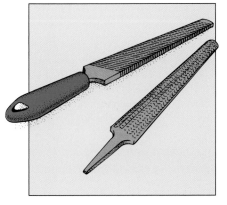

Figure 1-3:
Metal files are good for more than breaking out of prison.

✒ **Allen keys:** These L-shaped metal bars, often sold in sets (see Figure 1-4), are designed for turning screws or bolts that have hexagonal sockets in their heads. This tool also goes by the name *hex-key wrench*. Used to assemble everything from flat-pack furniture to bicycles, this tool was invented by a man named, umm, let's see . . . we'll have to get back to you on that one.

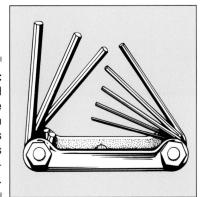

Figure 1-4:
Flat-packed furniture often requires Allen keys for assembly.

Gizmos and Gear

Tools alone don't lead to a life of joyful home improvements. You gotta have gadgets, too. Some really great gadgets are available to keep you organised, efficient, safe, and comfortable:

- **Teeny-tiny pocket notebook:** Keep a reference of your home improvement needs in your car or pocket and refer to it when you shop. Instead of jotting down notes on scraps of paper that you're more likely to lose than use, keep all this stuff in one place. Buying a new table? Jot down the dimensions of the old one. Need new vacuum bags? Make a note of the model number of your vacuum cleaner. Keep a record of paint colours and wallpaper patterns and a zillion other details in this little notebook.

- **Tool kit:** Keep a stash of the tools that you reach for most often in some kind of portable toolbox or crate. Be sure to include a stock of string, a pair of scissors, tough protective gloves, a tape measure, a torch, and other common household accessories. Many DIY jobs must be done on site, so having a tool kit that you can take with you to the project is invaluable.

- **Kneepads:** Cushioned rubber pads, held in place with elastic straps, protect your knee joints when you're crawling around on hard, debris-strewn surfaces.

- **Goggles or safety specs:** Wear goggles or safety specs when you're chipping away at loose brick or plaster, or anything that could make a rather nasty dent in your eye.

- **Dust mask:** Use a dust mask when you're sanding wood or plaster, or laying mineral wool insulation, to protect yourself from breathing in the particles.

- **Neon circuit tester:** Also known as a *mains-test screwdriver*, this cheap-as-chips item, pictured in Figure 1-5, can be a lifesaver whenever you have to work on an electrical switch, socket, or power source. Before you begin tinkering with a device, use this circuit tester to make sure that power isn't flowing to it.

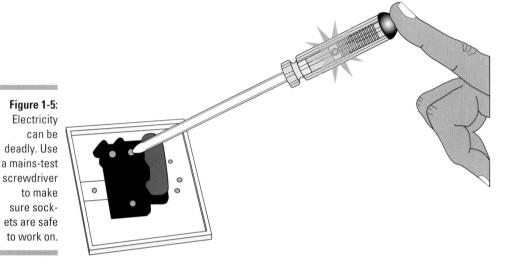

Figure 1-5: Electricity can be deadly. Use a mains-test screwdriver to make sure sock- ets are safe to work on.

 **Wire brush:** This item, shown in Figure 1-6, looks like a lethal tooth- brush. It's useful for scraping blistered paint, removing rust from metal, and taking corrosion off spark plugs.

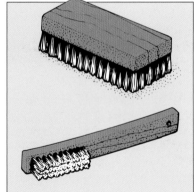

Figure 1-6: Wire brushes are particularly useful for removing rust.

✔ **Stud finder:** No, this tool isn't for finding hunky blokes (unless they're trapped in your walls). Wall studs are the vertical wood framing to which plasterboard is fastened. A stud finder, shown in Figure 1-7, is an electronic device that locates the studs behind finished walls, which enables you to find a sturdy place to hang pictures, mirrors, and shelves. Get a stud finder that also doubles as a pipe and cable detector.

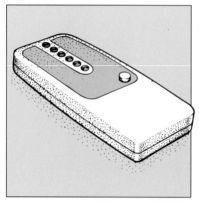

Figure 1-7:
Use a stud finder to avoid hanging heavy items over hollow plasterboard.

✔ **Ladders:** Get a stepladder for household chores, such as changing light bulbs and painting rooms; and get a taller self-supporting or extension-type ladder for outdoor maintenance like cleaning gutters and trimming trees. In general, aluminium ladders are lightweight and strong; wooden ladders are solid, heavy, and economical; and fibreglass ladders are strong, electrically nonconductive, and expensive. If you can afford it, fibreglass is the best choice.

Every ladder is given a *duty rating* – its maximum safe-load capacity. This weight includes you plus the weight of any tools and materials you wear and haul up the ladder with you.

Tools: To Buy or To Hire?

The top UK tool hire shop is HSS Hire, which has over 400 branches stocking over 2,000 tools. Get a copy of their free catalogue (08457 282828, www.hss. com), and you can compare the hire costs with tool purchase costs, enabling you to make an informed decision. Weekend hire rates are cheaper than mid-week, which is useful for home-improvers, and HSS can deliver bulky tools and equipment to wherever you need them.

Chapter 2

Being Safe and Prepared

*I*n this chapter, we offer time-honoured, proven safety practices blended with a host of new innovations, contemporary concepts, and the very best of today's high-tech electronic wizardry. When used all together, these measures ensure greater peace of mind for homeowners.

Practising Fire Safety

Fire has been a number one household danger ever since the day, many eons ago, when our prehistoric ancestors got the idea of bringing fire indoors for cave heating and dinosaur cooking.

The following points are worth noting with regard to residential fires:

✔ Careless smoking is the leading cause of residential fire deaths.

✔ Children playing with fire cause 25 per cent of fires with child fatalities.

✔ Household fire hazards include overloaded electrical circuits, faulty wiring, unsafe appliances, wood- and coal-burning stoves and boilers, electric and paraffin space heaters, unattended fireplaces, and the careless use of candles, lighters, and matches, especially by children.

Common sense can prevent fires

So what's your best defence against this household killer? Good old common sense:

- Exercise great care with all flammable materials, including fabrics (like curtains and furniture) near heat sources (like stoves, heaters, and open fireplaces) and especially combustible liquids (like solvents, cleaners, and fuels) – when both using and storing them.

- Don't overload electrical circuits or put too great a burden on individual sockets or lightweight extension cords. Overloading causes overheating, which leads to wire fatigue and a possible fire. Dimming or flickering lights, a power cord that's warm or hot to the touch, fuses that repeatedly burn out, and circuit breakers in the consumer unit that frequently trip are sure signs of an overloaded circuit.

- Don't use bulbs with a higher wattage than a lamp or fixture is rated for because the lamp can seriously overheat. Most modern light fixtures and lamps have a label on the fixture that rates the maximum recommended bulb wattage for that fixture. If you can't find the label, bring the lamp or information on the fixture to a lighting shop for recommendations on the wattage of bulb that you should use.

- Watch for faulty electronic equipment, malfunctioning appliances, frayed electrical cords, flickering lights, or fuses that blow and circuit breakers that trip repeatedly – they're all potential fire hazards.

- Never smoke in bed – or when you're tired or lying down.

- Never leave burning candles unattended.

- Make sure that any ashes have cooled before you throw them away. The careless dumping of ashes that are not fully extinguished starts many fires. This includes ashes from ashtrays, fireplaces, and barbeques. Hot embers can smoulder undetected in the bin for hours before igniting.

- Keep heaters at least a metre (3 feet) away from flammable items. Only buy portable units with tip-over shut-off switches and never have a heater on while you're asleep.

Smoke alarms: Gotta have 'em

A smoke alarm is considered to be one of the least expensive and best forms of life protection insurance you can buy. A working smoke detector doubles your chance of surviving a fire by warning you of a dangerous situation before it's too late.

Dealing with fire emergencies

After a smoke detector sounds a quick response and preplanned actions are your two best lifesavers.

Before opening any doors, look for smoke seeping around edges and feel the surface with your hand. The doorknob is another reliable indicator as to whether fire exists on the other side because metal conducts heat faster and more efficiently than wood does.

If it feels safe, open the door slowly and be prepared to close it quickly if heat and smoke rush in. Don't stop to get dressed, find pets, or collect valuables. Wasted seconds can cost lives. Shout loudly to alert as many people as possible to the fire. Gather your family members and exit immediately. If smoke is extremely dense, crawl on your knees and keep your mouth covered

with a towel or cloth, if possible. Once outside, use a mobile, neighbour's phone, or public phone box to call 999 for the fire brigade.

Families should develop and rehearse a home escape plan, with two ways out of every room. Store a fold-up fire escape ladder in every upstairs bedroom. Also include plans for a designated meeting place where everyone should gather once safely outside. After you're out, stay put until help arrives and never re-enter the house under any circumstances.

Rehearse your family escape plan regularly. After everyone knows what to do, perform run-throughs with your eyes closed – simulating darkness or smoke-filled passages – counting and memorising the number of steps to each and every turn and ultimately to safety.

For minimum coverage, have at least one smoke detector or alarm on every level of your home and in every sleeping area. You can also add alarms to hallways outside every bedroom, the top and bottom of all stairways, and often-forgotten places such as cellars, lofts, utility rooms, and garages.

Smoke detectors can be either

- **Battery-operated:** These inexpensive units can easily be installed anywhere. They require frequent inspection to determine the condition of the battery.

- **Mains-powered:** Installed by a qualified electrician, these units are much more dependable over the long term due to their direct-wired power source. But they should have an independent battery back-up so that they continue to operate during a blackout or an electrical fire that temporarily interrupts power.

Most smoke alarms have a hush-button feature that silences a nuisance false alarm and desensitises the unit for a few minutes until the air clears, when it resets itself.

PASSing on a fire

If you ever need to use a fire extinguisher, use the PASS method:

🖝 **P**ull the pin.

🖝 **A**im at the base of the fire.

🖝 **S**queeze the handle.

🖝 **S**weep the base of the fire from side to side, starting with the closest edge and working away from yourself.

Testing alarms and detectors

All smoke detectors and alarms have a test button that, when pushed, causes the alarm to sound. Also, most detectors have either a blinking or a solid light that glows to let you know that the alarm is getting power.

Once a month, get up on a chair or use a broom handle for extra reach and push the test button. If you don't hear anything, then your battery is dead. If after changing the battery, the smoke detector is still not working, immediately replace it with a new alarm, which you can buy from a hardware or DIY shop. Some battery-operated units have a built-in device that chirps when batteries get low, signalling the need for replacement.

The button test ensures that the batteries are working. However, it doesn't tell you whether the detector is operating properly. To find out, put two or three lighted matches together and then blow out the flame, holding the matches so that the smoke wafts up towards the unit.

Never remove a battery from your smoke alarm for use in another item, such as a radio, toy, or TV remote – it's too easy to forget to replace it!

While you're up checking your battery every month, also brush or vacuum the alarm to keep dirt and dust out of the mechanism. Never use cleaning sprays or solvents that can enter the unit and contaminate sensors.

Replacing alarms and detectors

After a period of ten years, a smoke detector has endured more than 87,000 hours of continuous operation, during which time the internal sensors have probably become contaminated with dust, dirt, and air pollutant residues. If your alarm or detector is more than ten years old, consider replacing it to maintain optimal detection capabilities of deadly smoke in your home.

Fire extinguishers

Most fires start out small. Often, you can put them out easily and quickly if you have a working fire extinguisher readily at hand. Manufacturers of home safety products recommend having one fire extinguisher for every 600 square feet of living area. The kitchen, garage, and cellar should each have an extinguisher of their own. Keep one in your car, as well.

Fire extinguishers are rated according to force and how much firefighting agent they contain – both of which determine how long the extinguisher operates when it's used and discharged. With most home extinguishers, the duration is short – so quick action and good aim are important factors in quenching flames while a fire is still in its early stage. (See the sidebar 'PASSing on a fire' for tips on using fire extinguishers.)

Always purchase fire extinguishers with pressure gauges. Check the pressure gauge at least once each month to ensure that it's ready for use at all times. If the fire extinguisher pressure is low and the model can't be recharged, dispose of it and replace it with a new unit.

Under no circumstances should you test the extinguisher by pulling the pin and squeezing the trigger – doing so can result in premature loss of pressure.

Fire blankets are recommended in kitchens for cooker fires – if your chip pan is burning, it's much safer to drape a fire blanket over the top of it than to blast the burning oil with a fire extinguisher!

Preventing Carbon Monoxide Danger in the Home

In concentrated form, carbon monoxide (CO) can be fatal when inhaled – killing in minutes or hours, depending on the level of CO in the air. In smaller doses, CO produces a wide range of flu-like symptoms ranging from red eyes, dizziness, and headaches to nausea, fatigue, and upset stomach. One telltale sign of mild CO poisoning is flu symptoms without a fever.

CO is an invisible, odourless, poisonous gas produced by the incomplete combustion of fuel – such as petrol, paraffin, propane, natural gas, oil, and even wood fires.

Typical sources of CO in homes are malfunctioning gas boilers, gas stoves, clothes dryers, and improperly vented fireplaces (especially gas fires vented into redundant chimney flues). Letting a car run in a garage means that exhaust fumes can collect and enter the home.

You can buy CO detectors and combination CO and smoke detectors for the home from DIY stores. As with smoke alarms, CO detectors can be battery operated, or mains powered. Units that plug into a direct power source should have an independent battery back-up in case of a power failure. Place CO detectors from 350 mm off the floor to face height on the wall and never near a draught, such as a window, doorway, or stairwell.

If you have only one unit, place it in the hall outside the bedroom area of your home. Invisible CO in concentrated form is even less likely to awaken a sleeper than thick toxic smoke.

Your CO detector should have a digital display with memory that indicates and records a problem, even when it's too small to trigger the alarm. A normal low level of CO in a home is zero. However, even a small reading – such as 25, 30, or 35 parts per million – indicates a problem that could escalate. If a higher level of CO is recorded, then immediately turn off the appliance that seems to be causing the problem, and call in a qualified heating engineer to investigate. The care and maintenance of CO detectors is basically the same as for smoke alarms. (See the 'Smoke alarms' section earlier in this chapter for more information.) Unlike using kitchen matches to test a smoke alarm, you can't test a carbon monoxide detector using an outside source – it's imperative that you test the test buttons provided on the equipment at least once each month.

Have your heating system, vents, chimney, and flue inspected (and cleaned if necessary) by a qualified person. Always vent fuel-burning appliances.

Other important maintenance procedures include checking and correcting any signs that indicate potential CO problems, such as

- A noticeably decreasing hot water supply
- A boiler that runs constantly but doesn't heat your house
- Soot collecting on, under, and around any appliance
- An unfamiliar burning odour
- Damaged brick, chimney discoloration, or a loose-fitting flue pipe

Protecting Your Home from Intruders

Fifty per cent of all home burglaries are due to windows or doors being left unlocked. Have properly installed, solid, and secure window and door locks strong enough to deter the average burglar.

One of the best ways to determine whether your home is secure from potential intruders is to imagine locking yourself out. Can you get in without using your house key? Be on the lookout for loose doorknobs and deadlocks, and shaky windows and doors (including the garage door).

Many break-ins can be averted. A number of whole-house alarm systems are available today, and – just as with smoke alarms and carbon monoxide detectors – they need occasional testing, checking, and tuning up. Most systems include a failsafe battery back-up, which you need to check and replace at regular intervals – at least twice annually. Many systems also have a fire-sensing capability that you must check and maintain as outlined in the 'Smoke alarms' section earlier in this chapter.

Most systems have a keypad for indicating system operation and points of intrusion, and a horn or siren installed indoors (in the loft) or outside under an overhang or eave. Follow the manufacturer's instructions for maintaining and checking these features at specified intervals – pay particular attention to all points that signal an intrusion when contact is broken.

Make sure that sensitivity levels are properly set to avoid both frequent false alarms (that eventually go unheeded) and a system that doesn't respond properly when it should.

Before ordering and installing an alarm, check with police to see if any restrictions or special conditions apply to alarms in your area. Most police forces discourage homeowners from installing a dialler-type alarm system that automatically calls the police when activated. A good alternative is to have your alarm monitored by a central reporting agency. Thus, if a false alarm occurs, the police won't be summoned, and you'll be off the hook for a false alarm fee and the embarrassment of having the police show up at your home only to find you in your dressing gown collecting the morning paper.

Maintaining Electrical Safety

Leave most electrical work to a qualified electrician. Call an electrician when you see any of the following signs:

- Habitually flickering lights
- A circuit breaker that repeatedly trips
- A fuse that repeatedly burns out

Any of these signs can mean a loose connection or a circuit that's overloaded, which can cause a house fire.

Testing Residual Current Circuit Breakers

A Residual Current Circuit Breaker (RCCB), more commonly known as a *Residual Current Device* (RCD), helps keep people from getting electric shocks when sorting out electrical problems. The easiest way to think of an RCD is to remember that a normal circuit breaker protects property, while an RCD protects people.

When an electrical fault occurs, the RCD detects that some of the current is going where it's not supposed to go and is creating a shock hazard. When this occurs, the RCD *trips*, preventing the flow of electricity, and offering protection against electric shocks in one-fortieth of a second – a short enough period that most healthy people aren't injured.

All RCD sockets have test buttons. Test each RCD socket in your home at least once a month. If the test doesn't trip the breaker, replace the RCD immediately, or get a qualified electrician to replace it for you.

Modern consumer units have an integral RCD which protects all the power circuits wired through it. To prevent *nuisance tripping* whenever a light bulb blows, the light circuits don't go through the RCD. Some people also make sure their deep freezers are on a non-protected circuit, so as not to lose a freezer-full of food should they be away from home when the RCD trips.

Due to the rising number of deaths from badly fitted electrical equipment, Part P of the building regulations now restricts what DIYers can and can't do with electrical wiring. If in doubt, hire a qualified electrician to do the work for you.

Chapter 3

Working with (And within) a Budget

*E*very home improvement project requires a budget. Whether you're painting a bedroom or gutting and remodelling a kitchen, you need to look at your current finances and make sure that you have enough money (or a way to get enough money) to pay for everything. Home improvement budgets can range from a few hundred pounds to tens of thousands, depending on the size and scope of the project. This chapter shows you how to establish a realistic budget that gives you a good shot at getting everything you want.

Establishing the Scope of the Project

Think about how the room can better meet your family's needs and life-style. Check out other homes (family's, friends', neighbours', and so on) for touches that work for them and may work for you, too. Scour decorating magazines to get your creative juices flowing. Use Table 3-1 to jot down your ideas.

Table 3-1	Determining What You Like and Don't Like
What Works in the Room I Plan to Remodel	**What Needs to Be Changed in the Room**

Don't forget to list the existing things in your home that do work and things you want to retain in the room. In most cases, you don't need to totally gut the area. Yes, you may make major changes, but you probably don't need to tear everything back to the wall studs.

After you make your lists, prioritise the items from most to least important, which will help you in the decision-making process. You may not get everything you want, but make sure to include everything you need.

Even if you have the skills to do a remodelling job yourself, you may not have the time. Your time is valuable not only to you but also to your family and friends. If the project's going to tie you up every weekend during the summer, but you could hire a professional to complete the job in, say, a couple of weeks, doing it yourself may not be worth it.

Looking at Things Room by Room

Remodelling projects take many forms, depending on which room is being made over. The following list looks at the rooms in a typical house, one by one, and shows you what you need to cover when assessing the situation for a remodel.

- **Living room:** Call it a living room, a front room, or a lounge – it's an important part of your home. You need to analyse a couple of critical things within this room's area for a remodel:

  - Does the existing floor plan work? The original architect had a specific layout in mind when designing the room, especially regarding traffic flow. You need to decide whether it works for you.

  - Is enough light getting into the room? Do the existing windows do the job when it comes to size, shape, and location? More light makes a space seem larger and more inviting.

✏ **Dining room:** People do a lot of entertaining in this area, like a living room, and it needs to work both size- and layout-wise, or you won't want to use it. Most people remodel their dining rooms to increase space. Put in a dining table, eight to ten chairs, a china cabinet, and maybe a sideboard, and you may not have enough room for your guests to sit down! For most people, remodelling a dining room involves taking out a wall from an adjoining room or extending an outside area to add floor space. Either way, this remodel is a major project and can cost you a substantial amount of money.

✏ **Kitchen:** The kitchen is the number-one remodelled room in the house – it's also the one that gives you the best return on your remodelling pound. You need to address cabinets, sinks, appliances, lighting, flooring, and decorating (paint and wallpaper) in a kitchen remodel. If you're replacing cabinets and flooring, be ready to spend thousands. After all, the cabinets are the most visible items in your kitchen, so you want them to look as nice as you can afford. The floor also needs special attention because it's probably the most used and abused floor in the house.

Beyond the obvious visual items, you need to make sure that the layout of your kitchen works. If, for example, you have a small kitchen but are a budding chef, you may want to find a way to enlarge the kitchen space. Enlarging space often means knocking out an adjacent wall. It also can be as easy as rearranging the kitchen's layout. A qualified kitchen designer can help you analyse your existing kitchen's layout, assess your wants for the new space, and create a new layout that gives you what you need. But be prepared to pay through the nose!

✏ **Bathroom:** Most people want a washbasin, toilet, and bath or shower to make a bathroom serviceable. But who wants only serviceable? Bigger is more comfortable, especially when two people are trying to get ready for work or a night on the town at the same time. A bathroom, like a kitchen, often necessitates a new floor plan to make things work better. Installing a whirlpool bath, repositioning a conventional bath, adding or enlarging a shower, repositioning the toilet, and even adding a second (or third) washbasin are possible remodelling steps. Yes, they involve a lot of work and planning, and a professional carpenter and plumber should probably handle them. However, making these moves will make your mornings less cramped and just may get your days off to a better start.

✏ **Bedrooms:** Most people remodel bedrooms to enlarge the space. Homeowners often take two small bedrooms and create one larger space by removing a wall. In some jobs, the homeowners add or enlarge wardrobe space. Both remodelling projects are considered very doable but usually require at least some good, hard consulting with a building or design professional.

✔ **Basement or loft:** If you're lucky enough to have a basement or loft, consider finishing the space – it's a great place for a playroom for the kids, or a home office.

✔ **Porches and patios:** Don't forget about outdoor spaces when considering a remodel. Patios and large decked areas can increase a home's usable living space – not to mention increase its value. You can usually do these additions fairly easily because you add them to the outside of the house. A remodel requires a space for the door, but beyond that, most of the work occurs on the outside.

After you've taken a hard look at what you want to remodel, list all the materials and equipment you're likely to need in Table 3-2.

Table 3-2	Listing the Materials You Need	
Room or Project	*Materials*	*Estimated Cost*

Getting Estimates and Prices

If your project involves structural changes to your house, you need to involve an architect, a builder, and possibly even an engineer. Any structural change can affect the stability of your house, and it must meet Building Regulations to ensure that the house remains structurally safe to inhabit. You also need to engage inspectors from your council's Building Control department. You can contact them by calling your town hall and asking for 'Building Control'.

Choosing builders is always a problem area. If you don't know anything about building, then we strongly advise that you engage an architect or chartered surveyor to plan and supervise the work for you. This includes finding the building contractor or tradespeople to do the work. For small jobs that you feel you can supervise yourself, make sure you get estimates in writing, including a written specification of the materials to be used, and sketches or drawings where appropriate. You can also try finding tradespeople through Trade Associations. These are not official bodies, and some people say trade associations are there to protect their members from the public! But at least they give you a point of reference to start chasing tradespeople if things go wrong.

Book I

Planning
Your Home
Improve-
ment
Projects

Choosing an architect or designer

If your project involves complex or detailed drawings and plans, don't count on having two or three free estimates to compare. Architects and most design and construction people don't create elaborate plans without being compensated – it's not like getting a price on timber from a couple of different builders' merchants. You need to select a single designer or architect to work with, so here's where you do your homework ahead of time.

Even though you won't get several drawings or bids to compare, you should meet with at least two designers or architects, and for two very good reasons:

☒ You need to see whether they can give you a rough plan that meets your wants and needs. If they can't understand what you're looking for, why would you hire them?

☒ You need to determine whether your personalities are compatible. This factor is critical to a successful remodel. You must be able to get along with the designer so that both of you can discuss suggestions and changes without becoming agitated. Homeowners too often fail to thoroughly feel out designers and architects before hiring them. Eventually, they end up having to make a switch halfway through the project. In all instances, the change in personnel costs not only time but also big money.

Pricing materials

A visit to a local builders' merchants or DIY centre is a great way to begin the step of pricing materials. Visit a couple of different shops: Competition is fierce, and you may be surprised by what a particular retailer or supplier can do for you, especially if the shop believes that it can get your entire order.

A thorough materials list is invaluable here. Providing the shop with a complete list enables them to do a *take-off* (an estimate of materials needed and their total costs). Give the list that you created in the preceding section to each retailer and see which one gives you the best prices.

Don't be afraid to ask one shop to match a competitor's price. Most retailers are willing to drop a few pounds to get your business.

After you have a couple of estimates in hand, do your homework. Don't pick a product or material simply because it has the lowest price. Make sure that the prices are for the same product or for products of equal quality. If you're not familiar with a specific type or brand of product, ask to see it and get the salesperson to explain its various features. Check what kind of guarantee the product comes with.

Another good source of product information is the Internet. Most manufacturers have Web sites to provide consumers with product information and evaluations, even if only their own evaluation. Also consider checking consumer magazines like *Which?* reports to see whether they've tested the type of products you're looking at. These reports are very fair at evaluating and rating all types of products, especially home products, such as appliances.

Some DIY shops offer installation as an option with the products they sell, so you save on labour costs.

Sticking to your budget

Establishing a workable budget usually means compromising on a few things. Here are some ways to make your budget numbers add up to what you can afford to spend:

- When pricing new products – for example, a whirlpool bath, an oven, or a fridge – consider getting one that has only the features you need and no extra bells and whistles. Buying a fridge is like buying a new car: The top-of-the-range model may be your dream machine, but the model a notch or two below probably does what you need it to do, and it's cheaper.

- If you're remodelling a bathroom or kitchen, consider leaving the waste pipes where they are, especially if your budget is tight. Moving waste pipes is time-consuming, which means a lot of money in labour costs (it's usually best to leave this task to a professional plumber).

- Do as much of the work as possible yourself. If you're replacing kitchen cabinets, for example, why not tear out the old ones yourself? Most homeowners can do this part of the project; plus, it's a great way to let off steam!

- If you're set on using some expensive materials, plan on paying a professional to do the installation rather than starting the project yourself and calling someone in midstream. In addition to the fact that you'll have to pay top whack because you need help immediately, you may also have to pay to have someone correct your mistakes.

Allowing for fun (and your mental health!)

You alone can't wrap up many remodelling projects in a weekend or two. Even if you bring in the pros, you can expect your home and lifestyle to be disturbed for at least a short while. To avoid total chaos and keep family members being nice to one another, allow room in your remodelling budget for eating out and maybe even sleeping away from the house.

Book I

Planning
Your Home
Improve-
ment
Projects

Unless your remodelling project is off in some remote area of the house, preparing meals and finding a suitable place to enjoy them probably becomes a challenge – especially if you're remodelling a kitchen. Meals can throw a budget way out of whack. Why? It's pretty simple, really. A family of four can easily spend £20 to £30 on an evening meal – and that's if you go the fast-food route. Go to a sit-down restaurant and it's more like £15 to £20 per person. So budget accordingly – and take up the offers from kind friends who invite you over for dinner.

If your project is going to last for a substantial length of time, plan a weekend away somewhere near the middle of the project's timeline. Go to a hotel for a couple of nights and relax. See a film or play, go to a concert – just do something other than remodelling! This short break may be the best gift you give yourself during the project. Yes, you'll spend some money, but this hiatus will bring you home rested and energised, ready to get your project completed.

 If you do build in a mid-project retreat, try to schedule it around a part of the project that can get you away from new fumes or odours – for example, if you're having floors refinished or walls painted.

Considering Financing Options

You have several financing methods to choose from when paying for the remodelling project if you don't have the cash on hand. This section looks at the options that work for most people and should work for you, too.

 Don't start a remodelling project before getting your finances in order. Most lenders require that the house be valued before they loan you money, and the house must be in sellable condition when it's valued. Your house can't have walls being removed or a bathroom or kitchen being torn out when the valuer comes to do the job.

 Don't use the following information as financial or investment advice, just as a starting point to help you find the best way to pay for your remodelling project. As you would with any financial matter, consult your bank, financial adviser, or accountant.

Remortgaging your home

For a remodelling project that's going to cost thousands or even tens of thousands of pounds, remortgaging the home is a popular method of paying for things. Many homeowners have built up considerable *equity* in their homes. Equity is your home's current assessed value minus the total amount of mortgages or loans against its value. Remortgaging is the process of paying off the existing loan based on the current value of the house.

Check with your current mortgage lender about getting a second mortgage through them, or check with any mortgage broker. Make sure to consult with a competent mortgage broker or your accountant before entering into a second mortgage. Second mortgage rates are generally a few percentage points higher than first mortgage rates. Finding a lender for remortgaging shouldn't be difficult if you have a good credit rating. Your bank is a good place to begin your search. Contact your current mortgage lender, too. The lender will be glad to talk to you, and going this route may make things easier because the lender already knows your credit history and is familiar with the property (your home). You can also contact a local estate agent. Estate agents are in constant touch with mortgage brokers who can give you a competitive current interest rate on a home mortgage.

Keep in mind that remortgaging your home is almost the same as purchasing it for the first time, so you need all the closing documents from the current loan, employment information, and so on.

Some lenders have been known to offer a second mortgage that's as high as 125 per cent of your home's current value. Although that may seem like an easy way to get all the money you need for your project, we would never recommend borrowing more than the current value of the property. If you do borrow more than your home's value and the market suddenly drops, you could be in big trouble – especially if you find yourself having to sell your home and end up selling it for less than the amount of the mortgages or loans against it.

Buying with low- or no-interest credit cards

An option that may be available to you is to open new low- or no-interest credit card accounts. Yes, doing so means adding another creditor or two to your credit record, but these cards also enable you to purchase things immediately without having to go to the bank. This option is handy when, for example, you see the bath or oven you want on sale for less than your estimate price and you decide that it makes sense to purchase it now, even if you don't need the item for several weeks.

Read the small print that describes the card's rules and regulations. Most of these cards offer very attractive up-front rates but hit you hard if you miss the payment date even once. Whenever possible, make your payments as soon as you can. Set up a direct debit to ensure the minimum payment is met.

Watching Every Penny to Avoid Overspending

The number-one problem with remodelling projects is going over budget. Most homeowners do their best to adhere to the budget they created, but unfortunately, a little overspending here and there adds up to going over budget. This section offers some suggestions to help you keep your spending in check.

Reviewing expenses regularly

Getting cost estimates for materials and labour is only part of the financial picture. You need to set up a filing or tracking system so that you can check what you're spending versus what you've budgeted. A number of budgeting and record-keeping computer programs are available. If you're computer challenged or don't have a home computer, you can find home record-keeping plans at most bookshops.

No matter what record-keeping method you choose, use it regularly! Update your records as you make purchases instead of saying, 'I'll take care of things on a weekly basis.' Continued purchasing without recording and reviewing expenses against your budget numbers is a quick and easy way to go over – or completely blow – your budget.

Hitting the sales

Shopping for remodelling materials is no different to shopping for everyday items – keep your eyes open for sale prices! For example, if you know that you're going to get new kitchen appliances and they're on sale now, grab 'em. Buying expensive items doesn't mean that you can't or won't find them at a good or sale price, so be vigilant about watching for bargains. You can also ask in shops about getting ex-display models at reduced prices. Don't be shy – they can only say no!

The same holds true for timber and other building materials. If you know you're going to need timber, plywood, roofing, or other building materials, contact the retailer you plan to use and make sure that you can get those sale prices when it's time to order. You may need to pay for the materials now, but at least you'll get the sale price, even if the materials aren't delivered immediately. And don't forget to consider second-hand or reclaimed materials. As well as looking funky, reclaimed timber, bricks, and roof tiles can sometimes (but not always) be cheaper than the new versions – especially if you buy at auctions, or from the small-ads section of your local newspaper or free ads paper. But before you buy, make sure you know the latest prices of new materials from your local builders' merchants, and don't assume that just because materials are second-hand they must automatically be cheaper.

Collecting items yourself

You can also save money on delivery. If the stuff isn't too tricky to collect and you have access to the right type of vehicle, consider collecting things yourself to avoid pricey delivery charges. Just don't try to handle anything more than you can safely carry and then unload. Delivery drivers are usually skilled at manoeuvring their vehicles in tight places, as well as unloading things quickly and safely.

If you do need to have things delivered and you're ordering all your materials from one retailer, see if they can reduce or even waive the delivery charge. Don't be afraid to try to wheel and deal – the worst they can say is no!

Book II
Basic Home Maintenance and Improvement

"I'm afraid it's a very serious blockage, madam."

In this book . . .

*E*veryone knows that a bit of filler or a coat of paint can make a home look better. But beauty isn't only skin deep. Filler and paint do more than meet the eye. This book helps you see beyond the obvious and shows you what to look for when it comes to keeping your home looking fabulous and keeping strong and sturdy.

Here are the contents of Book II at a glance.

Chapter 1

Repairing Walls and Putting Up Shelves

In This Chapter

▷ Making the most of your four walls

▷ Shelving clutter with storage and display

▷ Staying warm with the right insulation

*B*ritain is now a nation of stay-at-homers and some of us need to spend a little time getting our nests in better shape. These cosy little spaces that we call our homes have plenty of room for improvement. This chapter includes our best advice on how to fix up your corner of the cosmos.

You might want to wear a mask when working with plasterboard, as the particles from the board can really get up your nose!

Working on Walls

Just like every other part of a house, walls are susceptible to damage and the ravages of time. This section includes all you need to know to repair the walls of your home and add shelving where needed.

Filling cracks

Two types of cracks occur in walls or ceilings: Hairline and structural cracks. Faulty workmanship, defective materials, head banging, or drying shrinkage cause hairline cracks. Movement in the structure or frame of the building causes structural cracks.

In houses with brick walls, structural movement might be a once-only thing that occurs when the new house settles onto its foundations (called *settlement*), or it might be an ongoing problem, caused by ground movement (called *subsidence*). Subsidence is not usually the expensive horror story that some people make out. Softening of the ground due to leaking drains can cause it, or seasonal shrinkage of the ground in dry summers. It can be fixed, but if you suspect your home might be affected by subsidence, get it checked out by a qualified structural engineer.

In timber-framed houses, movement is the result of shrinking and swelling of the wooden structural members, such as studs or joists. This movement occurs seasonally, when changes in the temperature and humidity cause fluctuations in the moisture content of the framing timber. Cracks filled with filler or other brittle patching compound recur with these movements.

Wallboard or taping compound is used to cover taped joints in *dry lining* (plasterboard that's not plastered yet). *Filler* is used to fill holes and cracks in plastered solid or plasterboard walls. *Wallboard* is the larger size of plasterboard, used for walls, to distinguish it from *plank*, a smaller size used for ceilings.

Here's what you need to repair a crack in a plasterboard wall or ceiling:

- Filler knife
- Scraper, taping knife, or plastering trowel
- Premixed wallboard (plasterboard) compound and fibre (or paper) plasterboard tape
- Plastic container to hold the taping compound or filler
- Fine sandpaper

Cracks in corners may be due to a build-up of taping compound or paint. These hairline cracks are in the excessively thick material; they don't extend through to the reinforcing tape itself. To repair these surface cracks, fold a piece of sandpaper over the end of a scraper or taping knife and carefully sand away the excess material. By folding the sandpaper over the knife blade, you can keep the sanded surface smooth and flat; if you sand a soft, flat surface like plasterboard with your fingers backing the sandpaper, you may leave an uneven surface. Do not sand through the wallboard tape. After removing the excess material, use a small paintbrush to touch up the corner.

Follow these steps, shown in Figure 1-1, to repair a deeper crack with wallboard tape:

1. Clean out the interior of the crack so that no loose material is present.

2. **Apply a light coating of wallboard compound to the crack.**

   Premixed wallboard compound contains about 50 per cent water by volume, so it shrinks as it dries. For this reason, several applications are needed to build up a surface and overcome shrinkage.

3. **Embed the paper tape in the wallboard compound and scrape a scraper or filler knife along the joint to remove excess wallboard compound.**

   Don't leave wrinkles in the tape: If the crack isn't straight, cut the tape where the crack zigzags and apply the tape so that it's centred over the crack.

4. **Apply a thin coat of wallboard compound over the wallboard tape and smooth it with a wide taping knife to minimise sanding.**

5. **Let the patch dry completely.**

6. **When the wallboard tape and first coat are dry, use a scraper, taping knife, or trowel to apply a second, smoothing coat.**

   This application is intended to smooth and conceal the tape. Don't pile wallboard compound in a thick coat over the tape; you're not decorating a cake!

7. **Let this application dry completely and repeat with a third coat.**

8. **Use a sanding block to smooth the repaired area.**

Book II

Basic Home Maintenance and Improvement

Figure 1-1:
Apply a light coat of wallboard compound over the crack and then smooth tape into place with a wide knife (left). When the first coat is dry, apply a thin second coat (right).

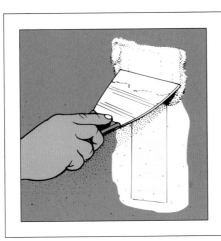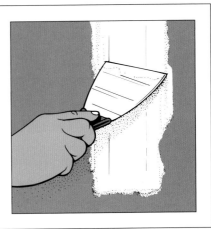

Repairing plaster cracks

The advice in this section for repairing cracks is intended for plasterboard or 'wallboard' construction, but you can follow generally the same patch techniques for plaster cracks.

When patching plaster with wallboard tape, you don't have to cut a V-shape into the crack to retain patching plaster, nor do you need to clean out the inside of the crack. Use a scraper or taping knife to clean away any broken plaster that's protruding out of the crack and then coat and tape as described for filling cracks in plasterboard.

Repairing nail pops

Wallboard nails often work themselves loose from the wall framing and appear as small, crescent-shaped cracks in the wall. This curious phenomenon, called nail pop, usually happens during the first year of a building's life, while the house framing is settling or drying out.

Nailing wallboard became outmoded the day that wallboard screws and screwguns were invented. Fastening wallboard takes fewer screws than nails, and fewer fasteners mean fewer pops. Also, 1-inch-long wallboard screws provide the same holding power as 1¼-inch-long wallboard nails, but with less penetration of the wood framing: Less wood penetration equals less pop.

When you see a popped nailhead or a small crescent-shaped crack, press with the flat of your hand against the wall and notice how the framing has shrunk away from the wallboard. Shrinkage in framing timber often causes nail pops. As timber dries out, it shrinks away from the wallboard, leaving the nailheads or screwheads protruding from the wall.

Follow these steps, illustrated in Figure 1-2, to repair a nail pop:

1. **Drive new drywall screws a few centimetres above and below the popped fastener or nail.**

   The wallboard pulls tight against the framing as you drive the screws into it. The screwhead should dimple, but not penetrate, the paper facing.

2. **Use a hammer and a long nail to drive the old fastener completely through the drywall and tight against the wall stud.**

3. **With a scraper, apply a coat of premixed taping compound over the dimpled heads of the old and the new fasteners.**

   Don't pile compound above the surface of the wall; smooth it so that it's flat on the surface.

4. **When the compound is dry, sand it with a fine sandpaper, feathering it to blend in with the surface of the wall.**

5. **Apply a light second coat of compound in the same way and then sand it smooth to match the surface of the wall.**

Figure 1-2:
Drive new drywall screws above and below a popped nail to pull the wallboard back to the wall stud (left). Before you patch the nail pop, drive the loose nail through the wallboard.

Book II

Basic Home Maintenance and Improvement

TIP

When you're patching popped nails, shine a strong light across the wall. The beam highlights any defects and reveals even the slightest nail pops. Set a floor lamp about a foot from the wall and use a 100-watt bulb with the lampshade removed. When subjected to strong side lighting, defects pop out like stars on a dark night.

Patching holes

Nail pops occur all by themselves. A hole in a wall is a different matter. You often find holes behind a swinging door, with a nice imprint of the doorknob, or where your little tyke ran his bike into the wall.

The challenge of patching holes in wallboard is bridging the gap of a small hole or anchoring a new piece of wallboard in a large hole. In times past, the only way to make those kinds of repairs was to cut away the damaged area to reveal the studs on either side and then nail the new patch into place on the studs. For years, people used the old cardboard-and-string trick (tying a string to a piece of cardboard and sticking it into the hole to use the cardboard as a base for the patching compound), but that's ancient history. Try some of these new ways for dealing with this age-old problem.

A bridge for small gaps

If the wallboard hole is less than 100 mm in diameter, hang a picture over it. Not good enough? Use self-adhesive plasterers' scrim to cover the hole. You can buy it in rolls at builders' merchants. Here's what to do:

1. **Use a sharp utility knife to trim away any loose or protruding wallpaper or loose pieces of wallboard.**

2. **Peel a length of scrim off the roll and position it over the hole, as shown in Figure 1-3.**

   Make sure that the patch is smooth.

3. **Use a scraper or taping knife to press the adhesive edges into place.**

4. **Apply two thin coats of wallboard compound, letting the compound dry between applications.**

5. **When the second coat is dry, sand the patch smooth so that it blends in with the surface of the wall.**

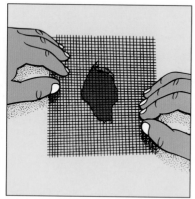

Figure 1-3: Smooth a patch over small holes and then cover it with several coats of wallboard compound.

Wallboard clips for large holes

The key to repairing a large hole is to make a clean cutout of the patch area so that you can insert a same-size piece of wallboard into the hole. You then screw wallboard clips into the surface of the surrounding wall to hold the repair piece in place. After you screw in the clips, break the tabs off of the clips and apply wallboard compound as you would for other repairs.

Follow these steps, illustrated in Figure 1-4, to install wallboard repair clips:

1. **From a piece of scrap wallboard, cut a patch that completely covers the hole in the wall.**

   Save yourself time and trouble – make the patch a square or rectangle, even though the hole may be a different shape.

2. **Place the patch over the hole and trace around it with a pencil.**

3. **Use a metal rule to guide your knife as you cut the wallboard along these lines around the hole.**

   If the patch is large, you can make the project go much faster by using a drywall saw, as shown in Figure 1-4, to cut the wall. Just be careful to avoid wiring and pipes that may be hidden behind the walls.

4. **With the sharp utility knife, cut away any protruding paper facing or crumbled gypsum core from the perimeter of the patch area.**

5. **Install wallboard clips on the sides of the hole and secure them on the edges of the damaged wall by using the screws supplied with the clips.**

   Space the clips no farther than 300 mm apart.

6. **Insert the wallboard patch into the hole and drive screws through the wallboard patch into each wallboard repair clip.**

7. **Snap off the temporary tabs from the repair clips.**

8. **Apply wallboard tape and wallboard compound to all four sides of the patch.**

9. **When the tape and first coat are dry, apply a second, smoothing coat.**

   This application is intended to smooth and conceal the tape. Don't pile taping compound in a thick coat over the tape. Otherwise, the repair will be as obvious as the hole was.

10. **Use a sanding block to smooth the repair area so that it blends with the surface of the surrounding wall.**

11. **Apply a coat of wallboard primer and let it dry.**

Book II

Basic Home Maintenance and Improvement

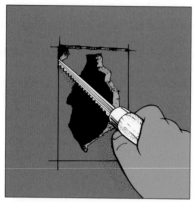

A. Using the replacement patch as a template, cut away the damaged wallboard. (Step 3)

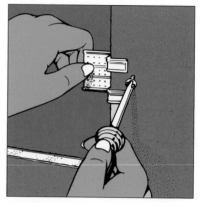

B. Push the wallboard clips over the edge of the sound wallboard and secure each clip with a wallboard screw. (Step 5)

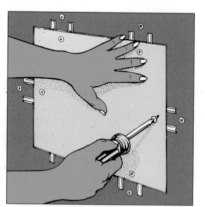

C. Place the wallboard patch in position and secure it by driving a wallboard screw into the wallboard clips. (Step 6)

Figure 1-4:
Repairing a large hole in a wall is easy with the help of wallboard clips.

Repairing sagging plaster on walls and ceilings

Older houses may have plaster walls and ceilings with wood lath for a base. The wood lath was installed with gaps, called keys, between each piece of lath. The plaster was forced between the spaced laths, and this keying action held the plaster in place.

As plaster ages, these keys may break away from the lath, and the plaster coating can come loose and sag away from the lath. Sagging is usually visible to the eye. If you have sags in a plaster ceiling, press upward on the area with the flat of your hand. If the plaster feels spongy or gives under your hand pressure, it's a sign that the key strength has been lost. If it's not repaired, the plaster ceiling can collapse.

Whether you patch or replace the sagging plaster depends on the extent of the damage:

- ✏ If the sagging is severe, meaning that it's hanging a few centimetres or more away from the lath base, or if it covers a large portion of the ceiling, your best bet is to remove the old plaster and replaster the ceiling, or cover it with wallboard. Not an easy do-it-yourself project.

- ✏ If the sagging is slight, or covers a small area, you can reattach the plaster to the wood lath by using long drywall screws fitted with plaster washers. A plaster washer is a thin metal disk that increases the size of the head of a drywall screw so that it doesn't pull through the plaster. You thread the drywall screw through a plaster washer and then drive it through the plaster and into the ceiling joists, wall studs, or wood lath. The screw and washer pull the loose plaster tight against the framing, restoring the ceiling. By surrounding the area with plaster washers, as shown in Figure 1-5, you can stabilise the plaster so that it doesn't sag any further.

Book II

Basic Home Maintenance and Improvement

To reattach the sagging plaster to the lath, drive the washer with a power screwdriver or drill so that it penetrates the wood lath, wall studs, or ceiling joists. To avoid cracking the plaster and creating an even bigger repair job, don't pull the plaster tight to the lath in a single motion. Instead, start a few washers around or across the sagged area and drive them snug against the plaster face. Then tighten each of them slowly, moving from one to another, so that the plaster gradually pulls tight against the lath. Tighten the screws just enough that the screwheads and washers bite into the surface of the plaster and do not stand proud of the ceiling. Then apply filler to hide them.

To repair large sags, follow these steps:

1. **Remove the loose plaster.**

2. **Install drywall screws and plaster washers around the perimeter of the loose area, as shown in Figure 1-5.**

3. **Install a cut-to-size piece of plasterboard over the exposed wood lath.**

   See the preceding section for instructions on patching wallboard.

4. **Apply primer and a coat of paint by following the directions earlier in this chapter in the section titled 'Filling cracks'.**

   Wallboard compound absorbs a lot of paint, so plan to give the patched area several coats of paint to make it blend in with the rest of the wall or ceiling.

Figure 1-5:
Install plaster washers around the edge of the damaged area to pull the plaster tight against the lath.

Decking the walls

When hanging something on a wall, consider both the surface of the wall and the size and weight of the object that you're hanging. For example, a lightweight framed poster doesn't require the holding power that a heavy mounted deer's head does. And fastening a hanger into hollow wallboard is a very different process from mounting something to a brick wall.

When you're shopping for the bits and pieces to hang pictures, know the following:

- The approximate weight of the object: Put it on the bathroom scales.
- The dimensions of the object: Get out a measuring tape.
- The type of wall surface: Is it wallboard, plaster, or brick?

As you look at various types of hanger hardware, read the package instructions – they usually spell out weight and dimension requirements. Hanging very large or heavy pictures on a timber stud wall always requires anchoring the picture hanger into wood framing, and you may need two or more hangers for support.

Hollow walls

Most partition walls have cavities created by the wall studs. Builders use these cavities to run electrical wires and plumbing pipes through the house.

Building regulations generally require that these be protected so that you can carefully nail and drill into most walls and be pretty sure that you won't damage one of these wires or pipes. But we recommend that before you drill, screw, or nail anything to a wall (or ceiling) you first use a pipe and cable detector. These are inexpensive hand-held battery-powered gadgets that bleep when they detect anything metal below the surface. Some models also have a switch that enables them to detect electric current, and even wood (see the nearby sidebar 'Finding the stud').

But remember: Use a pipe and cable detector first, and whenever you nail or drill into a wall, be careful. If, while drilling, you encounter unexpected resistance, STOP. Plasterboard, plaster, UPVC pipes, and wooden studs are rather soft compared to steel or copper pipes. Don't push harder on the drill; instead, back off and investigate the source of the resistance. You can't even begin to imagine the amount of damage you can cause if you drill into a copper water pipe.

Use the following items to hang lightweight objects on hollow walls:

- ✏ Small finishing nails and brads driven at a 45-degree downward angle into drywall or plaster

- ✏ Hook-type hangers that are held in place with a nail

- ✏ Adhesive hangers

To hang medium-weight objects, use one of these items (pictured in Figure 1-6):

- ✏ **Plasterboard fixings,** or hollow-wall anchors, are combination screws surrounded by casing. As you tighten the screw, the casing around the screw braces against the wall interior. Predrill a hole and insert and turn the screw to brace and tighten.

- ✏ **Cavity toggles,** another type of hollow-wall anchor, have spring-loaded wings that expand inside the wall. Predrill a hole, remove the winged toggle from the screw, and place the screw through whatever you want to hang. Then replace the toggle and insert the assembly into the wall. Tighten the screw to pull the toggle tight against the inside of the wall.

- ✏ **Plastic expansion plugs** (also known as wallplugs) fit snugly into pre-drilled holes in brickwork or blockwork. As you drive a screw into the plastic plug, the slotted base of the plug spreads and locks against the perimeter of the hole.

Book II

Basic Home Mainte- nance and Improve- ment

Cavity toggle

Plasterboard fixing

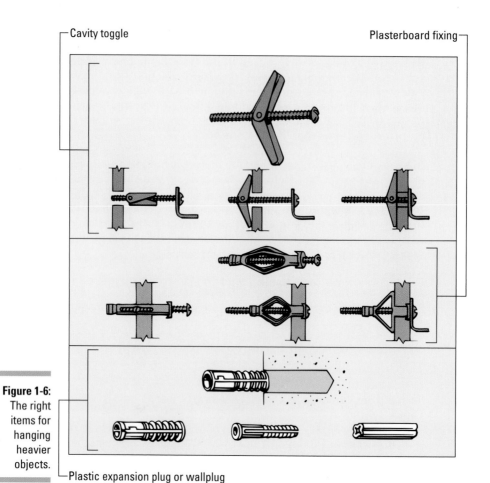

Figure 1-6:
The right
items for
hanging
heavier
objects.

Plastic expansion plug or wallplug

Brick and masonry surfaces

Penetrating hard surfaces, such as brick and concrete, is more difficult than getting through ordinary wallboard. For this job, you need an electric drill with a masonry bit to predrill a hole.

To hang lightweight items on a brick or masonry surface, follow these steps:

1. **Drill a hole in the masonry to the same depth and diameter as the anchor.**

2. **Tap the plastic plug or anchor into the hole.**

3. **Drive a screw through the fixture and into the plug to expand it and lock it inside the hole.**

Finding the stud

Where possible, anchor hardware into the vertical wall studs, not the space between them. Stud spacing is typically 400 mm, centre to centre. To find a stud, you can go the high-tech route and use an electronic stud finder – a gadget that locates studs in the wall by measuring the density of various points. When you pass the stud finder over a wall stud, a light or bleeper signals the location. Or you can use a pipe and cable detector – which will bleep when it finds the screws or nails that hold the wallboard or laths to the studs.

For a low-tech approach, check at power points, removing the cover plate if necessary. There's usually a stud on one side or the other. Or remove the shade from a lamp and set the lamp with bare bulb about a foot away from the wall to highlight fastener locations. Or get down on your hands and knees and look at where the skirting board has nailheads showing. Wherever you see a nailhead, especially if they appear to be 400 mm apart, it's likely that a stud's behind it.

To hang medium-weight items on a brick or masonry surface, do the following:

1. **Drill a hole in the masonry the same depth and diameter as the anchor.**

2. **Tap an expansion-type anchor into the hole.**

3. **Drive a screw into the anchor to expand it and lock it inside the hole.**

Building Shelves

A simple wall shelf adds form and function to a room. Use a shelf to display your loved ones' mugshots, or to store cookbooks in the kitchen. A shelving system that uses brackets and uprights to hold the shelves is a bit more costly and time-consuming to install, but it's a project worth tackling. And wardrobe shelving is downright rewarding because it puts you on the road to peace and order, knowing that, when you open your wardrobe door, you're not in danger of getting clobbered by falling objects. Whatever shelving you choose, it's always a treat to have a place for everything and everything in its place.

Putting up a simple wall shelf

A single small wall shelf like the one shown in Figure 1-7 consists of the shelf itself and brackets that are fastened to the wall. The shelf is either secured to the brackets or just rests on top of them. More than two brackets are needed for longer shelves.

Here's what's involved in installing a decorative wall shelf with two brackets and one shelf:

1. **Locate a wall stud and mark the location for the first shelf bracket on the wall.**

   No need to do this if you have a brick wall – just be careful no wires or pipes lie behind the plaster. Use wallplugs in brick or block walls.

   Follow the instructions in the 'Finding the stud' sidebar in this chapter to locate a stud in the wall. Then hold a shelf support bracket over the stud and use it as a template to mark the location of the mounting screws on the wall.

2. **Install the bracket with screws that are long enough to penetrate the wall stud by at least an inch or so.**

3. **Mark the location of the second stud.**

   Wall studs are usually placed 400 mm apart, so measure 400 mm from the bracket you just installed. Place a spirit level on the first bracket to extend a level line to the second stud and then hold the second bracket in position. Mark the location for the second set of mounting screws on the wall.

4. **Install the second bracket with screws that are long enough to penetrate the wall stud by at least an inch or so.**

5. **Install the shelf on the support brackets. Use short screws to secure the shelf to the brackets.**

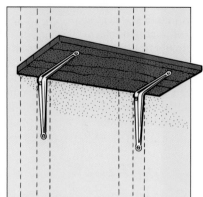

Figure 1-7:
Secure shelving brackets to wall studs to make sure the shelf can safely support a heavy load.

Installing a shelving system

A shelving system is made up of three basic components: Shelves, standards (long vertical slotted strips fastened to the wall), and brackets that fit into grooves along the length of the standards. Because the shelf sits on top of these brackets, you can adjust the height of shelving for a variety of configurations, as shown in Figure 1-8.

Figure 1-8: Choose a shelving system that you can adjust to hold different sized items.

Book II

Basic Home Maintenance and Improvement

Before you invest your hard-earned pounds in a shelving system, consider these shopping tips:

- Make a preliminary shopping/learning expedition to select a shelving system and pick up a planning brochure with the system's standard and bracket specifications.

- Decide how many shelves you want and how you want to arrange them. Make a sketch of the wall, noting the location of wall studs so that you can plan the design.

- Choose the standard size and shelf depth and style to fit the items you plan to store and display. Plan to space the standards about 800 mm apart and allow a maximum overhang of one-sixth of the shelf length.

- If you must fasten the shelf to a hollow wall, choose mounting anchors based on their weight-bearing capacity. Don't be embarrassed to ask for help!

- Read the instructions, noting how many uprights and brackets and what width and length of shelves are included. Most systems have brackets for at least two widths of shelving, so make sure that you buy the correct sizes. Some systems include the mounting hardware; some don't. Don't leave the shop without everything you need.

Follow these steps for installing a component shelf system with standards and brackets:

1. **Use a stud finder to locate the studs on the wall; they're usually placed 400 mm apart, but might be 450 mm or even 600 mm apart.** In older houses they might not be regularly spaced at all, but just spaced out approximately to fill the length of the wall!

    Plan to install each standard on the centre of the stud. Make light pencil marks on all the wall studs in the vicinity of the spot where you plan to install the shelving unit. (You may have to adjust the exact location slightly so that the standards are attached to the studs.)

2. **Mark the location for the top screw hole on the first standard and drill a small pilot hole through its top hole into the wall or stud.**

3. **Use a spirit level to straighten the standard so that it's plumb and then mark the location of another mounting screw.**

    To mark the spot for the next screw, place a pencil on one of the mounting screw holes in the bracket, as shown in Figure 1-9.

4. **Swing the bracket to one side and then drill a pilot hole for the mounting screw.**

5. **Reposition the upright and install the mounting screw with a Phillips-head screwdriver.**

6. **Locate the proper position of the second standard.**

    To position the second standard, place a shelf support bracket in the standard hanging on the wall. Then install another shelf support bracket in the same slot of a second standard. Hold the second standard over the next wall stud and then place a level (alone or on a piece of shelving) on the brackets and move the new standard up or down until the shelf is level, as shown in Figure 1-9.

7. **Mark the location on the wall of one of the mounting screws for the second standard and install it as you did the first one.**

8. **Repeat with the remaining standards.**

9. **Install the shelf support brackets into the standards.**

    These brackets usually tap into slots that lock them in place.

10. **Install the shelves.**

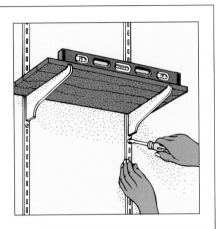

Figure 1-9:
A spirit level ensures that the first standard is plumb (left) and that subsequent uprights are level with the first one (right).

Book II

Basic Home Maintenance and Improvement

Adding a wire shelf system to a wardrobe

You can tame wardrobe clutter by installing a wardrobe organiser with ventilated wire shelves. You still have to hang up your clothes, but opening the wardrobe door is far less intimidating when you don't face a potential avalanche.

These systems are sold as individual components to fit any size wardrobe and as wardrobe kits designed for various sizes. For example, a kit for a 2.5m wardrobe may include four shelves, one support pole, a shoe rack, and mounting clips and screws.

Here's what you need to install a wire shelf system:

- A spirit level
- Screwdrivers
- Measuring tape and a pencil
- A hacksaw for cutting the metal shelving to length
- A free afternoon

Before you can install a wardrobe wire shelving system in your wardrobe, you have to do the following preparation:

1. **Remove all the stuff inside the wardrobe.**

   Just do it! Think of this as an opportunity to get rid of items that you don't wear or use. Donate the booty to charity or to anybody who can use it; just get rid of it.

2. **Remove the existing shelving and the clothes rod.**

   You may need a pry bar or claw hammer to remove the shelving if it's nailed to the walls; otherwise, it's a matter of unscrewing screws or fasteners or pulling out nails that hold the shelf and pole in place.

3. **Patch any nail holes that remain from the old shelving with a wallboard compound.**

   See the 'Patching holes' section earlier in this chapter.

4. **If the walls are dirty and dingy, give them a quick coat of paint.**

   Trust us. The extra effort will pay off every time you open the wardrobe door.

To install the shelving system, follow these steps:

1. **Read through the instructions that came with the shelving.**

2. **Determine the height for the main shelf, hold a spirit level at the approximate height, and mark a level line on the wall with a pencil.**

3. **Mark the locations for the wall clips.**

   Make a mark 65 mm in from either end of the shelf line and 12 mm above the shelf line. Then mark 300 mm intervals along a level line connecting the two marks.

4. **At each mark, drill a hole 6 mm deep and insert the wall clip, as shown in Figure 1-10.**

5. **Insert a screw into each wall clip and tighten them into the wall.**

6. **If your shelf system includes end caps for the shelves, to provide a nice finish to cut edges, put the end caps on one end of the shelf before measuring and cutting the shelf to length on the other side.**

7. **Put the other end caps on the cut end.**

8. **Hang the shelf on the wall clips, as shown in Figure 1-10.**

9. **Hold the shelf level with the lip of the shelf toward you and facing down.**

10. Position the wall brackets on the side walls and mark the holes.

11. Lift up the shelf until it's level (perpendicular to the wall) and drill holes for the anchors.

12. Insert the anchors.

13. Position the wall bracket, insert the screws, and tighten.

14. When both ends are installed, tighten the screws of the wall mounting brackets.

Figure 1-10:
Installing a wire shelving system is easy with special brackets with built-in wall anchors. The shelf snaps into the mounting bracket, and a screw threaded into the anchor locks it in place.

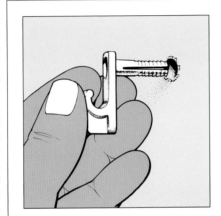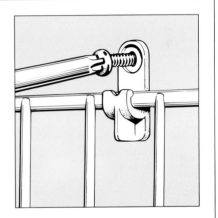

Book II

Basic Home Maintenance and Improvement

Chapter 2

Windows Don't Have to Be a Pane

*W*indows are designed to bring sunshine and fresh air into a building. Unfortunately, in some homes, windows have broken glass panes and rotted wood, or they rattle like a bag of bones and let in cold draughts. This chapter is a crash course in the basics of window maintenance and repair. Read on to discover how to improve or upgrade your windows, and how to adorn them with roller blinds and venetian blinds.

Know Your Windows

The most popular window style is the *double-hung window*, commonly known as a sliding *sash window*, shown in Figure 2-1. Double-hung windows have an upper and a lower sash (the inner frame that holds the glass panes in place) that move vertically in separate channels. The sashes are separated by a small piece of wood called a *parting strip*. The upper and lower sashes have *meeting rails* – where the top rail of the bottom sash and the bottom rail of the upper sash meet and are slanted and weather-stripped to form a tight seal between the rails. A locking mechanism secures the sashes together at the two parting rails to create a tight seal and to minimise air infiltration and heat loss.

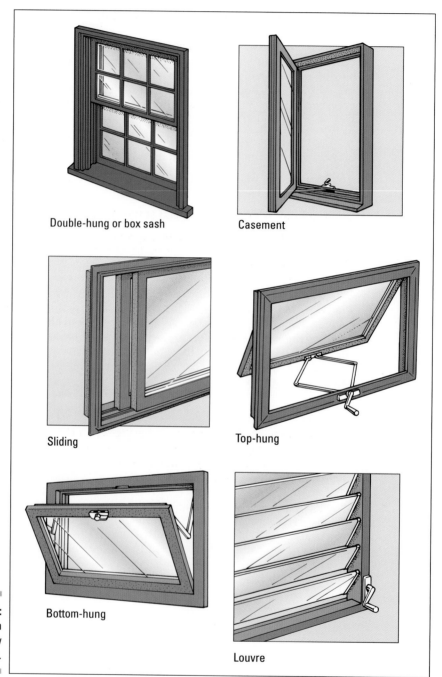

Double-hung or box sash

Casement

Sliding

Top-hung

Bottom-hung

Louvre

Figure 2-1:
Common
window
styles.

Other common window styles, shown in Figure 2-1:

- **Casement windows** have hinges on one side of the sash and swing outwards (or sometimes inwards). Because the entire casement sash swings outwards, these kinds of windows provide full ventilation and unobstructed views. Casement windows are easy to open, so they're commonly used where humidity or heat can build up, such as above kitchen sinks, in bathrooms, and on walls that connect to porches.

- **Sliding windows** open horizontally and bypass each other in separate tracks mounted at the top and bottom of the frame.

- **Top-hung windows** are hinged at the top and swing outward via a crank or lever.

- **Bottom-hung windows** are hinged at the bottom and swing inward.

- **Louvre windows** are made of a series of horizontal glass slats that are joined so that all the glass slats open or close together when the crank is turned. Louvre windows can be draughty, as the gaps between the slats let in air, even when closed.

Although they differ in design, basic maintenance is the same for all types of windows. By figuring out how your windows are supposed to work, you can keep them in tiptop shape and detect problems before they become serious.

Book II

Basic Home Maintenance and Improvement

Window Maintenance

At least once a year, put together a maintenance kit and inspect, lubricate, and clean each window. OK, OK, window duty isn't a great way to spend a weekend, but annual maintenance adds years to the life of your windows. Be sure that your maintenance kit includes:

- A small paintbrush for cleaning dirt and debris from the window channels

- A vacuum cleaner for sucking up loose dirt

- A roll of paper towels

- A can of spray lubricant, such as WD-40, for lubricating channels and locks

- A selection of both cross-head and flat-head screwdrivers for tightening any loose screws

First, open the window. Clean the debris from the windowsill with the paintbrush or vacuum cleaner. Then wet a paper towel and wipe down the sill to remove any residual dust.

If you have a **metal window frame**, inspect it for any loose hardware. Metal window channels or guides are attached to the side frames via small screws or brads. Renail or tighten loose guides. Check that the screws are tight in the window locks. Lubricate the locks with a shot of spray lubricant.

If window locks are jammed with paint, unscrew the locks and soak them in paint remover; then clean, polish, lubricate, and replace them. Use paper towels to wipe away any excess lubricant.

Modern sliding sash windows don't have ropes and sash weights the way older-model windows do. Instead, the sashes travel vertically in metal channels that are positioned on either side of the window. The channel on one side is spring-loaded, and the spring tension holds the window in position. But when you move the window sash to the middle of the frame and then pull sharply to the spring-loaded side, the sashes slip out of the frame easily, ready for repair or cleaning. This easy-access feature has been available on double-hung windows for several decades. To check your windows, press against the metal channel on both sides of the frame. If one side yields to hand pressure, your window sash can be snapped out of the frame. Use graphite or any other dry lubricant to grease the metal window channels in double-hung windows.

Casement or **awning windows** open via an arm, which may be a single linkage arm, double sliding arms, or a scissors arm. By opening the windows fully, you can disengage the arm from the track, which permits you to lubricate the arm and track or to free the window sash for easier washing.

Heave-ho: Unsticking a Stuck Window

If a window is stuck, the problem may be that the window channels need cleaning and lubrication, but the odds are that paint has run into the cracks between the window stops and the sash and is binding the window. Either problem usually yields to a simple solution.

The first rule of unsticking is this: If the window doesn't budge, don't force it. You may break the glass and cut yourself or damage the window beyond repair.

First, check that the window is unlocked. Then place a block of wood against the sash frame and tap the block lightly with a hammer while moving the block around all four sides of the frame. This trick may loosen up the window so that you can open it. Whatever you do, don't pound on the block, or you may crack the glass.

If the window resists your best open-sesame efforts, check for paint in the crack between the window sash and beads. Insert a knife blade into the crack, as shown in Figure 2-2. Using a light sawing motion, move the blade in the crack along the entire length of the window sash on both sides. Then cut any paint bond between the bottom rail and the sill.

A pizza cutter has been known to work just as well; don't hesitate to experiment!

If your sliding sash window still refuses to open, remove the beads along both sides of the sash with a small pry bar. You can then work the window sash free of the frame. Use fine sandpaper or a paint scraper to clean the edges of the sash and the edges of the beads. To lubricate the sash, rub a block of paraffin or a wax candle stub along the edges of the window sash and the stop. Push the sash back into place and refix the beads.

Book II

Basic Home Maintenance and Improvement

Figure 2-2:
Use a pizza cutter to open painted-shut windows.

Replacing Sash Cords

The sash weights in old double-hung windows are intended to provide balance so that, when the window is open to the desired position, it stays there. If the sash cord (or chain) breaks, the window can't stay in place. If you have to prop open your sliding sash window with a stick, chances are that the sash cord is broken and the window operates with all the controlled restraint of a guillotine.

To replace the sash cord, follow these steps (illustrated in Figure 2-3):

1. **Use a sharp knife to cut the paint line where the stop bead is attached to the frame.**

   Cutting this paint seal keeps the stop bead from breaking when you pry it off.

2. **Using a thin pry bar or a stiff putty knife, gently pry out the stop bead at each nail location.**

3. **At both sides of the frame along the upper sash, use the pry bar or putty knife to remove the parting bead.** The parting bead is the thin strip between the two sashes.

4. **Raise the lower sash so that it clears the sill; then swing out the sash.**

5. **Disconnect the sash cords from the slots at each side of the sash.**

   With the sash removed, you can see the sash weight access panels on either side of the frame.

6. **Use a screwdriver to remove the retaining screws and then pull off the panel cover.**

7. **Remove the sash weight from its space.**

8. **Use an aerosol lubricant such as WD-40 to lubricate the pulley above each access panel.**

9. **Feed the new sash cord over the pulley and downward until you can see the end of the cord through the hole at the access panel.**

10. **Tie the sash cord to the weight.**

    Pass the end of the cord through the hole in the top of the sash weight and then tie a knot in the end of the rope.

11. **Replace the weight in its compartment.**

    Pull the other end of the rope tight so that the sash weight stands up straight in the compartment.

12. **Attach the sash rope to the sash.**

The end of the rope that you have in your hand attaches to the window sash. Most sashes have a groove milled in the side that fits the diameter of the sash rope. Nail the cord into the groove so that the sash weight hangs about 75 mm above the bottom of the compartment when you put the knot into the recess and raise the sash all the way up.

A. Gently loosen the stop bead before pulling out the nails. (Step 2)

B. Access the window weights by opening the small access panel in the base of the jamb. (Step 6)

C. Remove the weight from the hollow area behind the window jamb. (Step 7)

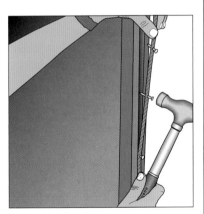

D. To reinstall the sash, nail the cord into the recess in the side of the sash. (Step 12)

Figure 2-3:
Replacing a damaged sash cord in a sash window.

Book II

Basic Home Mainte-nance and Improve-ment

While you have the window sash removed, replace both sash cords, not just the broken one. Why? Because the chances are they are both the same age, and if one has broken, the other is likely to break soon too. And few things are worse than overhauling your windows, and then having a sash cord break a few weeks later. After you replace the cords, position the top window sash back in the frame and renail the parting beads. Then position the lower sash and fix the stop beads.

Modern sliding sash windows have metal channels in which the sash sides, or *stiles*, move. These channels are spring-loaded, and one channel has tension screws that can be adjusted to hold the window in any open position. If your double-hung window refuses to stay open at the chosen position, increase the tension on the stiles by turning the adjustment screws counterclockwise with a screwdriver. When properly adjusted, windows open easily but remain firmly in place at any open position.

Crash! Replacing a Broken Window Pane

Replacing window glass is not a difficult task. Repairing the damage is only a bit more difficult than breaking the glass in the first place. Just gather the appropriate materials and tools and follow the steps for the type of window you're repairing.

You need the following materials to replace a broken pane:

- Replacement glass: Ask a salesperson at a hardware shop or glass merchant to cut a piece of glass exactly to size. Follow the steps later in this section to make sure that your measurements are accurate.

- Glazing putty: This material, available in the glass and painting departments, forms an airtight, watertight seal while allowing the pane to expand and contract in changing temperatures.

- A box of metal glazing sprigs: Sometimes called *glazier's sprigs*, these tiny headless nails hold the pane of glass in place.

You also need the following tools:

- Heat gun (available from tool hire shops) to soften the old glazing putty if it's still intact and as tough as cement

- Flexible putty knife

⤚ 25 mm OR 50 mm stiff steel scraper

⤚ Flat-head screwdriver

⤚ Pincers or pliers

When you work with broken glass, wear safety goggles to protect your eyes, and gloves to cover your hands.

Wood-frame window

To replace a broken glass pane in a wood window, first measure the size of the pane. Measure the exact length and width of the grooves in which the pane will fit and then have a new piece of glass cut so that it measures 3 mm short of the exact dimensions in both the length and width. This ensures a 1.5 mm gap on all four sides between the edges of the pane and the *rebate*, the groove cut into the edge of the wood where the glass pane rests.

When you have your tools and supplies ready, follow these steps, illustrated in Figure 2-4:

1. **Remove any remaining glass shards.**

2. **Use a heat gun to soften the old glazing putty.**

   Heat the glazing putty and scrape it away with a putty knife; if it doesn't lift off easily, apply more heat and try again. You may find that the putty around really old windows is as hard as concrete. Be patient – the heat will eventually soften all putty. Don't be tempted to chisel out the old putty unless you don't mind wrecking the window and creating even more work for yourself!

   As you remove the old glazing putty, you can see small metal glazing sprigs, which hold the glass in position until you apply the glazing putty.

3. **Use pincers or pliers to remove the old glazing sprigs.**

4. **Clean and inspect the rebate to ensure that no glazing putty, glass shards, or glazing sprigs remain.**

   Wear safety goggles as well as gloves; small chips of glass can cause permanent eye damage.

5. **Squeeze out a 3 mm bead of putty on the side of the rebate where the glass will sit.**

Book II

Basic Home Maintenance and Improvement

A. Wear heavy gloves when removing broken glass from the sash. (Step 1)

B. Hold the glass in place with glazing sprigs. Push the glazing sprigs into place with a putty knife or screw-driver. (Step 9)

C. Drag the putty knife blade over the glazing putty at a 45 degree angle to smooth the putty. (Step 11)

Figure 2-4:
Replacing a broken window pane.

6. **Carefully position the new pane in place against the putty. Press the glass down gently at the edges to bed the glass into the putty.**

   Allow the putty bed to spread out and form a moisture seal on the inside of the window between the glass and sash.

7. **Position the new pane in the rebates so that a 1.5 mm gap remains between pane and sash on all four sides.**

8. **Place at least two new glazing sprigs along each edge of the window sash surrounding the new glass.**

   Space the sprigs evenly around the perimeter, about 150 mm apart.

9. **Using the flat side of a putty knife or a screwdriver blade, tap the glazing sprigs into the wood sash.**

10. **Roll a glob of putty between your bare hands to form a 12 mm-thick rope and then press the length of putty along all four sides of the glass.**

11. **Holding the putty knife at a 45-degree angle, press and smooth the glazing putty against the glass and sash.**

12. **Allow the putty to dry and then repaint the putty and repair area.**
    Paint the putty as soon as you can, to keep it from drying out. In summer the putty should be firm enough to take a coat of oil-based paint within 24 hours; in colder weather you may have to wait 48 hours.

Book II

Basic Home Maintenance and Improvement

Don't use masking tape on the glass before painting because you want the paint to form a moisture seal between the glass pane and the sash. Allow the paint to overlap about 3 mm onto the glass to form the seal.

Metal-frame window

Some steel or aluminium window frames are welded together in one piece at the factory.

Glazing putty or some sort of rubber gasket (the same as is used to secure a car windscreen) holds the glass in place. Except for some minor points, which we explain, replacing a broken pane of glass in either type of metal-frame window is basically the same as for wood windows.

To replace the pane in a one-piece steel window, follow the instructions for replacing glass in a wood window with the exception of glazing sprigs. The glass pane in steel casement windows is held in place with glazing putty and spring clips rather than glazing sprigs. When you remove the broken glass from the metal frame, save these clips so that you can reinstall them later.

On some one-piece metal windows the glass is held in place by a rubber gasket. The gasket acts as a seal between the metal and the glass, eliminating the need for glazing putty. Use a screwdriver or putty knife to pry out the gasket. Carefully remove any broken pieces of glass from the frame and then replace the pane with new glass. Reverse the process and push the gasket back into the frame with a putty knife or screwdriver.

Screws placed at each corner of the frame hold together some metal window frames, including sliding sashes. Remove the screws, slide out the broken pane, slide in a new pane, and redrive the corner screws.

Other metal frames are held together by L-brackets placed at the four corners. The faces of these frames are dimpled over the L-brackets. To take these frames apart, you have to remove only one side. To do so, follow these steps:

1. **Drill a hole in the depression at both ends of one side of the frame.**

   Use a drill bit slightly larger than the diameter of the depression.

2. **Pull the sides of the frame apart and carefully remove any broken glass from the frame.**

3. **Replace the pane, making sure that you fully seat the new glass into the gasket surrounding the glass.**

4. **Push the corners together so that the L-brackets are in place and the joint is tight.**

5. **Use a small nail set or a punch and hammer to dimple the metal back over the L-brackets and lock the frame together.**

What a Rotter: Repairing a Rotted Windowsill

Windowsills are sloped outward so that water can run off the sill. Brilliant, eh? Still, if the paint is peeling and the sill is left unprotected, the wood may rot. If you have a windowsill that's rotted, probe the wood with a penknife or carpenter's awl. Wherever the awl penetrates easily, the wood is rotted. When you hit a point where the wood is difficult to penetrate, you've reached solid wood. If the wood is completely rotted, you'll have to replace the entire sill with a new piece of wood – a job probably best left to a skilled carpenter. If the rot is limited to a small area, you can make repairs by following these steps (illustrated in Figure 2-5):

1. **Using a wood chisel or sharp knife, cut away any soft wood.**

   Remove all the damaged wood down to the rot-free portion.

2. **Fill the damaged area with epoxy or polyester wood filler.**

   Filler bonds to sound wood and is very durable.

3. **Use a putty knife or small broad knife to shape the wood filler so that it matches the contours of the old sill.**

4. **Wait for the filler to set and then sand it smooth.**

   Follow the directions on the container; you want the filler to be rock-hard to the touch before sanding. Sand the repair area so that the new surface is smooth and level with the adjoining surface.

5. **Apply wood primer and paint to the repair area to match the existing finish.**

Book II

Basic Home Mainte-nance and Improve-ment

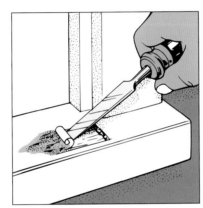

A. Chisel away all soft, rotten wood. (Step 1)

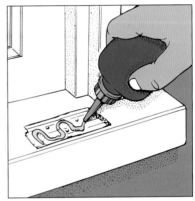

B. Apply the wood filler to the damaged area. (Step 2)

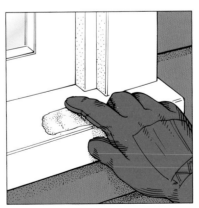

C. Smooth the filler and allow it to harden before sanding. (Steps 3-4)

Figure 2-5: Repairing a rotted window sill.

Energy-Saving Projects

Two of the easiest projects that you can do around the house happen to cut your heating bills. Weather-stripping and sealing fill in gaps and holes around doors, windows, and other places that leak air. Buttoning up the holes and plugging the leaks are must-do projects that couldn't be easier.

Weather-stripping, step by step

Weather-stripping is material that seals the gaps between moving components, such as the gap where a window sash meets the frame or stop bead. In addition to saving energy, weather-stripping blocks draughts and keeps out dust and insects. The thin barrier also blocks outside noise.

Weather-stripping comes in many shapes. It's available with a felt, PVC, or foam-rubber edge on a wood or plastic strip that you attach to the edge of a door or window with small brads. Some versions have an adhesive back so that you can install them without nails.

The easiest type of weather-stripping to install is the adhesive-backed V-seal type, available in a peel-and-stick roll. This type of weather-stripping is inexpensive and easy to install. To apply adhesive-backed weather-stripping to a double-hung window, follow these steps (illustrated in Figure 2-6):

1. **With a damp rag, clean the window frame or other surface where you plan to apply the weather-stripping and let dry completely.**

2. **Cut the strip to the length you want.**

    Use a measuring tape to find the length you need, or place the weather-stripping in position and cut a piece slightly longer. To fully seal the window, you need strips for each side of the inner and outer sash, the bottom of the inner sash, the top of the outer sash, and the outer *meeting rail.*

3. **Raise the inner sash as far as it will go.**

4. **Peel away the backing of the strip, except for a centimetre or so at the top.**

    Later, you have to push this part of the strip up between the sash and the jamb, which is easier to do if you leave the backing in place.

5. **Press the strip in place with the V facing inside.**

6. **Install the strip on the opposite side of the jamb in the same way and then close the window.**

7. **Remove the backing from the top of the weather-stripping that protrudes above the sash and press it in place.**

8. **Lower the outer sash as far as it will go and install the weather-stripping in this sash the same way that you did on the inner sash.**

   The only difference here is that you should leave the backing at the bottom of the strip in place until you raise the window.

9. **Raise the inner sash and apply a strip of weather-stripping to the bottom of the sash; then lower the outer sash and put a strip on top.**

10. **Lower the outer sash far enough to expose the inside face of the bottom of the sash; clean this surface and then apply a strip of weather-stripping with the V facing down.**

Book II

Basic Home Maintenance and Improvement

A. Raise the inside window sash and apply the weather stripping with the V facing towards the inside of the jamb.

B. Lower the sash and remove the backing from the top centimeter or so of the weather stripping and press it in place.

Figure 2-6: Installing adhesive-backed V-seal weather stripping.

C. Lower the outer sash and install the weather stripping in the jamb with the V facing inside.

D. Install weather stripping on the bottom of the inner sash, the top of the outer sash, and the inside face of the lower portion of the outer sash.

Modern windows often have a *kerf* – a slot into which the weather-stripping fits. The weather-stripping for these windows has a tubular edge on one side, with a felt or vinyl lip on the opposite side that closes and seals any crack. To replace this weather-stripping, pull or pry the tubular retaining edge from the slot in the window and then press the new weather-stripping into the slot.

Sealing, step by step

Mastic sealant is a filler material that seals a crack where two nonmoving components meet, such as where a wall meets the exterior window frame. Sealant seals the crack against air infiltration, prevents draughts, and keeps moisture from entering the crack and causing paint to peel or wood to rot.

Sealant is available in many formulations, including polysulfide, acrylic, and silicone. Unlike traditional oil-based sealants that are known to crack and fail within a very short time, modern sealants are warranted for 25 or more years. To avoid having to reseal each summer, choose a quality paintable silicone or acrylic sealant product. These sealants are *elastomeric*, which is a fancy word meaning that they remain flexible after drying and don't crack when weather changes, which causes either of the two joined components to expand and contract.

Sealant is available in a tube with a cone-shaped plastic nozzle. Because the nozzle gradually decreases in size from its base to the tip, you can squeeze out a bigger bead of sealant by cutting the nozzle shorter.

The sealant tube fits into a mastic gun. The gun has a trigger handle that you squeeze to apply pressure to the tube, forcing the sealant out of the nozzle. Mastic guns are available at DIY shops, builders' merchants, and decorating shops.

To seal a gap with mastic sealant, follow these steps:

1. **Use a putty knife or scraper to clean away any old sealant remaining around the gap.**

2. **Cut the tip off the sealant tube nozzle at a point where it produces a bead large enough to fill the gap.**

   A 6 mm bead is large enough for most cracks.

   To avoid too large a bead, cut the nozzle tip near the end, test the bead for size, and then cut off more if you need a larger bead.

   After you cut the tip, you have to puncture the seal in the end of the sealant tube before any sealant will flow. To puncture this seal, unscrew the nozzle, cut the plastic nipple off the end of the tube with a sharp knife, and then screw the nozzle back on.

3. **Apply a bead of sealant, moving the mastic gun at a measured pace along the gap and using continuous light pressure on the gun trigger.**

4. **Smooth the sealant.**

   You can use a teaspoon or wet finger to create a smooth surface.

5. **Wipe away sealant remaining on the gun, your hands, or other unwanted spots before it dries.**

Window Enhancements and Add-ons

Unless an exhibitionist streak runs in the family, most people want some kind of covering for their windows. For rooms where privacy is a prime concern, such as a bathroom or bedroom, impenetrable blinds might be appropriate. In other rooms, you might want floaty net curtains for protection from bright sunlight. Whatever the motivation, basic window coverings are easy to install, even for the not-so-handy.

Installing a window blind

Window blinds are spring-loaded so that they roll up or down and lock in the chosen position. The hardware consists of round support brackets at either end of the blind, as shown in Figure 2-7. You mount the brackets on the inside of the window frame. One bracket has a hole into which a round blind support is inserted; the opposite bracket has a slot to receive the flat support on the other end of the blind.

If you're replacing an old blind, measure the width of the old roller from end to end, including the metal tips, and then measure the length of the blind fully extended. Order a new blind of the same width and length.

Book II

Basic Home Maintenance and Improvement

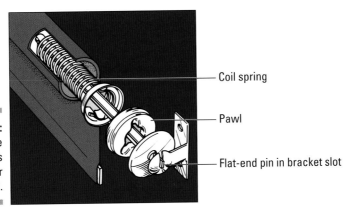

Figure 2-7:
The mechanics of a roller blind.

Coil spring

Pawl

Flat-end pin in bracket slot

To measure for a new blind, hold a rigid measuring stick across the top of the window. Place one end on the inside upper window frame and carefully extend the rule across to the stop on the other side. Order a blind 3 mm smaller than the measurement.

Measure the inside of the jamb and then subtract 3 mm to find the proper length. You can purchase blinds that are easy to cut to the exact length that you need.

To install a blind, follow these simple steps:

1. **Position the metal support brackets at opposite sides of the window. Mark the screw hole positions on the frame with a sharp pencil.**

   Allow enough room between the top of the window jamb and the blind for the roller to turn freely, remembering that when the blind is fully rolled up, it grows in diameter. Hold the blind up where you plan to install it. When you find the correct position for the first bracket position, make a pencil mark for the location of the screw hole. Measure the distance from the top and sides of the window frame and then use that measurement to locate the bracket on the opposite side.

2. **Secure the blind brackets to the window frame with small screws.**

   With a carpenter's awl, make starting holes in the wood. Hold the blind bracket in position and insert the screws.

3. **Slide the ends of the blind into the slots in the brackets.**

   Make sure that the blind is fully wound up when you install it, or it may not retract properly. If you pull the blind down and it doesn't fully roll up by itself, pull the blind down a foot or so and take it off the bracket. Rewind the blind on the roller and then reinstall it in the bracket.

To remove the blind, just push upward on the slotted end of the blind to free it from its bracket and then pull the round support from the hole in the opposite bracket.

Installing a venetian blind

Venetian blinds are mounted in U-shaped brackets that have snap-on covers to provide a finished look. Use them alone or with a fabric valance or cornice board covering the top of the window.

You can mount most venetian blinds outside the window frame (on the architrave of the window), on the wall (so that they cover the architrave), or on the inside of the frame between the window stops. Most mounting brackets have predrilled holes on both the ends and the backs of the mounting brackets. You use only one set of holes, depending on how you mount the venetian blinds.

Trim-to-fit blinds

Many large retailers sell inexpensive window blinds that you can cut to fit almost any window. These blinds are lightweight and flimsy (what do you expect for about £10?), but they may be just right for a quick fix or when you're on a tight budget.

You can't do anything about the length of these blinds, but you can custom-cut the width by using the score lines on the blind as guidelines. The steel blind roller slides together to fit the new width.

Install the brackets as we describe for regular blinds. (See the 'Installing a window blind' section in this chapter.) Insert the blind in the left bracket. Remove the plastic hem slat from the pocket and notice its score lines that match up with the score lines running the length of the blind. Hold the blind level under the right bracket, so you can determine the correct width. Then mark the width with a light pencil mark at the closest score line on the blind. Carefully begin to tear the length of the blind at its score line until the entire blind is done. Adjust the blind roller to fit the new width by pushing the end plug until it reaches the end of the blind. Then snap off the plastic hem slat to the same width and install it. Easy-peasy!

Book II

Basic Home Mainte- nance and Improve- ment

Before you purchase venetian blinds, decide whether you want to mount the blind inside or outside the window frame and then measure your windows using a folding wooden measuring rule or wooden measuring stick. The general procedure is to measure the width at the top, middle, and bottom of the window and use the smallest dimension for its width. Measure the length of the window to get the correct extension of the blind.

If you order custom blinds, you can indicate the length you want the blinds to be. If you buy blinds off the rack, you have to cut the blind cords to the proper length; usually, you want the bottom edge of the blind to rest on or slightly above the windowsill. Directions for cutting the blind cords for length are included in the venetian blind package.

 You can install small clips on both sides of the window to act as hold-down brackets to secure the bottom of the blinds so that they don't sway freely. These clips, secured with a small brad or finishing nail, are easy to reach but not noticeable.

To install a blind on the inside of the jamb, follow these steps:

1. **Measure and mark the locations for the U-shaped mounting brackets.**

   Position the mounting brackets at the top corner of the window jamb. Hold the brackets in place (paying attention to which is the right and which is the left bracket) and use them as a template to mark the location of the mounting screws with a pencil.

2. **Drill pilot holes for the mounting screws through the pencil marks on the window jamb.**

   Use a 2 mm drill or carpenter's awl to make starter holes for the screws.

3. **Use a screwdriver to install the mounting brackets with the screws provided.**

4. **Push the blind's header bar into the brackets, as shown in Figure 2-8, and secure it by closing each bracket.**

   Some designs simply slide into the bracket.

5. **If necessary, cut the blind cords to length.**

Figure 2-8:
To install a venetian blind inside the jamb, screw the brackets to the top or side of the jamb.

Driving small screws while reaching upward is an awkward and frustrating job that may introduce new and colourful words into your vocabulary. To make the job easier, use a cordless screwdriver, which is small and light-weight. You can use the toggle switch on a cordless to provide drive or reverse power.

Installing curtain rods and hardware

Rod-mounting brackets are often nailed to the window architrave or frame to hold the rods for lightweight curtains. To install curtain rods, refer to the 'Installing a window blind' section for directions, earlier in this chapter.

Installing rods to support heavy curtains can be a horse of a different colour. If you're mounting rods for heavy curtains on the architrave or the window frame, you can drive the hardware screws into the wood. But if you are fixing into the wall at either side of the window, then you need to drill holes using a masonry bit, and insert plastic plugs, also known as *Rawlplugs* or *wall plugs*, to take your screws.

Chapter 3

Doors: An Open-and-Shut Case

In This Chapter

▷ Caring for door hinges and locks

▷ Unsticking folding doors

▷ Keeping sliding wardrobe doors on track

▷ Installing and replacing door locks

▷ Keeping garage doors in tiptop shape

They swing open; they slide shut – simple acts you probably take for granted. But when they squeak or refuse to budge, you start to notice the doors in and around your house. To keep everything in good working order, perform the typical door maintenance and repair jobs in this chapter, and you won't hear another squeak from them.

Maintaining Locks and Hinges

You probably don't spend much time thinking about your doors – and if you do, you may want to seek professional help – but consider that a family opens and closes household doors thousands of times each year. The hinges and locks on the doors take a real pounding, so lubricate them at least once a year. To lubricate door hardware, you need:

✔ A can of aerosol (spray) lubricant such as WD-40

✔ Paper towels

✔ Slot and cross-head screwdrivers

✔ A hammer

Lubricating hinges

Interior doors typically have two or three hinges. Exterior doors are heavier than interior doors, so they have three or four hinges. To lubricate door hinges, first remove one hinge pin. Some hinge pins extend through the hinges, so you can use a large nail to tap them up from the bottom, as shown in Figure 3-1. Other hinges may require you to insert the blade of a slot screwdriver under the head of the hinge pin and then tap the handle of the screwdriver with a hammer to drive the pin up and out of the hinge.

Figure 3-1:
Using a nail to remove the hinge pin.

After you remove one hinge pin, drop a large nail in the hinge to temporarily replace the removed pin and prevent the door from sagging off its hinges. Lay the hinge pin on paper towels and remove any dirt. Spray the pin with a light coating of lubricant and replace it in the hinge. Repeat this procedure for all the hinges, one at a time.

Lubricating door locks

Many people put up with the aggravation of a sticking door lock for years – an annoyance that would try the patience even of Harry Houdini. Ironically, you can fix most stubborn locks in a matter of minutes.

First, clean the keyhole with a penetrating lubricant like WD-40. (Don't apply household oil to the key or cylinder because it attracts dirt and eventually gums up the lock.) Spray the lubricant into the keyhole itself and then spray it on the key. Slide the key in and out of the lock several times to spread the lubricant.

If this superficial cleaning doesn't free the lock, eliminate the aggravation altogether: Take about ten minutes to disassemble, clean, and reassemble the entire door lock. Here's how to remove and clean the most common type of door lock:

1. **With the door open, use a cross-head screwdriver to take out the two connecting screws that are located by the doorknob on the inside of the lock.**

2. **Remove the two screws that hold the lock faceplate on the edge of the door.**

3. **Slide the doorknob off the spindle, pull out the lock mechanism, and remove the latchbolt from its hole in the edge of the door, as shown in Figure 3-2.**

Book II

Basic Home Mainte- nance and Improve- ment

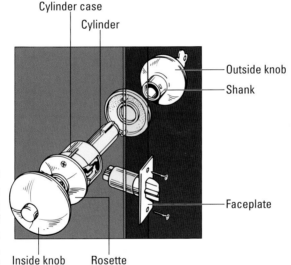

Cylinder case

Cylinder

Outside knob

Shank

Figure 3-2: The assembly of a modern door lock.

Faceplate

Inside knob   Rosette

4. **Lay the disassembled lock parts on layers of newspaper or paper towels.**

5. **Spray a light all-purpose household lubricant or silicone lubricant on all moving parts of the lock, flushing out any dirt from the latchbolt. Use powdered graphite from a hardware shop to lubricate the lock cylinder.**

   Spray until all the dirt is flushed from the assembly and then let the latchbolt assembly lie on the newspaper or towels until all the excess lubricant has dripped off.

To reassemble the door lock after cleaning and lubricating it, follow these steps:

1. **Insert the latchbolt assembly into its hole in the edge of the door.**

2. **Insert the exterior doorknob and spindle into its hole, aligning it so that the spindles and connecting screws pass through the holes in the latchbolt assembly, as shown in Figure 3-3.**

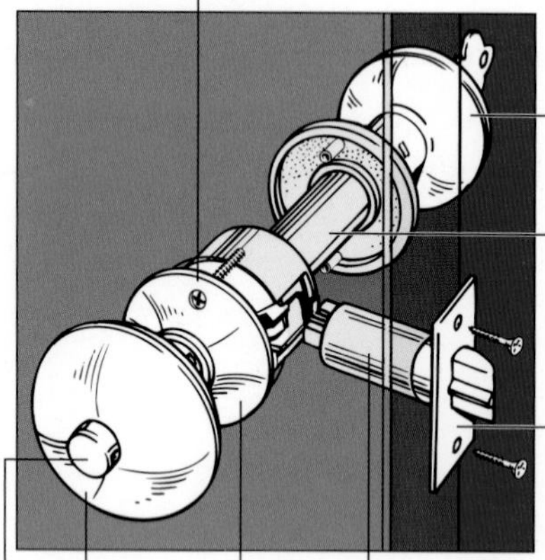

Attaching stems

Outside knob

Spindle

Figure 3-3:
Carefully
align the
spindles
when
reinstalling
a latchbolt
lock
assembly.

Faceplate

Inside knob   Rosette
Push button   Latchbolt assembly

3. **Drive in the latchbolt screws, but don't tighten them until the lock is completely assembled.**

4. **Slide the interior doorknob onto the shaft, aligning the screw holes, and then drive in the screws.**

   Turn the doorknob back and forth to check that the cylinder and latchbolt are engaged and in proper alignment.

5. **Tighten the screws on the latchbolt and recheck the alignment by turning the knob.**

6. **Test the lock by turning the knob and locking the lock.**

   If the lock doesn't work smoothly, loosen the screws, realign the cylinder and latchbolt, and try again.

You can lubricate deadbolts the same way. Remove the connecting screws, the faceplate screws, and then the knobs. Next, pull out the latchbolt assembly and clean and lubricate the lock as just described. To reassemble the lock, reverse the procedure.

Tightening loose hinges

Loose hinges can cause a door to stick, bind, or scrape the floor. Luckily for you, this is another common, easy-to-solve problem. First, check that the hinge screws are tight. Open the door, grasp it by the lock edge, and move it up and down. If you encounter movement at the hinge screws, they need to be tightened.

If the hinge screws have been loose for a short time, you may only need to tighten them with a screwdriver. But when hinge screws are left loose for a long time, the constant movement of the hinge plate and screws enlarges the screw holes. Eventually, the holes become so large that the screws can't stay tight. The result: Completely useless stripped screws!

If the door still moves even a tiny bit after you tighten its hinge screws, repair the enlarged screw holes. Repair one screw hole at a time so that you don't have to remove the door. Here's how:

1. **Remove the loose screw.**

2. **Dip the bare end of a wooden match or cocktail stick in some wood glue and tap it with a hammer as far into the screw hole as it will go, as shown in Figure 3-4.**

   If the screw is large, you may have to put several glue-coated matches in the hole.

Book II

Basic Home Mainte- nance and Improve- ment

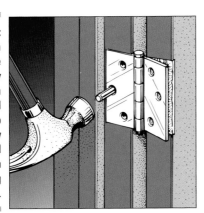

Figure 3-4: Tighten a loose hinge screw by driving a glue-coated match into the screw hole and then reinstalling the screw.

3. **Break or cut off the match(es) flush with the hinge plate and discard the heads.**

4. **After you've filled the void in the screw hole with the wooden match(es) and let the glue dry, drive the screw into the hole with a screwdriver.**

5. **Remove the next screw and repair its hole, continuing until you have fixed all the enlarged screw holes. Clever, eh?**

In place of a match, you can use wooden golf tees coated with glue to plug a stripped screw hole. Golf tees are tapered, so they fit easily into the screw hole. Let the glue dry and then cut off the protruding part of the tee.

Fixing Folding Doors

Folding doors suffer from another chronic condition: They tend to jump off their tracks or become misaligned and, consequently, don't open or open only partially.

Folding doors are arranged in hinged pairs that fold like an accordion toward both sides of the door jamb or frame when opened. Because folding doors permit you to open the doors fully and provide access to all storage, they're often used on wardrobes. They move via nylon rollers or pins mounted on the tops of the doors and travel on a track mounted at the top of the door jamb, as shown in Figure 3-5. The doors nearest the side jambs swing on pivot blocks installed at the top and, on some models, at the floor to keep the bottoms of the doors from swinging outward. To keep folding doors operating smoothly, clean and lubricate the track, rollers, and pivot blocks at least once a year.

Figure 3-5:
Folding doors have rollers that run along tracks and pivots that enable the panels nearest the jambs to swing open.

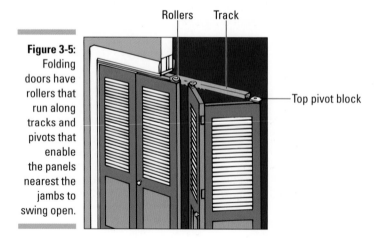

Rollers   Track

Top pivot block

To tune up folding doors and lubricate the top track, open the doors. Wipe the track with a clean cloth to remove dust. Use an aerosol lubricant to spray the track and rollers or pins. Apply the lubricant sparingly and be careful not to spray any clothes hanging in the wardrobe. Leave only a light film of lubricant on the parts; use paper towels to wipe away any excess lubricant.

If your folding doors *bind* (don't open or slide on their tracks easily), first check to see whether all the hardware is secure and working properly. If the parts are broken, replacement hardware is available at DIY centres. Check the hinges between each pair of doors. If the hinge screws are loose, use a screwdriver to tighten them. If the screw holes are stripped so that you can't tighten the hinge screws, remove the hinges and plug the screw holes following the steps we suggested for door hinges earlier in this chapter.

 Working on folding doors may be easier if you remove them from the door-frame first. To do so, unfold the doors and carefully lift them up and out of the frame. You may find this easier to do if you stand inside, not outside, the door. For example, to remove a folding wardrobe door, you may have to stand inside the wardrobe, see how the door sits in its track, and then lift it out.

If, when you rehang the doors, the gap between the door and the jamb is uneven, use a screwdriver or wrench to adjust the top pivot blocks and even the gap. Some folding doors have adjustable pivot blocks at the bottom corner.

> **Book II**
>
> **Basic Home Mainte-nance and Improve-ment**

Keeping Sliding Doors Smooth Operators

The two types of doors that are easiest to open don't have hinges at all; instead, they slide on tracks. Follow our simple repair and maintenance procedures to keep your sliding doors on track.

Getting your patio door to slide better

Patio doors slide horizontally – or at least they're supposed to. All too often, these big, pesky contraptions stubbornly resist opening, and getting outside becomes about as easy as dragging a fridge through a hedge.

The most common cause of a sticking patio door is debris in the lower track. This channel easily becomes clogged with dirt, leaves, and such because people and pets walk over it whenever they go in or out. Each time you vacuum your floors, use a small brush attachment or cordless vacuum to clean the sliding-door tracks. Apply a lubricant to both upper and lower tracks to keep the door hardware clean and operating freely.

In addition to cleaning and lubricating sliding-door tracks, you need to lubricate the door lock. The best way to lubricate any lock is to disassemble it and use an aerosol lubricant to flush away grime and coat the moving parts of the lock.

Sometimes, patio doors become hard to open even when the track is clean. The problem is usually that the rollers at the bottom of the door have started to rub against the track. The rollers at the top can also wear down, lowering the bottom of the door so that it rubs on the track.

Most sliding doors have a mechanism called an *adjusting screw* located at the bottom of the door ends. Turning this screw raises or lowers the roller, as shown in Figure 3-6. Give the screw a clockwise turn and test to see whether the door slides more easily. If the door becomes even harder to open, turn the screw in the opposite direction. After a bit of adjustment, the door should roll easily without rubbing on the bottom track.

Figure 3-6: A screw at the base of the door controls the clearance between the bottom of a sliding door and the track.

Maintaining sliding wardrobe doors

Sliding wardrobe doors operate on rollers that are positioned in tracks at the top jamb and floor, allowing the doors to bypass each other in the tracks (see Figure 3-7).

To clean and lubricate the hardware of a sliding wardrobe door, use a stiff brush, a toothbrush, or a hand vacuum to clean dust from the tracks. Use an aerosol lubricant to lubricate all the door rollers. If the rollers are damaged, install replacement rollers (available at DIY centres).

If the door doesn't hang level, leaving an uneven gap between the door and doorframe, look for an adjustable mounting screw at the inside top of each door. Use a screwdriver to adjust the mounting screw and even out the door.

A simple roller-and-track assembly.

A roller with adjustable clearance.

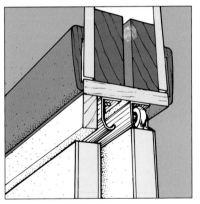

A two-track sliding door.

Removing a sliding door by lifting it up out of its tracks.

Figure 3-7: Sliding wardrobe doors.

Book II

Basic Home Maintenance and Improvement

Locking Up

If a door in your house looks good, but its lock wobbles or shows signs of wear, consider replacing the lock. Standard interior locks come in a variety of styles and finishes that can improve the look of the door as well as provide security.

Replacing standard door locks

If your locks are becoming worn or damaged, replace them with new units. Because door locks vary somewhat in design, remove the lock and measure the diameter of the opening and the distance from the centre of the hole to the edge of the door, which is either 60 mm or 70 mm. If you find an exact match, you won't have to redrill the lock holes.

To replace a standard door lock, see the directions in the 'Maintaining Locks and Hinges' section earlier in this chapter.

Installing a deadbolt

Many exterior doors are fitted with an ordinary cylinder lock that has a key-hole in the doorknob. This type of lock offers little resistance to a determined burglar (and what other kind of burglar is there?). The latchbolt of most standard locks extends only into the doorframe and a stiff kick from a booted foot can splinter most doorframes. And thieves can wrench out the exterior knobs of passage locks by using a pipe wrench. For added security, install a deadbolt lock on every exterior door.

Deadbolt locks have latchbolts that extend through the doorframe and into the wall stud next to the frame. A deadbolt lock has no exterior knob, so it's impossible to wrench the lock from its hole in the door. From the inside, you operate a deadbolt lock by turning either a thumb-turn lever (if you have a single-cylinder lock) or a key (for a double-cylinder lock). If you have small children in the home who may not be able to find the key in an emergency, choose a thumb-turn lock. Keep in mind, though, that if your exterior door contains glass panels, a burglar can break the glass, reach inside, and unlock a thumb-turn lock.

Preferably fit your front door with a five-lever mortise deadlock, though insurance companies accept a rim automatic deadlock. Both must be to British Standard 3621 or the equivalent European Standard EN12209.

Deadbolt locks are relatively inexpensive, and most come complete with a cardboard template that shows where to drill the cylinder and latchbolt holes.

Follow these general steps, illustrated in Figure 3-8, to install a deadbolt lock:

1. **Choose a position on the door for the lock.**

   Most standard locks are set at or near 36 inches from the bottom of the door. Install the deadbolt lock above the standard lock or about 44 inches above the bottom of the door.

2. **Use masking tape to affix the template to the door edge and face.**

3. **Use a bradawl or large nail to mark the centres of the holes for the lock cylinder (through the face of the door) and the latchbolt (into the edge of the door).**

4. **Use the proper size of hole saw to bore the hole for the lock cylinder.**

   Some manufacturers offer a kit that includes a hole saw with the lock set. Drilling the hole from both sides helps prevent the door from splintering. The hole saw has a centre pilot bit to guide the saw through the door. From one side of the door, drill until the tip of the pilot point pokes through the opposite side of the door, and then pull the hole saw out, position the bit in the hole, and finish boring the hole from the opposite side of the door.

5. **Use a 25 mm flat bit to drill the latchbolt hole into the edge of the door.**

   The flat bit is an inexpensive wood-boring instrument that looks like a paddle with a triangular point on the end. Attach it to your drill to cut a perfectly round hole into the wood.

6. **Cut a mortise, or recess, in the wood for the latchbolt faceplate.**

   The latchbolt faceplate must fit into a shallow mortise in the edge of the door. Cutting out this mortise isn't nearly as difficult as it sounds; all you need is a sharp 25 mm chisel and a hammer.

   To cut the latchbolt mortise, place the latchbolt in the hole and mark around the faceplate with a knife to indicate its outline on the end of the door. Use the chisel to deepen the marks to about 3 mm. Then, starting at the top of the faceplate outline, make a series of closely spaced chisel cuts inside the marks. A 25 mm-wide chisel blade will fit inside the outline. Tap the chisel with a hammer so that it makes 3 mm-deep cuts.

   Remove the resulting wood chips with the chisel blade. Then use the chisel to smooth the bottom of the mortise. Place the latchbolt in the door and check the fit of the mortise. If the faceplate is not flush with the door edge, chisel away a bit more wood.

Book II

Basic Home Maintenance and Improvement

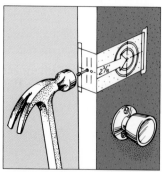

A. Drive a nail through the template layout marks to indicate the position for the lock-set holes. (Step 3)

B. Use a hole saw to bore the large hole for the lock cylinder in the side of the door. (Step 4)

C. Use a wood-boring flat bit to drill the latchbolt hole in the edge of the door. (Step 5)

D. Use a utility knife to mark the outline of the faceplate on the edge of the door and then make the shallow mortise to recess the plate. (Step 6)

E. Insert the keyed portion of the lock into the hole in the latchbolt. (Step 9)

Figure 3-8: Installing a deadbolt lock for extra security.

7. When the faceplate fits flush with the door edge, hold it in place and use it as a template for installing the two mounting screws.

8. Before installing the lock, apply a thin film of aerosol lubricant to all the moving parts.

9. Place the latchbolt in its hole and then insert the keyed portion of the lock so that the tailpiece extends through the hole in the latchbolt.

10. From the inside of the door, fit the inside cylinder so that the holes for the retaining screws are aligned with the exterior portion of the lock.

11. Use the two retaining screws to secure the two sides of the lock together.

12. Shut the door and use a pencil to mark the spot on the door jamb where the latchbolt meets the jamb.

13. Using the keep or striking plate (the metal plate that fits on the frame and holds the latch) as a template, trace and cut a mortise on the door jamb; then dig out the mortise with a sharp chisel.

14. Use a spade bit to bore a latchbolt hole in the centre of the mortise.

15. Use the screws provided to install the striking plate into the mortise.

16. Shut the door and test the fit by operating the deadbolt lock. If necessary, you can loosen the screws and adjust the lock set slightly so that the latchbolt passes easily into its hole.

Book II

Basic Home Maintenance and Improvement

If you replace entry door locks on several doors, buy locks that are keyed alike so that you can use one key to open both or all entry doors. If you're replacing only one lock, ask the dealer to rekey the existing lock so that one key can open both back and front doors. If you use separate keys for your home's entry locks, you can have a locksmith rekey the locks so that one key fits all.

Securing sliding patio doors

Because they're large and easy to force open, patio doors are common targets for intruders. Safeguard your residence by buying a locking device that blocks the track, preventing outsiders from forcing the door to slide open. Or create your own device by cutting a length of wood (such as a broomstick or a 50 x 50 mm wooden board) to fit snugly between the doorframe and the stile of the operable door.

You can enhance this safety feature by drilling a hole through one door and into the other and then inserting a long nail or bolt through the holes: This setup prevents intruders from prying the door up and swinging out its bottom to gain entry. If the existing lock doesn't work, check DIY centres for replacement locks.

To prevent a break-in through the door pane, install a tough window film (sold at glass merchants) that prevents the glass from shattering and resists forced entry.

Maintaining Garage Doors

Because garage doors are especially exposed to weather extremes, you should inspect and service them at least once a year. Most modern garage doors consist of a single-panelled 'up-and-over' metal door. The 'round-the-corner' garage doors consist of four or more panels that are hinged so that they can travel in a pair of tracks, as shown in Figure 3-9.

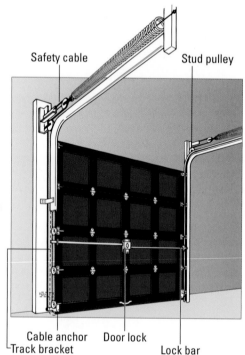

Safety cable   Stud pulley

Figure 3-9:
Lubricate
the major
parts of your
garage door
annually.

Cable anchor   Door lock
└Track bracket   Lock bar

Use an aerosol spray lubricant and wand to clean and lubricate all these moving pieces:

- **Combination hinge and rollers:** These gizmos are located at either side of the door, between each pair of panels. Apply lubricant to the roller and the hinge to which the roller is attached. Use lubricant sparingly; too much doesn't make the door work better, it just attracts dirt that will eventually gum up the works.

- **Hinges in the centre of the door panels:** The hinges that hold the centre of the door panels together don't have a roller. Apply lubricant to these hinges and then operate the door several times to distribute the lubricant to all moving surfaces of the hardware.

- **Lock mechanism on the door:** Spray lubricant into the keyhole and work the key several times to distribute the lubricant to the lock's moving parts. If your door is manually operated, lubricate the pair of locking latches at each side of the door.

If your garage door operates with an automatic opener, ensure that it's equipped with a safety-stop feature (available from garage door retailers – check out your *Yellow Pages*) that prevents damage to the door and protects young children from being trapped and injured under the door. The safety-stop mechanism on an older door causes the door to reverse direction if it meets any resistance as it closes. Newer models have a safety-stop mechanism that causes the door to stop closing if anything interrupts a beam of light directed across the door threshold.

Book II

Basic Home Maintenance and Improvement

Chapter 4

Roofs and Walls

In This Chapter

▸ Looking after your roof

▸ Stopping leaks before they begin

▸ Getting into gutters

▸ Caring for cladding

▸ Maintaining masonry

*Y*our home and its contents depend on the integrity of your roof and exterior walls in the same way that you depend on protective clothing to keep you dry in foul weather. Getting temporarily stuck in bad weather can make you uncomfortable and may even ruin your hair, but left unchecked, a roof leak – even a tiny one – can end up costing a fortune in damage to a home's interior and its precious contents. Damage to flooring, plaster, furniture, important papers, and more is no small matter.

Your Roof: The Fifth Wall of Your Home

Most people are pretty conscientious about maintaining the exterior walls of their homes. But rarely do you see anyone on the roof of a home unless the roof is being replaced. For some reason, people just don't pay as much attention to their roofs, which we think is a mistake.

Consider the roof as the fifth wall of your home that requires maintenance with the same regularity as the walls that support it. With proper care and maintenance, a roof can outlast its warranty without leaking a drop or suffering ugly damage.

If you aren't agile or athletic, or if you have a fear of heights, think about hiring someone else to maintain your roof. If you do go up there, wear rubber-soled shoes, which grip well. Never walk on a wet roof, and don't be afraid to wear a safety harness, too; it prevents broken bones and may even save your life.

Cleanliness is next to godliness

Streaks or discolouration can cause a perfectly good roof to look worn and tattered. So, for appearance's sake, use the following universal roof cleaning formula when your roof gets dirty. This concoction also gets rid of mildew or moss on your roof, which can cause extensive damage if left unattended.

You need these supplies:

- 250 ml liquid chlorine bleach
- 115 g powdered laundry detergent
- 5 litres hot water
- Bucket or large mixing bowl
- Garden hose
- Pump garden sprayer
- Safety glasses or goggles
- Stiff-bristle broom
- Stir stick (the kind for paint is fine)
- Tall ladder (the height you need depends on the height of your roof – see the nearby sidebar on ladders)

Do this project on a cool, dry day to ensure that the cleaner doesn't dry too fast on the roof. Wait until the weather's right and then follow these steps:

1. **Mix the hot water, bleach, and detergent until the soap granules dissolve and then pour the mixture into the garden sprayer.**

2. **On the roof, spray the cleaner on a strip about 1 metre high x 3 metres wide and let it sit for about 15 minutes.**

    Start work on the part of the roof farthest away from you so that you never stand on wet tiles. If the tiles are thin slate you may need a walkway to protect the slates from cracking if you tread on them. Modern concrete tiles are pretty tough though.

3. **If the cleaner begins to dry out, spray on a bit more.**

4. **Use a broom to scrub the area as needed to get it clean.**

5. **Rinse the cleaned area with fresh water.**

    Repeat the process until the roof is clean.

A few uplifting words about ladders

You can choose from as many different ladders as there are tasks that require them. They range from the small two- and three-rung stepstool type to the common 2- and 2.5-metre folding models, to the granddaddy of them all, the extension ladder.

If your home-maintenance budget can afford only one ladder, get a 2-metre stepladder, which gives you the length you need when tackling most home-maintenance and repair projects. However, if your ceilings are 3 metres or higher, you need a 2.5 metre ladder. If your project involves a multistorey roof, you need an extension ladder.

When buying a ladder, look for secure connections, metal-supported steps, and superior hinges. As the ladder ages, keep an eye out for loose connections, splits, cracks, and missing rivets.

Follow these ladder-safety tips:

✔ A sinking ladder can tilt and throw you to the ground. When working on earth or grass, you may need to stabilise the ladder

by placing the feet on boards or a sheet of plywood to prevent them from sinking into the earth. For added stability, place the bottom of the ladder away from the wall one-quarter of the ladder's length.

✔ When you're working on the roof, make sure that the ladder extends a minimum of 600 mm above the edge of the roof. The extension provides support so that you can steady yourself as you traverse from ladder to roof and vice versa. Firmly secure the top of the ladder so that it can't move.

✔ Never climb onto a roof from the gable end where the roof crosses the ladder rungs at an angle. Instead, mount the roof from a horizontal side. Make sure that the plane of the roof is parallel to the ladder rungs at the point where you leave the ladder to mount the roof.

✔ To maintain proper balance, keep your hips between the side rails when climbing the ladder or reaching out. Keep one hand on the ladder and the other free for work.

Book II

Basic Home Maintenance and Improvement

The naked truth about flashing

Roof flashing creates a watertight connection where the roof is adjoined to a wall, as when a first-storey roof connects to a second-storey wall. Roof flashing also creates watertight connections between the roofing and items that penetrate it, including plumbing pipes, boiler flues, skylights, and chimneys.

All roofs have roof flashing. Although most flashings are made of lead, some are made of galvanised sheet metal or aluminium. And that means rust or corrosion. And rust or corrosion means leaks.

To prevent flashing from leaking, you need to keep it from rusting. Applying a good coat of Hammerite metal paint every few years generally does the trick. After you apply the first coat of paint to your flashing, maintaining it is easy. You want to focus on removing any rust that appears and keeping the paint in good condition.

Follow these steps to remove rust from your flashing:

1. **Wash the surface with tri-sodium phosphate, or TSP, mixed to the manufacturer's specifications.**

   The TSP *etches* (chemically roughens) the painted surface.

2. **Use sandpaper or a wire brush to remove all rust.**

3. **Clean away the dust and use a paintbrush to apply a rust converter.**

   The rust converter acts as a primer while converting leftover rust to an inert material.

4. **Apply gloss paint or Hammerite metal paint as a finish coat.**

   We like to paint our roof flashings, vent pipes, and flue caps the same colour as the roofing material, making them less noticeable and more aesthetically appealing.

 One type of flashing, called vent flashing, incorporates a rubber grommet that seals the connection between the centremost portion of the flashing and a plumbing vent pipe. Keep this rubber grommet in good condition with a shot of rubber preservative every year or two.

Fixing Slipped or Damaged Slates and Tiles

The saying 'a stitch in time saves nine' was never truer than when applied to roofs. The average house roof contains 2,000 to 3,000 slates or tiles, and as long as each one does its job, everything's fine. But if just one slate or tile slips out of place or gets broken, then the water can get in and create big problems. So if you spot a slipped or damaged slate or tile, get it fixed fast.

Safety first

Roofs have an unfortunate habit of being high up off the ground, so in most cases, you are far better off getting an experienced roofer to do your repairs for you. Exceptions are bungalows and single-storey extensions to higher houses, where you can safely reach the lower courses of slates or tiles from a securely fixed ladder or scaffold tower. Some houses have safely accessible roofs you can reach without climbing a ladder, such as 'butterfly' roofs, where you can climb out of a roof window and stand on the valley gutter. The safest way to access the roof is when a competent scaffolding contractor has properly scaffolded the house.

Replacing a slate

The usual cause of slipped slates is 'nail sickness', which is a quaint term for rust. Each slate is fixed to its timber roof batten with nails, and when these nails corrode, nothing's left to stop the slate from sliding gracefully down the roof. Of course, it might be that the nails are perfectly OK, and the slate was cracked by the hefty boots of the bloke who installed the new satellite dish – but that's another story. Suffice to say that if your roof was last re-covered 60 years ago or more, and lots of slates have slipped, then nail sickness may be a real problem, and it's time to think about having all the slates stripped off and re-fixed to new timber battens by a pro.

If you just have one slipped or broken slate, you can do it yourself. You won't be able to fix the replacement slate with nails in the same position as the original, as the nail positions are hidden under the bottom edge of the slates in the course above. The replacement slate is held in place using a *clip*, which you can cut from a strip of lead sheet. Here's how to replace a slate:

Book II

Basic Home Maintenance and Improvement

1. **Remove the slipped or broken slate by sliding it gently downwards, so as not to disturb the overlapping course of slates above it.** If the nails are still in place in the batten, either pull them out with pliers or cut off their heads using a thin cold chisel or bolster or, better still, a purpose-made tool called a *slate rip*, shown in Figure 4-1.

Figure 4-1:
A slate rip.

2. Cut the clip from a piece of lead sheet – approximately 15 mm wide and 300 mm long – and fix the top end of the clip to the batten by driving a galvanised nail through the clip and into the batten, in the gap between the two slates in the course above.

3. Slide the replacement slate into position gently from below, and secure it by folding up the bottom end of the lead clip. See Figure 4-2.

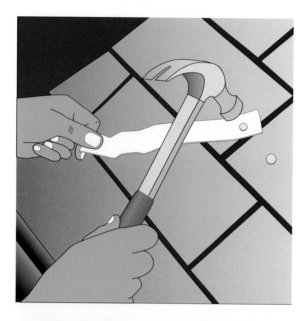

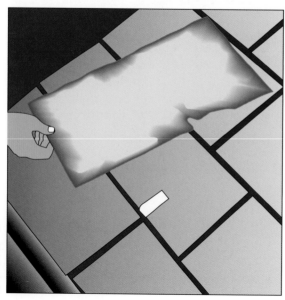

Figure 4-2:
Replacing
a slate.

Book II

Basic Home Mainte- nance and Improve- ment

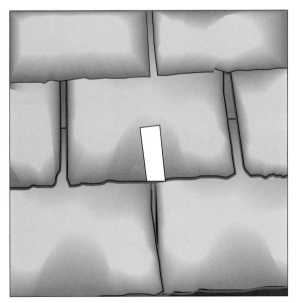

Replacing a tile

Roof tiles are generally easier to replace than slates, as older tiles are not nailed to the timber battens, but are hung onto the battens by nibs protrud- ing from their top edges. Modern tiles are nailed about every fifth one. Here's how to replace a slipped or damaged tile:

1. **Remove the tile by tilting up the tiles in the course above until you have enough room to wriggle the nibs free of the batten.** You may even be able to slide the tiles in the course above upwards (under the course of tiles above *them*), to give yourself room to work.

2. **Insert the replacement tile by sliding it into position gently from below, making sure that the nibs are firmly hooked over the timber batten.**

3. **Slide the tiles in the course above back into place, and make sure that they are also firmly hooked into position.**

Putting Your Mind in the Gutter

When it comes to your home, you'll be cursing not singing in the rain if you haven't maintained your gutters and drainpipes properly.

Cleaning gutters and drainpipes

Gutters, drainpipes, and rainwater downpipes filled with debris can clog up, causing roof leaks, rot, and structural damage. Once a year, get up on a ladder and give those gutters and rainwater downpipes a good cleaning. Gutters that haven't been cleaned for a while may be filled with a mud-like substance, which you can scoop out with a small garden trowel or putty knife. You may even want to invest in a *gutter scoop* (a trowel-like plastic scoop made for cleaning gutters).

After you remove the majority of the debris, flush the rest away by using a garden hose with a spray nozzle.

Patching leaks

When galvanised sheet metal gutters aren't regularly cleaned and painted, they tend to rust. As we mention earlier in this chapter, unpainted metal rusts, and rust results in leaks. Use the same technique on gutters that you use to maintain roof flashings. (See the section 'The naked truth about flashing', earlier in this chapter.)

If the gutter is sagging, replace the mounting brackets before fixing leaks. You don't want the gutter shape to change after you've fixed the leak. Doing so may cause a patch to open.

When a rusty area turns into a leak, try this quick repair:

1. **Use a wire brush or the wire wheel on a drill to remove as much rust from the area as possible.**

2. **Apply a coat of rust converter over the repair area.**

   The converter renders remnants of rust inert. Allow the converter to dry completely.

3. **Apply a 3 mm-thick coat of roof cement around the leak.**

   Before the cement dries, add a strip of aluminium foil to the repair area (like taping a sticking-plaster to your arm). Use a putty knife to gently flatten the foil and squeeze out the excess cement.

   The total thickness of the repair shouldn't exceed 1.5 mm. You can create a dam if you use too much roof cement.

   For larger repairs substitute a piece of sheet metal for the aluminium foil. Heating contractors typically have a bin full of scraps that are perfect for this type of repair. Chances are that you can get the scrap you need for a handshake and a 'thank you'. For badly damaged areas, sheet metal plates can be pop-riveted into place and sealed with liquid aluminium. However, you may want to leave this maintenance task to a sheet metal contractor.

4. **With the foil in place, use a putty knife to add another thin layer of roof cement to cover the patch.**

If the repair area is large, consider replacing the damaged sections. The style you have is probably still available. Gutter shapes haven't changed much over the years!

Occasionally, a gutter seam or joint opens, producing a leak. Catching this problem early on reduces the chance of rust and, possibly, a major repair. You can seal joints in aluminium and galvanised sheet metal gutters with silicone mastic and you can repair plastic gutters by renewing the rubber gaskets on the joints.

Cladding: Armour for Your House

Water can attack and damage wood cladding. Rendered (stucco) walls crack when the house shifts, as winter rains expand soil. Metal cladding dents easily. Vinyl (UPVC) cladding pits as it oxidises. Even brick chips and cracks with winter freezes and summer ground settlement.

No material is perfect, but you can take action to extend the life of your home's exterior.

Book II

Basic Home Maintenance and Improvement

Treating wood cladding

Treat wood cladding with an application of oil, stain, or paint to prevent rot. These materials act as a barrier, preventing water from coming into direct contact with the wood. Which finish you choose is mostly an aesthetic choice:

- Oil, a clear finish, is absorbed into the wood, filling all pores and voids, thereby displacing water that otherwise would be absorbed. Oil doesn't last as long as paint, but it doesn't chip or blister.
- Oil stain is the same as oil except that a pigment is mixed into the oil.
- Paint penetrates and protects in the same way that oil does. Additionally, paint coats the surface of the wood with a thin, durable, waterproof skin.

Head to Book III, Chapters 2 and 3 for all you need to know on painting and staining wood cladding.

Cleaning PVC-U cladding

PVC-U cladding (unplasticised polyvinyl chloride for those of you geeky enough to wonder) is a great-looking product. It doesn't warp, split, or buckle, and, according to several manufacturers, you never need to paint it. (Although several brands of exterior paint are now available that are designed for use on PVC-U cladding.)

PVC-U does have its shortcomings. The surface of PVC-U cladding etches in time. As the surface deteriorates, the pitting causes the material to become dull and prone to stain.

To prolong the life of your cladding, clean it regularly. Twice a year is good – once in the spring and then again in the autumn. Use a pressure washer with laundry detergent to get the surface sparkling clean. Most pressure washers have a plastic dip tube that you can use to blend in agents like detergents. Keeping the surface of the PVC-U clean won't prevent it from oxidising, but it will slow the process of deterioration.

Maintaining aluminium cladding

Pressure wash your aluminium cladding once or twice a year, filling the plastic dip tube on the pressure washer with laundry detergent. Your aluminium cladding will remain bright and shiny for years, and the task won't seem overwhelming.

If you want to paint your aluminium cladding, keep these tips in mind:

- Never scrape aluminium cladding. Aluminium has a smooth surface; sand it with 400- to 600-grit sandpaper.

- A zinc oxide primer (metal primer) is best for bare aluminium.

- Because an aluminium surface is smooth, spray-paint it for best results.

- Always patch an aluminium surface with a filler made especially for metal – like Isopon, used for cars.

Maintaining and Repairing Brick Walls

The majority of houses in Britain and northern Europe have brick external walls – mostly exposed face brickwork, but some covered with various cement-based coatings such as render, roughcast, and pebbledash. Brick walls have performed well over the years, and are highly prized by builders and property owners.

Brick walls do not require a great deal of attention, which is one of their great advantages. Most problems with brickwork arise when otherwise well-intentioned homeowners decide to start messing around with their brickwork by cleaning it, repointing it, or covering it with paint or waterproof sealants.

The brickwork in your house is very likely to be much older than you are, and it has survived okay up until now. So think very carefully before you start messing around with it.

Cleaning

Many architectural purists say that face brickwork should never be cleaned but should be left just as it is, as a memorial to all the history it has witnessed. Plenty of Victorian-era working-class houses in Britain have soot-stained brickwork as a lasting testament to those times when every room had a coal fire, and every chimney pot belched smoke into the atmosphere. The dark colour of the brickwork hasn't had any downward effect on the value of those properties, some of which are now in highly desirable parts of town.

Still, some people always want to restore a house to the way it looked when it was first built, and if you are one of those people, then who are we to stop you?

Book II

Basic Home Maintenance and Improvement

If you really want to clean your brickwork, then the best advice we can give you is please be gentle. Bricks may be tough, but they are not hard. So avoid pressure-washing and especially sand-blasting, which can blast off the face (or 'fire-skin') of a kiln-fired brick and expose its soft underbelly. And once that has happened, the elements can start to cause serious damage.

The only cleaning we recommend is gentle washing with water and a soft brush. And even then, wouldn't you be better spending the time on the parts of the house that really need your valuable care and attention – such as painting the outside doors and windows?

Repointing

Repointing is the process of scraping out the mortar from between the bricks (the *pointing*) and replacing it with fresh mortar. Repointing is often advised by mortgage valuation surveyors when older properties change hands, but it is very rarely needed. Moisture evaporation, salt efflorescence, and frost damage are concentrated in the mortar, leaving the bricks themselves undamaged. After many years – 80 to 100, say – the pointing might be weathered away to a depth at which it needs replacing. But until then, it is best to leave the pointing to do what it does best, which is allowing the brickwork to move and to breathe, thus preventing damage occurring in the bricks themselves.

If you do want to repoint the brickwork on an old house, then it is important to do it using the correct material, which is sand-and-lime mortar to match the original, and definitely not sand-and-cement, which is hard and impermeable, and responsible for a lot of damage to brickwork in older properties.

Here's how to repoint brickwork in an older house (before about 1950):

1. **Rake out the old pointing as gently as you can, trying to avoid damaging the edges of the bricks.** The usual hand-tool is a *plugging chisel* (shown in Figure 4-3) but this has to be used with care, as it can easily become jammed between two bricks, splintering them. If the brickwork has already been repointed with hard sand-and-cement mortar, the danger of damage is even greater. In this case, the best course of action is often to first use a 100 mm bolster chisel to break the bond between the pointing and the bricks, before using the plugging chisel to prise out the pointing in short lengths. Rake out the joints to a depth at least equal to their width (10 mm) in the mortar, and brush out any loose material and dust. See Figure 4-4.

For large areas, we recommend a diamond-tipped mortar raker (such as the EasyRaker), which is fitted in a disk cutter, and can also be used with a dust-extraction unit to minimise dust and debris getting into the house or annoying the neighbours.

Figure 4-3:
A plugging
chisel.

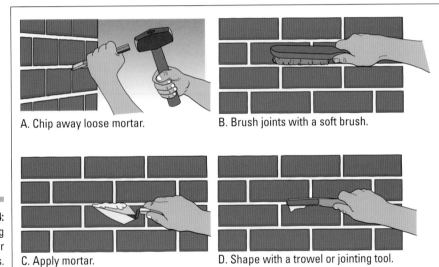

A. Chip away loose mortar.

B. Brush joints with a soft brush.

Figure 4-4:
Repointing
mortar
joints.

C. Apply mortar.

D. Shape with a trowel or jointing tool.

2. **Make your repointing mortar by mixing four parts coarse sharp sand to one part hydrated lime.** Hydrated lime is sold in 25 kg paper sacks at most builders' merchants. Mix the sand and lime dry, by hand (or rather, by hand-held shovel) on a flat surface, or in a normal drum mixer, and then add water to achieve a stiff paste.

Lime mortar benefits from being allowed to *slake* (hydrate) for a few days (or at least 24 hours), so cover it with plastic sheeting, or shovel it into buckets and pour in water until it is just covered with a layer of water. Lime mortar sets on contact with the air, so as long as the air is kept out, it will stay soft. Lime mortar matures and becomes more work- able the longer it is stored. (Cement mortar sets on contact with water, and must be used up within a couple of hours of being mixed.)

3. **Working in areas of around 1 sq metre, wet the joints lightly by spraying with water from a garden sprayer, and then push the lime mortar into the joints using a pointing trowel.** Try to reproduce the pattern made by the original bricklayers. The usual practice is to do the vertical joints first (known as *perpends* or *perps*) and then the horizontal joints (called *bed joints*). A common pointing pattern is a *struck joint*, where the perps slope slightly outwards from left to right, and the bed joints slope slightly outwards from top to bottom, to throw rainwater clear of the bricks below. But pointing might also be finished flush with the bricks (a *flush joint*), given a concave segmental finish (a *bucket-handle joint*), or a convex V-shape (*double-struck joint*).

Replacing damaged bricks

In a 100-year-old house, it's natural that every brick won't still be in perfect condition. (Your skin won't be perfect when you're 100, either.) The odd blemish here and there won't do any harm. But if the face of a brick is *spalled off* (flaked off) by frost damage, then you may wish to replace it.

Don't cover spalled bricks with a layer of sand-and-cement – it stands out like a sore thumb, and after a few years it falls off, taking even more of the face of the brick with it.

Make sure that you can buy replacement bricks to match the originals, otherwise you'll be in sore-thumb territory again. Don't forget that old bricks were made in a variety of imperial sizes, so you want the exact replacement size – definitely not modern metric-sized bricks, which are a little bit smaller in all three dimensions. Demolition yards salvage and sell good-quality bricks from your area. Don't be afraid to go down to the demolition yard with one of your removed bricks (see below) and ask for advice. Demolition men may look rough, but inside they're pussycats, and will be pleased to help you find the right bricks for your house.

Here's how to cut out and replace a brick:

1. **Use a 10 mm masonry drill bit (one that's at least 100 mm long) to drill a series of holes along the top and down one side of the brick.** Rake out the drilled mortar with a plugging chisel and lump hammer. If the mortar is harder than the brick, drill out the centre of the brick with a series of holes, and then use your plugging chisel to work outwards, removing the brick in small pieces.

If you have a dozen or more bricks to cut out, it's worth investing in a 100 mm EasyRaker bit. These diamond-studded tools fit in a standard disk cutter and, although they cost around £90 each, they make such short work of removing the bricks (around three minutes each) that we think it's absolutely worth the expense.

2. **Once you've removed all of the brick and the surrounding mortar, try your replacement brick in the hole for size, to make sure it slides in easily.** Then wet all around the sides of the opening with a garden sprayer. In hot weather, soak the replacement brick in a bucket of water for a few minutes, too.

3. **Use a small trowel or pointing trowel to spread a bed of mortar in the bottom of the opening, and on the top and sides of the replacement brick.** Then slide it into the opening, catching any displaced mortar with the trowel and pushing it into the joints to keep them full. A flat-bladed jointer is useful to push the mortar tight into the joints, or you can improvise with a piece of plywood, or even the blade of the plugging chisel. Pack in the mortar as tightly as you can all around the replacement brick. Rake all the joints out to a depth of around 10 mm, for pointing later on, after the mortar has set (following Steps 2 and 3 in the Repointing section before this one).

Repairing render

Render (the plaster covering your exterior walls) is really cool stuff. It doesn't rot, and compared to other types of finish, it's relatively easy to maintain. Some Victorian houses have parts of their brickwork covered with *stucco*, smooth render decorated with mouldings, or grooved to imitate large stone blocks. In the 19th century stucco was made with sand-and-lime, but in the early 20th century it was more likely to be sand-and-cement. Render/stucco is one of the easiest surfaces to prepare and paint. Unfortunately, its brittle, damage-resistant surface can be a drawback and when the house shifts, it can crack.

Repairing cracks

For cracks up to 6 mm wide, caulking solves the problem. Follow these simple steps:

1. **Clean all loose debris from the crack.**

2. **Use a paintable 50-year silicone caulk – and your finger – to make an invisible repair.**

   Don't use a putty knife. Doing so prevents you from matching the existing texture. With your finger, you can force the caulk in the crack to align with the irregular surface of the render.

Repair wider cracks and gouges with a latex patching compound, available from DIY shops. Follow the manufacturer's mixing instructions carefully because the amount of water you use changes the properties of the patching compound, which may lessen its ability to hold. Then, follow these steps:

1. **Clean all loose debris from the crack or gouge.**

2. **Use a latex patching product and a putty knife or trowel to fill the area.**

3. **Apply a second coat to match the surface texture.**

   Thin the patching compound to pancake batter consistency. Dip the end of a paintbrush into the mixture. Holding your hand between the wall and the paintbrush, slap the handle of the brush against your hand. The patching compound splatters onto the surface, matching the texture of the render. If the texture is flat, wait for the splattering to become slightly firm and then wipe it to the desired flatness with a putty knife or trowel.

Painting render

Really porous render absorbs litres of paint, causing you to use a great deal more paint than you really need to. If you're painting render for the first time, save paint by sealing the render with dilute PVA solution or, better still, a proprietary masonry stabiliser. Wait for either substance to dry before painting with a good-quality masonry paint.

Repairing roughcast and pebbledash

Some houses, especially those built in the 1930s, are characterised by having some areas of face brickwork, and other areas rendered, or finished with pebbledash or roughcast. *Pebbledashing* is a layer of dry shingle thrown against the final render coat, so that the pebbles stick to it, and is normally left unpainted. *Roughcast* is shingle mixed into the final render coat, which is thrown on, and left rough. Roughcast is normally painted over.

If your roughcast or pebbledash needs patching up, get your hands on this equipment:

- Club hammer
- Cold chisels
- Mixing board
- Buckets
- Shovel
- Plasterer's trowels
- Throwing shovel (a small coal shovel will do)
- Brush
- Sponge
- Plastering sand
- 10 mm pea shingle

✔ Ordinary Portland cement

✔ Slaked (hydrated) lime (see Step 2 in the Repointing section earlier in this chapter)

Here's how to repair a small area of roughcast or pebbledash:

1. **Hack off the roughcast or pebbledash to expose the area around the crack.** If you have more than one crack, or if the render sounds hollow when tapped with a hammer, then it may be necessary to expose a wider area. Otherwise, expose an area about 100 mm to 150 mm wide.

2. **Add the slaked lime to water, mixing until it is the consistency of thick cream.**

   Lime is a caustic material, so use protective goggles and gloves.

3. **Mix six parts of plastering sand with one part cement and one part slaked lime for the base coat.**

4. **Wet the exposed brickwork with a brush, especially around the edges of the repair.** Trowel on the base coat using a small plasterer's trowel. Apply the render until the area is filled, and then smooth it over.

5. **Once it has started to stiffen, but before it has gone hard (after about one hour), scrape off the surface of the base coat to the thickness of the shingle in the roughcast or pebbledash coat (about 10 mm).**

6. **Key the base coat to accept the roughcast finish, by scratching it with a sharp object such as a nail.** Leave the base coat to harden for at least 24 hours.

7. **Mix the roughcast coat as one part slaked lime, one part Portland cement, and two parts pea shingle.**

8. **Use the throwing shovel to apply the roughcast.** Use only the tip of the shovel, and make sure that the amount on the shovel is never more than one stone thick (10 mm). Throw the roughcast onto the wall with a flick of the wrist. Smooth off the edges of the repair with a soft brush, and clean off surrounding splashes with a damp sponge.

9. **For a pebbledash finish, follow Steps 1 to 6. Then apply another coat the same as the base coat (described in Step 3), and use the throwing shovel to flick dry pea shingle into it.** Use a plasterer's trowel or float to gently push the shingle into place to leave a flat surface.

Book II

Basic Home Maintenance and Improvement

Chapter 5

Dealing with Damp

In This Chapter
- Keeping moisture out of your house
- Knowing the difference between fungus and efflorescence
- Keeping your basement or cellar dry

This chapter tells you how to deal with one of the most common building problems: Dampness.

Is a Fungus Amongus?

One of the most common symptoms of dampness is a white powdery substance that appears on your walls. Although most people mistake the white powder for a fungus (fungus is typically green or black), it's really *efflorescence*, which is a growth of salt crystals caused by the evaporation of salt-laden water.

Efflorescence appears when mineral salts in the masonry, plaster, or mortar leach to the surface. Although efflorescence isn't particularly destructive, it's unsightly and on rare occasions can result in *spalling* – crumbling of the brickwork – or minor deterioration of the surface on which it grows. If your house was built in the last few years, then efflorescence might be simply the result of construction water coming to the surface and drying out. If you've got efflorescence appearing on older brickwork, however, or on internal plastered surfaces, then it is a sign of the passage of moisture, which needs to be diagnosed and rectified.

On outside walls, efflorescence is most likely to be *lime* (calcium carbonate) leached out from the mortar. It's harmless, and in most cases the natural action of the wind and rain removes it over a few years. To hasten its removal, wait for a spell of dry weather, and brush it off gently with a soft brush. Resist the temptation to wash it off with a hose, as this can bring even more lime to the surface and make the efflorescence look worse!

On internal plastered surfaces, efflorescence is probably *gypsum* (calcium sulfate), which you can more easily remove by wiping with a damp cloth. It is common for some efflorescence to appear on newly plastered walls – especially where pink gypsum plaster has been used on the inside of solid brick walls on older houses. Leave the walls to dry out thoroughly for a few months before decorating, wipe off any efflorescence that appears, and seal the plastered surface with dilute PVA solution (such as Unibond) before decorating.

Preventing Moisture from Building Up under Your Home

If you see efflorescence on your basement walls and/or your walls are perpetually damp and mildewy, you've got a moisture problem! A natural spring, a high water table, a broken water or sewer pipe, poor drainage, excessive irrigation, and poor ventilation are some of the most common causes of this problem.

What's a little water around and under the house going to hurt, you ask? Lots! Aside from turning your basement into a sauna, excess moisture can lead to a glut of problems, such as repulsive stinks, rotted timbers, insect pests, foundation movement, efflorescence, and allergy-irritating mould. We can't stress enough the importance of doing everything you can to keep excess moisture out of this area of your home.

Dealing with the rising damp myth

The problem with getting builders or surveyors in to diagnose your home's dampness problems is that a lot of ignorance exists about rising damp. Specialist 'damp-proofing' firms are often only too keen to tell you that your home has 'rising damp'. Treat their diagnoses with a healthy dose of scepticism. In most cases these firms use electrical moisture meters on the walls, but these meters are calibrated for use only on timber, and are almost guaranteed to give high readings when used to test masonry, plaster, and wallpaper. In many cases, we've seen rising damp diagnosed in walls that are actually completely dry, simply by misuse of these meters.

If your home really does have dampness problems, the best way of dealing with them is to use traditional good construction practices – lowering raised outside ground levels, and making sure that gutters and rainwater pipes are clear and draining away properly, and that the house is heated and ventilated.

Rooting out the cause of moisture

A musty or pungent smell usually accompanies efflorescence and excessive moisture. Start by checking for leaks in water and sewer pipes under your home. A failing plumbing fitting or corroded pipe is often the culprit. Fitting a replacement or installing a repair 'sleeve' around the damaged section of pipe almost always does the trick.

Believe it or not, a wet basement may be the result of a leaking toilet, bath, or valve located in the walls above. When it comes to finding the cause of a damp basement or sub-floor area, leave no stone unturned.

Overwatering plant pots, window boxes, and hanging baskets surrounding the house is another common cause of water down under. Adjusting watering time, watering less often, installing an automatic timer, and adjusting sprinkler heads are the simplest means of solving this problem. Better yet, move the plants!

Book II

Basic Home Maintenance and Improvement

Using gutters to reduce moisture

Rain gutters are more than a decorative element to the roofline of a home. Their primary purpose is to capture the tremendous amount of rainfall that runs off the average roof. Without gutters, rainwater collects at the foundation and eventually ends up in the basement. If you don't have gutters, install them. And if you do, keep them clean.

Make sure that your gutters and rainwater downpipes direct water a safe distance away from your house. Even worse than not having gutters and downpipes is having downpipes that jettison water directly into the ground next to the walls. Ideally, your downpipes should direct water into yard gulleys connected to the main sewer system, or piped to run into a nearby ditch or stream.

Some older houses have downpipes running into *soakaways*, which are basically just holes in the ground next to the house, filled with stone or builders' rubble, and covered over with soil. Over the years, soakaways become silted up, and instead of allowing water to percolate gently into the ground, they become mini-ponds, which can allow water to soak straight back through the footing or basement walls of the house. If your house has soakaways, we recommend digging them out and renewing them, or preferably relocating them three or four metres away from the house. You can dig a trench and add a bend and a length of plastic pipe to the foot of the existing downpipe to direct the water to the new soakaway. You can buy modern soakaways that are plastic cages that you bury in the ground.

See Chapter 4 for more on gutters.

Draining water away from the house

Be sure that the soil and hard paving around your home is at least 150 mm (two brick courses) below the level of the damp-proof course, and slopes away from the building. This helps divert most irrigation and rainwater away from the structure.

Lowering ground levels

A patio or path that slopes towards the home discharges water into the basement or sub-floor area, which in turn breeds dampness problems and rot. Unfortunately, the only sure way to correct this problem is to remove and replace the source, and replacing a path or patio can be pricey. If the previous owners of your home were unwise enough to install a new path or patio without bothering to remove the old surface first (a surprisingly common situation), then this will have raised the ground level, and presents you with a big problem. Ideally, you should dig it all up, and lower the ground levels, but we know this can be a daunting prospect.

A possible compromise is to lower the ground level immediately next to the wall, to a width of 300 to 400 mm, and pave this strip at the new lower level. It should be paved with a gradient so that rain water runs away to the nearest existing yard gulley or, preferably, you should fit some new yard gulleys in the lowered strip, connected with pipes that direct the water away from the house or into the main drainage system.

Giving the problem some air

Ventilation is another effective means of controlling moisture in a basement or sub-floor area. Two types of ventilation exist:

✔ **Passive ventilation** is natural ventilation that doesn't use mechanical equipment. Terracotta airbricks are often set into the walls below the level of an inside suspended timber floor. They can work well, as long as they're not blocked by raised ground levels (see 'Lowering ground levels' above), and as long as they're positioned to allow a through flow of air below the floor. This means having airbricks in both the front and back walls of a terraced house, and also making sure that you have ventilation gaps in the footings of any intermediate walls running up the centre of the house. Victorian builders often put just one terracotta airbrick or perforated metal vent in each of the front and back walls, so you can add extra airbricks to improve the ventilation. Modern plastic airbricks are the same size as the old terracotta ones (75 x 225 mm and 150 x 225 mm), and are reckoned to have about five times more ventilation area.

✏ **Active ventilation** involves mechanical equipment, such as an extractor fan.

Passive ventilation should be your first choice because it allows nature to be your workhorse and doesn't necessitate the use of energy to drive a mechanical device. You save on your electricity bill and help the environment by not relying on fossil fuel. Having said that, don't hesitate to use active ventilation if your crawlspace or basement needs it.

If you use passive ventilation, you must keep vents clean to allow maximum airflow. Thinning shrubbery, vines, and ground cover may be necessary from time to time. If your vents are clear and moisture is still a problem, you may be able to add vents.

All the passive ventilation in the world may not be enough to dry out some problem basements. In these cases, install an active source of ventilation, such as an extractor fan.

Saying 'oui' to a French drain

If the advice we gave in the previous sections doesn't help and you're still faced with a basement or sub-floor area that looks like a bog, it's time to call in a building engineer to determine whether the condition requires the installation of a French drain. A French drain is a drainage channel dug around the outside of the house, right next to the walls. Some older houses have French drains that are just filled with stone, but the modern version uses perforated plastic land-drainage pipes that are bedded on, and back-filled with pea shingle. The pipes are laid at a gradient to drain water clear of the house or away to the main drainage system.

If you already have a French drain, it still needs occasional maintenance. Clean the inside of the pipe once a year by using a pressure cleaner, which is a high-powered water blaster with a hose and nozzle for use within drainpipes. You can rent this equipment from a tool hire company, or a plumbing contractor or sewer and drain cleaning service can clean a French drain for you.

Chapter 6

Electrical Repairs and Replacements

In This Chapter

▷ Dealing with blown fuses and short circuits

▷ Wiring light switches and electrical outlets

▷ Bringing a broken lamp back to life

▷ Replacing a ceiling rose

▷ Adding a phone extension

*E*ver since that grand moment when Ben Franklin decided to fly a kite in an electrical storm, civilisation has had a curious fascination with and an addictive dependence on electricity. But what happens if you're suddenly thrown into darkness by an interrupted electrical service? What do you do then? Going to a friend's house to watch *EastEnders* isn't the response we're looking for. This chapter explains how to make all sorts of minor electrical repairs and improvements to your home.

On 1 January 2005 new Building Regulations came into force across Britain that drastically affected the regulation of DIY electrical work. Homeowners and DIYers are still allowed to work on domestic electrical systems, but by law they must now have their work approved and inspected by their local authority Building Control officer. The only exceptions are replacing a damaged or faulty light switch, power point, or lamp holder, with one of the same. So if you want to do anything more ambitious – such as extending your home's power circuitry, or adding light fittings where there were none before – then we recommend that you get the work done by a suitably qualified professional electrician.

Replacing a Fuse and Resetting a Circuit Breaker

You plug in your great new speakers, turn on the CD player, and suddenly the whole house goes dark. Hmmm, you've heard of blown fuses and short circuits, but how do you fix them? The first step is to locate your consumer unit and open it. (See the sidebar 'When it comes to electricity, always be prepared' for tips on finding and labelling your consumer unit.)

 Electricity flows through a pair of wires called a circuit. Electrical energy flows down one wire (the *live* wire) through the light, TV, or whatever you're running and then returns to the consumer unit through the other wire (the *neutral* wire). These wires are sized to carry a certain amount of electrical energy without overheating. But if you plug too many appliances into a circuit, the wires supplying this energy get very hot. And if the wires supplying the energy touch each other, they create a *short circuit* – a shortcut for the electrical power to flow through – and the wires begin to glow in a matter of seconds.

Each circuit is protected by either a *fuse* or a *circuit breaker*, both of which you can see in Figure 6-1. If a short circuit occurs anywhere in the wiring, if the wires overheat, or if an appliance malfunctions or catches fire, the fuse or circuit breaker shuts down power to that circuit. Additionally, the entire system is protected with a master or main fuse or breaker.

- **Fuses:** Houses that are more than about 30 years old often have fuses rather than circuit breakers to protect the wire circuits. To shut down a circuit in these homes, you have to remove the fuse. Shut off the power to the consumer unit before replacing fuses. Look for a big 'Master' or 'Main' switch (usually located at the top or side of the consumer unit); flick this switch to shut down the power to the entire house. Make sure you have a working torch on hand!

  If the fuses aren't labelled, look at the wire of each fuse to determine which one is blown. A good fuse shows an unbroken length of wire; in a bad one the wire will be burnt and broken. Replace the damaged length of fuse wire with a new piece of the correct size and rating (30 amp, 15 amp, or 5 amp). Restore the power by turning on the main switch.

  Have replacement fuse wire on hand at all times, or better still, replace the fuses with plug-in circuit breakers of the correct rating.

- **Circuit breakers:** Newer homes have circuit breakers – protective switches that enable you to fix short circuits without turning off the power. Circuit breakers simply switch off when they become overloaded. To reset a circuit breaker, simply flip the switch back to the 'On' position, or depress the button for the pop-out variety of circuit breaker. If the breaker shuts off again, you have a short or some other problem that needs to be fixed before you attempt to switch it on again.

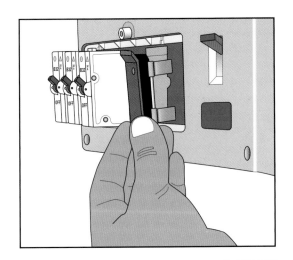

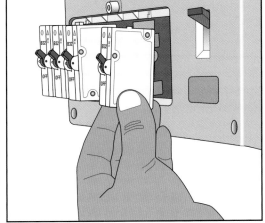

Figure 6-1:
Replace the
wires fuses
in an old
consumer
unit (top)
with circuit
breakers
(middle and
bottom.
A modern
consumer
unit has
miniature
circuit
breakers
(MCBs)
already
fitted.

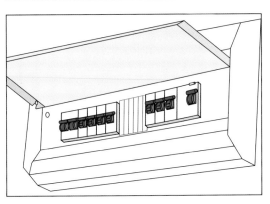

Book II

Basic
Home
Mainte-
nance and
Improve-
ment

When it comes to electricity, always be prepared

To prepare for electrical emergencies, familiarise yourself with the consumer unit – the circuit breaker box usually found close to your electricity meter. Have a torch with good batteries somewhere near the consumer unit to give you good light for looking at it – remember, the overhead light may not be working when you need to change a fuse or re-set a tripped circuit breaker.

The electrician who wired your house should have marked each circuit on the unit with a label telling which lights or appliances it controls. But things don't always happen the way they should, and you may find yourself with a unit of unlabelled breakers. Before a short circuit leaves you in the dark trying to guess which fuse or breaker controls what, get down to business and label those breakers yourself.

To label the breakers, plug a lamp into each power point and turn on all the lights in your house. Then go to your consumer unit and turn off each circuit breaker, one at a time. Have a helper call out which lights or appliances shut down and are, therefore, on that circuit. Label all the breakers with lists of what they control.

If you're on your own, plug a radio into the socket you're testing and turn up the volume so that you can hear it from the consumer unit. When the radio stops playing, you know that you've found the circuit that connects to that fuse or circuit breaker.

Working with live wires is never a good idea, and sometimes wires from more than one circuit may be present in a single outlet. So to ensure that the electricity is turned off on every circuit you come in contact with, purchase an inexpensive neon voltage circuit tester or mains-test electrician's neon screwdriver. This little screwdriver device lets you know whether a circuit has power running to it.

To use a mains-test neon screwdriver, hold the screwdriver blade onto the wire or brass terminal you want to test, and touch the button on the end of the screwdriver handle with your forefinger. If the circuit is live, current flows through the screwdriver, and through your finger to earth, and the little neon lamp lights up. Don't worry about getting an electric shock – the screwdriver contains a large electrical resistor, meaning that only a tiny fraction of the current flows through your finger.

Wiring Switches and Sockets

If a switch fails to function or a power point (commonly called a socket outlet or socket) no longer holds a plug securely, it should be replaced, but often people just want to upgrade, change style, or modify the configuration of outlets to meet changing styles or needs. Modern switches and sockets have screw terminals in the back to accept the end of the wire.

You can easily loosen the screws in the back of the device with a standard screwdriver (turning anti-clockwise). Here are descriptions of the wires and where they go (see the nearby sidebar too):

- The black (or blue) (neutral) wire connects to the terminal marked 'N'.
- The red (or brown) (live) wire goes to the terminal marked 'L'.
- The green/yellow or bare copper (earth) wire, if the device has one, attaches to the terminal marked 'E' on the switch or socket, and to the earth terminal in the back box.

Swapping a light switch

Most kitchen and bedroom switches are the one-way type and are designed to control a light or socket from a single location. Hallways, on the other hand, usually have two-way switches that are designed to control a light or socket from two locations (usually the landing light, so you can turn it on if you're upstairs or downstairs). Sometimes, an electrician places a three-way switch between two-way switches to allow control of lights from three separate locations.

Turn off the circuit breaker or fuse to a light circuit before you unscrew the *switch plate* (the plastic or metal square around the switch). Then test the wires with a voltage circuit tester or neon screwdriver to make sure that power isn't flowing to them.

Changes in cable colours

Until a few years ago, '2-core & earth' lighting and power cables in the UK were all coloured red (live), black (neutral), and green/yellow (earth). During the 1980s, in pursuit of European harmonisation, the flexible cables ('flex') used to connect drills, toasters, hairdryers, and other plug-in appliances were changed to brown (live), blue (neutral), and green/yellow (earth). From 1 April 2006, these new colours also applied to lighting and power cables in new installations. So for many years to come, if you unscrew a light switch or power point from its back box, be prepared to see either combination of colours.

For cable used for two-way lighting (lighting that you can turn on from two different places), called '3-core & earth', the old colours were blue, yellow, and red, with a bare copper earth, but from 1 April 2006 they changed to grey, black, and brown with a bare copper earth.

Confused? No wonder. If you're doing nothing more complex than replacing a light switch or power point, then you'll probably have no difficulty in just swapping the old connections for the new. But for anything more complicated, when in doubt, hire an electrician.

Replacing a one-way switch

To replace this kind of switch, follow these steps:

1. **Turn off the power to the switch at the main circuit breaker or fuse panel.**

2. **Unscrew the switch from the back box and pull it out with the wires still attached, as shown in Figure 6-2.**

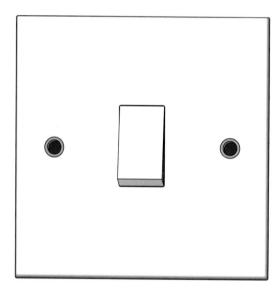

Figure 6-2:
A one-way switch.

3. **Use a voltage tester or neon screwdriver to make sure that the circuit is dead.**

   Two or three wires will be attached to the switch: An incoming live wire, which is red or brown, and a return wire, which carries the electricity to the fixture, which may be black, blue, or any other colour except green. And sometimes an earth wire, which is green/yellow or bare copper. There may be other wires in the box, but you are only dealing with the ones connected directly to the switch.

   You may find a black or blue wire that has red or brown tape on it connected to the switch. This tape indicates that the black or blue wire is being used as a 'switched live' wire, so that when the switch is on, it becomes live, and is no longer neutral.

4. **Compare your new switch with the one you're replacing to find the corresponding locations for the electrical screw connectors.**

   Because the power is off, you can match up the connectors the easy way: Instead of disconnecting all the wires at once and possibly getting confused, unscrew and connect one wire at a time.

5. **Attach the first wire you unscrew to the same-labelled screw on the new switch as it was on the old; do the same with the second.**

   To connect a wire to a terminal, strip off about 12 mm of insulation, using a wire stripper, pocket knife, or pincers. Push the exposed wire into the terminal, and tighten the screw with a screwdriver. If the back box is metal, make sure that the green/yellow earth wire is attached to both the earth terminal on the switch and the earth terminal on the back box.

6. **Gently push the new, wired switch back into the back box and screw it in place.**

7. **Turn on the power.**

Replacing a two-way switch

A two-way switch is one of two switches that control a single light or socket, shown in Figure 6-3. To replace a two-way switch, follow these steps:

1. **Turn off the power to the switch at the circuit or fuse panel.**

2. **Unscrew the switch from the back box and pull it out with the wires still attached. Then use a voltage tester to make sure that the circuit is dead.**

   A two-way switch has at least three wires and possibly four, depending on whether it has an earth wire. The new switch may have the electrical screw connectors in slightly different locations than the switch you're replacing. The connectors will be labelled 'L1', 'L2', and 'Common'.

3. **Remove the wires from the switch.**

Book II

Basic
Home
Mainte-
nance and
Improve-
ment

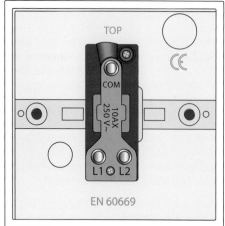

Figure 6-3:
A two-way
switch.

4. **Transfer one wire at a time from the old switch to the new switch.**

5. **If the back box is metal, make sure that the green/yellow earth wire is attached to both the earth terminal on the switch and the earth terminal on the back box.**

6. **Push the new, wired switch back into the back box and screw it in place.**

Replacing a three-way switch

If the switch is the centre switch of three switches that control a single light or receptacle, it's a three-way switch. Figure 6-4 shows a typical three-way switch.

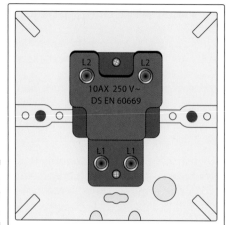

Figure 6-4:
A three-way
switch.

To replace a three-way switch, follow these steps:

1. **Turn off the power to the switch at the circuit panel or fuse box.**

2. **Unscrew the switch from the back box and pull it out with the wires still attached; then use a voltage tester to make sure that the circuit is dead.** This switch has at least four screw terminals. It may also have a fifth earth terminal (green/yellow).

3. **Transfer one wire at a time from the old switch to the new switch.**

4. **Attach the wires to the corresponding terminals of the new switch.**

   If the back box is metal, make sure that the green/yellow earth wire is attached to both the earth terminal on the switch and the earth terminal on the back box.

5. **Push the new, wired switch back into the back box and screw it in place.**

Replacing a standard switch with a dimmer switch

Replacing a standard single-pole or two-way switch with a dimmer switch is no different than replacing a standard switch. Remember: Dimmer switches don't work on most fluorescent fixtures, and low-voltage lighting requires special low-voltage dimmers.

Check the rating of the dimmer switch you purchase. Most dimmer switches can handle 600 watts of power. Count the number of light bulbs that the switch controls and add up the maximum wattage of bulb allowed for the fixture. For example, if the switch controls a light fixture that accommodates up to two 100-watt bulbs (200 watts total) a 600-watt dimmer will have no problem, but a string of seven recessed lights could overload the dimmer.

To replace a standard switch with a dimmer switch (shown in Figure 6-5), follow these steps:

1. **Turn off the power to the switch at the circuit or fuse panel.**

2. **Unscrew the switch from the back box and pull it out with the wires still attached; then use a voltage tester to make sure that the circuit is dead.**

3. **Remove the wires from the old switch, noting which colours are connected to the 'L1', 'L2' (if applicable), and 'COM' terminals.**

4. **Connect the wires to the dimmer switch, using the same L1, L2, and COM formation.**

Book II

Basic Home Maintenance and Improvement

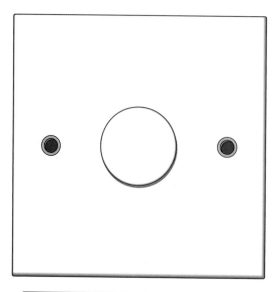

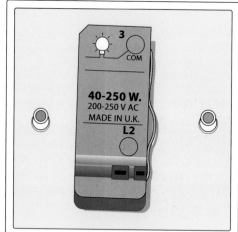

Figure 6-5:
A dimmer
switch.

5. Push the new switch back into the back box and screw it in place.

The body of a dimmer is larger than the switch being replaced. Don't just force it in. Often, you need to reposition or better organise the wires first to make room for it.

6. Turn on the power.

Replacing Double Sockets

The procedure for replacing a double (two-outlet) wall socket is the same as for replacing a switch. The only difference is that, depending on where the socket is located in the wiring of your house, it may have more wires attached to it than you find attached to a light switch.

If the socket is wired as a *spur* (a socket wired from an existing socket), it usually has only two (live and neutral) wires, and a third earth wire. If it is part of a *ring main* (the ring of wires delivering electricity from the consumer unit), two additional live and neutral wires will be connected to it in order to carry current to the next socket. Just rewire the new socket the same way the old one was wired. (See Figure 6-6.)

Book II

Basic Home Mainte- nance and Improve- ment

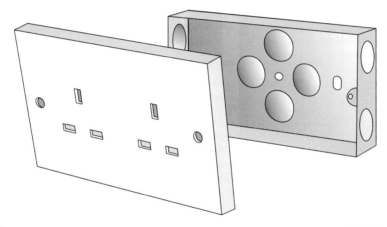

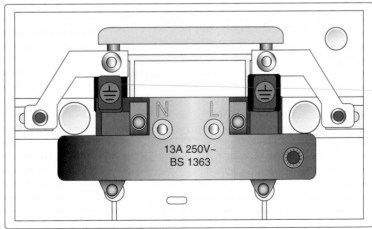

Figure 6-6: (a) A double 'two-gang' power socket. (c) A two-gang power socket wired into a ring-main, with two wires in each terminal.

Replacing a standard socket

To replace a standard double socket, follow these steps:

1. **Turn off the power to the socket from the main fuse or circuit panel.**

2. **Unscrew and remove the cover plate; then use a voltage tester to make sure that the circuit is dead.**

3. **Unscrew the socket from the back box and pull it out with the wires still attached.**

   Note where the red and black wires are attached to the old socket.

4. **Remove the wires.**

5. **Attach the wires to the terminals of the new socket.**

   If the back box is metal, make sure that the green/yellow earth wire is attached to both the earth terminal on the socket and the earth terminal on the back box.

6. **Push the new socket back into the electrical box and screw it in place.**

Replacing a socket with a residual current circuit breaker

A *residual current circuit breaker* (RCCB) is the same as an ordinary socket, except that it has a sensitive built-in circuit breaker and reset switch. Building regulations require that you install this device in outlets located in areas prone to dampness, such as bathrooms, kitchens, cellars, garages, and outdoors.

Normally, the amount of current flowing in an electrical circuit is the same in all the wires. For example, if your hairdryer takes 10 amps (a measure of the amount of electricity flowing in a circuit) to run, then 10 amps of current flow into the dryer through the hot (red) wire and 10 amps flow out of the dryer through the neutral (black) wire. If the dryer experiences a short, current could flow through your wet hand to, say, the tap handle as you turn off the water. If this happens, the amount of current going into the dryer exceeds the amount coming out because some of the electricity is going through you. The RCCB senses this discrepancy and trips open to stop everything before you frizzle.

Fortunately, these devices have a Test button on them so that you can check that they're functioning properly. Press the Test button, and the device trips and shuts everything down. To reset the device, press the Reset button.

You can install an RCCB socket in the same way you install an ordinary socket. To replace a standard double socket with an RCCB socket, follow these steps:

1. Turn off the power to the socket from the fuse or circuit panel.

2. Unscrew the socket from the back box and pull it out with the wires still attached; then use a voltage tester to make sure that the circuit is dead.

3. Note where the red, black, and green/yellow wires are attached to the old socket and then remove the wires.

4. Transfer the wires from the old socket to the RCCB.

   If the back box is metal, make sure that the green/yellow earth wire is attached to both the earth terminal on the socket and the earth terminal on the back box.

5. Push the new socket back into the back box and screw it in place.

Book II

Basic Home Mainte- nance and Improve- ment

Repairing a Faulty Lamp

As electrical appliances go, lamps are very reliable. But after a while, the socket may act up and cause the lamp to flicker, to be difficult to turn on, or to just refuse to light. You can purchase replacement lamp parts at any hardware shop or DIY centre. These parts are standard; you can buy lamp cord by the metre, and you can use just about any type of plug to replace the one on your old lamp.

If your present lamp has a three-way bulb in it (if you can turn the lamp on to several degrees of brightness), purchase a socket switch that's designed to control a three-way bulb.

To replace a lamp socket, follow these steps:

1. Unplug the lamp.

2. Remove the shade, bulb, and harp (the wired shape that holds the shade).

3. Snap off the socket shell from the socket shell cap, as shown in Figure 6-7.

   Some sockets have the word 'Press' stamped in two places on the shell. Squeeze the shell at those points and pull up to remove it. If the shell doesn't budge, push the end of a screwdriver between the base of the socket and the side of the shell and then pull the shell up and off the socket base.

4. Pull the socket switch up out of the shell base to expose enough of the switch to reveal the two wires attached to it.

   If the screws are loose, tighten them and reassemble the lamp. Loose screws may have been the lamp's only problem. If the lamp works after you tighten up the screws, great! If not, take it apart again and proceed with the following steps.

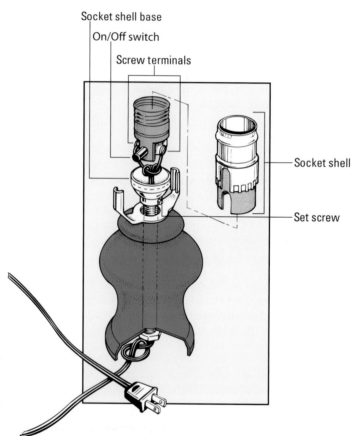

Socket shell base

On/Off switch

Screw terminals

Socket shell

Set screw

Figure 6-7:
Removing
the socket
shell.

5. **Unscrew the wires.**

   A lamp switch has brass screws to which the live (red) and neutral (black) wires are attached. Lamp cords, however, don't always have coloured wires in them.

6. **Loosen the socket cap set screw and then unscrew and discard it along with the old socket shell and socket.**

7. **Screw the wire leads to the new socket.**

8. **Place the new socket shell over the socket and push the cover down until it snaps into the new socket shell cap.**

9. **Replace the harp, light bulb, and shade.**

Replacing a Ceiling Rose and Bulb Holder

Most ceiling light fittings consist of a plastic ceiling rose, to which is attached either a screw-on lamp holder (called a *batten holder*) or a screw-on cover with a hole in the centre, out of which comes a length of flex attached to a separate lamp holder (called a *pendant fitting*). Because these fittings are sited directly above an incandescent lamp (a light bulb) they are subjected to a lot of heat over the years, and can become discoloured and brittle. You probably won't notice this until you try to unscrew the cover on the ceiling rose – probably to get it out of the way while you paint or wallpaper the ceiling – and find the whole thing crumbling apart in your hands. If this happens, don't panic. Just buy a replacement at your local DIY shop or electrical suppliers and follow the instructions below.

To replace a ceiling rose and bulb holder, follow these steps and refer to Figure 6-8:

1. **Turn off the power to the light circuit at your consumer unit by flicking the switch on the circuit breaker.** If you need lights and power in the rest of the house, turn off the main switch, pull out the fuse, and then turn the main switch on again.

2. **Unscrew the plastic cover on the rose and use a circuit tester or neon screwdriver to make sure that the circuit is dead.**

3. **If you have a pendant fitting, let the cover slide down the flex, and unscrew the two wires (red and black, or brown and blue) connecting the flex to the rose. If you have a batten holder, the bulb holder will usually come away as you unscrew the cover.**

4. **Make a sketch of all the different-coloured wires going into the existing ceiling rose, and the terminals they are connected to.**

5. **Loosen all the screws to the brass terminals, and gently pull the wires free. Undo the two woodscrews holding the rose to the ceiling, and remove it.**

6. **Feed the wires through the hole in the centre of the new rose (you may have to knock out one or more of the plastic blanks to make the hole).**

7. **Screw the new rose to the ceiling, using the same woodscrews and holes if you can. Make sure that the woodscrews do not catch or damage any of the wires.**

8. **Connect up the wires to the terminals as per your sketch, and screw the cover on.** With a pendant fitting, you have to thread the bulb-holder flex through the centre of the cover first, connect the two wires to their terminals, and then slide the cover up the flex and screw it in place.

Book II

Basic
Home
Mainte-
nance and
Improve-
ment

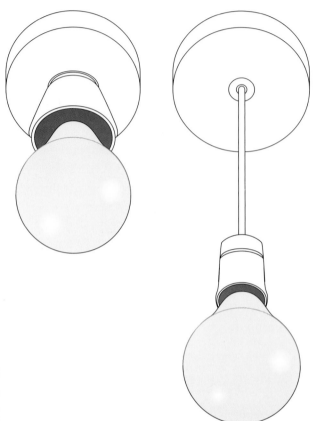

Figure 6-8: A ceiling rose.

Planting seeds of light

Those familiar glass globes that light up when electricity is passed through them are commonly referred to as light bulbs. But professional electricians know them as *lamps*. Electricians have a saying: 'Lamps hang from the ceiling; bulbs are planted in the ground.' So if you go up to the trade counter of your local electrical suppliers and ask for bulbs, don't be surprised if the bloke behind the counter directs you to the local garden centre. Depending on how your lighting circuits are wired, you might find that each ceiling rose is connected to the electrical system by only two wires, or by a bunch of three or four. This is because in some circuits – known as *loop-in wiring* – all the lights on one floor of the house are connected together on a ring, and the ceiling roses are used to connect them all together, as well as passing current through each individual fitting. In other circuits, these connections are made in separate junction boxes hidden in the ceiling, leaving only the live and neutral wires to connect up to the rose. Both systems work equally well, and the only thing you have to do is make sure you wire up the replacement rose in exactly the same way as the one you have taken off.

Wiring a Telephone Extension

We can get one thing clear from the start: The telephone system does not operate on mains voltage – so that scene in the James Bond film where our hero electrocutes someone by chucking a phone into the bath with him is just fantasy. Landline telephones pack about as much punch as a big torch battery, so connecting an extension socket or two shouldn't present any dangers – apart from the usual ones of falling off the stepladder or stabbing yourself with the screwdriver, that is.

However, because the amount of current flowing to your phone is so small, you have a limit to the number of devices you can route through a single line. Well, to be more precise, you have no limit to the number of phones, as long as you are only going to speak on one at a time, but there *is* a limit to the number of bells that will ring when someone calls you. Most homes can cope with a maximum of three or four phones (or faxes) on one line.

Book II

Basic Home Maintenance and Improvement

It's easy to fit extension phone cables to the master socket by using a converter plug or a 'socket doubler'. A converter plug has several metres of cable already attached to it, which you plug into the master socket, and then plug your existing phone into the outlet on the front of the converter plug. See Figure 6-9.

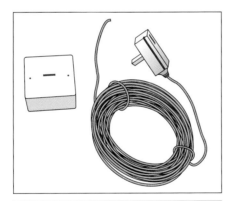

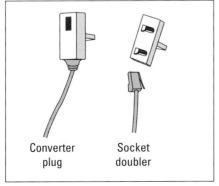

Figure 6-9: A telephone extension and converter plug.

Converter plug

Socket doubler

A socket doubler also plugs into the master socket, but you then have to plug both the existing phone and the plug on the end of the extension cable into the two outlets on the face of the socket doubler. You can buy both types of telephone extension kit from your local DIY shop.

Here's how to fit a converter plug or socket doubler:

1. **Work out the most convenient location for the position of your extension socket, and screw the back box to the wall or skirting board.**

2. **Plug the converter plug (or socket doubler and plug) into the existing master socket, and start running the extension cable towards the extension socket by the shortest convenient route.**

   The usual technique is to run the cable along the top of the skirting boards, and around door architraves, but it often saves time (and cable) to drill a small hole through the wall to get the cable into an adjacent room. Don't forget to use a pipe and cable finder to check for, you guessed it, pipes and cables before drilling a hole through a wall.

3. **Pin the cable to the skirting boards and architraves with small (0.5 mm) plastic cable clips.** These are often supplied as part of the extension kit, but you can also buy them separately in boxes of 50 or 100.

4. **When you reach your extension socket, cut the excess off the cable using wire cutters or pincers.** Strip about 6 mm of insulation from the ends of the wires, and attach them to the terminals according to the manufacturer's instructions.

5. **Fit the cover to the extension socket and plug in your extension phone.**

Book III
Painting and Wallpapering

"One case of chickenpox and the rest are victims of DIY rage."

In this book . . .

More people probably tackle painting and wallpapering than any other type of home improvement project. Applying a fresh coat of paint or hanging wallpaper is the easiest and most economical way to transform a room or a home's exterior and to make it uniquely your own. The chapters in this book take you through every step of the way – so get stuck in!

Here are the contents of Book III at a glance.

Chapter 1

Planning Your Painting Project

In This Chapter

▶ Choosing the right finish for the job

▶ Playing it safe with lead paint

▶ Estimating how much paint you need

▶ Selecting the right applicators

▶ Using the proper painting techniques

*W*ith good preparation and planning, any job – big or small – will go smoothly, and you'll reap the rewards of an attractive, long-lasting finish. This chapter walks you through the stages of planning a painting project, from selecting a finish to buying the right amount of paint to finding the best technique for the surface you're painting.

A Primer on Finishes

The greatest hurdle you're likely to face isn't on your walls or ceilings; it's in the aisles of your DIY store. Faced with mile-long shelves stacked to the ceiling with paints, stains, and other finishing products, you may stand there musing, 'How on earth do I know what kind to buy?'

Beyond the ornamental purposes that paint, varnish, and other finishes provide, they bond with wood or other materials to protect the surface from heat, moisture, sunlight, chemicals, dirt, stains, and even fire. Depending on the formula and the application, a finish prevents (or slows) degradation caused by weathering and sunlight, wood rot, mildew growth, and rust; limits expansion and contraction due to changing moisture content and temperatures; and keeps surfaces cleaner and, when they get dirty, makes them easier to clean.

Water-based or oil-based?

When you reach the paint department, you face a choice between the two major types of paint, stains, varnishes, and other clear coatings: oil-based and water-based. Oil-based paint produces more durable and washable surfaces, but because cleaning up afterwards involves using paint thinner (or white spirit), it isn't as user-friendly.

Water-based paint is the more popular choice because it's much easier to work with and cleans up with soap and water. Plus, water-based paint dries quickly and produces fewer odours.

The most common approach is to use oil-based paint on woodwork and *trim* (such as skirting boards and architraves), where a hard, durable finish can be washed frequently, and water-based paint on the walls.

First things first: Primers and sealers

Base coats include primers, sealers, and combination primer-sealers. You apply a base coat, or undercoat, under a *topcoat* (the top colour) to provide better adhesion and to seal and cover the surface for a more even application of the finish.

Certain topcoats don't require a primer when used on certain surfaces. For example, you don't need to prime when you're recoating well-adhered paint with an identical paint (water-based gloss over water-based gloss, for example) and you're not making a significant colour change. Fortunately, you don't need to remember these rules – just read the label on the tin of topcoat paint: It will specify primer requirements, if any, for various surfaces.

Before you paint, you need to prime all unpainted surfaces, patched areas, and spots that you make bare in the preparation stages.

Primer generally dries fast; some can be topcoated after as little as an hour.

Use a sealer or primer-sealer if you're painting a material that varies in porosity, such as newly installed plasterboard or a wood such as pine. The seal prevents the topcoat from being absorbed unevenly, which would give the finish a blotchy appearance or an uneven texture. Sealers also block stains. If you have kids, for example, you may have pen or crayon stains on your walls. To prevent bleed-through, apply a stain blocker, stain-killing sealer, or white-pigmented shellac. These primer-sealers are available in spray cans for small spots and in litre and 2.5 litre containers for large stained areas. You can also use primer-sealers to prevent the resin from wood knots bleeding through the topcoat.

Having had mixed results with the stain-sealing effectiveness of these products, especially when it comes to knots, we recommend that you apply two or three coats.

Categorising finishes

Sorting through the myriad choices of topcoat isn't as difficult as it may seem at first. Most fall into one of the following categories:

- **Exterior paints** are formulated to withstand the effects of weather, damaging ultraviolet radiation, air pollution, extremes in heat and cold, expansion, and contraction. Exterior topcoats include masonry paints (intended for the body of the house but may be used for trim), trim paints, and a variety of speciality paints, such as those for metal roofs, barns, aluminium or UPVC cladding.

  You can use some exterior paints indoors (read the label), but they aren't designed to hold up to scrubbing as well as some interior paints are. Never use an interior finish outdoors.

- **Interior paints** include ceiling and wall emulsion in a range of sheens from matt to gloss, trim paints, and enamels in higher gloss ranges. Consider using special interior paints that contain fungicides for high-humidity areas such as kitchens and bathrooms. Interior textured paints, intended for use on ceilings and walls, contain sand or other texturing materials.

- **Interior and exterior stains** are formulated for interior, exterior, or interior/exterior use. Although people associate stains primarily with wood, they are also available for concrete. Stains intended for interior applications offer little or no protection and must be topcoated with a protective, film-forming sealer finish such as varnish, or with a separate sealer and a wax or polish. Exterior stains have water-repellent and UV-reflecting qualities.

- **Varnish** offers more protection than other sealer/finish approaches, such as shellacs, oils, and polishes. However, varnish masks the beauty of the wood more than these alternatives do. Furniture oils are penetrating, wipe-on finishes with a satin lustre. Oils offer little moisture or stain resistance, but you can easily conceal scratches by recoating. This quality makes oils a good choice for wood that takes a beating – but only if stains and water aren't big concerns.

- **Speciality finishes** are formulated for specific and usually demanding applications. Whenever a project seems to go beyond the basics, look for speciality products. Primers are made for galvanised metal and aluminium. Masonry sealers protect brick and stone. Special paints (two-part epoxy and two-part urethane) are used when a particularly strong bond is required or when a finish must stand up to extreme abuse, such as on garage floors.

Book III

Painting
and Wall-
papering

Lead, the environment, and you

Lead, an extremely toxic substance, was present in paints in Britain until 1992, when its use was banned. An estimated 75 per cent of homes built before 1992 contain lead-based paint. If your home has lead-based paint, exercise caution whenever you make repairs around the house.

If you're planning to paint, refinish, or wallpaper, and any of the repair or prep work will remove or disturb lead paint or create dust, the best advice is: Don't do it yourself. Don't allow an unqualified painting contractor to do the work, either.

We have no doubt that this advice is sound for large projects, such as stripping all the paint off your exterior cladding or interior trim. On the other hand, we recognise that it's neither practical nor realistic to expect homeowners not to work on certain smaller projects just because they involve lead paint. But before you start work, read the advice leaflets from the British Coatings Federation (www.coatings.org.uk, 01372 700 848), and use a 'lead test' kit from decorators' suppliers, or DIY stores.

When you do prep work involving lead finishes, never dry-sand or dry-scrape (that is, without wetting the surface as you sand or scrape), and never use propane torches or heat guns to remove lead-based paint.

Choosing an Exterior Finish

Unless you're building a new home or re-cladding an existing one, your choices for what finish to use are dictated to a degree by your cladding and the type and condition of any existing finish. For example, some finishes work better on smooth, painted wood, and others work better on rough, stained wood. So the first step is to narrow the options to the appropriate finishes. Next, choose the finishes that offer you the right combination of qualities. Finally, choose a colour.

Exterior water-based paint

Water-based is the hands-down favourite for most painted exterior surfaces because it's easier to use and more environmentally friendly than oil-based paint. Water-based paint is more elastic and remains flexible, so it won't crack as the materials to which it's applied expand and contract. Oil-based paint, on the other hand, becomes brittle with age. Water-based paint has superior colour retention over most oil-based paint – it doesn't fade as much. The paint film also permits interior moisture vapour to pass through, so water-based paint is less likely to peel due to moisture problems. You can apply a water-based topcoat over either water-based or oil-based primer.

Exterior oil-based paint

On a few surfaces, oil-based paint may be a better choice than water-based. For example, if a house has numerous coats of oil-based paint, it's generally best to stick with oil-based. Believing that oil-based-painted surfaces are generally easier to clean and have more sheen than water-based paints, some professionals use water-based on the body of the house but prefer to use an oil-based finish on trim or other high-contact areas, such as doors. We think that the advantages of water-based outweigh the purported advantages of oil-based-based paint in the vast majority of applications. We're inclined to agree with the professionals, however, who say that oil-based paints, especially primers, are better to use on problem areas.

Don't use oil-based paint over a water-based topcoat: It's likely to peel off even a well-prepared water-based finish because the water-based expands and contracts too much for the relatively rigid oil-based film.

Paint versus stain

If you have new cladding or cladding that has been treated only with a semi-transparent stain, your options are wide open. However, you can't stain over previously painted surfaces.

Book III

Painting and Wall-papering

As a general rule, paint is the preferred finish for smooth cladding, trim, and metal cladding like steel or aluminium because it offers maximum protection from UV radiation and moisture. Stains are commonly used on natural wood cladding, especially rough-sawn boards, and on other exterior wood surfaces, such as decks and fences.

Although paint lasts longer than stain, paint finish builds up and may peel or otherwise fail; if it does, you're in for a lot of work. Stains, on the other hand, may not last as long, but thanks to the penetration, they just weather away. Over the long haul, less cost and work may be involved if you choose stain – it's easier to apply, and preparation is usually limited to simple power-washing.

Exterior stains and clear coatings

Stains and clear coatings are the most natural-looking protective finishes for wood. Exterior stains and varnishes have fungicides, offer ultraviolet (UV) protection, and have more water-repellent qualities, too.

You can only apply stains over new or previously stained surfaces – not painted ones.

Oil-based semitransparent stains are a good choice for new wood cladding, decks, and fences. These stains have a linseed-oil base, which offers good penetration of new wood (especially rough-sawn surfaces) while revealing the wood's grain and texture. For best protection, use two coats of semi-transparent stain on new wood surfaces.

If your goal is to conceal discolouration, solid-colour stains have more pigment than semitransparent stains and tend to hide the wood grain. This characteristic makes solid-colour stains a better choice to finish pressure-treated wood that has a pronounced green or brown tint, which semitransparent stains may not cover.

Choosing the Right Interior Paint

Interior paints come in different gloss ranges, or sheens. Some manufacturers get a bit more creative in naming sheens, but the most common are

- **Matt:** This paint is at the low (dull) end of the sheen spectrum. Matt is often used on walls and ceilings because it reflects a minimum of light off the surface, reducing glare and helping to hide small surface imperfections. This paint is generally not considered washable.

- **Eggshell, low-lustre, and satin:** These paints have increasing amounts of sheen, making them a little more dirt-resistant than flat paints, and washable. The slight sheen is generally noticeable only when the surface is lighted from the side. These paints are a good choice for walls in hallways, children's bedrooms, playrooms, and other high-traffic areas.

- **Semi-gloss:** This paint has still more sheen, making it even more washable. Walls in kitchens, bathrooms, and children's rooms are good candidates for semi-gloss paints.

- **Gloss and high-gloss:** These paints dry to a durable and shiny surface. High-gloss paint has an almost mirrorlike sheen. Gloss paints are the most dirt-resistant and scrubbable choice for interior trim and most woodwork. Gloss enamels are particularly hard and are an excellent choice for doors, furniture, and cabinets because the surface can withstand heavy cleaning. Some gloss enamels, called deck or floor enamels, are specifically designed for wearing surfaces, such as floors.

Finding the Perfect Interior Stain

If you think that variety is the spice of life, you're going to love shopping for wood stains. Stains are available in a wide variety of wood tones, as well as pastels. Your hardware shop probably has samples so that you can see how various stains look on real wood.

Let your decor and tastes determine which stain is best for you. For nicely grained wood, such as oak, a penetrating stain that enhances the grain pattern is a good choice. For furniture, cabinets, or mouldings made of less attractive wood, or for mismatched pieces of wood, consider using a dark stain to conceal more.

Can't find the perfect colour? Play chemist and mix together different stains from the same manufacturer to make your own unique stain. If you decide to experiment, be sure to mix enough stain to do the entire job. Measure and record the proportions carefully because if you run out of stain in the middle of a project or if you need to mix up a batch for a future repair, matching the tone without a formula is difficult.

You can also make your own pigmented stain by thinning oil-based paint with white spirit. For example, for a deep black stain, mix thin flat-black oil-based paint with white spirit. Start with a 50-50 mix and add white spirit, testing often on a scrap of wood until you get just the result you want.

Estimating How Much Paint to Buy

To estimate the amount of paint you need for a project, consider how much surface area you want to cover. Dust off a maths formula that you probably learned in primary school: length (in metres) x width (in metres) = area (in square metres). Virtually all paints and other coatings describe coverage in terms of the number of square metres (area) that 1 litre covers. The coverage varies by product and is printed on the label.

You also need to consider the condition of the surface. A rough, porous, unpainted surface absorbs much more paint than a primed or topcoated surface. Similarly, a six-panel door requires more paint than a smooth, flat door.

Estimating isn't an exact science. Keep in mind that you can usually return unopened standard colours, but not custom ones, so it's more important to be accurate when using custom colours.

Although you don't want to waste paint, a reasonable amount of leftover paint is handy for touch-ups.

Follow this process to figure out how much paint to buy:

1. **Find the total area of the surface you want to paint.**

   For walls, just add together the length of all the walls and multiply the result by the height of the room, measured from the floor to a level ceiling. The number you get equals the total area.

Book III

Painting and Wallpapering

Ceiling measurements are usually fairly straightforward – just multiply the room's width by its length. Add this number to the area of the walls or leave it separate, depending on whether you're planning to use different-coloured paints for the ceiling and the walls.

If the room has a cathedral ceiling, it has some triangular wall sections (usually two identical ones on opposite walls). Dust off one more maths formula: area (of a triangle) = ½ base x height. Measure from the top of the wall to the peak of the triangle. Multiply that number (the height) by ½ the width of the wall (the base) to get the square metreage of the triangle. If your room has two identical triangles, either double the number or multiply the height by the entire width.

Measuring a home's exterior is more complex, but the procedure is basically the same. Just break up the surface into rectangles, multiply length by width for each rectangular area, and total them up.

Don't bother to climb a ladder to measure the height of a triangular gable wall section; count the rows, called courses, of cladding from the ground. Measure the exposure (the distance from the bottom of one course of cladding to the bottom of the next course) on cladding that you can reach easily, and then multiply that number by the number of courses to come up with the height measurement. To calculate the area of a triangle, multiply the height by the width, and divide by two.

2. **Account for windows and doors.**

   To figure how much of the total area is paintable, you need to deduct for the openings – windows and doors. Unless you have unusually large or small windows or doors, you can allow 2 square metres for each door and 1.5 square metres for each window. Add up the areas of the openings and subtract that total from the total area.

   On the exterior, however, don't make any deductions unless an opening is larger than 10 square metres. This general rule helps to account for some of the typical exterior conditions described in Step 5.

   If you plan to paint the doors, use the following rules. Allow 2 square metres for each door (just the door, not the trim); double that if you're finishing both sides.

3. **Calculate the total area of the trim.**

   Generally speaking, you need about 1 square metre of paint to cover the sash and trim of a standard-sized window.

4. **Make a preliminary calculation of litres required.**

   Knowing the area to be covered, divide the total square metreage of paintable area by the coverage per litre, which is stated on the label. For example, if you're painting walls with a paint that covers 20 square metres per litre, you divide the paintable wall area by 20 to find the number of litres of paint you need for the walls.

5. Factor in surface conditions.

Out go the formulas for this final step. The coverage stated on the label applies under typical circumstances. A litre of quality water-based topcoat applied over a primed or painted smooth surface, for example, covers about 20 sq m But you use more paint if you're painting walls or ceilings that are unfinished, porous, heavily patched, or dark in colour. Plan to apply a primer and a topcoat or two.

If you're painting problem surfaces, allow 25 to 50 per cent extra in most cases. To allow 50 per cent more paint, multiply your total painted area by 1.5. To allow 25 per cent more paint, multiply the painted area by 1.25. On a large project, like painting or staining an entire house, seek the advice of experienced paint shop personnel. If you're using custom colours, which usually can't be returned, be conservative and plan a second trip if you need more.

The Workhorses of Painting: Brushes and Rollers

Indoors or out, most painting tasks call for one or more of the big three applicators – brushes, rollers, and pads. (Actually, painting has four workhorses, but the fourth, the paint sprayer, is out in its own pasture.) You can use all three applicators with oil- or water-based finishes, so the surface you plan on painting is the primary determining factor. These applicators produce slightly different textures, which can be a second reason for choosing one type over another. See Book 3, Chapter 3 for tips on painting and paint effects.

Book III

Painting and Wall-papering

Brushes

A good brush gives you the desired result with the least amount of work. Price and feel are the best indicators of quality, and you need to consider the size, texture, and shape of the surface you're finishing. Keep these points in mind:

✏ Check to see that the *ferrule*, or the metal band that binds the brush fill (see below) to the handle, is made of noncorrosive metal; otherwise, rust may develop and contaminate the finish. The ferrule should be nailed to the handle.

✏ The handle should feel comfortable in your hand.

Brush fill, as the brushing material on a paintbrush is called, is very important and falls into two main categories:

- **Natural bristle brushes,** sometimes called hog bristle or China brushes (the hogs are from China), are the best, but you can use them only for oil-based paints because the bristles soak up water and get ruined. Hog bristle has a rough texture that picks up and holds a lot of paint, and the ends are naturally split, or flagged. A flagged brush, which looks a bit fuzzy at the tip, allows each individual bristle or filament to hold more paint without dripping and to apply paint more smoothly.

- **Synthetic brushes** are made of nylon, polyester, or a combination of synthetic filaments. Nylon bristles are more abrasion-resistant than natural bristles, hold up to water-based paints, and apply a very smooth finish. Although you can use nylon brushes with oil-based paints, poly-ester brushes hold up much better to solvents, heat, and moisture and as such are better all-purpose brushes. The best synthetic brushes blend nylon and polyester filaments and are an acceptable compromise for use with exterior oil-based painting.

Regardless of which type of brush you choose, look for a mix of short and long bristles with flagged tips. As the flagging on longer bristles wears, the shorter bristles take over. Don't use brushes whose bristles are all cut to the same length. Bristles should feel full, thick, and resilient. If you fan the brush and tug lightly on the bristles, no bristles should fall out. Also, choose brushes with bristles that are contoured or chiselled to an oval or rounded edge. A chiselled-tip brush cuts in better around trim.

After you know what type of brush fill you want, you need to choose the right style.

Here are the four standard brush styles:

- **Enamel (varnish) brushes** are generally available from 25 to 75 mm wide. The brush fill is designed to have superior paint-carrying capacity and has a chiselled tip for smooth application. Use these brushes for trim and woodwork.

- **Sash brushes** look like enamel brushes. These brushes, too, are avail-able in 25 to 75 mm widths, but the handle is long and thin for better control. Although laying paint on flat surfaces may be easier with a flat sash brush, an angular sash brush is okay for flat surfaces and is much better for *cutting in* (carefully painting up to an edge) and getting into corners.

- ✔ **Wall brushes** are designed for painting large areas, including exterior cladding. Select a brush according to the size of the surface you're painting, but avoid brushes over 100 mm wide – they can get awfully heavy by the end of the day.

- ✔ **Stain brushes** are similar to wall brushes, but they're shorter and designed to control dripping of watery stains.

Rollers

A paint roller is great for most large, flat surfaces and is the runaway favourite for painting walls and ceilings. A roller holds a large amount of paint, which saves you time and the effort of bending and dipping. (The only bending and dipping we like to do while painting involves a bag of crisps and a bowl of salsa.) See 'Roller Techniques' for tips on using your roller.

When you buy a roller, choose one made with a heavy wire frame and a comfortable handle that has an open end to accept an extension pole. Don't buy economy-grade rollers that tend to flex when you apply pressure and result in an uneven coat of paint. Choose a heavy, stiff roller that doesn't flex and enables you to apply constant pressure.

A 225 mm roller is the standard size, but you can buy smaller sizes for smaller or hard-to-access surfaces such as behind radiators. If you're painting the town, you can find a 450 mm length.

The soft painting surface of a roller is called a *sleeve* or cover. The sleeve slides off the roller cage for cleaning and storage. Used properly, a quality roller sleeve leaves a nondirectional paint film that looks the same on an upstroke as it does on a downstroke. Clean a sleeve thoroughly after every job, and it'll last for years.

Look for rollers with bevelled edges. These rollers are less likely to leave tracks – lines or beads of paint that form on the surface at the edges of the roller. Don't cut corners here, either; a cheap roller sleeve sheds fibres, and you'll spend more time picking fibres out of wet paint than you will actually applying the paint. Wrap masking tape around a new roller and then peel it off along with lots of loose fibres that otherwise would end up on your wall or ceiling.

Book III

Painting and Wall-papering

You can buy two kinds of sleeves:

- Natural sleeves, made of lambswool, are preferred for oils because they hold more paint.

  Lambswool shouldn't be used with water-based paints because the alkali in water-based paints detans the sheep leather and makes it vulnerable to rot.

- Synthetic sleeves, usually made of polyester, can be used for both oil- and water-based paints.

The *nap length* (the length of the woolly fibres on the sleeve) you choose depends on the type of job you're undertaking. Check out Table 1-1 for pointers.

I have the power! Taking painting to the next level

If you plan to do a big painting job, you may want to check out the power-painting systems: Power rollers and spray systems.

If you're facing a major interior paint job, like when you move into an empty house, or if you plan to paint the exterior of your home with a roller, power rolling is definitely worthwhile, saving time and providing an even finish.

Power rollers have an electric pump that draws paint directly from the tin; they are either mains- or battery-powered. Power rollers use air pressure to push the paint from a reservoir to the roller, where it seeps out of little holes in the roller-sleeve core and saturates the fabric. The techniques for a power roller and a manual one are the same except that you don't have to reload a power roller. You just roll away and occasionally push a button or pull a trigger to feed more paint to the applicator. Instead of filling a roller tray with paint, you either fill a reservoir or pump directly from the tin.

Other than cost (a battery-powered paint roller starts from around £35, compared to a manual one you can pick up for under a fiver), the principal downside of this equipment is the increased setup and clean-up time. You also end up with a fair amount of waste every time you clean, as you have to wash the paint out of much of this equipment.

The next level is paint-spraying. Paint-spraying is fast and excellent for working on complex exterior surfaces, such as rough-hewn wood, concrete, shutters, fences, detailed roof trim, and wicker furniture. Compressor-driven and airless sprayers atomise paint, which means that the paint breaks up into many tiny particles. These particles float in the air and can be carried for long distances on a breeze, so make sure you're not spraying near anything (or anyone) that would be damaged by getting splattered. Wear goggles and protective clothing while spraying, and only spray in well-ventilated areas. Whichever sprayer you use, read the instructions carefully and practise on an inconspicuous area of the wall. You can buy or hire paint-spraying equipment – expect to pay around £20 for the gun and £100 for the compressor, or they cost around £40 per day to hire.

Table 1-1	Picking a Nap Length to Suit Your Job
Nap Length	*Job*
6 mm	For very smooth surfaces like flat doors, plastered walls, and wide trim
10 or 12 mm	For slightly irregular surfaces like drywall and exterior cladding
18 mm or longer	For semi-rough surfaces like sawn timber
25 or 32 mm	For rough surfaces like concrete block and render

Foam painting pads

Painting pads are rectangular or brush-shaped foam applicators, with or without fibre painting surfaces. Some people find pads easier to use than brushes and they paint a nice, smooth coat on trim and leave no brush marks. We especially like one that has rollers on the edge to guide the pad when cutting in ceilings and interior trim.

On the downside, pads tend to put paint on too thin; they don't hold as much paint as rollers or brushes and aren't as versatile. Using a pad makes it harder to control drips and to apply an even coat on a large surface. Given the time most people need to develop techniques, it may be better to stick with a brush and/or roller for most applications.

Brushing Up on Techniques

Knowing how to use a paintbrush is largely intuitive – rocket science it ain't. In this section, we show you a few techniques and tricks that can help you get better results with less fatigue.

It's all in the wrist

Painting can be tiring and messy, but if you use the techniques we describe in this section, you can get the best out of your efforts.

Book III

Painting and Wall-papering

To hold and load your brush:

1. **Hold the brush near the base of the handle with your forefingers just barely extending over the ferrule (the metal band that binds the brush fill to the handle).**

   For detail work, you probably want to use your good hand, but otherwise swap hands often. Alternating hands takes a little getting used to, but the more you do it, the less fatigued your muscles become and the faster you paint. Changing bodies works well, too.

2. **Dip your brush about a third of the way into the paint and tap it (don't wipe it) on the side of the tin to shake off excess.**

   Fully load your brush. Don't overload it, but don't shake off any more paint than necessary to get the brush to the surface without dripping. This brush-loading technique enables you to paint a larger area without having to move your setup.

To lay on an even coat of paint with a paintbrush:

1. **Unload the paint from one side of the brush with a long stroke in one direction, horizontally or vertically.**

2. **At the end of the first stroke, unload the paint from the other side of the brush.**

   Start in a dry area about a foot away from the first stroke and brush toward the end of the first stroke.

3. **Keep the brush moving, varying the pressure of your stroke to adjust the amount of paint being delivered to the surface.**

   The more pressure you apply, the more paint flows out of the brush, so start with a fairly light touch and gradually increase the pressure as you move along. If you must press hard to spread paint, you're probably applying it too thin.

4. **Brush out the area as needed to spread the paint evenly.**

   Oil-based paint requires more brushing out than water-based, but don't overwork the finish, especially when using varnish.

Minimise brush marks and bubbles with a finishing stroke – a light stroke, as long as possible, in one direction and feathered at the end. To feather an edge with a brush:

1. **Start your brush moving in the air, lightly touch down, and continue the stroke.**

2. **Slow down near the end of the stroke and, with a slight twisting motion, lift the brush from the surface.**

3. **Continue in the same fashion in an adjacent area.**

4. **Immediately brush the paint toward the previous wet-feathered edge to blend those two surfaces.**

5. **Spread and level the paint with additional strokes and feather a new wet edge.**

   You can't maintain a wet edge everywhere if you're painting a large area, so start and finish at corners, edges, or anywhere other than the middle of a surface so that the transition won't be noticeable. To slow drying, avoid painting in direct sunlight or on very windy days.

May I cut in?

Cutting in describes two quite different painting techniques. In one sense, cutting in refers to the process of carefully painting up to an unpainted edge or an edge of a different colour or sheen, such as the joint between a doorframe and a wall.

Cutting in also refers to using a brush or other applicator to get into corners that a roller or larger applicator can't get into, such as where the ceiling and wall meet. Accuracy isn't an issue here, so work quickly. Just remember to feather the edges and to paint to the feathered wet edges as soon as possible, especially when applying oil-based paint (see the preceding section).

Book III

Painting and Wall-papering

Secret weapon: Backbrushing

For some applications, you can take advantage of a roller's speed, but you should follow up with a brush — a technique called backbrushing. Backbrushing smoothes out roller stipple, pushes out air bubbles, and works the paint into the surface for a better bond. These examples show you when to use this technique:

- Rollers leave a slightly stippled paint film that's fine for walls and cladding, but you may not like it on a door or cabinet. A short-fibre pad or wide brush levels the finish on a door or trim nicely.

- On exterior surfaces, where a good paint bond to the surface is important, a roller doesn't do as good a job as a brush. Nothing works paint into a surface quite

like a brush. We recommend backbrushing to work spray-applied penetrating and solid-colour stains into exterior surfaces.

Backbrush immediately after you apply the finish and while it's still wet. Dip your brush in the finish just once to condition it, but wipe it against the side of the tin to remove the excess. You don't need to add finish; just work what's already there.

One final tip: When a project calls for backbrushing, use a team approach — one person with a roller and another with a brush. You'll fly through the job. Don't forget to swap tasks on big jobs to avoid the fatigue associated with each task.

When cutting in carefully up to an edge, remember that you have the best control if you use an angled sash brush. Use the edge of the brush, not the face, and follow these steps:

1. **Lay the paint on close to, but not right on, the edge that you want to cut in.**

   Keep in mind that more paint is on your brush when you start a stroke, so apply less pressure and/or stay a little farther away at the outset. For the same reason, apply more pressure and move closer to the edge you want to cut in as you lay on the paint with a long stroke or two. Lay on the paint evenly and uniformly close.

2. **Start a finishing stroke, varying the pressure to push the paint that you left on the surface in the first pass right up to the edge.**

   It may take a couple of passes, but with practice, you'll be able to apply a finishing stroke in one long stroke.

You may need to reshape a brush that has lost its shape from being used on edges this way. Just dip it in paint and wipe both brush faces several times against the edge of your paint bucket.

Roller Techniques

You can work faster with a roller than with a brush. The most important thing to remember is that a roller spreads paint so efficiently and easily that the tendency is to spread it far too thin.

The best way to ensure that you don't spread the paint too thin is to use a methodical approach:

1. **Load a roller fully by dipping it about halfway into your paint reservoir.**

   Roll the roller very lightly on either the sloped portion of your roller tray or the roller screen, depending on your setup. This technique coats the roller surface more evenly while removing excess that would otherwise drip on the way to the surface.

2. **Unload and spread the paint in an area of about 1 square metre.**

   On large surfaces, especially rough ones, unload the paint in an N or other three- or four-leg zigzag pattern; then spread the paint horizontally and make your light finishing strokes vertically. Figure 1-1 shows this three-step zigzag process.

3. **Reload the roller and unload another pattern that overlaps the just-painted area.**

   Spread the new paint, blend the two areas, and wind up with finishing strokes.

Figure 3-1:
Roller on the paint in a zigzag pattern, roll it out horizontally, and finish with light vertical strokes.

Normally, you don't need to feather the wet edge when you're rolling on paint because you overlap and blend each section before the paint dries. However, a few exceptions exist:

- If you're unable to start or finish an edge at a natural breaking point, such as a corner or the bottom edge of a course of cladding, you may need to feather the edge.

- When you roll paint onto large surfaces where one painted area must sit while you're working your way back to it, you may have difficulty blending if you don't feather the edge.

- Although oil-based paint takes longer to dry than water-based, blending one area with another is harder with oil-based paint unless you do it almost immediately.

Book III

Painting and Wall-papering

To roll a feathered edge:

1. **Start the motion in the air, lowering the roller to the surface.**

2. **Roll with light pressure until you near the edge.**

3. **Gradually reduce pressure and lift the roller off the surface as you pass into the unpainted area.**

Feather when touching up with a roller to blend in the newly painted area, which almost always has a slightly different tone than the surrounding area. In fact, feather more than usual: After you feather an edge as just described, use a nearly dry roller to make a few very light passes over the touched-up area, extending at least 300 mm into the unpainted area.

Indispensable painting accessories

You need more than a brush or roller to paint. You need to accessorise. We've found the painting accessories listed here to be particularly helpful.

- Swivel/pot/ladder hooks: A must for exterior house painting, a pot hook lets you securely hang a paint tin or bucket on your ladder, and it swivels to allow you to rotate the tin for convenient access.

- Extension poles: Spend a couple of quid on an inexpensive handle extension that screws into the end of a roller handle. You can roll from floor to ceiling without bending and with less exertion, and you avoid constant trips up and down a ladder. Some poles have adjustable heads to which you can attach a paintbrush for hard-to-reach spots or a pole sander for sanding ceilings and walls.

- 25-litre bucket with roller screen: An alternative to a roller tray is a 25-litre bucket with a roller screen, a metal grate designed to fit inside the bucket. The rig is ideal for large jobs because it saves you the time you'd spend refilling the paint tray. The bucket is easier to move around and not as easy to step into. At break time, drop the screen in the bucket and snap on the lid.

- Trim guard or paint shield: This edging tool is very useful for painting around windows, doors, and painting skirting boards. Press the metal or plastic blade of the guard against the surface you want to shield from fresh paint. Don't forget to wipe the edges clean frequently to avoid leaving smears of paint.

- Clamp lamp: These inexpensive lamps let you direct light where you need it.

- 5-in-1 tool: The Swiss Army knife of painting tools, it can scrape loose paint, score paint lines for trim removal, loosen or tighten a screw, hammer in a popped nail or other protrusion, and scrape paint out of a roller sleeve.

- Paint mixer: This inexpensive drill attachment does a faster and more effective job than a paint stirring stick – it's so easy that you might actually take the time to stir as often as the instructions say to!

Chapter 2
Preparing Surfaces for Painting

*W*e're not going to beat around the bush: Properly preparing the surface for a finish is often the most time-consuming, difficult, and least rewarding part of a painting job. If you're thinking, 'Fine. Let's skip this part of the work and the book,' think again. Any painter worth their colours will tell you that the key to a successful painting job is preparation. This chapter describes what you need to do and how to get it done in the most efficient way possible. The rest is up to you.

Don't become another DIY accident statistic by balancing on a chair to reach the tops of walls. Chapter 3 deals with using access equipment safely and effectively.

Preparing Exterior Surfaces

Although good-quality paint and proper application techniques are important, surface preparation is usually the most important factor in determining the success of a painting job. This section is devoted primarily to the process of preparing the exterior of a house before you pick up a paintbrush.

Here's an overview of the proper sequence for preparing a house for repainting:

1. **Repair or replace any loose, missing, rotten, or damaged wall surfaces, woodwork, or trim (such as skirting boards and architraves).**

2. **Remove any peeling or loose paint.**

   Hand-scraping and power-sanding are the usual ways to do this job, but sometimes you need to use power-washing, chemicals, or heat.

3. **Treat any mildew problem with either a bleach-detergent solution or a commercial house cleaner that contains a mildewcide.**

4. **Prime bare wood or other problem surfaces that require primer.**

5. **Patch nail holes and seal gaps and cracks with paintable caulk or exterior-grade filler.**

6. **Pressure-wash the entire exterior to remove sanding dust, dirt, and grime.**

Proper preparation varies according to the type and condition of the exterior surface, as well as the type of finish you intend to apply. Here are some tips for dealing with the problems associated with typical exterior surfaces:

- **New wood cladding:** Brush the wood clean, working from the top down. Caulk after you stain or prime. If you plan to paint or use a solid-colour stain, set any nails that the carpenters missed below the surface and fill the nail holes with caulk.

- **Weathered wood cladding:** Stain bonds well to unpainted wood that has weathered. If you plan to paint, then sand or power-wash the wood to remove any grey, weathered surface and to smooth cladding that has been exposed to the weather for more than a few weeks. (See the section 'Saving time by power-washing', later in this chapter.) You may have to remove as much as 3 mm of the grey, weathered surface to get to the nonweathered, natural-coloured wood. If you're staining, use a wood restorer or power-wash the wood to bring it back to its natural colour so that staining produces the desired colour.

- **Old painted cladding:** Scrape off loose paint, using a scraper. Then power-sand to feather the hard edges left by scraping (as shown in Figure 2-1), prime any wood made bare in the process, and caulk all joints. Also, push in any popped nails and fill the holes with caulk.

Figure 2-1:
Feather the edges of the scraped areas by sanding.

✏ **Concrete and masonry:** Unfinished, fully cured concrete can be finished with concrete stain or paint after being cleaned with a power-washer to remove dirt, stains, and any residue from old sealers. If you're repainting, use the same type of paint: Oil-based or water-based masonry paint. Although you can scrape or sand small areas of peeling paint off concrete or masonry surfaces, doing so dulls scrapers and chews up sandpaper very quickly. If you're working on a large area, consider sand-blasting or stripping with a chemical remover.

Clean out cracks with a heavy-duty vacuum cleaner or brush before caulking the cracks. Do the same when using a concrete patch and mist the surface before applying the patch.

✏ **Render:** In many cases, a masonry cleaner – available at any DIY shop – is all you need to renew a rendered (or stucco) surface. Hose off the loose dirt and, while the surface is still wet, apply the cleaner to lift the remaining dirt. Then scrub with a stiff brush. If the render still looks dingy, consider having a render contractor redash the finish, a process in which a new cement surface is either sprayed or brushed onto the render. (See Book II, Chapter 4 on how to make repairs to render.)

Power-washing render or stucco, especially old stucco, is risky. The force of the water can blast the finish off, turning a simple cleaning job into a major repair.

✏ **Glossy finishes:** Paint doesn't bond well to glossy surfaces, including painted ones. If a cleaned painted surface still shines, you must dull it. Sanding is a surefire approach, but it's time-consuming and especially difficult on detailed areas of trim, windows, and doors. Brush-on deglosser, available for both oil- and water-based paints, is a much easier way to dull the surface.

✏ **Iron railings, cladding, and so on:** Clean the metal to remove dirt, grime, and oil before priming with a rust-inhibiting (direct-to-metal) primer. Follow the paint manufacturer's cleaning guidelines. Generally, you can use a 50-50 vinegar and water solution for all metal except galvanised steel. Clean new galvanised metal with white spirit before priming with special galvanised metal primer.

Rust often occurs under the paint on these surfaces, causing stains and a bumpy finish. Eventually, the finish flakes off. There are two basic approaches to preparing rusty metal for paint: You can eliminate rust by sanding, grinding, or sandblasting. Or, when removing every last spot of rust is impractical, you can use a wire brush to scrape off only the loose, flaking rust and then treat the metal with a chemical to neutralise the corrosion. Results with chemical neutralising vary, so always apply anti-rust metal primer on bare metal. You also can apply a paint conditioner, such as Penetrol, to rusty areas before you apply paint. The conditioner seals the rusty areas and provides a better paint bond.

- **Aluminium or PVC-U gutters and cladding:** Avoid painting aluminium and PVC-U gutters. If you do paint, scuff-sand for better bonding, and use specialist paint, such as PVC-U paint.

- **Aluminium cladding:** A good cleaning is generally all that aluminium cladding needs before you paint.

Scrubbing the house down

The secret to a long-lasting paint job is cleanliness. The ideal time to clean is after you finish scraping, sanding, spot-priming, and caulking – and after a long nap. Allow two to three days for drying before you paint.

In addition to the many commercial cleaners available, you can make two widely recommended homemade cleaning solutions:

- For general cleaning, mix 50 grammes of laundry detergent or trisodium phosphate (TSP) in 5 litres of water. Scrub with a stiff brush and rinse thoroughly with water.

- To remove mould, mildew, algae, and lichen, mix 1 litre of household bleach and 50 grammes of detergent with 3 litres of water. Spray on with a garden sprayer. If necessary, cover the area for about an hour to prevent it from drying out. Rinse well with water and repeat as necessary.

Saving time by power-washing

Washing your house may seem like an insurmountable job, but an electric or gas-powered washer is one of the most useful and labour-saving machines homeowners can get their hands on. Plus, power-washers (also called pressure-washers) are just plain fun to use.

Small electric power-washers (or pressure-washers, as they're also called) sell for as little as £70. Gutsy gas models cost two to four times as much. You can also hire a killer unit for about £30 a day. If you hire, you may want to share the hire cost with a neighbour – cleaning the exterior of two houses in a day is entirely possible.

Virtually risk-free uses of a power-washer include preparing concrete and asphalt surfaces for protective coatings and restoring a slimy green or severely weathered wood deck to its original beauty. Other applications may present risks both to you and to your house. For example, if you have an old house with little or no insulation, loose-fitting windows, or very old cladding, especially wood shingles, skip the power-washer and wash the house by hand, instead.

Handling a power-washer

Power-washers usually have a control to vary the pressure of the water stream. For most cleaning projects, especially on wood, 800 to 1000 psi (pounds per square inch) is adequate. On less vulnerable surfaces, you can go up to a maximum of 1,500 psi. Read the power-washer's operating instructions or request a demonstration from the company you're renting it from.

The jet of water spraying from a power-washer can be lethal. Exercise good judgement when using a power-washer, and most important, never use it near other people or pets. If you're on a ladder, keep one hand on the ladder and be prepared for the considerable kick that occurs when you pull or release the trigger.

Depending on the application, some cleaning solutions can be used with power-washers that add chemicals into the water stream from a detergent bottle or through a siphon hose. Read the label carefully: Many solutions contain chemicals that can damage the washer and/or put your health at risk when used with a power-washer.

Preparing the site and using safety precautions

High-pressure water finds its way into any unsealed opening in its path, so make sure to protect everything you don't want to spray. No matter what you're washing – cladding or decking – follow these basic guidelines:

- Wear waterproof gear, wellies, and safety goggles.
- Use dust sheets or large sheets of polythene to catch paint chips.
- Test pressure adjustment, spray pattern, and working distance on an inconspicuous area.
- Practise your spray angle by holding the sprayer to the surface until you get the even results you want. Overlap passes for even cleaning.
- Don't swing the wand in an arc; you'll get uneven results because you're closer to the surface in the centre of the arc.

Battling mildew stains

A brown, grey, or black stain on cladding or trim may be simple grime, or it may be mildew. To test whether a stain is grime or mildew, try washing the stain away with water and detergent. If the stain doesn't wash away with water and detergent, it's probably mildew.

Book III

Painting and Wall-papering

Because mildew is a fungus growth, it thrives on moisture and dirt, so keep the cladding open to the sun and air. Don't store firewood or other materials close to the house. Prune tree branches that shade the house. If you have recurring mildew problems, power-wash the house's exterior once a year and apply a mildewcide solution every two to three years.

Handle bleach and mildewcide solutions with care. Read label warnings, and always wear protective clothing, especially neoprene gloves and goggles. Protect plants by watering them down well and covering them if possible before you power-wash the house and watering them well again afterwards.

Cleaning chalking surfaces

Some exterior paints, such as those used on aluminium cladding, intentionally *chalk* for self-cleaning. Wipe the surface with the palm of your hand. If the paint colour comes off on your hand, the paint is chalking. Scrub off the chalk with a strong solution of water and detergent (or a nonphosphate TSP alternative). You can also use a commercial wood cleaner to remove chalked paint. Water pressure alone doesn't do the trick.

As you scrub the surface, work from the bottom up to avoid streaking. Rinse frequently with clear water, and allow the surface to dry before painting.

Cleaning stucco, render, and other masonry

Efflorescence, mould and algae, lichen, and stains from chalking paint or rusting metal are problems that you need to attend to before painting masonry, which includes surfaces such as stucco, brick, and concrete block.

First, eliminate the sources of the problems. Overhanging trees can cause mould and algae; a deteriorating chimney cap can allow water to penetrate behind the brick and cause efflorescence. Rusting may result from the use of various metals reinforcing materials in masonry construction, such as wire mesh or steel structural materials over windows and doors. Even if the metal isn't visible, the rust stains may bleed through to the surface. If the paint on cladding above masonry is chalking, it washes down onto the masonry and stains the surface.

In most cases, you need to scrub the surface with a chemical cleaner. See the introduction to this 'Scrubbing the house down' section for cleaning solutions to use for general cleaning and for removing mildew, mould, and lichen. For efflorescence and other stubborn stains, mix 200 ml of 10 per cent brick-cleaning acid in 5 litres of water. (Brick-cleaning acid is available at your local builders' merchants.) Heavy stains may require up to a 1:1 solution, but the risk of damage to the surface increases. Scrub the surface with a stiff brush and rinse thoroughly with water. Strong acid solutions must be neutralised with a 1:10 bleach-water solution to stop the etching otherwise caused by the acid.

Add the acid to the water (instead of the water to the acid) or it will spatter. Because the acid vapours can burn your lungs, keep your distance from the acid by using a long-handled brush to scrub the surface. Wear protective gear, including a respirator, heavy neoprene gloves, and splash-proof goggles, and read the label for additional handling instructions.

Sealing cracks and holes with caulk

Filling cracks and holes in your home's trim and cladding before painting not only makes the paint job look better, but also makes the paint last longer. Cracks and holes in any surface collect water, which eventually causes paint to peel.

Caulk is a term for a substance designed to seal a joint between two surfaces and to fill small holes. Use top-quality caulk outdoors, where it needs to withstand extreme temperature changes and remain flexible for 30 to 50 years. Before caulking joints between dissimilar materials, make sure that the manufacturer recommends the caulk for both materials. If you're going to paint the area, the caulk must be paintable. If you're unsure whether a caulk is suitable for a particular application, contact the manufacturer's customer service department.

Book III

Painting and Wall-papering

The best time to caulk is after you scrape, sand, and prime. Caulk adheres better to primed surfaces, and the gaps, cracks, and holes are more evident.

Scrape away any peeling paint adjacent to the caulked areas. If doing so exposes any bare wood, recaulk all cracks between any two nonmoving materials. Let the caulk cure for a few days before power-washing the exterior.

Don't caulk the horizontal joints on cladding where the cladding courses overlap. The cracks between two courses of cladding provide ventilation points to let moisture escape from the cladding and from inside the wall. In fact, one of the often-recommended cures for a moisture problem involves inserting numerous wedges between cladding courses to create a larger gap through which moisture can escape. For the same reason, don't try to fill the joints between courses with paint.

Patching surface cavities before painting

Fix small holes in cladding with an exterior patching compound, available in a premixed form (much like interior filler) and in a dry powder form that you mix with water. Just make sure the package states that the patching compound is for outdoor use.

To patch holes and depressions in cladding of any kind, follow these steps:

1. **Clean the hole or depression you plan to fill.**

   Roughen the area you want to patch with 80-grit sandpaper for a better bond.

2. **Fill the area with patching compound.**

   Apply the compound to the hole or depression in one direction and then smooth it in a perpendicular direction so that it's level with the original surface.

3. **Allow the compound to harden and then sand it smooth.**

   Compound shrinks, so a second coat may be necessary. Be sure to remove the dust from sanding the compound before you apply a second coat.

To repair large cracks and damaged trim, remove any rotten wood with a chisel. Use a two-part polyester-based compound (similar to filler for use on cars) to make the repair. Two-part fillers come with a thick paste base and a small tube of hardener. Mix the hardener with the paste according to the manufacturer's directions. The filler sets within three to five minutes, so mix only as much as you can use straight away, and clean your tools immediately after use.

Use a putty knife to apply the compound to the damaged area and level it with the surface. This filler doesn't shrink as much as premixed exterior fillers do, but you still may need to apply several coats to fill a large hole. When the filler hardens, it's suitable for rasping, sanding, or drilling.

When the compound has set firm but isn't completely dry, you can easily shape or smooth it with a Surform tool or rasp.

Preparing Interior Surfaces

Most interiors will look better if you just slap on a fresh coat of paint. However, you'll get results that are even more striking, and a longer-lasting paint job to boot, if you take special care in cleaning and preparing the surfaces. Preparation includes making minor repairs to the walls, ceilings, and woodwork, and scraping and sanding to remove any loose paint.

Cleaning a room for painting

Unless you know that you'll be undertaking messy repairs or surface preparation work, start work with a thorough cleaning. The goal is to strip the room of all dirt and cobwebs and to clean the skirting boards, windows, and door linings. A vacuum cleaner with a crevice tool can catch the cobwebs and dust. While you're at it, vacuum up dust and dirt around radiators and heating ducts. Open the windows to remove all dirt and debris from inside the sill.

If walls and woodwork have dirt or grease on them, wash them with a sponge and a phosphate-free household cleaner. Then rinse the surfaces with clear water and let them dry.

Preparing kitchens and bathrooms for painting

Paint's number-one enemy in a kitchen is grease, which clings to walls, ceilings, cabinets, and other woodwork. Use a household detergent to remove grease. Keep in mind that wood cabinets don't like harsh detergents or water, so work quickly and dry the surface immediately. If you intend to paint wooden cabinets, they need special attention; see the section 'Repairing and preparing to recoat painted wood' later in this chapter.

In addition to dust and dirt, bathrooms often have mould or mildew stains. Give the bathroom the same general cleaning that you would any other room, but to kill mildew, try a solution of 1 part household bleach and 3 parts water. Sponge or spray on the solution and let it sit for at least 15 minutes. Repeat the process if necessary until the stains are gone.

Bleach isn't good for painted surfaces. After it does the deed on the mildew, stop the bleaching action by rinsing the surface well with a neutraliser, such as clean water or a solution made up of 3 parts water to 1 part vinegar. Also, bleach is caustic and splashes easily, especially when you're working overhead. Wear goggles, rubber gloves, and old clothes.

Book III

Painting and Wallpapering

Clearing the way

As you empty a room for painting, the idea is to clear the room as much as possible so that you have free and easy access. Move out as much furniture as you can. You may want to leave that tank of a sofa or other large pieces that may chip your walls or woodwork when you move items out or, worse, back in after you paint. Just make sure that everything remaining is in the centre of the room and protected by dust sheets. You need room to move a ladder around and enough floor space for your paint setup – and make sure that you can reach the entire ceiling if that's the area you're painting.

Go through the following checklist to get your room ready for the big makeover:

- Take down pictures and other wallhangings. If you plan to return them to the same locations after you paint, leave the picture hooks in place; if it's time for a change, carefully pull the nails straight out. If you have plaster walls, twist them out with a pair of pliers to avoid chipping out the plaster.

- If the room is very large, stack the furniture in two areas with space between them. In a smaller room, pile everything in the centre, at least 1 metre away from the walls. Cover all furniture with dust sheets.

- Remove any rugs. Put plastic dust sheets under your paint supply and mixing area, but cover the floor with quality canvas dust sheets, which are less slippery to walk on than plastic ones. Use two layers of dust sheets on carpeting for added protection.

- Minimise the amount of tedious work painting around electrical switch plates and socket covers. Remove plates and covers and place a strip of wide masking tape over the switches and sockets to protect them. Also remove or lower light fixtures. Keep all the small parts together in a container. Make sure everything is turned off at the mains!

- If you're painting doors, mask the hardware (such as the handle) or remove it. Removing and replacing hardware takes less time than painting around it, and you eliminate unsightly glitches and don't waste time cleaning paint off hardware later. See the section 'Making final preparations' later in this chapter to find out the best ways to mask hardware.

- Even if you're painting during the day, you need good electric lighting, and you may need power for tools. Plug an extension cord into a nearby room or hallway to bring power to the room.

Before you remove outlet covers or light fixtures, shut off the power at the circuit breaker. Remember, wall sockets and lights are usually on different circuits. Double-check that the power is off by using a neon circuit tester or plugging in a lamp or other electrical device that you know is working. Place tape over the breaker as a reminder to others that the power is off.

Smoothing the walls

After you take down all the pictures and remove or cover the furniture, it's time to repair damage to the walls. The best way to spot all the problems is to shine a bright light across the wall at a sharp angle and to circle areas that need attention with a light pencil mark.

You probably have a few minor chips or nail holes to repair. Fix small holes with filler applied with a putty knife. When the filler is dry, sand the patch smooth with fine sandpaper on a rubber or padded sanding block. Because filler tends to shrink, you may need to add another coat to fill the remaining indentation.

Popped nails are an all-too-common problem. The nails, which were originally set below the surface and concealed with joint compound or skim plaster, pop out enough to make a bump or even break the surface. See Book II, Chapter 1 'Repairing nail pops' for how to fix the problem. If there are cracks in the walls or ceilings, see Book II, Chapter 1 'Filling cracks'.

Repairing and preparing to recoat painted wood

Woodwork is one of those details that make a difference. If the woodwork doesn't look good, the whole room can look shabby, even if the walls and ceiling are perfect. In this section, we describe how to make your woodwork look new again.

Patching chipped or gouged wood before painting

If the wood is chipped, gouged, or otherwise damaged, and you plan to paint, you can make an easy, invisible repair by using a two-part polyester resin compound:

1. **Clean out any loose material and scrape off any finish so that the patching material will bond better.**

2. **Mix the hardener (part one) with the filler (part two) as directed and apply it with a putty knife.**

   Generally, you want to overfill the hole.

3. **Use a rasp or Surform tool to shape or level the material as soon as it sets hard but before it cures (dries) completely.**

4. **When the material is fully cured, sand the patch to smooth and blend it in with the surrounding area.**

5. **Apply a primer to the patch and any bare wood before you paint.**

Book III

Painting and Wall-papering

Making paint stick to panelling and cabinets

Factory-finished wood cabinets and panelling require special preparation for painting. To ensure that the paint adheres properly to factory-finished panels or to waxed or varnished board panelling, follow these steps:

1. **Clean the wood especially well to remove dirt, grease, and wax.**

   For panelling, use a solution made of equal parts of household cleaner and water. For cabinets and panelling that are beyond cleaning with a mild detergent solution, try a solvent, such as white spirit.

2. **Take the shine off the surface by sanding lightly or with a chemical deglosser, especially on irregular or moulded surfaces.**

If you sand the wood, put an exhaust fan in the window of the work area and open a nearby window outside the room. The fan prevents sanding dust from going anywhere but outdoors.

If you use a chemical deglosser, remember to apply paint within half an hour or the deglosser loses its effectiveness. Apply a thorough coat of deglosser on varnish or polyurethane finishes.

3. **Wipe the surface well with a *tack cloth*, a sticky cheesecloth for removing sanding dust.**

   The oil in a tack cloth may interfere with the proper adhesion of latex finishes. If you plan to use latex, just use a cloth dampened with white spirit or water.

4. **Prime the wood.**

   Mix a bonding additive such as PVA with your primer or use an alcohol-based primer-sealer or other special bonding primer tinted to the approximate colour of the topcoat. See Chapter 1 for advice on choosing the primer and topcoat.

If you're painting cabinets, remove the handles and knobs so that you don't have to paint around them.

Toiling with wooden windows

The amount of work required to prepare windows for painting can vary from a good cleaning to everything short of replacement. This section looks at the most common problems and their solutions.

One problem you may encounter is a stuck sash window. You can solve this problem by cutting through the paint film with a trimming knife or even a pizza cutter.

Another common window problem is peeling paint where the wood meets the glass. Failure to create a paint seal between the glass and the wood allows condensation and window-cleaning chemicals to seep into the joint. To remove loose paint, follow these steps:

1. **Scrape or sand the area to remove loose paint.**

   Wrapping sandpaper over the edge of a putty knife makes it easier to sand close to the glass without scratching it.

2. **Apply a stain-killing primer to water-stained wood before applying a topcoat.**

   Avoid this problem in the future by using proper window-painting techniques, which we describe in Chapter 3.

Other window repairs, including replacing sash window cords, are covered in greater detail in Book II, Chapter 2.

Making final preparations

You're probably champing at the bit to dive in and get painting, but with just a few more final preparations you can do a really great job.

Priming and sealing

Spot-priming improves the bond of the topcoat to surfaces such as bare wood and metal. It also seals the surface of unfinished or patched areas so that they absorb topcoats to the same degree that surrounding areas do. If you try to just topcoat, the patch area will have less sheen than the area around it, making the patch more noticeable. This advice applies to patches and repairs to plasterboard, plain plaster, and trim. Therefore, spot-prime these areas, being careful to feather the edges of the paint into the surrounding areas.

See Chapters 1 and 3 for feathering and other painting techniques. For information on how to prepare previously wallpapered surfaces for paint or wallpaper, see Chapter 5.

Sealing cracks with caulk

Caulk (also sometimes called sealer or filler) covers a multitude of sins and prevents many problems from occurring – it has a consistency like thick toothpaste, which makes it easy to spread and fill small holes and narrow cracks. When it dries, caulk becomes firm but remains flexible and can tolerate movement between materials that expand, contract, or otherwise move in relation to one another. If you're painting, choose a quality paintable acrylic latex caulk or a siliconised acrylic latex caulk. Buy caulk in cartridge form to fit a caulking gun for super-easy application.

Cracks show up better after priming, and caulk adheres better to primed wood, so complete any priming before you caulk. For a neat job, caulk all joints. Caulk all the joints between trim and wall surfaces to prevent penetration of moisture vapour into walls.

Cut the tips of two tubes of caulk. Cut a very small opening in one tube and use it for narrow cracks at joints between the woodwork and walls and window stops and frame joints. Cut the tip of the second tube with a larger opening for caulking wider cracks. Apply caulk by squeezing the trigger as you pull the tip along the joint. Use as little caulk as needed to fill the crack, or the excess will spread out onto the surface and be visible. Use a wet fingertip to fill very small holes and smooth the caulk. Allow adequate curing (drying) time (read the label instructions) before you paint.

Book III

Painting and Wallpapering

Masking

Take a little time to mask areas that you don't want to paint. We especially like these materials:

- **Painter's tape:** This tape, available in various degrees of tackiness and width, is designed for masking. Painter's tape seals well but comes off much easier than regular masking tape does. Read the label to choose the correct type for your situation.

- **Pretaped masking paper or plastic:** The self-stick edges adhere to surfaces such as the tops of window and door trim for a straight painting edge. The paper or plastic, which ranges in width from a couple of inches to many feet, drapes the surface. The seal isn't as reliable as that of painter's tape.

Don't use regular masking tape because it has too much adhesive, making it harder to remove; plus, paint bleeds under it more easily, creating a rougher edge.

After you apply painter's tape, keep these tips in mind:

- Press the edge with a putty knife, a block of wood, or another hard material to seal it. Sealing the edge prevents paint from bleeding under the tape.

- Remove the tape as soon as the paint has dried to the touch. Generally, you should wait three to four hours but not more than 24 hours before removing the tape. It's especially important not to leave the tape on for longer than 24 hours if the sun might bake the tape on or if the tape might get wet.

- When you remove the tape, slowly peel it back at an angle away from the painted surface to avoid peeling off the freshly applied paint.

When you plan to paint walls and ceilings, consider masking the following areas:

- The tops of skirting boards
- The tops of windows and door casings
- The tops of dado rails
- Ceiling roses

When painting or finishing the following areas, follow these recommendations:

- When painting skirting boards, mask hardwood flooring.
- When finishing or painting flooring, mask the skirting boards.
- When painting doors and windows, mask all hinges and other hardware, unless you can remove them completely.

Sanding stripped or unfinished wood

Sanding is no one's idea of fun, but you must smooth new wood or wood that has been stripped of its finish before you can apply a stain or finish. In addition to removing imperfections and making the wood look and feel smooth, sanding takes off a thin top layer of wood, enabling stains and other finishes to penetrate evenly.

If you need to remove deep scratches, start with 80-grit (medium) or even 60-grit (coarse) sandpaper; otherwise, start with 120-grit (fine) sandpaper. Work your way up to at least 150-grit, and preferably 220-grit, making sure that all scratches left by the coarser-grit sandpaper are removed at each stage.

Smoothing by hand or with a power sander

Whenever possible, use a sanding block or pad that conforms to the shape of the surface being sanded: Flat for flat surfaces, concave for outwardly curving profiles, and so on. Holding the sandpaper in your hand usually produces uneven results because you exert more pressure in some places than you do in others. Just as foam sanding pads are available that conform to irregular surfaces for hand sanding, accessory pads, such as cork sanding blocks, are available that conform to gently curving surfaces for some finishing sanders. If you have a lot of detail work to do, such as when refinishing the mouldings in many rooms, you may want to purchase a profile sander, which has a variety of rubber sanding block attachments to conform to irregular surfaces.

The *electric palm sander* and its more aggressive cousin, the *random orbit sander*, are finishing sanders that make wood smooth faster – a lot faster – than sanding by hand. These power sanders are ideal for smoothing flat surfaces such as wide skirting boards and tabletops. A palm sander costs $20 or more but is well worth the investment: You not only save time and effort but also do a better job. Somehow, when you're hand-sanding, you usually decide a lot sooner that the surface is smooth enough.

Exercise extreme caution when sanding veneered furniture or cabinets, especially if you're power-sanding. Wood veneer is thin, sometimes very thin. You often don't have a clue that you're about to sand too far. Suddenly the material under the veneer, such as particleboard, appears. Staining doesn't help disguise the damage, and sometimes it makes the damage stand out like a sore thumb. Also keep in mind that sometimes what appears to be wood veneer is convincing plastic laminate – and can't be sanded unless you plan to paint it.

Book III

Painting and Wallpapering

Knowing when enough is enough

To make sure you sand with a light hand, try these tips:

- Make a series of light pencil marks across the surface and sand the area until the pencil marks are all gone.
- Sidelight the surface to make imperfections more evident.
- Cover your hand with a thin sock or a pair of tights and wipe it over the surface. The sock or tights will snag on rough spots.

The rule is to follow the grain of the wood as you sand. This means that you sand along the length of a board rather than across it so that you don't scratch the surface. However, if you must remove a lot of wood to get out deep scratches, start sanding on a diagonal to the grain until the imperfections are gone. Then sand with the grain until you remove all the diagonal sanding scratches.

Getting furniture-quality results

To achieve a super-smooth surface on a beautiful door, cabinet, or other piece of wood that's new or has been stripped of its finish, try the following furniture maker's method for final sanding:

1. **Wipe down the surface with water or methylated spirit to intentionally raise the grain; it will feel peach-fuzzy.**

2. **Sand the fuzzy surface until it's smooth.**

3. **Repeat Steps 1 and 2 one or two more times. With most woods, the grain no longer rises after repeated sanding.**

Another trick that furniture makers use is to apply a liberal coat of a clear sanding sealer, a liquid product available at DIY and paint shops that you brush or roll on before the final sanding.

Sanding to a super-smooth surface with open-grained woods, such as oak, is especially difficult. You need to fill the wood pores. Specialist woodworking shops sell grain fillers in a variety of wood tones for the purpose. Apply the filler by rubbing it on with a rag across the grain. As the filler starts to dry, rub off the excess, at first across the grain and then with the grain. Press hard at each stage to force the filler into the open-grained surface. Filling the grain isn't necessary if you're planning a wax finish because the wax itself will do the job nicely.

Use sanding sealers and filler only after you apply stain.

Chapter 3

Painting, Finishing, and Cleaning Up

*N*ow's the time to reap the rewards of all your preparation. Painting and finishing go fast, and with every brushstroke, your projects get closer and closer to completion, and hopefully look better and better. This chapter walks you through the process of actually applying paint: On the outside, from cladding to windows and doors; on the inside, from floor to ceiling and everything in between.

Preparing to Paint the Exterior of Your Home

You did your homework and chose just the right finish and colour for your house's exterior. You worked hard to repair and prepare the surfaces. But now you're having a hard time keeping up your enthusiasm. Your house, which didn't look all that bad to start, now looks terrible, scraped and sanded everywhere.

Cheer up! Now comes the relatively easy part – applying the paint. The work goes quickly, and seeing the house transformed before your eyes is very satisfying.

Safety precautions

✓ Use extreme caution around electrical power cables, especially if you're using an aluminium ladder. Don't forget to look for them when moving a ladder. Also, get help moving a heavy extension ladder so that you're in full control of it, and not the other way around.

✓ Expect bees, wasps, or bats to fly out of cracks in the fascia boards. Hopefully they won't of course, but always be prepared! Keep one hand on the ladder so that you're less likely to fall when you're startled. You can't run, so protect yourself with a long-sleeved shirt, long trousers, and a hat or painter's hood. Tap suspicious areas with a broom handle before you get too close, and use wasp spray that you can aim from a safe distance.

✓ Don't assume that you have good ventilation just because you're outdoors. There may be little or no air movement. If you're working with products that suggest application in a well-ventilated area, wear a respirator.

✓ Don't overdo it on a hot day. Drink plenty of water (or a sports drink) and take breaks to avoid heat exhaustion.

Using ladders safely outdoors

As tedious as it is to stop repeatedly to move the ladder, never overreach. When using a stepladder, the trunk of your body must remain entirely within the ladder's rails. If you use an extension ladder, a good practice is to crook the elbow of your free arm around the rail of the ladder (for example, your left arm around the left rail) and reach out with your free arm only as far as this grip allows.

Always open a stepladder fully and lock it in place before climbing on it. Don't lean an unopened stepladder against a wall to climb on it. Never lean a ladder against guttering.

Set up your extension ladder so that the bottom is the proper distance away from the house wall – approximately a quarter of the working length of the ladder. Ladder rungs are spaced 250 mm or 300 mm apart, so just count the number of rungs from the bottom to the point where the ladder rests against the house to determine its working length. Divide that number by four to determine how far from the wall you should position the bottom.

Always tie ladders at the top to stop them slipping sideways. If you are working on or near a window then you may be able to pass a rope around the central stile of the window and tie it to one of the rungs. Otherwise, pass the rope in through the window and tie it to a bed leg or other piece of heavy furniture.

Several ladder accessories make your work easier and safer. Although an accessory from one manufacturer may work for a ladder made by another, your best bet is to buy ladders and accessories from the same manufacturer. You may find the following accessories helpful:

- A **stand-off,** shown in Figure 3-1, gives the ladder more lateral stability and allows you to centre a ladder over a window so that you can paint the entire window without moving the ladder. In addition, if your house has roof overhangs, it stands the ladder off the wall so that you can safely paint the overhang without bending backward. We recommend the Laddermax stand-off, available from `www.laddersareus.co.uk`, which also doubles as a tray for holding paint tins and tools while you're working off a ladder.

- A **stabiliser** is a bracket or pair of legs that bolts to the bottom of the ladder to stop it slipping or sinking into soft ground.

If you use a ladder without any of these attachments, always make sure that the feet are level, and on a firm base. Try to set the feet on a concrete path or paved area, and stop them from slipping by resting a sack of sand or a couple of concrete blocks against them. If the feet of the ladder have to be on lawn or earth, place a board underneath them, and stabilise the feet by driving a stake into the ground and lashing the ladder to it.

Scooting safely up scaffolding

Scaffolding allows you access to a wider area. You can use two ladders to support a scaffold plank (see Figure 3-1). The equipment is available at tool hire shops. A wood or aluminium plank sits on a pair of ladder jacks, which hook onto the rungs of each ladder. Although this setup is relatively safe at low to moderate heights, we don't recommend it for first-storey work (above two metres). Without guardrails or fall-arrest protection, such as a safety harness, you could fall. These protections just aren't feasible for do-it-yourselfers.

For work above two metres height, we recommend you hire or buy a scaffold tower. This is an arrangement of alloy sections and platforms that slot together to provide a safe working platform at whatever height you build it to, up to about eight metres. Because it's composed of sections, you can easily put up a scaffold tower and take it down, carry it around in the back of an estate car (or on a roof rack), and store it in a garage or shed. Any serious DIY homeowner should think about buying one – or for occasional big outside building jobs, you can hire a scaffold tower cheaply for a week or weekend from a tool hire shop.

Book III

Painting and Wall-papering

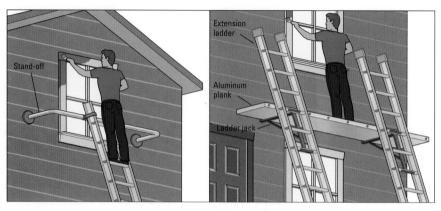

Figure 3-1:
A ladder jack scaffold enables to paint a large area.

Consulting the weather forecast

Coordinating an exterior paint job with the weather and your schedule can be quite difficult. First, you must wait for warm weather to allow a house to dry out after winter and early spring. Most paints and other finishes require that the temperature be at least 50 degrees and preferably above 60 degrees Fahrenheit (10C to 15C). Next, you need at least a couple of days of sunny weather to dry the house after rain or pressure-washing. You need another good day if you're priming. Finally, you need a nice day to apply the topcoat; an ideal day sees temperatures between 60 and 85 degrees Fahrenheit (15C to 30C) with no wind.

Differences between water-based and oil-based finishes may affect your decision of when to paint. Although you can apply most oil-based finishes even if you expect rain within a few hours, don't try it with water-based finishes. On the contrary, you can apply water-based on a slightly damp surface, but you're asking for paint blisters if you try it with an oil-based.

Whatever type of paint you use, allow the specified drying time between coats – or more if the weather is cool or humid. If you apply the topcoat over a primer too soon, paint failures such as surface crazing and blistering occur.

The best time to paint a surface is after the sun has warmed it but when it's no longer in direct sunlight. If you paint a hot surface, the paint dries too quickly. Then, as you go back to adjacent areas, you end up brushing over paint that has begun to dry. The result is distinct brush marks. Painting in the direct sun also may cause a variety of more serious failures, including cracking, flaking, blistering, and wrinkling – and that's just on the back of your neck.

Avoid painting or applying any surface coating outdoors on a breezy day. Windborne pollen, dirt, insects, and other debris lodge in the wet paint. The wind may also dry water-based paint too fast, causing the finish to crack or flake.

Planning your painting sequence

In most cases, you should paint the body of the house first and then paint the trim, windows, and doors. (As you paint the trim, you automatically cover any areas on the trim that were inadvertently painted with cladding paint.) Use a large brush, roller, or sprayer on the body of the house. For the trim, use a smaller brush, such as an angled sash brush, which helps you paint with more precision. Paint from the top down to minimise touch-ups for those inevitable drips.

Time is money to the pros, so they plan their ladder moves carefully. Professionals plan their work by painting everything within reach at one time: Cladding, trim, gutters, and all, even if they're using different colours or types of paint. The harder the setup, the more advisable this approach may be. This technique is the obvious one if you're using scaffolds or trying to manoeuvre around shrubs and have to level the ground to set up a 10-metre extension ladder. But at lower heights with less setup, follow the cladding-first rule.

Making last-minute preparations

After you get the brush out, you don't want to stop to remove outdoor light fittings or take time to tie back a bush that's in the way. Before you start to paint, make sure that your path is clear and that you've removed everything in the way. See Chapter 2 in this section for more preparation steps.

Book III

Painting and Wall-papering

Always place dust sheets below the area you're painting. This step takes only a moment and saves a great deal of clean-up time later. Use linen dust sheets or buy heavy paper dust sheets to cover under the area where you're working. Plastic dust sheets are slippery to walk on, especially when they're wet, so only use them under your painting tools.

Mix paint well before you use it. Mixing is difficult in a full container, even if you use a paint-mixing drill accessory. There may also be slight differences in colour between the paint in one tin and another, which won't be noticeable until it's too late. To overcome this problem, use a mixing process called *boxing*. Mix at least 10 litres together in a large container; then, when you've used about half, add a new 5 litres, and so on.

Before you carry that large tin of paint up a ladder, think about the mess it will make if it falls. You're better off pouring about a litre of paint – or just enough to cover the area within reach of the ladder – into a smaller tin or paint kettle.

Tooling up for the job

Refer to Chapter 1 in this section for descriptions of the different paint applicators and tips on buying and using them.

Which applicator you need often depends on what you're painting and the type of finish you're using. A paint pad, for example, is especially appropriate for painting cladding because the top edge of the pad paints the bottom edges of the cladding while the face of the pad paints the face of the cladding. A stain brush holds watery stain better than a paintbrush. If a roller cover is sized to suit the cladding, laying on the paint will go much faster. If you use a roller, go back with a brush to get the undersides and to remove the stippled texture left by the roller.

Have to hand sandpaper, a scraper, a wire brush, wood putty, a putty knife, and caulk so that you can clean and patch any defects you missed during preparation. Don't forget some rags to wipe off spatters.

Priming the surface

On most unpainted exterior surfaces, you need a primer coat followed by two topcoats of paint. (See Chapter 1 of this section for information about choosing these finishes.) We also recommend this procedure for any painted surface that requires significant scraping and repairs. However, if you're painting over existing paint that's still sound, a single coat of 'one-coat' acrylic water-based paint applied properly offers adequate protection and coverage.

You can apply quality water-based acrylic paint over any oil- or water-based-painted surface that's in good shape. If the paint is sound, you generally need to prime only scraped or repaired areas. You can also use a stain-blocking primer in lieu of regular primer to seal knots in board cladding or trim and to cover stains that you can't remove, such as rust.

Make sure that your primer is appropriate for the surface you're painting and that the primer and topcoat are compatible. How do you know? By telling your supplier what you're painting, reading the label, and (though not always necessary) using the same brand of primer and topcoat.

If you already have three or more coats of oil-based paint on the house, use oil-based house paint. Using water-based may cause the old paint to lift off the substrate.

Dealing with rust stains

You may have stains from rusty nails on the original paintwork. Use a bradawl or other pick to remove any caulk or glazing compound wherever rust stains are visible and hammer in any nails that are exposed. Then use a stiff-bristled brush to coat nailheads with stain-blocking, rust-inhibiting metal primer before covering them with caulk or exterior filler.

Painting the Exterior of Your Home

It's finally time to dive in and start to paint. Now comes the really satisfying bit.

Cladding

Although cladding is certainly the largest area to paint, the work goes surprisingly fast, even if you're using a brush. And if you use a sprayer, you move so fast that you have to be careful not to bump into yourself! This is your reward for doing such a good prep job.

Book III

Painting and Wallpapering

Painting wood cladding

Consider a few tips for painting wood cladding:

- **New or untreated wood cladding:** Coat new wood cladding as soon after installation as possible. Untreated wood requires a primer and two topcoats, if painting, or two coats of stain. Previously untreated or bare cedar may bleed tannin through a paint finish unless you seal the surface with an oil-based primer-sealer (preferably two coats) before applying a 100 per cent water-based topcoat. Knots should be treated with a special knotting compound.

- **Rough lumber:** Airless spraying works best for painting or staining rough surfaces, but brush the finish as you apply it. *Backbrushing*, as this technique is called, gets paint into areas that the roller or sprayer misses and works the finish into the surface. Brushing also results in a more uniformly stained surface and gives you the chance to brush out drips and runs. If the wood is already painted, use a roller followed by a brush.

- **New, smooth wood:** Some new cladding that's installed with the smooth side out doesn't accept stain well and sometimes is even too shiny for paint or solid-colour stain, which is like thin paint. Sand the wood with 100-grit paper and then stain or paint. If you plan to use a penetrating stain, you can let the cladding weather for six months to a year and save yourself the sanding work.

Choosing finishes for decking

Unfinished decking usually requires annual applications of a protective coating. A clear water repellent (also called a water sealer) prevents the problems associated with the constant wetting and drying of wood by helping it maintain a more even moisture content. Some water repellents contain mildewcides; none blocks damaging ultraviolet (UV) rays that cause wood to fade and crack. Semitransparent stains with UV protection limit the effects of UV radiation to a small degree. Some clear wood finishes also contain UV-blocking particles. Solid-colour stains and paints offer the greatest UV protection, but solid-colour stain wears on walking surfaces, and paint is likely to peel.

Decking needs abrasion-resistant stain; don't paint it. Even railings are easier to maintain if you stain rather than paint them. Renew stained decking every two to three years. You can apply clear water repellent or, even better, a water repellent with UV blockers over a semitransparent stain as a maintenance coating between stain applications.

You can treat the largest decking in a matter of minutes using a low-pressure garden sprayer or similar tool. For best results, follow up with a bristle-type pad on a long handle.

Painting PVC-U cladding

PVC-U cladding doesn't have a surface coating of paint. The colour is continuous through the material. Painting eliminates one of the primary advantages of this cladding material, namely that it's maintenance free. Nevertheless, if you can't stand the colour or it has become dull with age, painting is an option.

Use a light colour when painting PVC-U cladding. Dark colours cause excessive expansion and contraction because they soak up the heat, resulting in paint failure and buckled cladding. Use special PVC-U paint (sold in all good decorators' merchants) and follow the manufacturer's instructions.

Painting concrete, brick, or render

You can paint brick, render, concrete, or concrete block with exterior water-based paint after you clean the surface to remove accumulated grime. (See Chapter 2 in this section for information about cleaning these surfaces.) Use a finish with a satin sheen to make cleaning easier the next time.

Think twice before you tamper with unpainted brick, because removing paint from brick is nearly impossible. Instead, use a water-repellent sealer or stain, both of which offer some weather protection but don't peel.

You can paint stucco or render with an acrylic water-based product. You need to seal some masonry, especially highly alkaline surfaces such as stucco, with an alkali-resistant masonry primer. Moisture from the ground and from the house's interior rises to the exposed portion of the masonry and escapes harmlessly when the masonry is unpainted. If you paint the masonry, make sure that you use a water-based product that allows moisture vapour to pass through. Use a sprayer, long-nap roller, or rough-surface painting pad/brush to paint a masonry surface.

Windows and doors

Pay special attention to windows and doors. These elements attract the most attention and are the most vulnerable to paint failure because of all the joints where water can enter if the seal fails.

Windows

The outer surface of a window is painted with gloss paint to provide weather protection.

Here's the sequence to follow:

1. Begin painting the wood next to the glass, using an angled sash brush (also called a cutting-in brush).

2. Paint the stiles and rails of the sash.

3. Paint the window frame and architraves.

4. Open the lower sash to paint the exterior windowsill.

Book III

Painting and Wall-papering

TIP Don't paint the edges of the sliding sash. When these surfaces are painted, they tend to stick to the frame. This advice is especially important when you're painting a window with a sash that slides in PVC-U channels. Even a little paint on the edge of the sash can make it stick shut. Instead, seal these areas with a clear penetrating wood sealer to prevent moisture from entering the sash.

If you're painting a window sash while it's in the frame, use a brush that has very little paint on it to coat the outside edge of the sash. The dry-brush method prevents paint from running into the crack between the sash and the exterior stops, where it may cause the window to stick. Also, move the window sash frequently as it dries to prevent the window from sticking. If the window does stick, try using a craft knife or thin-bladed scraper to cut through the paint that glues the sash to the exterior stop.

To form a moisture shield between the glass and the sash, overlap the paint by about 1.5 mm onto the glass. If you have a steady hand and a quality angled sash brush, apply the paint freehand and wrap a clean cloth over the tip of a putty knife to clean off any mistakes. For the mere mortals, mask the glass before you paint, or use reasonable care and plan to use a razor scraper after the paint has dried. If you decide not to mask, you can use a trim guard to protect the glass, but don't push too tightly against the glass or you won't get the desired overlap.

If you leave masking tape in place and it gets wet or the sun bakes it on, it's nearly impossible to remove. Apply painter's tape when you're ready to paint, not before, and remove the tape before you move on to the next window.

Entry doors

Choose a semi-gloss or high-gloss oil-based paint for exterior doors, which get a lot of use and abuse. Water-based enamel also holds up well. If the door was previously painted with a high-gloss paint, use a deglosser to dull the finish and clean the surface. If a wood or metal door has never been painted, or if you expose bare wood or metal by sanding, apply the appropriate primer.

You're much less likely to have drips and runs if you take a few moments to remove the door and lay it flat on sawhorses. Use a shoebox to keep all the hinges and screws together.

Make sure that you paint the bottom and top of a wooden door. If you don't, moisture can enter the door and cause it to swell or warp. A convenient mini-pad paint applicator lets you paint the bottom edge without removing the door.

If the door has a flat surface, paint it with a 50 or 75 mm-wide brush, pad, or roller. A roller typically leaves a stippled finish that may not be acceptable on surfaces when viewed up close. If you use a roller for speed, plan to back-brush with a brush or pad. (See Chapter 1 for more on backbrushing.)

If the door is panelled, use a brush and paint the panels first. Then paint the horizontal cross pieces (the *rails*), and finally paint the vertical pieces (the *stiles*). Paint with the grain as you do when sanding. To avoid applying too much paint in a corner, brush out of the corner rather than towards it. As you paint, check often for drips and excess paint in inside corners and brush out the excess paint before moving on. Refer to Chapter 1 for information about paint applicators and techniques for using them.

Finishing things off

Before you store painting tools and equipment, make one final inspection, making sure that you didn't miss spots or overlook drips. Make sure you remove all masking or painter's tape. If it bakes on or gets wet and dries, it can be nearly impossible to get off.

Cleaning up the garden

Your outdoor clean-up is minimal if you're careful to use dust sheets during preparation and painting. Be careful not to contaminate the ground with paint chips, especially if they contain lead.

We've found it helpful to use a wet/dry vacuum cleaner to pick up paint chips that escaped our dust sheets. If you're careful and hold the nozzle just above the ground, you can pick up paint chips and sanding dust without sucking up too much soil or an occasional squirrel.

Removing drips and spills

While drips and spills are fresh, wipe them up with water (for water-based emulsion) or white spirit (for oil-based gloss paints). Use denatured alcohol (methylated spirit) to clean up alcohol-based coatings, such as some fast-drying primers. If the paint has dried but not fully cured, use methylated spirit on water-based emulsion or white spirit on oil-based gloss paints.

On glass and other relatively nonporous surfaces, you're often better off letting the spatter dry and scraping it off with a razor scraping tool. Use caution to avoid scratching the surface. A little paint spatter is much better than a ruined pane of glass.

For fresh spatters and spills on masonry and other porous surfaces, flood the surface with water or thinner and scrub, scrub, scrub. Repeat the process as needed, using clean thinner each time. If the paint has dried, try a paint-and-varnish remover.

Painting the Interior of Your Home

After you finish all the heavy and dirty prep work described in Chapter 2, you're ready for the fun part: The room transformation.

When painting a room, the usual top-down sequence works best: Ceiling, walls, woodwork (including windows and doors), and then the floor. Of course, it's common to paint only the walls and the ceiling and just give the trim a good wash, thanks to the durability and scrubability of gloss paint.

The argument for painting walls before trim is that you're likely to spatter wall paint onto the trim while rolling paint on the walls. But if you want to paint the trim first, go for it! If you get wall paint on the trim it's relatively easy to wipe off, and gloss trim paint covers flat wall paint much better than the other way around. You may also find that cutting in around already painted trim by using a brush or edging pad on the wide wall surface is easier than brushing the narrow edge of the trim – we do.

If you're planning to put two coats on the trim, you may want to paint the first coat before you paint the walls so that it's dry by the time you apply the second coat. If you have a lot of trim to paint, you may want to paint the windows straight after you roll the ceiling. Then break from that meticulous work for some big moves with a roller on the walls before going back to finish the doors and skirting boards.

Book III

Painting and Wall-papering

Ceilings and walls

Interior ceiling and wall painting is a project that's best divided into two: Cutting in and rolling. (Having two people do the work is nice – especially if you're not one of them!) One person uses a brush to cut in, or outline, all the areas that a paint roller can't cover without getting paint on an adjacent surface. The other member of the team spreads paint on the ceiling and walls with a roller. If the ceiling and walls are the same colour, you can cut in both at the same time. Otherwise, work on the ceiling first. (For a detailed description of these techniques, see Chapter 1 in Book III.)

If you're painting with a partner, have the person with the brush, who we'll call the outliner, start by spreading a 50 mm band of paint on the ceiling, all around its perimeter. Overlap marks result if the cut-in paint dries before you blend in the rolled area with the cut-in area, so don't let the outliner get too far ahead of the roller. You also want the roller to roll over as much of the cut-in band of paint as possible. The textures that a brush and a roller leave are quite different.

For a perfect paint job, follow the brush and roller techniques described in Chapter 1. To apply paint to broad, flat surfaces, such as walls and ceilings, use a 225 mm roller and either a shallow roller pan or the bucket-and-grid setup, also detailed in Chapter 1.

Before you use a new roller, wrap it in masking tape and then peel off the tape to get rid of any loose bits that might stick in the fresh paint.

Attach a pole extension or broomstick to your roller. This device enables you to do the work with less neck strain, with less bending, and without the need for ladders, staging, stilts, or platform shoes.

When rolling walls, keep these tips in mind:

- **Begin in a corner.** For ceilings, paint a big 'W' pattern about 1 metre wide. For walls, paint a roller-width coat of paint from top to bottom. Then smooth out your work by rolling lightly a 1 metre-square area on the ceiling or from ceiling to floor on walls. Continue to work your way across the ceiling or along the wall in this fashion.

- **Don't skimp on paint.** By applying a single ceiling-to-floor vertical stripe or 'W' pattern of paint per roller of paint and then smoothing only that area, you will assure adequate coverage.

- **Frequently step back and observe your work from several angles, checking for overlap marks and missed spots.** Adequate lighting is important here. As long as the paint is wet, you can go back over an area without creating noticeable overlap marks.

Decorative paint effects

Get your creative juices going by transforming walls with different paint effects. We start off by practising on a scrap of wallpaper or board, and then graduate on to a corner of the spare room that'll be hidden by the wardrobe. Don't try sponging or stencilling the lounge walls until you're absolutely confident of your ability, and are sure that you and your family will be happy with the effect!

Colourwashing

Colourwashing gives a soft, dappled, watery colour to a wall, and is popular with people who want an old-fashioned rustic appearance. Apply a basecoat of light-coloured distemper, and then brush a much thinner topcoat of colourwash (usually a darker colour) on top of it. You can buy distemper from some specialist decorating and artists' suppliers, or make it yourself in the traditional way from chalk ('whiting'), water, and rabbit-skin glue.

Dragging, stippling and sponging

Use these quick and easy effects to make a dramatic difference to your walls.

- **Dragging** is a technique using a stiff brush to produce an effect similar to the grain of wood. Apply an eggshell base coat, then cover it with a tinted translucent oil glaze (sometimes called *scumble*). Make vertical and horizontal brush marks in this glaze.

- **Stippling** uses similar materials and technique to dragging, but instead of using a stiff brush to leave brush marks, use a softer brush to dab the wet glaze surface, leaving a dappled effect (which is actually lots of tiny pinpricks of colour).

- **Sponging** uses ordinary water-based emulsion paint as a basecoat. Dab a topcoat of oil-based scumble onto it in a rough pattern using a sponge. After the topcoat is dry, you can sponge on a second colour, giving a marbled effect.

Book III

Painting and Wallpapering

Stencilling

Stencilling uses cut-out patterns in card or plastic to produce more uniform patterns on a wall. Start with a basecoat in either water-based emulsion (for walls) or oil-based gloss (for woodwork), and then apply a different-coloured paint on top, using the stencils to provide the pattern.

Woodwork

When painting wooden windows, doors, and interior trim, make sure that you keep your work area clean and free of draughts and airborne dirt to prevent dust and lint from settling on the wet paint. Getting professional results depends on good prep work, as described in Chapter 2. If the wood is bare, apply a primer. (For information on choosing a primer, refer to Chapter 1.)

If you're painting over already painted or varnished woodwork, prepare the surface as described in Chapter 2 and apply one or two coats of paint, always sanding between coats. If the finish has a glossy sheen you're not keen on, sand it or use a deglosser.

Working on windows

Paint the operational part of the window, the sash, first. Then paint the frame and the casing. (*Casing* is the top and sides of a window frame.) Paint the interior windowsill (called the *stool*) last. While you're working on the sash, paint any interior horizontal and vertical dividers (called *muntins*) before you paint the stiles and rails that make up the frame of the sash.

Don't paint previously unpainted surfaces. Instead, coat these surfaces with a clear, penetrating wood sealer to prevent moisture from entering the sash.

Taking an orderly approach to double-hung windows

Paint older double-hung sash windows in place. If someone's painted the upper sash shut or the pulley/counterweight system needs repair, correct the problem before you start painting. When you're ready to paint, follow these steps:

1. **Reverse the positions of the lower, inner sash and the upper sash, leaving both slightly open, as shown in Figure 3-2.**

2. **Using an angled 40 mm sash brush, paint the lower exposed portion of the outer sash.**

3. **After the paint dries, return the upper and lower sashes to their normal positions, but don't close them completely.**

4. **Paint the remaining portion of the outer sash and the entire inner sash.**

   Don't paint the outside-sloped portion of the window (the sill). This area is an exterior surface, and you must paint it with an exterior paint.

5. **Switch to a wider 60 mm angled sash brush to paint the casing.**

6. **Cut in the architrave where it meets the wall. Then do the stops, which form the inner edge of the channel for the inner sash, finishing with the face of the architrave.**

7. **Paint the window board (the internal sill).**

8. **After the sash has dried, paint the channels.**

   Slide the sash all the way up to paint the bottom half of the channels and, when the paint dries, slide the sash all the way down to paint the upper half. If unpainted metal weather-stripping lines the channels, don't paint the stripping.

Figure 3-2:
Reverse the sash on a double-hung window to paint the lower half of the outer sash first.

To save all the waiting, we often paint the lower half of the window channels before we start painting the walls and ceilings so that it can dry while we cut and roll. As soon as the channels are dry, we stop rolling and do the upper half of the channels.

As you're painting around the glass, lay the paint on in the middle of the area you're painting rather than starting in a corner. Then, with less paint on the brush, work from the corners out, dipping your brush into the paint you initially laid down as necessary.

As with painting the exterior window trim, use a brush with very little paint on it to coat the vertical, outside edges of the sash to prevent the window sticking.

Working on casements from the inside out

Follow the same procedure for a casement window, with one exception – paint the outer edges of the sash first so that they start drying ASAP. Don't close the window until it's completely dry.

Start by partially opening the window so that you can remove the operating mechanism from the sash. After you paint the outer edges of the sash, cut in the glass perimeter and then paint the face of the sash. Next, crank the window wide open to access and paint the frame. Finish by cutting in the casing and painting the frame and the face of the casing.

You need to overlap paint onto the glass slightly, especially on the lower third of each pane, to prevent water that condenses on cold glass from soaking into the wood behind the paint. This process causes the paint to peel and eventually leads to wood rot.

Book III

Painting and Wallpapering

Pausing for breath

If you want to take a break, wrap your brushes, rollers, or pads in cling film and stick them in the fridge until an hour or so before you're ready to paint again.

You can also leave a brush in solvent. If you do so, keep the bristles off the bottom by attaching a paint stick to the handle with a rubber band so that the stick extends below the bristles.

Doors

Doors take a lot of use and abuse, so for best results, choose a durable finish that has a semi-gloss or gloss sheen. Semi-gloss or gloss makes cleaning easier and holds up to frequent cleaning. You need to lay down at least two topcoats to get a uniform appearance. If the current finish on the door is a glossy paint, use a deglosser to dull the finish.

Leave doors hanging on their hinges while you paint them so that you can paint both sides at the same time. You can remove most modern lock sets in less than a minute (and replace them in under two), so removing them for painting is easier than masking. Make sure that you do one or the other.

You must seal all surfaces of new doors to prevent moisture from entering the door and causing it to warp. This step is critical for a solid-wood door or a solid-core veneered door. We even recommend sealing for hollow-core doors, which aren't as prone to warping. Slip a mirror under the door to see if the bottom edge has been painted. If it has not, either use a mini-painting pad that enables you to paint the bottom edge or remove the door from its hinges, apply a sealer to the bottom edge, and rehang the door to paint the rest of it.

Paint a raised-panel door, shown in Figure 3-3, with a brush, and paint with the natural grain of the wood.

Putting on the finishing touches

Before you pack away the paint and equipment, remove any masking tape and check carefully for spots that need a touch-up. Look for paint drips, too. Drips and runs take time to form, and despite your best efforts to keep checking just-painted surfaces, you may find some. You must wait until drips and runs dry completely before you scrape, sand, and retouch the area with paint.

Figure 3-3:
Paint the
top pair of
door panels
first, then
the wood
around
them.

First paint the top pair of panels and the wood (stiles, muntins, and rails) around them. Then move to the next lower pair of panels, and so on.

If you find paint on the glass in windows or doors (and you probably will), use a single-edge razor or a razor scraping tool to scrape it off. Before you scrape the paint off the glass, score the paint with the point of a utility knife and then scrape up to the scored line. Doing so prevents you from accidentally peeling paint off the wood. If you're trying to maintain a 1.5 mm overlap on the glass (see the 'Windows' section, earlier in this chapter), hold a wide filler knife against the wood as you score, as shown in Figure 3-4.

Book III

**Painting
and Wall-
papering**

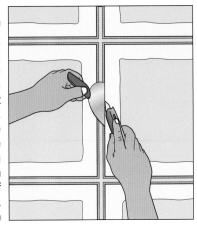

Figure 3-4:
Score a
paint line
before you
scrape paint
off glass.
The wide
filler knife
protects a
1.5 mm
border of
paint.

Be careful while scraping glass. Hold the razor at a low angle with its entire edge on the glass and work slowly to avoid scratching the glass.

Next, reinstall hardware, fixtures, and socket covers that you removed when preparing the room. Finally, move the furnishings back in, and please, don't chip that fresh paint!

Cleaning Up the Mess

Post-painting clean-up shouldn't be as big a chore as painting itself. You want your brushes and rollers to last you a while, so it's worth looking after them properly to extend their life.

Choosing tools to help you

Gathering some basic cleaning items will help make clean-up a breeze and extend the life of your painting tools. To make the task easier, arm yourself with the following items:

- **Solvents:** The proper solvent for cleaning up water-based paint is warm, soapy water. The best solvent for cleaning up oil-based paints, enamels, and oil-based varnishes and stains is white spirit, or paint thinner. Use methylated spirit to clean up shellac or other alcohol-based coatings, such as some fast-drying, stain-killing primers. If your brushes have a build-up of dried paint, use a special brush cleaner solvent or paint remover (or a dustbin!). Some paints require special solvents. Always check the label directions.

- **Brush comb or wire brush:** To get a brush really clean, open up the bristles with a brush comb or wire brush to allow the solvent to get into the heel of the brush, where paint tends to hide. Lay the brush on a flat surface and brush the bristles from the heel towards the tip. These tools are indispensable when trying to restore an old brush with dried paint in it.

- **5-in-1 tool:** The curved side of this multipurpose tool scrapes paint off roller covers before you clean them or dispose of them.

- **Heavy-duty rubber gloves:** An essential clean-up accessory. You need to use your hands to work the paint out of a brush, and you don't want to get any more paint or solvent on your hands than is absolutely necessary.

Using the three-container approach

Cleaning an applicator such as a brush or roller involves these steps:

1. **Scrape as much paint out of the applicator and into the original paint tin as possible.**

2. **Brush or roll out as much paint as you can onto newspaper.**

3. **Clean the applicator in the appropriate solvent (water or white spirit).**
   Clean water-based applicators under running water, but to conserve solvent or *thinner* – and limit environmental problems – use the three-container approach below for cleaning up applicators used with oil-based paint.

The idea behind using three containers is that you wash out as much paint as possible in each container before moving on to the next. At each step, the brush gets cleaner, and by the time you get to container number three, nearly all the paint is out of the applicator, so the solvent in the third container stays relatively clean and effective. Used thinner, after the paint has settled out, can be recycled. Use any suitable plastic cartons or glass jars, but mark them clearly and lock them away from mischievous kids.

Follow this simple step-by-step process:

1. **After you've scraped the excess paint into the original tin and wiped the applicator on some newspaper, wash the applicator in solvent in container 1. Take time to work the applicator with your fingers (don't forget your gloves) or by brushing the applicator back and forth on the bottom of the container.**

   This step gets the solvent deep into the applicator, such as the heel of a brush or the foam backing of a pad.

2. **Remove all excess liquid before moving on to the next container.**

   With brushes and rollers, the most effective approach is to use a brush spinner. With pads, draw the applicator firmly across a straightedge, such as a paint stick that's held over the container.

3. **Repeat Steps 1 and 2 using container 2 and then container 3.**

   Blot a pad on an absorbent towel.

4. **When the applicators are completely dry, store them properly.**

   See the section 'Cleaning and storing applicators', later in this chapter.

Book III

Painting and Wall-papering

5. **Recycle chemical solvents.**

   Pour all the solvent from container 2 into container 1. Then rinse out container 2 with solvent from container 3, and pour that into container 1. Wipe the two empty containers clean with rags or paper towels. Put a lid on container 1 and let it sit for a few days, or until all the paint has settled to the bottom of the container. Pour off the now-clean solvent into the original solvent container using a funnel. Scrape the settled paint onto a newspaper and allow it to dry before throwing it away.

Although warm, soapy water removes most water-based paint from brushes and rollers, some paint residue is often left behind. Rinse the tool with a brush cleaner and spin it dry before hanging it up for storage.

Cleaning and storing applicators

When the brushes are clean and dry, put them back in their original sleeve or wrap them in heavy paper secured with string. If possible, hang brushes for long-term storage or make sure that they're flat.

Use the full three-container approach for cleaning rollers and paint pads. Place these tools on their edges to dry on an absorbent towel and then store them in a plastic bag.

Cutting down on waste

Avoid waste by storing finishes properly and by recycling applicators, solvents, containers, and dust sheets. Save a little paint for touch-ups, but get rid of larger quantities. Return any unopened tins of non-custom-mixed finish. Pass unwanted paint or solvent on to others who can make good use of it or recycle it at waste disposal facilities.

Cleaning oil-based paint from your skin and hair

The only way to get dry oil-based paint off your skin and out of your hair is with solvents. Solvents are toxic and absorb quickly into the skin, so try to remove paint from your skin before it dries. At that point, the friendlier, natural citrus-based cleaners are effective; some are general cleaners, and others are made specifically for cleaning hands and skin. If you do use solvent, follow up with a mild grease-cutting washing-up liquid and rinse well. Use hand lotion to restore the moisture robbed by the cleaning process, or use disposable gloves.

Seal leftover paint in the smallest tin possible so that it takes up less room and the finish doesn't dry out. (Buy small, empty paint tins or use ones that you've recycled.) Label unmarked containers with relevant information, such as colour, sheen, room/location used, solvent, and any special instructions for use. For a better seal, lay cling film across the top of the tin before you put the lid on. Tip a paint tin upside down momentarily before storing it right side up or store it upside down for an airtight seal.

Protect paint and solvents from freezing or very high temperatures.

Disposing of paint and solvent safely

Oil-based paint and solvent and sludge from chemical removal of oil-based paints (especially lead-based finishes) are hazardous wastes. Never pour these materials onto the ground or into a sewer system. Local authorities typically regulate disposal of paints and solvents. Some authorities accept oil-based paint in the regular rubbish collection, but only after it has been allowed to dry; others have special collection sites or collection days. Contact your local authority to find out about disposal in your area.

Book III

Painting and Wall- papering

Chapter 4

Choosing Wallpaper and Preparing Walls

*W*allcovering adds rich texture and interest to the walls in your home that paint alone doesn't. You can choose from a virtually unlimited variety of patterns and styles in fabric, foil, natural grasses, papers, wet-look vinyls, and dozens of other materials. A room papered with your favourite pattern is a welcome sight that draws you inside; wallpaper is one of those little things that make a big difference.

You can buy wallpaper from DIY shops, online, or from catalogues filled with pages of . . . wallpaper. Look out for adverts in home improvement magazines to order wallpaper catalogues.

If you want to browse a selection of wallpaper without leaving your armchair, check out www.wallpaperdirect.co.uk. It has heaps of wallpapers to choose from and can send free samples direct to your door.

A first-time do-it-yourselfer can wallpaper a room perfectly. Trust us! However, the chosen wallcovering, the condition of the surface, the complexity of the room (whether the walls are straight!), and how many thumbs you have all determine the degree of difficulty.

In this chapter, we explore your options.

Choices, Choices: Looking at Different Wallpapers

In spite of its name, wallpaper isn't always made of paper. The material and coatings used to make and colour the wallcovering determine its appearance (natural, shiny, metallic, or wet, for example) and greatly affect how easy or difficult the covering is to hang. And the differences aren't restricted to the front of the wallpaper – you have to consider the other side too. You can either paste the wallpaper yourself, or buy prepasted wallpaper. We go through all your options so you can choose the right paper for the right room.

The front

The material and coatings also determine how durable, stain resistant, and easy to clean the wallcovering will be. A paper may be washable or scrubbable (or neither), which is usually determined by how much cleaning the paper or colour can handle. You can occasionally sponge a washable wallcovering with warm, soapy water. Scrubbable coverings are made of tougher stuff and can take more frequent washes – ideal for hallways, stairways, and toddlers' rooms, where smudges (and worse) are inevitable, in addition to kitchens, where spills and grease tend to build up on the walls.

Here's how your choices look:

- **Standard wallpaper** is generally easy to hang. Just be careful not to tug on the paper too hard as you position and reposition the sheets on the wall. Standard wallpaper tears quite easily, gets dirty easily, and is relatively difficult to clean because it lacks a protective coating. However, if money is an obstacle, you'll be thrilled to hear that wallpaper is generally cheap.

- **Vinyl-coated wallpaper** has a paper backing and a paper surface that's sealed with a liquid vinyl. This seal makes the wallcovering washable, meaning that you can safely sponge it off with soapy water.

- **Solid-sheet vinyl wallcoverings** consist of vinyl bound to a cloth or paper backing. These wallcoverings are the most rugged, stain resistant, and scrubbable and make an excellent choice for kitchens.

  Vinyls are the easiest type of wallcovering to hang, and they're durable, soil resistant, and easy to clean. They're even easy to remove.

- **Foils and Mylars** have a thin, shiny metal coating, and reflect a great deal of light. This feature makes them a good choice for small rooms with little or no natural light. The wall surface must be in nearly perfect condition, however, because the wallpaper's shiny surfaces accentuate any imperfections.

Even though hanging reflective wallpaper on walls with imperfections isn't a good idea, you can improve the results by first covering the walls with a heavy lining paper, which is designed to smooth small cracks and imperfections. Foil and Mylar papers are expensive, and lining paper installation can be a bit advanced for an inexperienced do-it-yourselfer, so we recommend that you call a pro for this job.

✓ **Grasscloth, hemp, and other cloths-on-paper** are richly textured, woven coverings with laminated paper backings. All are good choices to cover less-than-perfect walls, but they are expensive and relatively difficult to hang. If you are experienced and want to try one of these natural-looking coverings, discuss the installation requirements in detail with the wallpaper salesperson.

✓ **Textured wallpaper** is a good choice for covering walls that have minor surface imperfections. Flocked paper has raised, velvety patterns. Washable flocks are easier to install than nonwashable ones, but both are expensive, and installation generally requires a pro. Anaglypta and woodchip wallpaper, though not very trendy these days, are both excellent for hiding uneven walls. *Anaglypta* is a tough white or cream paper embossed with a raised pattern. *Woodchip* wallpaper is thick, durable paper embedded with small pieces of woodchip to provide a knobbly surface. You usually have to paint over these types of wallpaper.

The back

Your primary concern is rightly focused on the front side of the wallcovering. After all, that's the side that shows. However, what's on the back counts, too.

The two primary differences on the back sides of wallcoverings and what they may mean to you are

✓ **Prepasted or unpasted:** Perhaps the most obvious difference on the back of wallpaper is the presence or lack of paste. The vast majority of in-stock wallcoverings are unpasted. You usually activate prepasted wallpaper by dipping the paper in a water tray, as you find out how to do later on. Another type of wallpaper is 'paste-the-wall'. As you can guess, this requires you to paste the wall in sections, rather than the paper.

✓ **Dry-strippable or peelable:** This feature is of greater concern down the road when you, or the next occupant of your home, want to remove the paper. *Dry-strippable* paper peels off in its entirety. *Peelable* paper (usually vinyl) peels off but leaves behind its paper backing. This backing can be papered over (assuming that it's in good shape) or removed before painting. Keep in mind that strippable wallpaper or the paper backing of peelable wallpaper is easily removable only if the wall underneath was properly sealed before installation. See Chapter 1 in Book III for additional information about primers. See the 'Removing Wallpaper' section later in this chapter for all you need to know about ripping the stuff off the walls.

Book III

Painting and Wall-papering

Selecting a pattern that suits the room

Without a doubt, the most important factor in choosing wallpaper is choosing a pattern you like. You also must make sure that the pattern works in the particular room that you plan to paper.

Some basic aesthetic guidelines to consider when you're selecting a pattern are

- Vertical stripes or patterns make the ceiling appear higher.

- Horizontal stripes or patterns seem to widen a room and bring ceilings down.

- Large patterns generally don't look good in a small room because they tend to overpower the space and make it seem smaller. A large, open pattern looks best in a larger space.

- A mini-print or a paper with a small pattern or geometric design suits smaller dimensions.

- Dark colours make a room seem smaller.

- Wallpaper with a light background makes a room look larger.

- A pattern of ducks ice-skating makes any room look silly.

Matching repeating patterns

If you look at a roll of wallpaper, you see that patterns repeat themselves every so often along the length of the roll. This is called a *vertical repeat*. The pattern on one strip may align with another adjacent pattern horizontally or at an angle. How the designs on one strip are positioned in relation to the same designs on adjacent strips is called the *pattern match*.

Pattern matches come in five types: Random match, random texture, straight-across, half-drop, and multiple drops. (The term 'drop', in this sense, refers to how much the pattern drops to match the adjacent strip.)

The following list describes the five types of pattern matches shown in Figure 4-1.

- In a random match, such as a vertical stripe, you don't need to match patterns, but you do need to install each drop with the same edge always on the left.

- Random texture wallcoverings, such as grasscloth, don't have a pattern; therefore, matching is not necessary. However, the left and right sides of a roll often have shading differences that can cause problems. Installing the paper as it comes off the roll juxtaposes a light edge with a darker one, making the shading difference more obvious. To overcome this problem, manufacturers often recommend flipping every other drop.

✔ Straight-across patterns line up and match horizontally but may also be laid diagonally on a wall. The pattern always looks the same on every drop from the ceiling or other horizontal elements, such as a dado rail and the tops of windows.

✔ Half-drop patterns line up or match on a 45-degree diagonal line rather than a horizontal one. Each strip is positioned so that it's above or below the adjoining strips at a distance equal to one-half the vertical repeat. Every other drop looks the same at the ceiling.

✔ A multiple drop (called ⅓ multiple drop, ¼ multiple drop, ⅕ multiple drop, and so on) is similar to a half-drop; the difference is that the amount you offset on each strip varies. The higher the multiple (3, 4, 5, and so on), the less often a design repeats itself at the ceiling line. This type of pattern is great for out-of-level ceilings but can be very confusing.

Random match

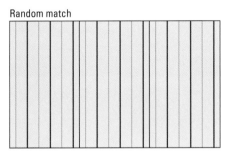

Random texture

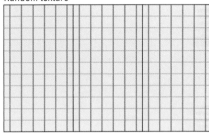

Book III

Painting and Wall-papering

Straight-across

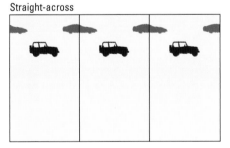

Conventional half-drop

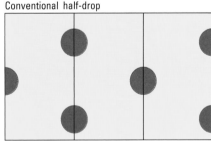

Multiple drop

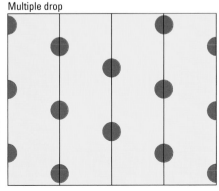

Figure 4-1:
Different types of wallpaper patterns.

Hanging wallpaper with a low vertical pattern repeat (a few centimetres versus half-a-metre or more) is easier and wastes less paper.

Buying Wallpaper

In many cases, calculating how many rolls of wallpaper you need is very straightforward. Just calculate the area you need to cover and divide that number by the area that each roll covers. So get out your tape measure and a pad of paper.

Sketching the layout

Make a simple sketch of each wall in the room, including any doors, windows, or other openings. Measure the dimensions (the width and height) of each wall and opening. Then calculate the area of each by multiplying width x height. Add up all the wall areas and then add up all the opening areas separately. For the total area to cover, subtract the total area of the openings from the total area of the walls and multiply that number by 115 per cent to allow for waste.

Estimating the number of rolls to buy

For random texture, random, or straight-across patterns in a typical room, you can easily work out the number of rolls you need. A standard roll is 10.05 m long and 0.53 m wide. Divide the area to be wallpapered by the coverage of the roll.

If your project is complex and involves lots of cutting, irregular openings, or an out-of-square room, or if your wallpaper has a tricky pattern or is otherwise a difficult type to hang, we strongly recommend that you let an experienced salesperson estimate your needs. The salesperson can evaluate the pattern repeat, the pattern match, the length and width of the wallpaper, the complexity of the job, the size of the rolls, and other factors to determine the amount of wallcovering you should buy.

When you buy wallpaper off the shelf, or when you receive paper that you preordered, make sure that the pattern numbers on all the rolls are the same and that the pattern is what you ordered. Also verify that the dye lot (or run) of all the rolls is the same. Each time the factory does a new run of the paper, changes can occur in the colouring, quality, or appearance of the coating.

Keep a permanent record of this information. If you have to order additional paper, be sure to request the same pattern number and dye lot.

Tooling Up for the Task

The tools you need for wallpapering may vary from our suggested list. For example, even if we suggest a Stanley knife (a breakaway razor), your utility knife with a sharp blade may work fine.

This list and Figure 4-2 show you the tools, supplies, and other items that a do-it-yourself paperhanger typically needs:

- Long spirit level (600 mm, 900 mm, or 1200 mm)
- Wallpaper paste, activators, or water tray (as required)
- Stanley knife
- Bucket, sponges, and clean rags
- Linen dust sheet (for areas you'll be walking on)
- Flat, hard work table (a half sheet of plywood on sawhorses is fine)
- Metal straightedge (such as a 150 mm taping knife or a paint shield)
- Pasting brush and bucket (for prepasted activator or unpasted paper)
- Pencil
- Plastic dust sheet (to cover everything that's not covered by your linen dust sheet)
- Plumb and chalk line (for marking a plumb line to start off your first piece of wallpaper vertically. You can use a long spirit level and pencil for this, but professionals swear by a plumb line. With a plumb and chalk line you let the line settle down, and then 'snap' the line so that it strikes the wall, leaving a vertical chalk mark.)
- Seam roller
- Sharp scissors
- Smoothing brush or plastic wallpaper smoother
- Filler, primer/sealer, sizing, and lining paper, all as needed for preparing the walls
- Stepladder
- Tape measure
- Bright anglepoise lamps and extension leads

Book III

Painting and Wall-papering

Plumb and chalk line

Break-away razor knife

Seam roller

Smoothing brush

Figure 4-2:
Helpful wall-papering tools.

Choosing Your Wallpaper Adhesive

If you choose to use unpasted wallpaper, it goes without saying that you need to apply wallpaper paste to get the paper to stick to the wall. Wallpaper paste is generally available premixed in standard and heavy-duty versions. Standard is fine for most wallpaper, but some types – heavy grasscloths, for example – require greater holding power. Tell your salesperson the type of paper and the surface you will apply it to, and he or she will tell you whether the wallpaper requires a heavy-duty adhesive.

If you're applying vinyl over vinyl or intend to put a border on top of vinyl paper (see Chapter 6 for more information about borders), you need a vinyl-to-vinyl adhesive, which bonds to just about any surface without priming.

Clearing and Cleaning the Room

To get the room ready for work, remove as much furniture as possible. Ideally, you want a completely empty room, but you can get by with a good 1 metre of work area in front of the walls. In addition, you need a work area where you can set up a table to roll out, measure, and cut wallpaper into strips.

A primer on primers

The key to good wallpaper adhesion is the proper condition of wall surfaces. If you start with a perfectly clean, painted or papered wall, you're likely to get good results with any pre-pasted wallpaper. However, you're *guaranteed* to get good results if you first apply an acrylic wallpaper primer/sealer to the wall. A primer/sealer not only promotes adhesion but also makes it easier to strip the paper off when you get tired of it or when the next owner prefers another wall finish. Primer/sealer makes it easier to position the wallpaper without stretching it, and that means fewer seams opening up when the paper dries.

If you're papering over a painted wall, use 80- to 100-grit sandpaper to sand oil-painted and glossy surfaces before sealing them, but be careful to not sand into the lining paper behind them.

If you're papering over new plasterboard, applying a coat of primer/sealer is a must. If you don't start with a primer/sealer, which soaks into and seals the paper surface of the plasterboard, you'll never be able to remove the wallpaper without doing serious damage to the plasterboard. If your walls have ink, lipstick, crayon, nicotine, or other stains on them, seal the stains or they will bleed through both the primer/sealer and the wallpaper itself. For this task, you need an acrylic pigmented stain-killing primer/sealer. However, stain-killers are not wallpapering primer/sealers, so you must follow up with a primer/sealer made for wallcoverings.

Acrylic all-surface wallcovering primer/sealer goes on white but dries clear. *Pigmented acrylic* all-surface wallcovering primer/sealer is more expensive than the clear stuff, but it helps cover dark or patterned surfaces and helps prevent the colour or pattern from showing through the paper. It's a good idea to tint a primer to the approximate colour and shade of the wallpaper background so that the wall colour doesn't show as much if the seams open slightly. Both primers perform equally well on porous and nonporous surfaces.

A coat of wallcovering primer/sealer takes two to four hours to dry, so paint it the day before papering or at least a few hours before you hang the paper. Be sure to read the instructions from the wallcovering and paste manufacturer.

Book III

Painting and Wall-papering

Turn off the power and remove the covers on electrical power points and light switches and cover the face of each fixture with masking tape. Also, remove any heating grates or wall-mounted light fittings. See 'Clearing the way' in Chapter 2 of Book III for more on preparing the room for decorating.

Removing Wallpaper

If you want to feel a sense of power, stand in a large room with the world's ugliest wallpaper and imagine that you can change the destiny of that room. (Dynamite is not an option.) In a perfect world, you could gently pull at a loose seam and the old paper would miraculously peel off the wall, leaving no residue or adhesive – just a nice, clean surface.

In the real world, that scenario is very unlikely. Removing wallpaper is messy and time-consuming, but very satisfying.

Knowing what you're up against

Before you can determine the best approach, you need to know the type of wallcovering and the type of wall surface that's under the wallpaper. In most cases, walls are either plasterboard (gypsum sandwiched between layers of paper), plaster smoothed over lath (either strips of wood or metal mesh), or plaster on masonry. You can usually tell what you have by the feel (plaster is harder, colder, and smoother than plasterboard) or by tapping on it (plasterboard sounds hollow, and plaster doesn't). When in doubt, remove a power point cover to see the exposed edges.

Remember that plasterboard is more vulnerable to water damage; you must avoid overwetting it. And use care when you're scraping because plasterboard gouges more easily than plaster.

What about the wallpaper? Be optimistic – assume that the paper is dry-strippable. Lift a corner of the paper from the wall with a filler knife. Grasp the paper with both hands and slowly attempt to peel it back at a very low angle. If all the paper peels off, you're home free.

If the wallpaper doesn't peel off, or if only the decorative surface layer peels off, you must saturate the wallpaper or the remaining backing with water and wallpaper remover solvent and then scrape it off.

Some papers, such as foils or those coated with a vinyl or acrylic finish, are not porous. If you're removing such wallpapers, you must scratch, perforate, or roughen the entire surface to permit the solution to penetrate below the nonporous surface to the adhesive layer (see 'Choosing a removal technique', later in this chapter). You can test for porosity by spraying a small area with hot water and wallpaper remover. If the paper is porous, you should see the paper absorb the water immediately. After the paper is wetted, you can scrape it off.

Now that you know what you're dealing with, you can choose an appropriate removal technique for the entire surface. Depending on your situation, choose one of three wallpaper-removal approaches: *dry-stripping*, *wallpaper remover*, or *steam*. Read the how-to for each approach later in this chapter in the section 'Choosing a removal technique'.

Preparing for the mess

All wallpaper-removal approaches are messy, so take the necessary precautions to protect your floors. For all removals except dry-stripping, we recommend that you lay down a 1-metre-wide waterproof barrier around the perimeter of the room, taped to the skirting board.

For extra precaution, tape down two layers of plastic on the floor. That way, you can roll up the top layer with all the paper goo, and the second layer will protect the floor while you sponge the adhesive residue off the wall. Also, keep plenty of old dry towels or rags around to mop up in case (or should we say when) your protective measures fail.

Water will probably end up dripping down the walls and under your feet. For that reason, you need to tape over switch and socket covers or shut off the circuit breakers at the consumer unit. Use an extension cord to bring power from another room for work lights and for the steamer, if you choose to use one.

Gathering tools and supplies for removing wallpaper

You need only a few basic tools and supplies for wallpaper removal. The following list describes the various tools that are available; see the following section for the specific tools you need based on the removal technique you plan to use.

Book III

Painting and Wallpapering

- **Razor scraper:** This push-type wallpaper-scraping tool (about 75 to 100 mm wide) looks like a putty knife but has a slot for replaceable blades so that you always have a sharp edge.

- **Wallpaper scoring tool (such as the Zinsser Paper Tiger):** This nifty gadget has small spiked wheels that perforate wallpaper, allowing water or steam to penetrate the surface and soak the paper right through.

- **Wallpaper remover:** Although warm water may do the trick (and is certainly the bargain option), you can turn to commercial wallpaper-removal solvents if you need to.

- **Spray bottle or paintbrush:** Use one or both of these tools to get the water/remover solution onto the wall.

- **Wallpaper steamer:** This is a cheap (£30 or less) and useful tool that will cut your wallpaper stripping time drastically, and lessen the chances of your damaging the wall by over-enthusiastic scraping. You can use it for removing paint and softening vinyl flooring adhesive, too.

- ✏ **Plastic and linen dust sheets:** You need both types to adequately protect your floors from the watery mess.

- ✏ **Wide masking tape:** Tape the plastic dust sheets to the skirting boards to avoid ruining your floors.

- ✏ **Water bucket, towels, rags, and wall sponges:** After removing the old wallpaper, wash down the walls well.

Choosing a removal technique

The technique you use for removing the old wallpaper depends on what kind of paper you're taking down and what kind of surface is underneath (refer to 'Knowing what you're up against', earlier in this chapter). The following sections outline the steps involved in the different approaches.

Dry-stripping

If a wallpaper is dry-strippable, you just need to loosen each strip at the corners with a scraper and slowly peel it back at a 10- to 15-degree angle, as shown in Figure 4-3.

Figure 4-3:
Starting from a corner, pull off wallpaper at a very low angle.

Don't pull the wallpaper straight out or you may damage the underlying surface, especially if it's dry-lined (unplastered) plasterboard.

After you remove all the paper, follow the adhesive-removal procedures that the next section describes. If only the top, decorative layer peels off, leaving a paper backing behind, it's a peelable paper. Dry-strip the entire top layer and then follow the steps in the next section to take off the backing and adhesive.

If you plan to repaper and the old backing is secure and in good condition, just hang the new wallcovering on top of it.

Soaking and scraping it off

To remove nonstrippable paper or any paper backing that remains after dry-stripping, turn first to steam or warm water and then wallpaper-removal solvent if steam or water is not strong enough. Soak the surface with water or wallpaper-remover solution using a spray bottle (normally used for misting your plants) or a wide brush or sponge. Then scrape the sodden paper off with a wide scraper.

Don't wet a larger area than you can scrape off within about 15 minutes. You shouldn't let water soak into dry-lined plasterboard walls for longer than that, or it may cause unnecessary damage.

If the wallpaper is nonporous, you must roughen or perforate the surface so that the remover solution can penetrate and dissolve the adhesive. To roughen the surface, use coarse sandpaper on either a pad sander or a hand-sanding block. You can also use a toothed perforating wheel or another perforating tool devised for use on wallpaper applied over plasterboard. Rounded edges on these tools help ensure that you don't cause damage that may require subsequent repair. Don't use the scraper after the wallpaper is wet, though; you may damage the plasterboard.

If you're successful in using the soak-and-scrape approach, skip to the 'Finishing off' section. If not, it's time to pull out the big gun: A wallpaper steamer.

Giving it a steam bath

You're talking major work if you must remove more than one layer of wallpaper or remove wallpaper that has been painted over. And if the wallpaper was not applied to a properly sealed surface, removing it without damaging the wall can be next to impossible. For these tough jobs, you may have to hire a wallpaper steamer (about £5 a day) or buy a do-it-yourself model (about £30). A wallpaper steamer is a hotplate attached to a hose extending from a hot water reservoir that heats the water and directs steam to the hotplate, as shown in Figure 4-4.

Book III

Painting and Wall-papering

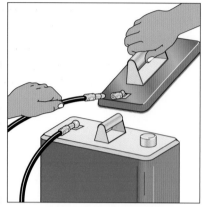 

Figure 4-4:
Using a wallpaper steamer to steam and scrape away old paper.

Although you can use a steamer and wallpaper scraper with relative confidence on plaster walls, use caution on plasterboard, which is much more vulnerable to water damage and is more easily gouged.

Keep a baking tray handy to put the hotplate in when you're not using it.

Starting at the top of the wall, hold the hotplate against the wall in one area until the wallpaper softens. Move the hotplate to an adjacent area as you scrape the softened wallpaper with a scraper. When you've scraped one area, the steamer usually has softened the next area, depending on the porosity of the paper.

The water that condenses from the steam can drip and burn you. To prevent hot water from dripping down your arm, stand on a stepladder when you're working above chest height. Wear rubber gloves and a long-sleeved shirt, too.

Finishing off

After you remove all the wallpaper and any backing, the walls are usually still quite a mess, with bits of backing and adhesive residue still clinging to them. Wash off any remaining adhesive residue with remover solution or with a nonphosphate cleaner in water, using a large sponge or sponge mop. You can use an abrasive pad or steel wool on plaster, but use caution on plasterboard. Avoid overwetting or abrading the paper facing. Use a scraper to get rid of any little bits and bumps.

Rinse your sponge often in a separate bucket of water, squeeze it out, and rewet it in the removal or cleaning solution. Continue washing this way until the walls are clean.

When the walls are completely dry, make any necessary repairs and do surface preparation work, as described in Chapter 2 of Book III.

If you're planning to paint the woodwork in the room to match the new wallpaper, or if your ceiling could stand a fresh coat of paint, paint before you hang. Getting wallpaper adhesive off a painted surface is no problem, but removing paint spatters from wallpaper is tough.

Book III

Painting and Wallpapering

Chapter 5

Hanging Wallpaper

*H*anging wallpaper is usually a relatively simple process. For more on choosing wallcoverings and factors that may complicate wallpapering, see Chapter 4. With a bit of planning and the help of this chapter, you should end up with beautifully papered walls.

Plan Before You Hang

Planning is essential for wallpapering. You'll get in a really sticky mess if you dive right in without first thinking carefully about things like where to hang your first – and last – sheet.

Locating seams

To avoid unpleasant surprises that result from poor seam placement or having patterns cut off in awkward places, plan before you start hanging wallpaper. Take a few minutes to evaluate the room to determine where you want each seam to fall and where the patterns will begin relative to the ceiling or the corners of a room. Ask yourself:

✔ **Which is the dominant wall?** That wall is the one most on display. Plan to lay seams where they'll be the least noticeable. Although seam planning should start on the dominant wall, don't start papering on that wall until you get into your stride.

✔ **How are windows, doors, or focal points (such as a fireplace) spaced on the wall?** Try to minimise the impact that any one special feature has on the wallpaper layout. For example, if the wall has two windows, a symmetrical approach works best. Simply start by centring a seam or strip on the wall between the two windows and work your way out to the corners.

✓ **Where do you want the kill point?** The *kill point* is the final seam. Because you'll be working around to the kill point from two directions, you need to cut one or both of the last two strips to fit the remaining unpapered space. This means that the pattern probably won't match at the final seam. A good inconspicuous place for the kill point is usually anywhere over an entry door, where the eye isn't usually drawn.

✓ **Are the ceilings and walls reasonably level and plumb?** Ceilings that aren't level and walls that aren't plumb present a problem when you're wallpapering. Because the patterns on the paper are truly horizontal and vertical, they make out-of-whack walls and ceilings even more noticeable.

✓ **Does the wallpaper pattern need special attention?** With a large pattern, cutting the paper vertically at a corner of a room may cause a noticeable break in the pattern. To overcome that problem, start working from the centre of the wall or from another spot.

In cases where precise placement of seams is important, you must know the expanded width of the paper. Most papers expand a per cent or two after the paste is wetted or applied, while some papers don't expand at all. Paste and book a foot-long, full-width cut-off for the specified time. (To find out how to do this, you have to read ahead in this chapter to 'Pasting the wallpaper'.) Then measure the width and use that figure, not the dry width, for laying out your seams.

Working around wonky ceilings and walls

If you have a ceiling that is badly out of level, avoid a straight-across pattern that will emphasise its wonkiness. Instead, consider a vertical pattern, such as stripes, or a drop-match pattern (one where every other strip starts with the same pattern). The larger the drop, the less evident any horizontal pattern elements are. Similarly, if you have out-of-plumb walls, avoid vertical patterns because a vertical pattern may start to lean.

Finding a starting point

If you plan seam placement, then start wallpapering wherever you want, with one exception – avoid starting with either of the two strips that lie on either side of the final seam (the kill point). You want these two drops to be the last ones you do because both drops may have to be cut simultaneously, which requires that they both be wet enough to peel back and reposition.

It's usually easier for a right-handed individual to work counterclockwise around a room and a left-handed person to work clockwise. Wherever you start, don't rely on a corner of the wall or the edge of a door and window trim to guide the first piece. Instead, use a plumb and chalk line (or a spirit level and pencil) to create a straight, vertical (plumb) guideline (see Figure 5-1). Position the plumb or level at the desired location. When you're ready, hang the first piece about 3 mm from the guideline.

If an out-of-level ceiling calls for it, you can establish an out-of-plumb vertical guideline by taking the following steps and checking out Figure 5-1:

1. Measure about 1200 mm down from the ceiling at each corner and snap a chalk line between the two points.

2. Use a framing square (or any object that you know has a square corner, such as a plywood scrap or set square) to draw a line perpendicular to the chalk line.

3. Extend the out-of-plumb line by using a pencil and a straightedge until the line runs from floor to ceiling.

Book III

Painting and Wall-papering

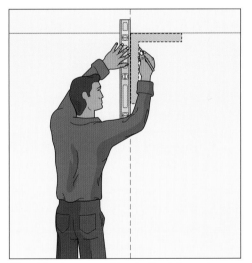

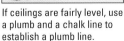

Figure 5-1: Making a guideline.

If ceilings are fairly level, use a plumb and a chalk line to establish a plumb line.

When following an out-of-level ceiling is better than hanging paper plumb, make a guideline that is perpendicular to the ceiling.

At Last You're Ready to Paper

With the planning complete and your first guideline established, it's time to hang the paper. First you need to reverse-roll every roll of wallpaper.

Reverse-rolling enables you to inspect every roll for imperfections and lessens the paper's tendency to curl or roll up during the pasting process. If you find flaws, you have two options: You can return the roll immediately (you can't return a cut roll), or you can keep it if you determine that you have enough paper to cut out the defect.

To reverse-roll, draw one end of the roll up onto and down the length of the table, pattern side up. Then reroll the paper so that the pattern faces in. After it's fully rolled, roll the entire roll back and forth under the pressure of your outstretched hands. Then unroll the entire roll in large concertina folds at the base of the table so that the top end of the pattern is on the top of the pile. Now, you're ready to cut.

Cutting strips of wallpaper

Cutting wallpaper involves two steps: First, you rough-cut the wallpaper before pasting and then you trim the wallpaper when it's in place for a precise fit. When you rough-cut, first draw the paper, design side up, onto your table. Then cut a strip to size with a pair of large scissors. Always pull the top of the strip up to the same end of the table for cutting and leave a 50 to 75 mm allowance at the top and bottom of each strip. Keep these other points in mind, too:

- ✓ **For papers without a vertical pattern repeat, such as woven coverings and those with vertical stripes, or for papers with a vertical repeat of less than 75 mm,** just measure the height of the wall and add about 125 mm (total) for top and bottom allowances. For example, cut 2.625 m strips for a 2.5 m wall.

  When installing every other strip upside down is called for (such as for grasscloths and other woven wallcoverings), clip the upper-right corner of every top as you cut it so that you know which way is up (or down) when you hang it.

- ✓ **For papers with a vertical pattern repeat of more than 75 mm,** place the paper on the floor at the base of the wall and, while holding the paper against the wall, carefully pull up enough paper to reach the ceiling. Move the paper up and down to adjust the position of the most dominant pattern, such as the largest flowers in a floral pattern. Then mark the paper at the intersection of the ceiling. Take it down for cutting. First, cut the top 50 to 75 mm above your mark. Then measure and cut the bottom so that the full strip is 125 to 150 mm longer than the height of the wall.

If the vertical pattern repeat is more than 75 mm, always use the pattern as your guide instead of just cutting a measured amount from the end of the roll. You'll be less likely to make errors or generate unnecessary waste.

✏ **For a straight-across pattern** (one in which the pattern placement is the same distance from the ceiling for every strip), cut all full-length strips so that they're identical to the first – that is, the same length and always starting at the same point on the pattern.

✏ **For paper with a half-drop pattern** (see Chapter 4 for a description), every other strip (strips 1, 3, 5, and so on) is cut at one point on the pattern. To determine where to cut the alternating strips (strips 2, 4, 6, and so on), roll out the paper side by side with the first strip and align the patterns correctly, making sure that the top of the uncut paper extends above the top of the odd strip. Then mark and cut the top and bottom of the even strip in line with the odd strip. Measure and cut all future even-numbered strips from this point above the dominant pattern.

When you're cutting alternating strips at different points on the pattern, as you do for drop patterns, keep the different strips that have been cut in separate piles, all orientated the same way.

Don't cut all the strips at once. If you cut the first one or two drops (strips) wrong, you've cut them all wrong. To avoid a scenario where you're wondering whether perhaps it would be cheaper to lower the ceiling than to buy new paper, we suggest a more cautious approach. Cut only the first two strips; use them to mark the next two as a pattern for future strips, but don't do any more cutting until you've hung the first two strips successfully. Even then, don't cut all the strips. Instead, do enough for one wall at a time.

Pasting the wallpaper

After you cut the first drop, it's time to activate the paste on a prepasted wallcovering or apply paste to an unpasted wallcovering. The procedures are generally quite straightforward, but be sure to follow the manufacturer's instructions for the particular wallcovering that you're hanging. For example, the instructions may tell you to gently fold over the paper (without creasing it) and let it relax for a time before you hang it – a process called *booking*.

During the time that wallpaper relaxes, it may expand as much as 25 mm or more. After the paper is hung and it dries on the wall, it tends to pull itself nice and tight on the wall, but the adhesive causes it to hold its expanded size. Booking the paper keeps the paper moist during this relaxing time.

The success of your project depends on the proper application of the right adhesive. For example, if you apply too much adhesive on grasscloth or fabric coverings, the paste seeps through the backing and onto the decorative surface. Too much adhesive can also cause excessive shrinking or slow drying, which can create mildew problems. Adhesive too thin and – you guessed it – the wallcovering won't stick or the edges will curl. The backing of the wallcovering and the type of wall surface determine the type of adhesive you should use, how thick it needs to be, and how much you should apply, but you need to consider other factors, too.

Applying the paste

Use a standard wallpaper paste for unpasted wallcoverings unless the manufacturer recommends a heavy-duty paste for the particular wallcovering you've chosen. You can buy premixed paste, or a packet of dried paste that you mix in with water. Then follow these steps:

1. **Lay one or more cut strips on your pasting table with the pattern side facing down.**

2. **Position the top of the first strip at one end of the table and apply the paste to at least the top half of the paper.**

   Use a short-nap paint roller or pasting brush to spread the adhesive as uniformly and smoothly as possible.

3. **Book the top half of the strip by folding the pasted surfaces together.**

4. **Slide the booked end down the table so that you can paste and book the rest of the strip.**

5. **Loosely fold or roll the booked strip if the manufacturer recommends resting time before hanging.**

If you are using a 'paste the wall' wallcovering, follow the manufacturer's instructions carefully, particularly with regard to wall surface preparation and using the correct paste.

Activating prepasted wallcoverings

The dry paste on the back of a prepasted wallcovering must be activated (liquefied) by soaking the wallcovering in water or by brushing on a prepaste activator, which is like a thinned wallpaper paste. If you're using a prepaste activator, follow the same procedure as described in the 'Applying the paste' section above.

If you're using the water-soak method, follow the manufacturer's guidelines:

 ⮞ **If the instructions say to go directly from water to wall,** place the water box in position at the base of the wall. Submerge the loosely rolled strip in the water bath for the specified time and then hang it as described in the 'Hanging the wallcovering' section, later in this chapter.

✏ **If the instructions say to book the wallcovering,** loosely fold the back of the strip together so that the pasted sides are over each other as follows:

1. Fold the bottom end to about one-half or two-thirds of the way up the paper.

2. Fold the top down just to meet that point. Be careful not to crease the paper at the folds.

3. With the pasted sides together, fold the strip in half or roll it up loosely and set it aside to relax for five to ten minutes, as suggested by the manufacturer.

The following tips help you lessen the chances of making an error when you hang the booked strip on the wall:

✏ Follow the same sequence and procedure every time you book and fold or roll a strip.

✏ When you book, fold, or roll a pasted strip, make sure that the end that will hang up to the ceiling is on the top of a fold or the outside of the roll.

✏ Lay a booked strip down to relax facing the same direction every time.

Hanging the wallcovering

Be brave! It's time to put the paper on the wall. To hang the drop, follow these steps:

1. **Grasp the top edge and peel open the fold that you made when booking the paper.**

   Leave the other half booked for the time being.

2. **With one hand on each edge a few centimetres down from the top, hold the drop in place on the wall.**

   Align the edge about 3 mm away from the vertical guideline and locate the top with the dominant pattern at the planned distance from the ceiling. This procedure automatically leaves a 50 to 75 mm allowance at the top and bottom.

   You don't want the edge right on the guideline because the chalk or pencil line may show through the seam. If the edge is not a uniform 3 mm from the guideline, peel the paper back as needed to reposition it; do the same to remove any large folds or air bubbles. Do not force badly misaligned paper into position by pushing it. Doing so stretches and

Book III

Painting and Wall-papering

may tear the paper and may also result in an open seam when the paper dries. If the paper needs only a slight adjustment, push carefully with two outstretched hands, or three if you have them.

3. **Smooth the upper half of the strip as shown in Figure 5-2.**

   Make your first strokes vertical ones, up and down, along the guideline. Then brush horizontally from the guideline towards the opposite side and finish with diagonal strokes.

4. **Grasp the bottom end and peel it apart until it hangs straight.**

   Smooth the strip as shown in Figure 5-2. (On subsequent strips, you'll work from the seam as you now work from the guideline.)

Continue with the remaining drops – paste-book-hang, paste-book-hang – one next to the other.

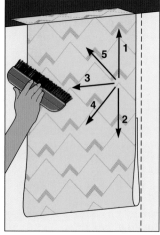 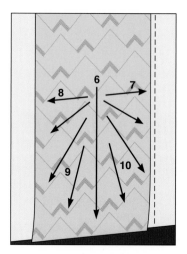

Figure 5-2: Use a wide brush to smooth the paper.

Trimming the paper

Trim the allowance at the ceiling and skirting board (see Figure 5-3) by using a Stanley knife guided by a metal straightedge, such as a taping knife or paint shield. Change blades often to ensure that you're using only the sharpest blade, or you may tear the paper. Alternatively, you can crease the paper at the ceiling-wall corner, peel it back to cut along the crease with sharp scissors, and then smooth it back onto the wall.

Before you move on to the next drop, remove any adhesive from the face of the wallcovering with a damp sponge. Wiping up wet paste is easier than getting it off after it dries. Also, wipe adhesive off the ceiling, skirting board, and other trim.

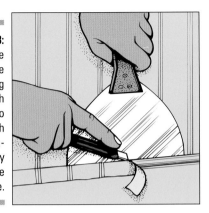

Figure 5-3:
Trim the allowance by using just enough pressure to cut through the wallpaper cleanly in a single stroke.

Smoothing seams

The seaming method you choose depends in part on the location – midwall or at the corners.

The two edges of a **midwall seam** should touch but not overlap. As you hang each drop, position it right next to the preceding one so that the edges just touch. If you don't get it quite right, peel the paper back as needed to reposition it. If the paper still needs a slight adjustment, push carefully with two outstretched hands. Do not force badly misaligned paper into position by pushing it. Overworking the paper stretches it, and when the paper returns to its normal expanded size, the seam will open. This is the numero uno cause of open seams. You may also tear the wallcovering.

Use a seam roller to seal the seam. Be firm but don't press so hard that you roll out all the adhesive. As you finish hanging each drop, always make a point to check the previous seam. If the edge has lifted, lightly reroll it. If it has pulled apart slightly, smooth the paper towards the seam or give it a little tap towards the seam with the smoothing brush.

At **inside corners** (and sometimes at badly out-of-plumb outside corners), use a wrap-and-overlap seam, in which one drop wraps the corner about 12 mm and the other drop overlaps the first drop and ends right in the corner. For details on how to make this seam, see the sections 'Papering inside corners' and 'Papering outside corners', later in this chapter.

Book III

Painting and Wallpapering

Papering around awkward obstacles

When you turn a corner or paper around an obstacle, such as a window, you need to make what's called a *relief cut* in the paper. Only one cut is required at right angles. When papering around rectangular obstructions, such as sockets or light switches (if you can't remove them), you need to make four cuts; one cut must originate from each corner, and the cuts should connect to form an X. You need to make many closely spaced relief cuts around a curve, such as an archway or the base of a round light fixture.

To make a relief cut, smooth the paper as close to the obstacle as possible. Then make the cut in place with a razor knife or crease the paper at the edge of the obstacle and peel it back to make the cut. See Figure 5-4.

The following situations call for relief cuts:

- **Inside and outside wall corners:** Smooth the wallcovering up to the corner. Make a relief cut out from the corner. Start the cut precisely at the ceiling-wall-corner intersection and extend it to the edge of the paper. Then you can wrap the corner.

- **Electrical switches and sockets:** Paper over the opening. Starting at each corner, make a diagonal cut so that all cuts connect to form an X. Then trim the flaps by making cuts from corner to corner around the perimeter.

  In the preparation stages for wallpapering (see Chapter 4), you should have shut the power off, removed cover plates, and taped over the face of the sockets or switches.

- **Window, door, and fireplace trim:** Cut the paper, leaving a 50 mm allowance at the trim. Smooth the paper up to the side of the trim and crease it into the corner formed by the trim and the wall. Make a diagonal relief cut starting precisely at the 90-degree corner of the trim and extending out to the edge of the paper. You can then smooth the paper over the trim. After you smooth the paper and roll the seam, trim the flaps with a razor knife and straightedge as described in the 'Trimming the paper' section, earlier in this chapter (see Figure 5-4).

- **Round or curved obstacles:** Smooth the paper up to the closest edge of the obstacle and make a relief cut up to that edge. Smooth a little more and make one relief cut on each side of the first cut. Continue smoothing and cutting.

- **Handrail or pipe:** Assuming that you can't simply remove an obstacle that you can't go around, such as a handrail or a pipe penetrating a wall, you must make a single cut from the obstacle to the nearest edge of the paper. Then you can proceed with the multiple relief cuts as described for round or curved obstacles. As you complete the circle, smooth and seam the long cut as you would any seam. (Refer to the section 'Smoothing seams', earlier in this chapter.)

  Sometimes, the pattern itself suggests where a cut can be least conspicuously located – along the stem of a flower or the edge of a line in a geometric pattern, for example.

✔ **Behind radiators:** Measure the positions of the radiator brackets and slit the wallpaper from the bottom as high as the top of the brackets. Use a *radiator roller* (a long-handled paint roller with a 100 mm sleeve) to push the pasted wallpaper flat to the wall surface behind the radiator, before trimming off at the top of the skirting board.

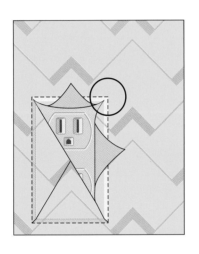
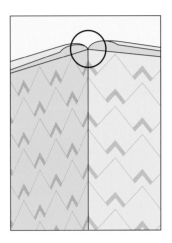

Book III

Painting and Wall-papering

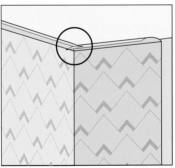
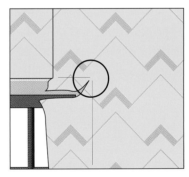

Figure 5-4: Relief cuts enable you to paper around obstacles.

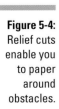

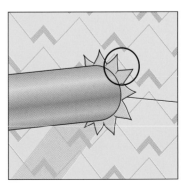

Papering inside corners

Never wrap wallpaper more than 12 mm around an inside corner. Even if the walls are perfectly plumb, the paper will pull away from the corner as it dries, making it vulnerable to tearing or wrinkling. Instead, make a wrap-and-overlap seam. Use the wrap-and-overlap seam for out-of-plumb outside corners, too, as shown in Figure 5-5 and in the following steps:

Figure 5-5:
Use a wrap-and-overlap seam at inside and out-of-plumb outside corners.

1. **As you reach the last strip before a corner, measure and cut the strip lengthwise so that it will wrap the corner about 12 mm.**

2. **Hang the strip but peel it back from the corner a few millimetres.**

3. **Measure the cut-off piece. Create a vertical guideline that's about 3 mm shorter than the narrowest width of the cut-off piece. Apply the straight edge of the next drop on the vertical line on the adjacent wall, allowing the cut edge to wrap the corner.**

4. **After you smooth the second drop into place, trim it at the corner with a Stanley knife guided by a metal straightedge.**

5. **Discard the trimmed paper and peel the paper back from the corner enough to enable you to reposition the first drop.**

6. **With the first drop wrapping the corner and smoothed into place, smooth the second drop over the first.**

   Smooth the paper with a side-arm seam roller, which has no frame on one side of the roller so that you can get into corners with it.

Papering outside corners

If the corner is perfectly plumb, you can just round it. If the corner is out of plumb, you can use the wrap-and-overlap technique as described in the preceding 'Papering inside corners' section, but with two differences. First, instead of wrapping the first drop about 12 mm (Step 1), wrap the corner at least 75 mm to ensure that it stays put. Second, instead of having the second drop end right at the corner (Step 4), measure, cut, and position it so that it stops about 6 mm shy of the corner. (See Figure 5-5.) Both cuts are located by measurement and made on the cutting table, not in place.

Applying the final strip

As you close in on the *kill point* – the location you planned for the final seam (see 'Locating seams' at the beginning of this chapter) – stop when you've done all but the drop on either side of the last seam. At that point, the unpapered gap on the wall measures a bit less than the width of two rolls. When applied, therefore, one drop will overlap the other, and you must double cut to make the final seam. Plan this cut at a location where the pattern mismatch will be the least noticeable. For example, if there's open background on both drops at any point where they overlap, make the cut there, as shown in Figure 5-6.

Planning this double cut is easier when the paper is dry. Place two strips on your worktable so that, together, the width is equal to the width of the unpapered wall area. Position the top layer so that you can locate the best place for a seam. Mark or measure the location and make the cut after you hang both strips.

Book III

Painting and Wall-papering

Figure 5-6:
Using the double-cut method to make the final seam.

A. Overlap the first drop and cut through both pieces using a knife guided by a metal straightedge or level.

B. Peel off the cut-away pieces of both drops.

C. Gently but firmly seal the seam with a seam roller.

Quick Fixes for Wallpaper

Two of the most typical repairs for wallpaper are fixing seams that lift off the wall and pull away, and patching torn or stained areas. These problems are surprisingly easy to repair – after you know how.

Sticking down seams

To reglue the edges of wallpaper that have pulled away from the wall, use wallcovering seam sealer. This sealer comes in a small, squeezable tube with an applicator at the tip, so it's easy to apply. The best part is that the sealer dries clear, leaving no telltale signs of the repair work.

Work through these simple steps to bond those loose edges of wallpaper:

1. **Gently peel back the loose wallpaper without stretching or tearing it.**
2. **Sponge to soften the old glue with a clean wet rag.**

   Wipe away as much of the old paste as you can reach on the back of the paper and the wall.
3. **Carefully put the nozzle of the opened tube of seam sealer behind the paper and squeeze the seam sealer onto the wall.**
4. **Gently smooth the edge of the wallpaper against the wall, removing any excess sealer with a damp rag or sponge.**

   Hold the paper carefully and firmly in place for several seconds.
5. **Seal the edges with a seam roller to apply light pressure.**

   If more sealer oozes out of the seam, wipe it with a damp rag or sponge.

Repairing a tear or stained area

Things may look bad, but you can easily patch a torn or stained area of wallpaper – easily, that is, if you have extra wallpaper to cut a patch the size of the damaged area. For a problem area larger than about 300 mm square, you're better off replacing the whole strip (which we talk about in Chapter 4).

For small patches or stains, begin by assessing the pattern and how it relates to the damaged area so that you can cut a patch piece that will blend in. Follow these steps, which are illustrated in Figure 5-7, to correct the damage:

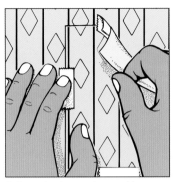

A. Cover the damaged area with a large scrap of wallpaper, lining up the patterns, and affix it with drafter's tape. (Steps 1 and 2)

B. Cut around the damage with a razor cutter, pressing through both sheets. (Step 3)

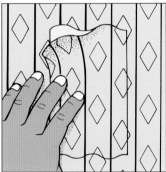

C. Remove the damaged piece, and replace it with the new cutout. (Steps 4 to 7)

Figure 5-7:
Patching damaged wallpaper.

Book III

Painting and Wall-papering

1. **To make a patch piece, unroll a piece of matching wallpaper on a flat surface and cut an area large enough to cover the damage.**

2. **Hold the patch piece over the damaged area and secure it with masking tape or drafting tape, which doesn't stick as tightly as other tapes.**

   Carefully align the pattern on the patch with the damaged area.

3. **Use a razor to cut through both the patch piece and the paper underneath.**

   It's important to cut through both layers in a single pass for a clean cut with sharp edges.

4. **Untape the patch piece, remove the damaged wallpaper, and clean the area so that it's free of old wallpaper paste.**

   Check out Chapter 4 for tips on doing so.

5. **Coat the back of the patch with wallcovering adhesive (or seam sealer for a small patch) and position it carefully.**

6. **Hold the patch in place until it feels secure and then use a damp sponge to smooth the paper and wipe away any excess adhesive.**

7. **Seal the edges of the patch with a seam roller.**

   Roll it gently so that you don't squeeze out the adhesive or seam sealer. When the patch dries, you won't be able to find it.

Border Incidents

You can use borders in all kinds of ways. Apply a border at the ceiling, as a dado rail, or as a detail around windows or doors. Most borders are pre-pasted and strippable and sold in rolls of 5 or 7 metres in length.

Here's how to determine how many spools you need:

1. Measure the length of the area you intend to border.

2. To determine the number of spools without a waste factor, divide that figure by the length of the spool you're buying.

3. Add about ½ metre for every spool to allow for matching and an additional ½ metre for every corner or mitre, such as when you border windows.

You can apply a border to any painted wall or on top of wallpaper that has been up for at least two days. Generally, borders look best on neutral backgrounds, but many patterned papers have borders with coordinating colours or patterns.

In a small room, a border at the ceiling level makes the space look larger. But don't assume that a border has to go at the ceiling-to-wall joint, which can be rough. For a different look, you can place a border 50 mm or so below the ceiling. Placed at chair-rail height (600 to 900 mm from the floor), a border tends to make a room look smaller because it divides the walls. If you have a really large room, though, that may be just the effect that you're looking for.

Making your borders straight as an arrow

Even some newly built homes have walls and ceilings that are not true (level, plumb, and square), but you can establish a horizontal guideline with a spirit level and measuring tape to act as a guide for hanging a wallpaper border.

To establish a level line below the ceiling, use a measuring tape and a spirit level to establish guidelines on the walls around the room as follows:

1. **Use masking tape as an experiment to help decide where you want to position the border.**

   Affix the tape lightly at different heights to see the different effects the border will have on the room.

2. **After you decide where you want the border, mark the location on one wall at a corner.**

   Measure down from the ceiling or up from the floor – whichever is shorter.

3. **Hold the level flat against the wall at the point you marked and adjust the level until the bubble is centred.**

4. **Draw a light pencil line on the wall at that mark.**

5. **Work your way around the room, using the level in the same manner to create a line on all the walls.**

Hanging borders

Before you hang the border, make sure that the walls are clean and remove electrical outlet covers if you're installing the border around them. Plan the job to begin and end in the least conspicuous point of the room so the joint of the two end pieces is less noticeable, which in many rooms is a corner behind a door.

To hang a border, follow these steps:

1. **To hang a border that's not prepasted on painted walls, use either premixed wallpaper adhesive or mix up packet paste with water.**

   For hanging a prepasted or non-prepasted border on top of a wallcovering, use a vinyl-to-vinyl adhesive for better adhesion. Apply the paste with a wallpaper brush, paint roller, or clean paintbrush to the back of the border. Coat the paste evenly, especially on the edges.

Book III

Painting and Wallpapering

2. **Fold the wet pasted sides together accordion-style to keep the adhesive moist.**

3. **Carefully align the top or bottom edge of the border just on top of the guideline to conceal it, unfolding the folded strip as you work along the wall.**

4. **Gently but firmly, smooth the border onto the wall with a smoothing brush or a large, damp sponge.**

5. **As you continue to hang the rolls of the border, butt the joints together so that they're smooth and evenly aligned.**

   If the pattern doesn't match exactly, overlap the new roll over the previous one until the pattern aligns. Then cut through both layers with a sharp Stanley knife, guided by a ruler or other metal straightedge. This process, called double cutting, ensures a perfect match every time. (Refer to Figure 5-6.) Then peel back the border to remove the cut-offs and press the ends back into place.

6. **When you get back to the point where you started, overlap the end of the border onto the beginning for cutting.**

   Peel it back and overlap it again as needed to find the least conspicuous spot to double cut the border. Usually (but not always), you want to cut at a point where there is little to no pattern.

7. **Lightly roll any seams with a seam roller.**

Using corner mitre cuts on borders

Use a mitre cut – cutting two pieces at a 45-degree angle so that, when joined, they meet at a right angle – where a horizontal border joins a vertical one. A mitre cut is a double cut because you cut two overlapping pieces at once. In an outside-corner mitre cut, a border outlines a door or window; in an inside-corner mitre cut, a border turns and runs up the side of a door or window. Follow these steps, as shown in Figure 5-8:

1. **Cut the horizontal border to extend at least 50 mm or so beyond the corner of the window or door casing.**

   Don't press down firmly, because you will trim and peel back the border.

A. Apply a horizontal border and lay a vertical border over it. (Steps 1 and 2)

B. Align a straight edge diagonally across the intersection. (Step 3)

C. Cut through both layers with a razor knife. (Step 4)

Figure 5-8: Use a double-cut mitre cut for a border that outlines a window.

D. Remove the cut-away pieces and apply the vertical border. (Steps 5 and 6)

E. Seal the edges with a seam roller. (Step 7)

2. **Cut the vertical border and hold it so that it overlaps and covers the horizontal border, forming a small cross.**

   Cut both strips too long, so that you can match up the pattern by moving the vertical strip up and down or the horizontal strip back and forth. Although you can certainly get a perfect match on one side of a door, you just as certainly won't get a perfect match on the other side. As you move the one horizontal and two vertical pieces, you strike a compromise that looks best at both corners. Although borders are often placed up against the architrave, no rule says that you must position them this way. You can also space the borders an equal distance from all sides of the architrave.

3. **Use a filler knife or ruler to lay a straightedge on a diagonal line from the corner at the trim to the opposite corner.**

4. **With the straightedge to guide you, carefully cut through both layers of the border with a Stanley knife.**

5. Remove the bottom horizontal cutaway piece by lifting the vertical border and then carefully removing it.

6. Reapply the vertical border so that it forms a perfect mitred joint with the horizontal border.

7. Carefully press the two joining edges together and seal them with a seam roller.

   The seam roller presses the edges tight against the wall.

8. Let the joint dry and then use a damp sponge to lightly remove any adhesive that may have oozed out from the seam.

Book IV

Carpentry, Woodworking, and Flooring

"Well — That's a good start!"

In this book . . .

Over the years, the ability to handle small carpentry jobs can save you a great deal of money. More importantly, you can make small repairs before they turn into big ones.

This book explains the basics of how to work with wood – drilling, fastening, finishing, and so on – and how to read diagrams if you'd like to create something yourself, such as a bookcase or a table. This book also contains a chapter on repairing and installing floors, which today's easy-to-work-with materials make doable for a typical do-it-yourselfer.

Here are the contents of Book V at a glance:

Chapter 1

Flooring: Keeping a Leg Up on Foot Traffic

The most used and abused interior surface of a home is the floor. No matter what type of flooring material your home has, it takes a beating every day.

This chapter shows you how to refurbish, repair, replace, and install new flooring. We also discuss where to use and where not to use specific flooring types. From hardwood to carpet and from sheet flooring to ceramic and vinyl tiles, this chapter's got you – well, your floor – covered.

The Subfloor: A Solid Base

Whether you're installing flooring in a room for the first time or tearing out and replacing old flooring, a solid, smooth subfloor is critical for successful installation. So it all starts at the bottom: The subfloor.

The subfloor is the material – either wood or concrete, depending on where it's located in the house – that serves as the bottom layer of support for the flooring. Homes built from the 1970s on generally have plywood or chipboard subfloors. Older homes, say from the early 1960s and before, often have individual 25 x 150 mm boards as subflooring. Both types form a solid base, and both can be damaged and require repair. The following sections take a look at the problems you might run into when inspecting and prepping a subfloor.

Fixing low spots in the subfloor

A new floor should be smooth and level. But over time, houses shift and settle, and low spots in the subfloor sometimes develop. The best way to check for low spots is twofold:

- Do a quick visual inspection; you can usually see any significant low spots.
- Lay a long spirit level or straight edge in various places over the entire floor, get down on your hands and knees, and look for spots where the subfloor and level or straight edge don't touch.

To eliminate a minor low spot, fill the area with ready-mix self-levelling compound, which you can get from a DIY shop. This stuff is easy to use because it's premixed; you simply spread it on the floor and smooth it with a floor trowel. Feather the edges of the patch. After the patch dries, use a spirit level to make sure that you've levelled the low spot. If the level is still off, fill in with additional compound until you get it right.

Making repairs to subflooring

Water can damage a kitchen or bathroom floor beyond the repair of a levelling compound. Water can cause the subfloor to rot or, in the case of plywood sub-flooring, *delaminate*. Delamination occurs when the individual layers of plywood separate. Water can also damage board subflooring by warping it.

A damaged subfloor results in an uneven finished floor surface. If you find rot, delamination, or warping, you must replace the damaged areas.

To replace damaged single-board subflooring, remove the damaged section of the board. You may be able to get away with replacing a small length of the board, or you may have to replace the entire board. Replacing the entire board makes the repair easier because the joints at the end of the board will fall directly over the floor joists, and you can screw them (or nail them, although screwing them is easier) in place. If you're replacing only a section of the board, cut out the section so that the ends of the new board's length fall over the middle of the floor joist. If they don't, the ends will be hanging free, and you won't be able to secure the joints to anything below. This setup creates weak spots in the subfloor.

Replacing damaged plywood subflooring is fairly easy. Most of the damage we've seen has required replacing an entire piece of plywood, although you can cut out a smaller section and replace it. When replacing an entire sheet of subfloor, you need to remove the nails or screws that secure it to the joists. If the fasteners are screws, you're in luck: Simply remove them with a powered drill/driver. If the subfloor is nailed down, a little more work is involved, but it's doable for most people.

Use a claw hammer or nail puller to get under the head of the nail and loosen it slightly from the floor joist into which it's driven. You won't be able to pull the nail out completely by using the claw hammer. The nails used for securing subflooring, called *ring-shank* or *cement-coated* nails, are meant to be driven into wood but not to be removed easily. A ring-shank nail has a series of rings on the shaft or shank that hold the nail in the wood. To pull up these nails, you need a tool called – surprise! – a *nail puller*. Its design gives you enough leverage to pull out even ring-shank nails.

Installing board or plywood subflooring is the same. Set the material into position and secure it with 60 mm-long screws. We recommend using screws because doing so is easier and faster than using nails, and you can remove screws more quickly and easily, too.

Understanding underlay

All types of flooring require an underlay to be installed over the subfloor. The subfloor provides overall structural support and strength, and underlay creates a level surface and helps prevent squeaks and uneven wear on vinyl or sheet flooring, and even keeps the finish on wood floors from cracking.

For most wood floors and vinyl or sheet flooring, a 3 mm- or 6 mm-thick plywood underlay is adequate. Check your flooring's installation specs to see which thickness of underlay it requires. If you use the wrong underlay, you void the warranty on the flooring.

Underlay for ceramic tiles is completely different. Because of the weight of the tiles, grout, and adhesive, a stronger, thicker underlay is needed. For most installations, tile backerboard (most commonly cement board but also gypsum and other materials) is recommended. Cement boards are made of cement-based materials and are usually 12 mm thick. They come in 900 x 1200 mm sheets, not 1200 x 2400 mm sheets like plywood does, so one person can handle them. However, even the 900 x 1200 sheets are a handful, especially in tight quarters, such as a bathroom. Cement board is secured to the subfloor with cement board screws or ring-shank nails specifically made for use with cement board. Be sure to use the manufacturer's recommended fixings.

If you plan to use an existing underlay, make sure that it's in good shape – free of loose pieces, low spots, and damage. You inspect underlay the same way you inspect subflooring, and make repairs the same way, too. Look for low spots and repair or fill them. Secure any loose spots and get rid of those squeaks now!

Book IV

Carpentry, Woodworking, and Flooring

Check to see what the flooring manufacturer's installation instructions say about how to deal with joints between pieces of underlay. Most flooring companies recommend, and in some cases require, that you fill every joint with filling compound to eliminate gaps between pieces of underlay, especially if you're installing sheet flooring. Filling the gaps creates a single, smooth, flat surface for the flooring and reduces the likelihood of high or low spots.

Hardwood Flooring

Something about the beauty and warmth of a hardwood floor just can't be topped. Whether it's a natural or synthetic wood floor, the rich colour and grain of the wood really add class to a room.

Refurbishing: When hardwood only needs a touch-up

Regular dusting or vacuuming keeps most wood floors looking good for years. Occasionally, however, the flooring needs an extra boost to gets its original look back. We're not talking about stripping and refinishing a wood floor or even a light sanding and recoating with finish; we're talking about simply using the cleaning product recommended for your flooring.

Before you delve into stripping your hardwood floor (covered in the next section), try this technique:

1. **Rub a small area with 0000-grade steel wool dipped in methylated spirit.**

2. **Wipe it dry to remove any wax.**

3. **Damp-mop the area and apply a coat of paste wax.**

If this process brings the floor back to life, do the rest of the floor in the same manner. This three-step process may seem like a lot of work, and it does take time, but it's easier and neater than sanding and stripping and may make your floor look the way you want it to.

 Don't try this method with synthetic wood flooring. The finishes on these products aren't designed for rubbing with an abrasive, such as steel wool, or cleaning with common cleaning products such as soap, floor polish, or scouring powder. Damp-mop the synthetic wood floor with a bit of vinegar in water. Just be careful not to flood the floor. A wrung-out damp mop will do the trick.

Refinishing: Making your floor look new again

If you tried refurbishing and your floor still looks less than great, you probably need to refinish the floor. This process involves removing all the old finish (wax and stain). To do so, you need a walk-behind floor sander, which you can hire. Also hire a handheld power edge sander for sanding tight against walls and in corners and doorways. Both units have a vacuum and dust bag system to minimise the amount of sanding dust left behind.

A walk-behind sander has a large rotating drum that evenly removes the finish – if you use the correct series of sandpaper grades and operate the sander properly. Tool hire shops have the three grades of sandpaper you need for successful floor refinishing: coarse, medium, and fine. The large sheets are designed to fit tight against the drum. Some sanders have a slot into which you tuck the sandpaper; other models have a screw-down bar that secures the paper. After the paper's in place, you tighten the drum with a wrench (supplied with the sander). For safety, wear a dust mask and eye and ear protection.

Some rooms may have a small piece of concave or convex moulding along the base of the skirting boards. For best results (and the least damage), we recommend removing the moulding. Doing so gives you maximum access when sanding and refinishing where the floor meets the wall.

Sanding off the old stuff

The most important idea to remember when sanding hardwood floors is to sand with the grain of the wood, maintaining an even pace. Sanding across the grain leaves gouges that not only look horrible but also are almost impossible to remove. Use the sandpaper in successively finer grades: Start with coarse to remove the toughest of the nasty finish and work your way to fine.

 When operating the floor sander, lift the drum of the sander off of the floor and then turn on the power. If you start the sander with the drum resting on the floor, it's likely to damage the floor, and it could take off and shoot forward almost uncontrollably.

When you get to the end of the section you're sanding, or if you need to stop before that point, raise the drum and turn off the power. Make sure that the drum has stopped spinning before you set it down. Also, make sure that each sanding pass overlaps the adjacent pass. Doing so ensures that you don't miss any spots, plus it reduces the chance of gouging or leaving a ridge.

A floor sander can get only so close to the walls and into the corners. For these areas, we recommend an *edge sander*. These units use the same grades of sandpaper as floor units, but the sandpaper is disk shaped. Again, keep

Book IV

Carpentry, Woodworking, and Flooring

the unit off the floor and then start the sander. Gently lower the unit onto the floor and remove the finish. Sand with the grain and be sure to overlap the adjacent sanded area.

Corners can be especially tough to sand, and you may have to use a sanding block or paint scraper. A paint scraper works well for removing the finish in a corner. Follow that step by using a sanding block, again with the same succession of sandpaper grades. This way, you achieve a smooth, sanded surface from power-sanded to hand-sanded areas.

Filling nicks and gouges

Now is also the time to fill any nicks or gouges in the floor. Use wood putty and a broad knife to fill any spots. Let the wood putty dry according to package directions and then lightly sand the areas smooth by hand with medium or fine sandpaper.

Sucking it up

After you've completed all the sanding, you must remove all the dust from the floor, trim, and walls. Yes, dust will settle on the walls. A lot of dust. Wipe down the walls and trim once to get the dust onto the floor, and then use a damp rag on the trim to remove any residue. You don't want any dust falling onto the floor later, when the new finish is drying. Let the dust settle, and then vacuum.

A standard shop vacuum with a dust filter will do the trick. You can also hire a heavy-duty vacuum from where you rented the sanders. Use the vacuum's brush attachment to pick up all the dust and reduce the chance of blowing it around the room.

After you vacuum, wipe the entire floor surface with a *tack cloth*, a wax-impregnated piece of cheesecloth designed to pick up and hold dust residue.

Selecting a finish

The type of finish you choose depends on the look you want for your floor. Durability is also an issue. Your choices are

- **Polyurethane,** either oil or water based, comes in various degrees of lustre. Polyurethane, or poly, has a sort of plastic look, which some people don't like at all. Both poly finish types darken or even yellow the wood's appearance, although some newer water-based products don't darken as much and leave the floor as close to natural as possible. Poly finishes are excellent for high-traffic and high-moisture areas, such as a kitchen or bathroom, because they resist water staining and abrasion. On the downside, if the finish gets nicked or gouged, it's extremely difficult to spot-repair. You'll need to resurface the entire floor to get an even appearance.

- **Varnish** comes in a variety of lustres, from matt to glossy. Varnish is very durable but is slightly softer than polyurethane. The higher the gloss, the more durable the surface. Varnish often darkens with age, so keep this fact in mind. On the up side, you can make spot-repairs to varnish.

- Penetrating **sealer** offers the most natural-looking finish. It brings out the grain in wood; however, it may darken over time. This sealer is also available in various wood colours. Penetrating sealer offers good protection, especially when waxed. However, it's less durable than polyurethane or varnish. It's the easiest of the three to spot-repair, though, and you can usually buff out scratches. You should wax floors treated with penetrating sealer once a year.

Putting on a new face

Ideally, you want to seal the floor on the same day you finish sanding to prevent the open wood surface from absorbing moisture. For best results, apply the stain (if desired) and sealer with a sheepskin applicator. Be sure to apply the sealer evenly, and use enough to cover the surface. But be careful not to apply too much. Excess sealer doesn't soak into the wood – it pools on the surface. If you fail to remove it, the sealer leaves an ugly spot.

After the sealer has dried, follow these steps:

1. **Buff the floor with No. 2 (fine) steel wool.**

2. **Vacuum and wipe the floor again with a tack cloth.**

   Removing all the dust between finish coats is critical, or you'll have a rough and ugly floor.

3. **Apply the first of two coats of finish wax or other floor finish, such as polyurethane or varnish.**

   Follow the directions on the finish container for drying time between coats.

4. **Apply the final coat.**

   Wait at least 24 hours after the final coat dries before moving furniture back into the room.

Repairing damaged hardwood flooring

Your floor may be in generally fine shape, with a damaged spot or two. If you find damage or stains, it may be easier and more effective to make small repairs than to refinish the entire floor. This section explains how to repair small areas of damage to hardwood flooring.

Book IV

Carpentry, Woodworking, and Flooring

Replacing a strip or plank of flooring

If a strip or plank of flooring is damaged and is beyond being saved by sanding and filling, you have to replace it. Some floors use a tongue-and-groove design for connecting adjacent strips. This design makes replacing a single strip or plank challenging, but not impossible.

First, look for any nails in the damaged board and drive as far through the board as possible by using a hammer and *nail set*, a pointed tool that you place on the head of the nail and then strike with a hammer, driving the nail into the wood. Carpenters use nail sets to drive nails flush with trim without damaging the trim with a hammer. After you've cleared the nails, it's time to remove the damaged board and install a new one. Follow these steps:

1. **Use a carpenter's square to mark a perpendicular line across the section of the board to be removed.**

   If you're removing the entire strip, skip this step.

2. **Use a 12 mm- or 10 mm-diameter drill bit and power drill to drill holes along the line.**

3. **Use a wood chisel to split the damaged board into two pieces.**

   Doing so makes removal easier.

4. **Pry out the damaged board.**

   If you take a strip out of the middle you can pry the remaining pieces away from the adjacent boards before prying them up. Remove any additional boards the same way but cut them so the end joints are staggered.

5. **Square up the drilled ends with a very sharp wood chisel, and remove any exposed nails or drive them in out of the way with a nail set.**

   You want the ends of the good sections smooth and square for easier installation.

6. **Cut a replacement strip to the same length as the one you removed. As needed, cut off the bottom side of the groove on the board.**

   Removing the bottom groove enables you to install a board between two others by inserting its tongue side first and then lowering its groove side into place. If you don't remove the bottom groove, you won't be able to get the board past the tongue of the adjacent board.

7. **Test-fit the strip to make sure that it fits.**

   If it doesn't fit, recut the board.

8. **Remove the replacement strip and apply construction adhesive to the back of the strip. Install the strip and gently tap it into place.**

   Use a scrap piece of wood to protect the strip's surface while tapping it into place. Nail the board with 50 mm-long ring-shank flooring nails and drive the heads just below the surface with a nail set.

Matching the finish of the new strip to the existing flooring may be difficult, but give it a shot before you refinish the entire floor.

Dealing with stains

Most stains on hardwood floors are very dark, even black. You don't need to try to get rid of the entire stain in one attempt. Getting rid of the blemish may take several tries.

Follow these steps to remove a stain:

1. **Sand off the old finish.**

2. **Mix oxalic acid crystals (sold at DIY centres and paint and hardware shops) in water, following the package directions.**

   Wear eye protection and acid-resistant rubber gloves.

3. **Soak a clean white cloth in the acid mixture. Then press the cloth on the stained area and let it set for about an hour.**

4. **Lift the cloth and check to see whether the stain has been bleached away. If it hasn't, repeat the process.**

   This process may take several applications, but eventually the stain will be bleached away.

5. **After the stain is gone, rinse the area with household vinegar to neu-tralise the acid. Wipe away any excess moisture and allow the area to dry completely.**

6. **Apply a matching oil-based stain lightly to the bleached area.**

   Use several coats, if necessary, to match. Don't try to match the colour with only one application. You can always darken the area with additional coats, but you can't lighten it after it becomes too dark. If you think the stain is too dark, wipe the area immediately with a cloth dampened with white spirit. Doing so will remove some of the stain and lighten the area.

   After you've achieved the desired colour, allow the area to dry overnight.

7. **Apply the topcoat finish and blend into the adjacent areas.**

Getting rid of nicks and scratches

You can usually cover up these little eyesores with coloured wax filler sticks. Simply clean the nicked or scratched area thoroughly and rub the wax filler stick over the damaged spot. Let the wax dry for a few minutes and then wipe it with a clean cloth. Most of the time, getting coloured wax into a nicked or scratched area is all you need to do to make the damage disappear – at least to those who don't know that the area was damaged before. Use the same stuff to fill nail holes in a patched floor after the topcoat is applied.

If a nick or scratch is really a dig or gouge, use wood filler and stain and try to match the existing floor colour.

Replacing a Wooden Floor

This section walks you through a typical hardwood floor installation.

Choosing the right flooring type for your project

Wood flooring is just that – all wood, either solid wood or laminated, like plywood. Most wood floors today are made of oak, which is strong and has an obvious grain. Other types of wood, such as ash and maple, are becoming popular. Softer woods, such as pine, fir, and cherry, aren't as common because they don't stand up to much wear.

- **Wood flooring** comes in strips with a variety of widths. If the flooring is 75 mm or wider, it's called *plank* or *board* flooring. *Parquet* flooring, which is made up of 225 mm to 450 mm squares of pre-made 'tiles' or wood strips, is also quite popular.

- **Laminate or synthetic wood flooring** is a combination of layers of material laminated together. The top layer is made of cellulose paper impregnated with clear melamine resins for durability. The second layer is a paper layer called the *design layer*, which has a pattern printed on it to give the appearance of wood. This layer is strengthened with resins. The third layer, the *core*, is made of chipboard or fibreboard. The bottom layer is made of paper or *melamine* (a plastic-like sheet material).

In a high-traffic area, laminate is a good choice because of its durability. But if you want the colour, richness, and warmth of wood, a real wood floor is the right choice for you.

Installing a prefinished hardwood floor – the way the pros do it!

A popular type of wood flooring uses a tongue-and-groove system to connect adjacent boards. Many systems are nailed down too, and others use glue to secure strips together. The glue method is called a *floating floor* because the flooring literally lays or floats on a thin cushioned underfelt. You can find complete installation instructions for a floating floor at DIY and flooring shops. This section shows you the general steps for installing a nailed-down wood floor on a wood subfloor and underlay.

Begin the installation at the longest wall and follow these steps:

1. **Place 12 mm temporary spacers between the first board and the wall to allow for seasonal expansion of the flooring.**

2. **Nail the first board to the underlay at the wall.**

3. **Continue installing boards, applying wood glue to the grooved edge of each piece of flooring just before installing it onto the adjacent piece.**

4. **To mark the first course for cutting, turn it so that the tongue along the edge of the board is against the wall.**

   You'll turn the plank to match the others after you cut it to length.

5. **Mark the turned board and cut it to length.**

   If you're cutting with a circular saw, turn the decorative face of the board down to avoid splintering.

6. **Turn the cut board into the correct installation position and install it at the end of the row.**

7. **Secure the tongue side of this row to the underlayment.**

   Drive the nails at a 45-degree angle through the tongue. Be careful not to split the tongue.

8. **Begin the next row with the leftover piece of the cut board.**

   Make sure that the piece is at least 200 mm long. If it isn't, use another board, but make sure that the first joints of each row of boards are staggered for a good-looking appearance and to keep a minimum of 200 mm of plank length between the joints.

9. **Place a scrap piece of flooring against the tongue of the board to act as a buffer board and tap the boards together with a hammer before nailing.**

   The block keeps the hammer from damaging the tongue.

   TIP

   The easiest and fastest way to nail wood flooring is with a *power flooring nailer*, an angled nailer that drives the nail through the tongue at the correct angle and depth. Use one as soon as you are far enough away from the wall to fit it against the course being installed.

10. **Continue this process to complete the job.**

    You may need to cut the final row of boards lengthwise because not every room's width exactly accommodates the various widths of flooring. Remember to leave a 12 mm expansion gap on this side of the room, too. The best technique is to cut a long board with a table saw, but you can use a circular saw. If you do use a circular saw, use a saw guide to keep your cut line straight. A length of 25 x 100 board clamped to the flooring works well as a cutting guide.

11. **Install the skirting board.**

When you fit a board around a corner or an irregular shape, such as a doorway, measure the length and depth of the obstruction that will protrude into the board. Use a combination square for accurate measurements. Then remove the marked area with a hand-powered coping saw or jigsaw.

 Doorways can be a problem because the door's jamb and architrave extend to the underlay. The best-looking and easiest approach is to cut off the bottom of the jamb and trim by using a flush-cut saw or hand-saw. Place the saw on top of a scrap piece of flooring as you complete the cut – this ensures a straight cut and one that removes just the right amount.

Ceramic Tile

Ceramic tile is one tough flooring product. In fact, tile is the toughest of the bunch – it withstands stains, liquids, and high traffic. Ceramic tile is easy to take care of and comes in a variety of sizes, colours, and patterns. On the downside, drop a large pan and you could easily be faced with a cracked or broken tile that you need to replace.

Replacing a damaged tile

Replace a cracked tile as soon as possible – not only for the appearance, but also to maintain the floor's integrity. Even one cracked or missing tile weakens the strength of the grout between the tiles, which can lead to adjacent tiles and grout becoming loose.

Follow these steps:

1. **Wearing eye protection and heavy-duty work gloves, remove the damaged tile with a hammer and cold chisel.**

   Starting at the edge of the tile and grout, break the tile into smaller pieces rather than trying to take out the tile in one big chunk. After all, the tile's a goner anyway. Just be careful not to chip the surrounding tiles.

2. **Use the cold chisel to scrape the old adhesive off the floor.**

   Remove as much adhesive as possible so that the new tile adheres properly.

3. **Apply thinset mortar to the back of the new tile by using a wide-blade putty knife.**

   Spread the adhesive right out to the edges.

4. **Set the tile firmly in position and level it with the surrounding tiles, and then tap it into place with a hammer and wood block.**

   You may need to apply more mortar if the tile isn't level. Use a short block of scrap wood to protect the tile when tapping with the hammer.

5. **After the mortar has set (usually a couple of hours), use a rubber grout float to spread the grout and fill the gaps between the tiles.**

   Hold the float at a 30-degree angle to the tile and work the grout into the gaps from all directions, and strike off the excess with the float nearly perpendicular.

6. **Wipe off any excess grout with a damp grout sponge.**

   Use as little water as possible and a light circular motion. Try not to rub or disturb the grout lines at this point. Just remove the grout on the face of the tile.

7. **After the grout has set slightly (about 15–20 minutes), go back with the grout sponge and clean up the grout lines.**

   This time, wipe parallel to the grout lines. Rinse the sponge often and wring it out well for best results.

8. **Buff off any light grout haze left with cheesecloth or a soft cloth when the grout is set.**

Replacing cracked or missing grout

Cracked or missing grout looks bad, and it's a good way for otherwise solid tiles to become loose.

Whether the grout is cracked or missing, you need to remove enough grout so that the new grout has solid grout to bond to. Follow these steps:

1. **Use a grout saw to scrape out the old grout.**

   A grout saw is a short-bladed hand tool that does a great job, although you will work up a sweat! Work the saw back and forth to loosen and cut out the old grout. The grout may come out in pieces, or it could turn into powder. Either way is fine – just get it all out.

2. **After the old grout is completely out or is back to solid material, vacuum out the joints.**

3. **Spread new grout into the joints by using a rubber grout float, as described in Steps 5 to 7 in the preceding section.**

Book IV

Carpentry, Woodworking, and Flooring

TIP

Regrouting a tile floor with a different-coloured grout also gives an old floor a new look.

Installing a ceramic tile floor

This project may appear to be beyond the abilities of most homeowners, but most DIYers can handle it. Just don't rush it – have a little patience! The materials are relatively easy to work with, and you can rent the tools, even the big ones.

Install ceramic tiles over a subfloor that's no less than 30 mm thick. A thinner subfloor causes the floor to flex due to the weight of the tile. A flexing subfloor results in cracked tiles and grout – and a lot of headaches. Most tile manufacturers recommend installing a cement backerboard instead of any other type of underlay, such as plywood. The boards come in 900 x 1200 mm sheets and are available where tiles and grout are sold.

Getting down to business

Ever wonder how a professional tiler always seems to get those tiles at a perfect 90- or 45-degree angle to the wall? They cheat! Not really, but they do use a pair of perpendicular reference lines for establishing a layout instead of relying on measurements from walls, which are neither straight nor square to each other. To ensure the reference lines are square, they use a 3-4-5 triangle rule as follows:

1. **Establish your first reference line by measuring across opposite sides of the room. Mark the centre of each side and then snap a chalk line between the two marks.**

2. **Measure and mark the centre of that line. Then use a pencil, a framing square, and a straightedge held against its shorter leg to mark a second line perpendicular to the first line.**

   Before snapping a second line across the room, make sure that the angle you formed is truly 90 degrees.

3. **Measure out 300 mm from the intersection and mark the pencilled line. Then measure out 400 mm from the intersection and mark the spot on the chalk line. Measure the distance between the 300 mm and 400 mm marks.**

   The distance should be 500 mm – the 3-4-5 rule. If it isn't, make an adjustment and pencil a new line. Now snap a chalk line across the room that falls directly over the pencilled line.

After you have reference lines, use them to establish layout lines, which guide tile placement. Dry-set two rows of tiles to extend from the centre to adjacent walls. If the last tile in a row would be less than half a tile, plan to shift the first course to be centred on the reference line rather than next to it. Snap your layout line a half tile away from the reference line. Repeat the procedure for the other row.

Laying out your tiles at 45-degree angles instead of 90 isn't that difficult. You just need a couple more layout lines. Mark the two layout lines as you would for a 90-degree job and then follow these steps:

1. **Measure out the same distance (for example, 1 metre) on the perpendicular lines.**

2. **From these points, make marks 1 metre out at right angles to the original lines.**

3. **Snap a chalk line through these new marks and through the intersection of the two original layout lines.**

   The two lines are now your layout lines for a 45-degree pattern.

After you establish your guidelines or layout lines, it's time to install the tiles. Follow these steps and check out Figure 1-1:

Figure 1-1: Laying border tiles around a room requires careful measuring and cutting.

1. **Before you think about setting the tiles in place with mortar, make sure that the layout is even from side to side in both directions. To do so, dry-fit the tiles along the layout lines in both directions and make sure that the finished layout looks good to you.**

   One important measurement to note is the width of the tiles that meet the wall. Make sure that you never have less than half of a tile's width at the wall. If you do, adjust the layout until you get an adequate end tile size. After you establish this, snap a new layout line to follow.

2. **Pick up the loose tiles and set them aside.**

3. **Use a notched trowel to spread thinset mortar (used to secure floor tile) over a 1 metre-square section at the intersection of the layout lines.**

   Trowels come with different-sized notches, so check the tile manufacturer's recommendation for the correct size.

Work in small, square sections – say, 1 metre x 1 metre. If you work with a larger section, the mortar may harden before you put the tiles in place. Be careful not to cover the layout lines.

4. **Begin laying tiles at the centre point of the two layout lines, setting each tile into the mortar by tapping it gently with a rubber mallet.**

   Use plastic spacers at each tile corner to maintain even grout lines between the tiles. Spacers are available where tiles are sold.

5. **Continue laying tiles until you've covered the mortared area.**

6. **Continue the process by applying mortar to another section and then laying tiles.**

7. **Fit the last tile in the row at the wall.**

   This step usually requires that you measure and cut the tile. First, set a scrap tile against the wall – it allows space for grout. Next, place a loose tile directly over the last full tile you laid (this is the tile you'll cut to size). Then place another tile on the loose one and up against the tile on the wall. Mark the loose tile and cut it to fit along the edge. (We discuss cutting in just a bit.)

8. **After all the tiles are set in the mortar, mix the grout according to the manufacturer's instructions and install it by using the rubber grout float.**

   Use a sweeping motion, pressing the grout into the gaps.

9. **Wipe away the excess grout with a grout sponge. Let the grout dry slightly and then wipe off the haze that appears.**

Cutting tiles

For most ceramic floor installations, you need a tile cutter, which you can buy or hire. To make a straight cut with a tile cutter, simply place the tile face up in the cutter, adjust the cutter to the proper width, and score the tile by pulling the cutting wheel across the tile's face. Then snap the tile along the scored line. Chapter 9 in Book IV has more on cutting tiles.

If you need to make a cut-out, say to go around a corner, mark the area you plan to cut out. Secure the tile in a vice or clamps – cushion the vice jaws to protect the tile from scratches. Cut along the marks with a *tile saw*, which is a hand-saw that's similar to a coping saw, except that it has a carbide saw blade designed for cutting ceramic tile.

If you need to make a round or circular cut, mark the area and then use a tile nipper to nip out small pieces of tile until you reach the line. A tile nipper is similar to a pair of pliers, but it has hardened cutting edges for cutting through ceramic tile.

Sheet Vinyl Flooring

Sheet vinyl is a popular flooring choice for bathrooms, kitchens, and hallways. Sold in 2- and 4-metre widths, sheet vinyl's pretty durable, easy to maintain, and not too expensive.

Using a template to cut your piece

Most manufacturers sell an inexpensive template kit for laying and cutting vinyl flooring. Follow these steps to use the template:

1. **Cover the entire floor with overlapping paper template sheets, large or small. Tape every piece together with masking tape.**

   The resulting template is the shape of the area you plan to cover.

2. **Carefully lift up the template, place it on the unrolled vinyl flooring, and trace the outline onto the flooring with a felt-tip pen.**

3. **Remove the template and cut the flooring with a utility knife with a new blade.**

   Change the blade often for smooth, even cuts.

4. **Place the vinyl flooring in position and slide the edges under the door casings.**

   Be careful when positioning the vinyl – you don't want to nick or tear it.

   You may find it helpful to cut off the door casings at the bottom by using the method described in the wood flooring section, earlier in this chapter.

Cutting a seam

Try to install your sheet flooring in one large piece. However, many areas are wider than 4 metres, which is the width that sheet flooring comes in. If you need to make a seam, plan to place it along a pattern line and not in a high-traffic area of the room. Follow these steps to cut a seam:

1. **Overlap the sheets by about 50 mm.**

2. **Match the pattern and tape the sheets together with masking tape.**

3. **Hold a straightedge tightly and make several passes with a utility knife to cut through both layers of flooring.**

Gluing it down

You need to glue down the flooring in an efficient yet unhurried manner. The adhesive begins to set after a while, but you have plenty of time to do it right as long as you work in a logical order. Follow these steps:

Book IV

Carpentry, Woodworking, and Flooring

1. **Pull up half of the sheet and roll it loosely.**

2. **Use a V-notched trowel to spread the recommended adhesive around the edge of the room and wherever a seam will lie.**

3. **Let the adhesive set for about 10 to 15 minutes until it gets tacky.**

4. **Unroll the flooring over the adhesive.**

5. **Press the flooring against the underlay with a rolling pin.**

   You can also hire a floor roller. Work around the entire area, including the edges and seams.

6. **Use a seam roller on each seam to ensure a solid bond of adhesive under both pieces of flooring.**

   A seam roller is slightly smaller than a floor roller. Roll it slowly along each seam to ensure that each seam is completely flat.

Repairing a damaged spot

To repair a damaged spot of sheet vinyl flooring, you need to have a scrap piece of the flooring available.

Try to make a patch repair along a pattern line, which does the best job of hiding the cut lines. Here's what to do:

1. **Determine the size and shape of the cut-out you want to make.**

   For regular, straight patterns, size the patch so cuts are made along the 'grout lines'. For overall patterns, make a diamond-shape patch.

2. **Cut the patch material slightly larger, lay it over the damaged floor, align the pattern, and tape it in place with masking tape on all sides.**

3. **Make a guided double cut through the patch and the flooring and remove the damaged flooring.**

   If the floor is adhered in this location scrape all adhesive off the underlayment, being careful not to damage or lift the surrounding flooring.

4. **Brush adhesive on the back of the new piece and, if the surrounding flooring is not adhered, on the underlay about 25 mm under the flooring edges.**

5. **Position the patch in the same orientation it had when it was cut and roll it with a rolling pin. Clean off any adhesive on the surface.**

6. **Press the seams together and hold them in place with masking tape.**

7. **Wait half an hour before removing tape and applying the recommended seam sealer according to directions.**

Carpet

Ah, the pleasure of digging your toes into rich, plush carpet. Carpet is still the most widely used floor covering in most homes. The best carpets are made of wool or a mixture of wool and manmade fibres. Wool carpet is very expensive. However, blends of nylon, polypropylene, acrylic, rayon, and polyester help keep carpet prices reasonable. Plus, these blends are more durable and stain resistant.

Installing carpet isn't difficult, technically. The process is challenging, however, because of the size of the rolls and the often-limited workspace. Carpet typically comes in 4 metre widths, which makes a roll of carpet heavy and hard to handle, even for an average-sized room of 4 metres x 4 metres.

 If your carpet needs a seam, or you want your stairs carpeted, call a pro to install it. You'll be much happier in the long run. A competent installer plans for seams to occur in low-traffic and low-visibility areas. All seams are cut using the double-cut method described in the previous section and the pieces are joined with seaming tape. The installer places the tape under the seam and then lifts the carpet to melt the adhesive on the tape with a seaming iron. Then he presses the carpet down onto the tape and pinches the pieces together before the adhesive cools.

Laying carpet with underfelt

This type of installation requires no glue or adhesive to hold the carpet and underfelt (underlay) to the floor. You do, however, need to secure it to the floor at the perimeter to prevent the carpet from moving and forming lumps or bumps.

Install the wooden tack strip, which runs around the perimeter of the room. Nail the tack strip to the subfloor with its points angled towards the wall. The small points sticking up out of the wooden tack strip grab the carpet and hold it down once you stretch it over the tack strip. Space the tack strips away from the wall at a distance equal to the thickness of the carpet.

Next, place the carpet underfelt within the tack strip layout and then staple it to the subfloor. The underfelt is easy to trim with a utility knife. You can seal the joints that form where two pieces meet with duct tape.

Loosely lay out the carpet in approximately the correct position. The less moving this monster of a piece, the better. Getting the carpet over the spikes of the tack strip requires the use of a carpet stretcher and carpet kicker. These tools are easy for a professional to use but can be tricky for a novice to use correctly.

Book IV

Carpentry, Woodworking, and Flooring

Laying cushion-backed carpet

This type of carpet is easy to install. Simply lay the material out in the room, cut it to fit, and then glue it down. You can cut cushion-backed carpet easily with a utility knife. The adhesive is easy to spread with a trowel. This carpet is also somewhat forgiving because you have a little time to reposition the carpet if it moves while you're laying it.

Patching a hole in carpeting

Cigarette burns and tough stains can cause permanent damage to carpet. If the blemish is on the surface fibre only, use a nail clipper or small manicure scissors to clip away the damaged fibre a small bit at a time.

If the damage is deep or the carpet is torn, replace a section of the carpet as shown in Figure 1-2. Cut a replacement patch by using a straightedge and a utility knife to make a straight cut-out around a damaged area. Then install a replacement patch cut to the same size, using double-stick cloth carpet tape to hold the patch in place.

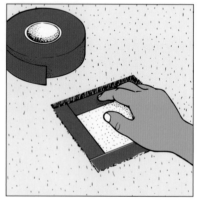

Figure 1-2: Replacing a patch of carpet.

A. Use a framing square to guide the utility knife as you cut an area around the damaged carpeting and a patch from a matching piece of scrap carpet.

B. Outline the bare spot with double-stick cloth tape to hold the replacement patch securely in place.

The tape, sold in widths of 40 mm and 50 mm, is available at DIY centres and hardware stores. Cut the tape to size to outline the perimeter of the patch area. Peel the protective paper from the face of the peel-and-stick tape and press the patch of carpeting into the repair area to ensure full contact between the carpet patch and the adhesive tape. Carefully separate the carpet fibres between the patch and the surrounding fibres. Give the adhesive time to set and then use a comb or brush to blend the carpet pile between the carpet and the patch.

Rather than cutting your own patch, take out the guesswork by using a *doughnut*. A doughnut is a circular cutting tool with a razor blade cutter fixed to the perimeter, and a centre rotating pin to anchor the cutter in place. The tool cuts shapes that are 75 mm in diameter and it costs about £10.

Silencing Squeaks

Whenever possible, fix annoying floor or stair squeaks from below. If, however, the bottom of the floor area or staircase is covered, you have to fix it from above.

Fixing a squeak from below

You have a few ways to eliminate squeaks from below. Which method you use depends on what the problem is. Take a look at each method (and see Figure 1-3):

- **Strutting:** Squeaking over a large area may indicate that the floor joists are shifting slightly and are not providing enough support to the subfloor. To solve or moderate this problem you can install strutting between the joists, which stabilises them and stiffens the floor system. Typically, you use one centred row when joists span between 3 and 5 metres, and two equally spaced rows for longer spans.

    Before a subfloor is installed, you can install either metal or steel herringbone strutting, which is installed at a diagonal between two adjacent joists and holds them in place when weight is put on the floor. You nail steel strutting from the top of one joist diagonally to the bottom of the adjacent joist. You wedge wood strutting between the two joists and then nail it to each joist.

    For existing floor systems, horizontal strutting or blocking is more feasible.

Book IV

Carpentry, Woodworking, and Flooring

✔ **Blocking:** Cut and nail short lengths of wood the same dimension as the floor joist (such as 50 x 200 or 50 x 250) to fit snugly between the joists in a perpendicular row. You nail through the joist into the ends of the block with 100 mm nails and stagger block positions so that you have nailing access from both ends.

✔ **Shims:** Use shims (small pieces of wedge-shaped wood) to fill a small gap between the top of a joist and the subfloor. If the floor joist isn't tight against the subfloor, simply apply glue and tap tapered shims between the joist and subfloor until it is just snug. Do not overdrive the shims, which actually lifts the subfloor, causing more squeaking.

To stop a squeak, apply glue to a wood shim or shingle and drive it between the floor joist and subfloor.

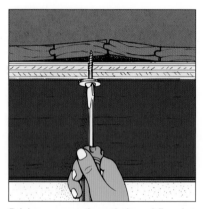

Driving a screw through the subfloor into the finished flooring can pull the boards together, stopping a squeak.

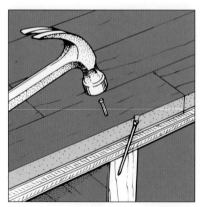

Figure 1-3:
Three ways
to stop
squeaks.

If the underside of the floor is inaccessible, drive finish nails through the flooring at an angle to silence a squeak.

Fixing a squeak from above

If you can't access a squeak from below, you don't have much choice but to tackle it from above. Check out Figure 1-4 to see how these tricks work.

Figure 1-4:
Methods for fixing squeaky stairs.

Stop squeaking stairs by gluing and then screwing wood blocks between the risers and treads.

If you can't get to the underside of the staircase, drive lost head nails into risers at an angle to help silence squeaks.

✓ **Squeaks in floor joists:** First, locate the floor joist so that you have something to nail into. Doing so involves drilling a small-diameter hole through the floor and then probing with a bent coat hanger. It's best to drill the probing hole near a wall or in another inconspicuous area. After you've located a joist, you can measure every 400 mm and you should find the next joist, then the next, and so on. After you've located the offending joist area, drill an angled hole from both sides through the flooring and subfloor and into the joist. This is a 'by feel' type of job, but it should work. Drive screws into the joists in the pilot holes to silence the squeak.

✓ **Squeaks on stairs:** The most common squeaks on stairs occur where the front of the upper tread rests on the top of the riser just below the tread. The best way to silence this type of squeak and anchor the tread to the riser is to drive flooring nails at opposite angles through the tread and into the riser. If the treads are hardwood, drill pilot holes first, and then drive finish nails into the risers and use a nail set to recess the nails. Use wood putty to fill the nail heads.

Book IV

Carpentry, Woodworking, and Flooring

Chapter 2

Drilling, Driving, Fastening, and Gluing

In This Chapter

▶ Holding your work together before you commit to it

▶ Finding the best drill to buy . . . and some to hire

▶ Figuring out which hammer is right for the job

▶ Exploring basic spanners, pliers, and other gripping tools

▶ Creating a tight hold with clamps and glue

▶ Looking down the barrels of stapling and caulking guns

Carpentry and related work, such as hardware installation, invariably involves assembly and, one way or another, attaching things together. In this chapter, you find out about the tools and techniques involved in this work – and how to use them safely without gluing your fingers together or nailing your shoes to the floor.

Trial Assembly Pays Off

You may have heard the old tip 'Measure twice and cut once'. The extra moment it takes to double-check your measurements often prevents disasters, or at least saves the time required to correct problems that arise from an error in measuring. The same principle applies to the assembly stage. Double-check your cut, positioning, or fit before final assembly. Make a habit of doing a trial assembly or dry-fit before you nail, glue, or screw parts together.

If you're nailing, a dry-fit can be as simple as holding the work, such as a piece of trim or length of cladding, in place to make sure that it fits well before driving any nails. In other situations, you may need to tack the piece in place, which is what carpenters call securing together a workpiece with a minimum number of nails, driven just deep enough to hold the work in place but shallow enough that they can be removed easily if the piece must be repositioned or recut.

Trial-fitting is especially important when glue and adhesive are involved. After you apply glue or adhesive, you're, well, stuck if the work doesn't fit. At best, you'd have glue all over a piece you need to recut. At worst, you'd drip glue all over the place and then track it through the house. Always trial-fit before assembling with contact cement (which sets instantly) and other fast-drying glues. Disassembly without damaging the work is difficult or impossible.

Don't think you're home free just because you're using screws. Sure, you can easily remove them, but you've still got the holes you made in the process. Even if you can recut a too-long board or use a too-short board, the holes may not be where they need to be. Similarly, if you need to move the piece slightly, you may need to plug and redrill the holes in the base material. So hold, tack, brace, or clamp the work before you drill pilot holes or drive screws.

Drilling and Power Driving

Today's 13 mm variable-speed reversible drill/driver, available in plug-in and cordless models, uses steel screw-driving tips to drive in or remove screws and various bits and accessories to drill holes, sand wood, mix piña coladas, and other important carpentry tasks.

For decades, the electric drill has been the top-selling power tool and the first power tool that most people buy. Not long after the drill's emergence, the makers added variable-speed triggers and reversing motors. This new tool, called a drill/driver, is more versatile. One tool performs both high-speed and low-speed drilling operations and, most significantly, drives and removes screws easily.

More recent improvements have put the drill/driver at the top of everyone's power tool wish list. Batteries replace cumbersome and inconvenient electrical cords, adjustable clutches let you control the torque (driving force), and with a keyless chuck, you can change bits or accessories in a flash. Simply grasp the keyless chuck with one hand and activate the tool with the other, in forward or reverse, depending on whether you're installing or removing a bit.

Having made driving screws almost as easy as pounding nails, the drill/driver brought on a parallel change in screw design and a dramatic reduction in swollen thumbs. Tapered, slotted-head wood screws have been widely replaced by straight-shank, cross-head screws. The changes also have spawned a line of screw-driving accessories, the most significant of which is the magnetic bit holder.

In addition to using a bog-standard electric drill, you can also purchase or hire other drills for a particular task. A hammer drill, for example, adds a high-speed pounding force to the rotary action for drilling concrete, tiles, your mother-in-law's roast potatoes, and other hard materials. A right-angle drill fits in tight places that a standard drill won't because the shaft (and therefore the bit) is perpendicular to the body.

Accessorising your drill/driver

Accessories turn your hole-drilling tool into a grinder, a sander, a carving tool, and even a fluids pump. Explore the many possibilities, but start with these essentials:

- **An index of high-speed steel twist bits:** Buy a large index (a metal box with labelled slots for various-size bits). Depending on your budget and the amount of use you anticipate, you'll also need a small set of bits that you can add to as needed or bite the bullet and go for a full 64-bit set.

- **A set of spade bits:** These flat, wood-boring bits are required for deeper holes and holes with diameters larger than 10 mm. They work better at high speeds.

- **A set of multibore or screw pilot bits:** Although many situations allow you to drive screws without the necessity of drilling pilot holes, most often you try to avoid those loveliest of sounds – wood splitting and screw heads snapping off. These multi-duty combination drill bits eliminate the need to change bits because one bit bores the clearance (or shank) hole and the pilot hole, and when called for, the countersink and counterbore, all in one easy step.

- **An assortment of Pozidriv and standard bits and a magnetic bit holder:** Start with the following five bits: Pozidrive (#1 and #2) and slotted (5, 6, and 7 mm). Buy bits for more exotic screws, such as the Phillips, square-drive, and Torx, as needed. The purpose of the magnet is to hold the screw and free up your other hand for more important things, such as holding the work, digging for the next screw, or scratching your nose.

- **A set of carbide-tipped masonry bits:** Buy bits ranging from 5 mm to at least 10 mm. These bits usually come in a handy plastic storage box. Use masonry bits for concrete, brick, other masonry products, plaster, and tile. (Never use steel twist bits on masonry materials – they'll quickly become dull and produce more smoke than a cheap cigar.)

Book IV

Carpentry, Woodworking, and Flooring

The following are accessories that you may well need some day, but we suggest that you purchase them as the need arises:

✔ **Holesaw:** A holesaw is primarily for cutting large holes in metal or wood. (If you thought that a holesaw is twice as big as a 'half saw', please put down this book before you hurt yourself.) One type has a cup-shaped cutter with teeth along the rim. Another has band-type blades. Each type of cutter fits on a spindle, called a mandrel, which also holds a pilot bit that enters the work and holds the holesaw in position as the large cutter enters the work. Holesaws come in several sizes, up to 100 mm or more. You're likely to need one to bore a 50 mm-diameter hole in a door for a lockset, and to cut holes in ceilings for downlights – it's the only practical, affordable tool to make that size hole.

✔ **Dowelling jig:** In many woodworking projects, wooden dowels reinforce joints. You drill holes in the mating pieces and insert a dowel. The dowelling jig precisely locates the holes and sets the depth, so that when you join the pieces, they align perfectly. Today, professionals favour the biscuit jointer, but then, who wouldn't favour anything relating to biscuits. A biscuit jointer is worth the investment if you do a lot of woodworking, but dowelling is fine for the occasional woodworker. Dowels are circular, and fit into drilled holes. Biscuits are shaped like . . . er . . . biscuits, and fit into slots. A biscuit jointer cuts the right sized and shaped slots.

✔ **Sanding, grinding, and other abrading tools:** Take advantage of the drill's versatility with these accessories that enable you to shape and smooth wood, clean and debur metal, remove paint, and perform a host of other tasks.

✔ **Portable drill stand:** Precision or repetitive drilling is ideally done on a drill press, a heavy piece of stationary equipment that few remodelling professionals even own. If you don't have a drill press, lock your drill into one of these handy, portable stands for easier and more accurate drilling.

✔ **Bit-extension tool:** Lock a twist drill or spade bit into the end of an extension shaft to extend the reach or to drill very deep holes. This tool gets a lot of work when you're rewiring. To fish wires from one place to another, you often need to drill holes at an angle through a wall, into a stud cavity, and through a floor or ceiling joist bay to the floor below or above – a distance of 300 mm or more.

✔ **Flexible shaft:** You can literally drill around corners by securing your drill bit in the end of a flexible shaft. It's not something you use every day, but it can come in very handy.

Watch your speed!

After you determine the proper bit to use, it's time to put on your safety goggles and, if required, a dust mask. Then work out the speed that you want that bit to turn and the amount of pressure to exert (called feed pressure). We suppose you can memorise a chart full of specs on the optimal speed for drilling holes in dozens of common materials, but all you really need is one general rule, a little common sense, and some trial-and-error. In general, the larger the hole and the harder the material, the slower the speed you want to use; and if your drill doesn't spin as fast as it should, ease up on the feed pressure and take a little more time.

In some cases, you may find it easier to start slow and pick up speed after you establish the location. Similarly, stepping up from smaller-diameter bits until you reach the desired hole diameter is a useful trick when drilling in concrete, masonry, metal, and other hard materials. Lubrication – oil for metal drilling and water for concrete or masonry drilling – cools the bits and improves the efficiency of the cutter.

When drilling into masonry, always use a carbide-tipped masonry bit. Start with a 5 or 6 mm diameter bit and step up the bit size a little at a time until the hole is the desired diameter. Your bits work more efficiently and more accurately and last longer with this method.

Assuming that you're using the proper bit/cutter and that it's sharp and properly secured in the tool, adjust your drilling speed and feed pressure if any of the following warning signs pop up:

- The bit or other cutter fails to do its job.
- The bit or cutter jams or turns too slowly.
- The bit or cutter overheats, as evidenced by smoke or blackening of the workpiece or bit.
- The drill motor strains or overheats.

As long as you can maintain control, you can often drive screws at a drill/driver's maximum speed. A screw gun, a single-purpose professional tool designed exclusively for driving screws, operates at speeds two or three times faster than the fastest drill/driver. However, if a screw is going in at a billion miles a second, you can't rely on the reaction of your trigger finger to stop the bit at just the right point. You're likely to drive the screw too deep, strip the screw head, snap the screw in half, or damage your workpiece – or all the above. Better drill/drivers have an adjustable clutch, which limits the torque – when the screw is seated, the bit stops turning.

Use your head. Slow down if you're not sure. Do you really want to drive a brass slotted screw into an expensive piece of hardware at high speed? Of course not. There are even occasions when it's best to pull out an old-fashioned screwdriver.

Book IV

Carpentry, Woodworking, and Flooring

Drilling techniques

When accurately locating a hole, called spotting, it's often helpful to create a small indentation to guide the bit's initial cut and prevent it from spinning out of control like a drunken figure skater. The harder the surface and the greater the accuracy required, the more advisable it is to spot a hole before drilling. In soft wood, this step is as simple as pressing the bit or a sharp pencil point into the wood. In hard wood, you may want to use an awl. In metal, you probably have to use a hammer and centre punch. To further prevent the bit from wandering off course, hold the tool perpendicular to the surface. If you need to drill at an angle, tilt the drill after the bit has started to penetrate, or clamp an angle-guide block onto your work.

To make an angle-guide block, drill a hole through a block of wood with the bit you intend to use. Then cut the bottom of the block at an angle that equals the angle of the hole you want to drill. If, for example, you want a hole angled 30 degrees off vertical, then cut a 30-degree angle on the bottom of the block.

Grip the drill firmly, with two hands if possible, for better control. Heavy drills have higher torque and may even include a side handle so that you can control the tool if the bit jams in the work and the drill keeps turning. Whenever possible, clamp workpieces that may not be heavy enough to stay put under a drilling load.

A drill tends to splinter the exit hole. To prevent this splintering from happening, ease up on the pressure so that the drill is doing all the work. Or even better, take time to back up your workpiece with a piece of wood scrap before you start drilling. Any splintering will occur on the scrap, not the workpiece.

Driving Screws

Despite the overwhelming popularity of the electric drill/driver, screwdrivers are still an essential item for every homeowner. You've probably heard the saying 'Use a tool only for its intended purpose'. Very often, you can injure yourself, ruin a tool, or damage your work if you fail to heed that advice. However, if using a screwdriver for a task other than driving screws were a crime and the punishment were banishment from hardware shops, the aisles would be empty, and paint tins would be forever full.

The first rule for driving screws is to use a driver that matches the type and size of screw you're driving. The majority of screws are either cross-head screws, which have a cross-shaped recess in the head and require a Phillips or Pozidrive screwdriver, or slotted screws, which have a single slot cut across the diameter of the screw head and require a standard driver.

You get the best deal and are prepared for most screwdriving situations if you buy an assortment of screwdrivers. At a minimum, you need two standard drivers, a 5 mm cabinet and 6 mm mechanic's, and two cross-head drivers, a 100 mm #2 and a 75 mm #1.

Alternatively, you can buy a 4-in-1 or 6-in-1 driver. The 4-in-1 has a double-ended shaft, two 5 mm and 6 mm standard, and #1 and #2 Phillips or Pozidriv interchangeable bits (tips). In the 6-in-1 model, the two ends of the shaft serve as a 6 mm and 7 mm nutdriver. Buy other size screwdrivers as needed. One advantage of these multidrivers is that they accommodate different bits; when you run across screws with square holes, star-shaped holes, or other tip configurations, you need to buy only the appropriate tip, not a whole other tool.

Avoid the bargain racks when looking for screwdrivers. Shop for named brands and look for tempered (heat-treated) tips.

The way to use a screwdriver is essentially obvious, but we have a few points worth mentioning. First, don't hold the tool between your knees or teeth – you'll get lousy torque pressure. Always match the driver to the fastener. Failure to do so inevitably deforms the screwhead, sometimes to the point where you can no longer twist it out or in. This is particularly true with brass screws (which are easily damaged because brass is relatively soft) and when the screw is unusually tight or even stuck.

If you're trying to draw and fasten two things together with a flathead screw, for example two pieces of wood, join the two pieces together and use one of the following approaches:

- Clamp the two pieces together and, using a bit that's a little smaller than the diameter of the screw, drill a pilot hole as deep as the screw is long. Finish by using a countersink bit to bore a conical hole that suits the screwhead. Clamping is necessary because the screw tends to force the two pieces apart as it enters the second piece.

- Alternatively, bore the appropriate pilot, clearance, and countersink holes before driving the screw. Using a bit that's a little smaller than the screw's diameter, bore a pilot hole that's equal to the screw's length through both pieces. Then, using a bit that equals the diameter of the screw, bore a clearance hole through the top piece only. A screw pilot or multibore accessory bit bores all three holes at once and is available in sets to suit various screw sizes.

Predrilling for screws is always best and makes driving screws by hand much easier. Predrilling is essential for most finish work (where neatness is important) and to prevent splitting when screwing into hardwoods, plywood, end grain, or near the ends of a board. On many occasions, however, you may not need to drill pilot holes or countersinks, especially if you use a drill/driver. The best screws to use in wood without pilot holes have bugle heads (similar to flathead screws), straight shafts, and coarse threads.

Book IV

Carpentry, Woodworking, and Flooring

Lubricate screws (especially brass ones) with wax to make them easier to drive. Don't use soap, as it tends to corrode screws.

Although you can buy a depth gauge for drill bits, a piece of tape (masking, electrical, duct, or whatever) wrapped around the shaft of a bit tells you when to stop drilling.

Sometimes, it's hard for beginners to drill holes at the desired angle – usually perpendicular to the surface. If accuracy is critical, hold a combination square (or a block of wood that you know is cut square) on the surface and against the top of the drill. As long as you keep the drill centred on your guide and in contact with it, the hole will be accurate.

Whenever you need to bore many holes in identical locations in more than one piece of wood, use a template. Take, for example, drilling screw holes to locate knobs on a number of cabinet doors, or drilling a series of holes in the side of a bookcase for plug-in shelf supports. For knobs, the template may be a board with a hole drilled in it that fits over the corner of a cabinet door so that the hole lies in precisely the same spot on each door you place it on. For shelf supports, the template may be a 600 mm-long strip of 6 mm hardboard with a series of holes so that you only need to align the template with the front or back edge of the bookcase side to drill holes in the exact same spots every time.

You must locate hinges accurately if one half is to mate well with the other, and to ensure that the door is located precisely in its opening. Pilot holes for hinge screws must be exactly centred, or they tend to push the hinge off mark or the screwhead won't sit flush with the hinge. Any irregularity in the wood grain can push an unguided drill or punch off the mark. A self-centring pilot drill or self-centring punch has tapered ends that fit into the countersink of a screw hole in the hinge, automatically centring the drill bit or punch. One size fits all for the punch, but the drill accessory comes in several sizes to suit #6, #8, and #10 screws.

The Nail Hammer: The Quintessential Carpentry Tool

Nail hammers come in two basic types: The one you bought and the one you borrowed from your neighbour three years ago. Just joking. Actually, the types include the curved-claw hammer, which has a curved nail-pulling claw, and the ripping-claw hammer, which has a straight claw.

For general use, we recommend a 16-ounce, curved-claw hammer with a fibreglass handle. Like wood, fibreglass cushions the vibrations to your hand and arm but has the added advantage that it won't break under tough nail-pulling conditions. The curved claw on this hammer gives you good nail-pulling leverage (see the section on 'Pulling nails' later in this chapter). This hammer is also heavy enough for most nailing projects, including framing work, as long as the project is modest in scope – such as studding a cellar wall.

For a big framing project, you want a heavier hammer. Although it's heavier to hold, the added weight (and usually a somewhat longer handle) of a 20-ounce ripping hammer does more of the work for you, whether you're driving large nails, banging things apart, or fine-tuning a dented bumper. When a project involves demolition, you can easily force the claw of a ripping hammer between two materials that are fastened or glued together.

Taking precautions

When you want to bang on something other than a nail, think twice before reaching for your nail hammer. When you need to 'persuade' something into position but might damage it by using a metal hammer, reach for a rubber mallet.

Never strike one hammer against another. The hardened steel can chip off a small piece of metal and send it flying at such great speed that the shard can embed itself deep into your body and presents a particularly great danger to your eyes. Plus, you'll never get through an airport metal detector without setting off the alarms.

For the same reason, don't use a nail hammer to strike cold chisels, masonry chisels, punches, or other hard metal objects, with the exception of nail sets, which are designed to be struck with a nail hammer. Avoid using a nail hammer on concrete, stone, or masonry, too. As a general rule, don't strike anything harder than a nail with a nail hammer.

Plus, such abuse ruins the face of a nail hammer. If you look closely at the face of a hammer, you see that it isn't flat. A quality nail hammer has a shiny, slightly convex face with bevelled edges to minimise surface denting. Some ripping or framing hammers have a milled face (chequered or waffled), which makes it less likely that you'll slip off the head of a nail that you don't strike squarely.

For cold chisels and centre punches, use an engineer's hammer (also called a ball peen hammer). For masonry chisels, concrete, and masonry, use a lump hammer. See Figure 2-1.

Book IV

Carpentry, Woodworking, and Flooring

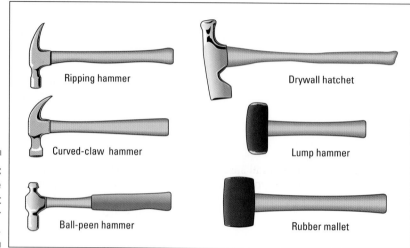

Figure 2-1:
Choose
the right
hammer for
the job.

Driving nails (into wood, not from the shop)

Like all carpenters, we've had our share of smashed fingers and bent nails. But you can avoid them most of the time by driving nails the right way. Whether you're nailing a hook for a picture or nailing a 50 x 100 to a garage wall, follow these basic steps for ouch-free installation:

1. **To have proper grip, grasp a claw hammer almost at the end of the handle and with your thumb wrapped around the handle.**

   Thinking that they'll gain more control, beginners often make the mistake of lining up their thumb on the handle. Not only does this grip fail to improve accuracy, but it's also inefficient and may cause injury to your thumb. The one exception to this rule is when you're nailing sideways across your body in a technique called nailing out.

2. **Start the nail by tilting it slightly away from you and giving it one or two light taps. Then, move your fingers out of harm's way and drive the nail with increasingly forceful blows.**

   You want the handle to be parallel to the surface at the point that it strikes the nail. For rough work, drive the nail home – that is, until the nail draws the pieces tight and is set slightly below the surface. For finish work, stop when the nail is just above the surface. Finish the task with a nail set so that you don't risk damaging the wood. (See the section 'Putting on the finishing touches', later in this chapter.)

The rules are a little different for a 20-ounce ripping or framing hammer. Unlike a claw hammer, you grasp the handle a little higher – about a quarter of the way up from the end – and keep a little looser grip. Also, take a bigger backswing and use a more forceful downswing. With the heavier hammer and the added driving force, keeping your other hand well out of harm's way, preferably behind your back, becomes imperative.

If a nail driven straight in would penetrate out from the back of your workpiece and you don't want to use a shorter nail, you may be able to drive the nail in at an angle. Carpenters often use this technique when they nail up doubled wall studs or headers over framed door and window openings. Nailing at opposing angles improves the holding power significantly.

Because of their small size, brads and tacks are difficult to hold safely when starting the nail. If you have a tack hammer, use it, but if you must use a claw hammer, save your fingers by using long-nose pliers to grasp the nail while you give it the tap or two required to get it started.

Face-nailing and toenailing

Face-nailing and toenailing (shown in Figure 2-2) aren't horrible punishments that carpenters inflict on plumbers who cut too-big holes in their floor joists. Rather, they describe the two common ways of nailing objects together.

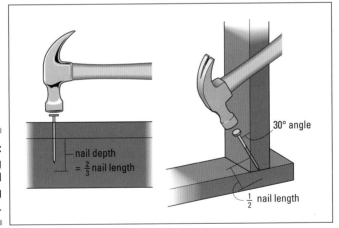

Figure 2-2:
Face-nailing
(left) and
toenailing
(right).

30° angle

nail depth
= $\frac{2}{3}$ nail length

$\frac{1}{2}$ nail length

Book IV

Carpentry, Woodworking, and Flooring

Most often, you nail through the face of a board and into the backing material. This is called face-nailing. As a general rule, nail through the thinner member into the thicker one whenever possible. The deeper that nail goes into the backing, the more holding power it has.

Here's a good guideline to follow when you need to figure out the proper length of a nail: A nail should penetrate into solid backing material at a depth equal to twice the thickness of the member being attached. For example, if you're nailing an 18 mm-thick furring strip on a plasterboard-covered wall, you want to use at least a 50 mm nail (2 × 18 mm + 13 mm for the plasterboard).

When you want to secure one piece of timber to another at a 90-degree angle, such as a wall stud to a sole plate or top plate, you have one or two nailing options, depending on whether you have access to the top of the T. Face-nailing through one board into the end of the mating board is typically the easiest and preferred technique. If you don't have access, or if the board is so thick that face-nailing through it would be impractical, you must toenail (or skew nail) through the end of one board into the face of the other board.

Driving the first nail at such an angle tends to push the board off its mark, so as you drive the nail, you need to back up the board (typically with your foot). It also helps to drive the nail to where it just penetrates one board and then reposition it as necessary before driving one sharp blow. In fact, you may want to assume that driving will tend to push the board past its mark and compensate for that by positioning it a little to the opposite side of the marks.

Blind-nailing

Blind-nailing may sound dangerous, but it's nothing to worry about. The term describes any nailing technique in which the nail is hidden from sight without the use of putty or wood fillers. In its most common form, the technique is used to secure tongue-and-groove boards, such as solid wood panelling. Nail into the tongued edge of the board at a 45-degree angle. When you install the next board, its groove conceals the nail, and so on across the wall or floor. The first and last boards typically must be face-nailed as described in the preceding section.

Putting on the finishing touches

In finish work, you generally want to sink the nail head slightly below the surface, as shown in Figure 2-3, and later fill the depression with putty, caulk, or wood filler so the nails don't show. For this task, you need a nail set, which comes in sizes ranging from 1 mm to 3 mm to suit various nail head sizes. Buy a set of three and you're ready for any nail you're likely to encounter in home carpentry.

Whenever you need to hold one tool and strike it with another, your fingers are vulnerable. (Theoretically, you can ask for nail-holding volunteers, but you won't get much interest.) Generally, holding the nail as you hammer isn't a problem when setting finish nails because you need a relatively minor blow to drive the nail. Such light hammering is easy to control and does less damage if the blow is off the mark.

When nail-setting heavy round wire nails, such as you may need for face-nailed decking, a heavier blow is required. After mashing our fingers a number of times, we adopted an old carpenter's nail-setting trick, and it hasn't happened since. Lay a 75 mm round wire nail flat on the surface with its head over the centre of the nail head to be countersunk. With your fingers holding the nail a safe distance from the head, strike the edge of the nail head, and it will set the nail below. The process tends to mush the nail head, so after rotating the head a couple of times and setting half-a-dozen nails or so, use a new nail.

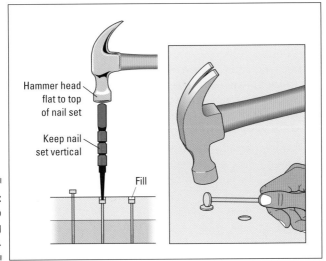

Figure 2-3:
Two nail-setting approaches.

Pulling nails

When it comes to pulling nails, you have many techniques and tools to choose from. The ones you choose depend on whether you need to protect the surface, whether the situation allows you to pry the materials apart, whether you can talk someone else into doing this job, and several other factors. To be prepared for most situations, you need a nail hammer, one or two cat's paw-style nail pullers, and a couple of pry bars.

Try one or more of the following techniques, according to your needs:

✔ **Remove the board and then the nails.** Most often, the easiest way to take things apart is to either bang or pry them apart or give them to a two-year-old child. Take, for example, trim removal. To do this job while minimising the damage to either the trim or the surface to which it's nailed requires a pry bar with a straight, wide blade that's thin enough for you to drive it between the materials – a trim bar. (You may want to grind the end of this tool to an even thinner taper to make it easier to insert.) Drive the tapered end of the trim bar behind the trim between two nailing locations. Pull gently towards you and work your way over towards the nailing locations. Then pry the trim still farther out, using the other end of the trim bar or a larger pry bar, working your way all along the board.

Book IV

Carpentry, Woodworking, and Flooring

To protect the wall and increase leverage, insert a shim; a thin, stiff material, such as a stiff-blade putty knife; or a wood block between the pry bar and the wall, as shown in Figure 2-4.

Virtually all nailing, demolition, and nail-pulling operations require you to wear proper eye protection.

✓ **Pry nails from removed boards.** If you've pried a board off a surface and nails remain in the board, tap the pointed ends to drive the heads above the opposite surface, at least enough so that you can pull them from the face with a hammer claw or the bent end of a pry bar. If you're trying to avoid damaging the face of the board (as you might for trim that you've removed and plan to reuse), pull the nails through from the back. It's easy for finishing nails, and with enough force (and soft wood, such as pine), you can pull common nails out backwards, too.

To pull the nail, use a hammer as described in the bullet point 'Side-to-side technique', later in this chapter. Alternatively, pincers work well, especially with finishing nails. Grasp the nail shaft with the jaws of the pincers as close to the surface as possible. Roll the pincers over to one side, then the other, but don't grip too hard or you'll cut the nail.

✓ **Pry a little, then pull a little.** If you want to protect the surface and can pry a board a little above the surface, do so. Then drive the board back with a sharp hammer blow. The goal is for the board to go back in place and leave the nails standing proud (or humiliated). Protect the surface from the hammer blow with a scrap of wood. Then pull out the nails with a pry bar.

✓ **Pull nails from the face.** If you can't get behind a board to pry it free, you must attack the nails from the face of the board. For this task, you need a claw-type nail-puller. For rough work, where damage to the surface isn't a concern, a cat's paw, which has a relatively wide head, works well. But to minimise damage, you need a puller with a narrower head and sharper jaws that don't need to be driven so deeply into the wood in order to bite into the nail head. This style also has sharper claws that bite into the shaft of a nail; the wider paw generally needs a head to pull on. You can also find mini versions of these tools for small finish nails.

Position the puller with the points of the claw just behind the nail and drive it down into the wood and under the head of the nail. Pull back on the tool with a steady, controlled motion to pull it at least 13 mm above the surface. Then use one of the following approaches with a hammer or pry bar.

• **Standard approach:** After the nail's head is above the surface, hook onto it with a hammer claw (or with the V-notch on the bent end of a pry bar) and pull the handle of the tool towards you to pry out the nail.

Don't jerk a hammer in an attempt to free a nail that's too stubborn to be pulled out with a steady, smooth motion. With the loss of control comes increased risk of injury. The sudden force may break a wooden hammer handle or snap the head off the nail, making it even harder to remove. (Try the next technique if you accidentally snap the head off.) Instead, use a pry bar or nail puller, which gives you the additional leverage required.

- **Side-to-side technique:** If the nail is long or if you need to protect the surface, slip a scrap of wood under the hammer, as shown in Figure 2-5, to add leverage and enable you to pull out a long nail entirely. To pull large or headless nails, carefully swing the claw into the nail with enough force to make it bite into the shaft as close to the surface as possible. Then push the hammer over sideways, and the nail will come out about 25 mm. Reposition it and push sideways in the opposite direction to pull it another 25 mm. If you have a good-quality hammer with a sharp claw, it won't slip off the nail's shaft. After you've sufficiently loosened the nail, use the standard pull-towards-you approach to pull it out the rest of the way.

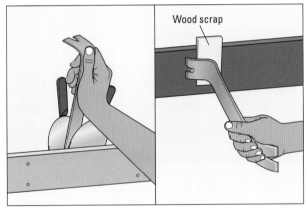

Figure 2-4:
Minimising damage to a board being removed.

Wood scrap

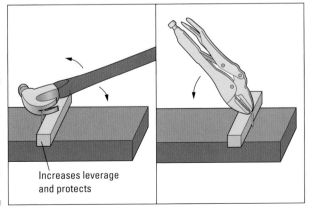

Figure 2-5:
A block of wood increase leverage and protects the surface.

Increases leverage and protects

Book IV

Carpentry, Woodworking, and Flooring

Fastening with Staples

A staple gun is handy for many remodelling projects, such as securing insulation, ceiling tiles, or plastic sheeting, as well as for such household repairs and projects as recovering a seat cushion or attaching outdoor fairy lights. The tool is available in manual and electric models. Each staple gun has pros and cons, but given the typical limited use, it probably doesn't matter which you choose.

Most staple guns allow staples to be fired into the air, so you risk eye injury if you use them improperly or without care. Although an electric stapler may have a safety catch on the trigger, it's very easy to fire a staple accidentally – too easy, in our opinion. Make a habit of setting the safety lock after every series of shots and when you store the tool. The temptation to play 'guns' with an electric model suggests that you keep it out of the hands of unsupervised children – better yet, keep it out of their hands, full stop.

A dial on the hand-powered model regulates the force of the blow. The harder the material you're stapling into and the longer the staple, the more force you need. To ensure that all the force that you set is delivered, press the stapler down firmly as you fire the staple. If an occasional staple stands proud, give it a tap with a hammer – not the stapler.

Getting Down to Nuts and Bolts

Product installations often involve nuts and bolts, and many carpentry projects make use of lag bolts and a variety of other metal anchors and fasteners that you can't grab with a screwdriver or nail hammer. In addition, you'll often find that you need a firm hold on a variety of non-fastener items such as pipes, product and machinery parts, wiring, hardware, and so on. These tasks all require one of the following gripping tools.

Pliers: Grippy, grabby, and pointy

Slip-joint pliers have toothed jaws that enable you to grip various-sized objects, like a water pipe, the top of a gallon of mineral spirits, or the tape measure you accidentally dropped into the toilet. Because its jaws are adjustable, slip-joint pliers give you leverage to grip the object firmly. This tool is on everyone's basic list of tools, but to be honest, few people use it very often. Instead, we prefer locking pliers (commonly known by the brand names Mole Grips or Vise-Grips). Locking pliers easily adjust to lock onto pipes, nuts, screws, and nails that have had their heads broken off and practically anything that needs to be held in place, twisted, clamped, or crushed.

For occasional minor electrical work and repairs, every tool kit needs a pair of long-nose pliers (often mistakenly called needle-nose pliers, which have a much longer, pointier nose). Long-nose pliers cut wire and cable, twist a loop on the end of a conductor to fit under a screw fitting, and, turned perpendicular to the wires, do a fair job twisting wires together. Pincers probably have some real electrical value that has eluded us for many years, but they're invaluable nail pullers and cutters.

Spanners: A plethora of options

Carpentry work often involves minor plumbing work, primarily the temporary removal of piping connections for work such as installing cabinets and fishing the pet goldfish out of the bathroom sink's U-bend. And all sorts of projects involve nuts and bolts and similar fasteners. A spanner is the primary tool for this work.

An adjustable spanner is included in most basic tool kits because it accommodates any size nut – metric or imperial – and small to moderate-size pipe fittings. On the downside, adjustable spanners don't grip as well as fixed-sized spanners. Don't waste your money on a cheap one. Get a good-quality tool.

For a better grip, choose a spanner that's sized for the fastener or fitting. Combination spanners, which have one open and one closed (boxed) end, are sold in imperial and metric sets and in sets that include both. For most carpentry work, you need only a small assortment (six to ten).

For many projects, you can avoid the imperial/metric debate altogether by purchasing a nice combination socket set. Socket spanners not only are sized for specific fasteners (which helps fight the age-old rounding-off-the-hex-head problem), but they also offer a ratcheted handle that enables you to tighten or loosen a nut without repositioning the tool every half-turn or so, as is required for combination wrenches.

Set screws, fittings, and other fasteners have hexagonal-shaped recesses that require an Allen key (also called a hex key or hex wrench). These metal bars come in several shapes – straight, L-shaped, and T-shaped (where the top of the T is a handle). Although you can buy Allen keys individually – they may even come with a product that requires one for assembly, adjustment, or maintenance – it's best to start with a matching set or two. On the rare occasion that you need one that's not included in a set, buy it separately. Straight sets fold into a handle like a penknife. L- and T-shaped sets come in a plastic case or little pouch. The L-shaped ones are more versatile because the shorter leg of the L gets into places that the longer straight or T-shaped ones can't.

Book IV

Carpentry, Woodworking, and Flooring

Clamping Stuff Together

Clamping is an essential part of many carpentry projects. Clamps hold your work in place while you tool the workpiece with saws, drills, sanders, and other tools. (Some types of clamps are traditionally called *cramps*, for reasons lost in the mists of time.) Clamps also hold together two or more objects in precise alignment while you drill pilot holes and install fasteners. In the final stages, clamps hold things together while you wait for glue/adhesives to cure, in some cases reducing the number of fasteners required or eliminating the need for them altogether. The number of clamps a project requires varies widely, but typically, you need one every 200 mm or so along the joint.

Because carpentry and woodworking projects assume an endless variety of shapes (flat, square, 90- and 45-degree corners, cylinders) and sizes (long, short, big, small), you need a variety of clamps and ones that offer versatility. Dozens of types exist, but a few basic clamps have proven their worth. (See Figure 2-6.)

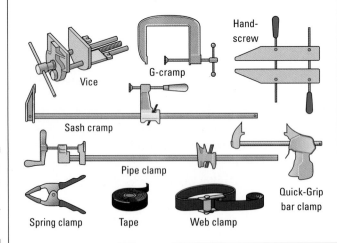

Figure 2-6:
Choose the right clamping tool for the job.

A G-cramp, named for its shape, comes in sizes that describe the maximum open capacity of the jaw, from 18 mm to 300 mm. It's the primary clamp that woodworkers use. Most jobs require a minimum of two clamps, so make a practice of starting out with at least a pair of a particular size, and buy more as needed. G-cramps exert tremendous force: You never need to use anything other than your hand to tighten them. Prevent damage to your workpiece by placing a wood scrap between the clamp and the work. If they're heavy enough, such boards also serve to distribute the force more evenly.

- **The edge G-cramp** is a variation of the G-cramp. This clamp is designed to hold wood strips against the edge of another board, such as a plywood shelf or kitchen counter. To use it, lock the G onto the board and then tighten the edge screw against the edging strip.

- **Pipe clamps** consist of one fixed crank screw (head stock) and one movable jaw (tail stock) mounted on a pipe. The crank screw threads onto the end of the pipe, and the movable jaw slides over the pipe, locking onto the pipe when pressure is exerted. You can use any length pipe and easily move the clamps from one pipe to another to suit the project.

- **Sash cramps** (so called because they are long enough to clamp together the component parts of window sashes) work like pipe clamps, but the bars aren't interchangeable and therefore aren't as versatile. Both types may be equipped with rubber pads to prevent them from damaging the work.

  If you put all the movable jaws on one side of the workpiece, they tend to make the work bow up at the middle. Counter this tendency by alternating the clamps from one side to the other. If that doesn't solve the problem, you can straighten a bowing surface by easing up on the clamp pressure just a bit, inserting a thick block of wood on the workpiece under the pipe at the midpoint, and tapping a shim between the block and the pipe. Check for straightness with the edge of a framing square or other straightedge.

  If you need to use a pipe clamp for a non-rectangular workpiece, such as a round or triangular tabletop, cut a jig that, when clamped against the opposite edges of the work, yields a rectangular shape for the clamps to lock onto.

- **Spring clamps** work like giant clothespegs for quick clamping and releasing of projects where clamping is near the outer edge and the boards aren't too thick.

- **A handscrew** has parallel wooden jaws that won't damage wood workpieces as readily as a steel clamp. It exerts tremendous power with little effort on your part, but most important, it won't apply twisting force, which tends to move your pieces out of alignment. The jaws also can adjust to accommodate work where the two faces are uneven or not parallel to each other.

- **Web clamps** wrap around irregular surfaces and exert inward pressure. Perhaps the most common application is gluing chair legs and the spindles that span between them. Loop the web around the work and thread it through a ratcheted metal fixture, much like you put a belt through its buckle.

When clamping glued work, use just enough pressure to squeeze and hold the parts together. Too much pressure squeezes out too much of the glue, resulting in a weaker bond.

Book IV

Carpentry, Woodworking, and Flooring

Getting Sticky with It: Adhesives and Glue

You need to use adhesives to make strong furniture that holds together. Only a few years ago, you didn't have many choices for adhesives, but nowadays the options are almost limitless. In this chapter, we cover the most commonly used adhesives for woodworking. The chapter also examines when and how to use each of them, as well as how to clean up when you're done.

Cluing in to gluing: Understanding how glue works

Adhesives work one of two ways: Mechanically or chemically. The type you choose depends on what material you glue and what type of joint you're gluing.

- **Chemical bonding:** Chemical bonding requires that the surfaces being glued together have even contact without gaps. These glues require an undisturbed surface area in order to bond properly. That said, these glues will work with some voids, but not substantial voids. Chemical bonding adhesives include wood glues (yellow and white) and hide glue.

- **Mechanical bonding:** If the items you want to glue together have large gaps, you're better off using an adhesive with mechanical bonding characteristics. These types of adhesives include epoxies and plastic resins, and the latest *grab* or *Gripfill*-type adhesives . Their advantage is that they actually fill the voids between the joints and create a lasting bond when gluing less-than-perfect joints.

As for which type of adhesive works best on a specific joint, have a look at the next few sections.

Working with wood glue

You have two glues to choose from when working with wood glue:

- **White wood glue:** The standard for gluing up wood. It's inexpensive and easy to work with, and it creates a strong, lasting bond. Technically, white glue is a polyvinyl-acetate (PVA) adhesive and creates a chemical bond, but 'white glue' is just so much easier to remember.

- **Yellow wood glue:** A newer version of white glue, yellow glue, also known as *panel adhesive*, is slightly thicker, dries quicker, and is more resistant to heat and moisture.

Wood glues are often available in two grades – external (waterproof) and internal. Waterproof external wood glue should not be used for furniture or exposed internal work, as it can stain the wood and be hard to cover up with paint.

Knowing when to use wood glue

White and yellow glues are chemical bonding glues, so they require joints with a substantial surface area and few voids. If you machine your joints with some degree of care and use the best joints for the job, you can use wood glue without hesitation for nearly all your woodworking tasks.

If you intend to expose your finished project to moist conditions, choose a waterproof yellow glue.

Applying wood glue for best results

To apply wood glue, wipe or brush a thin, even coat on both surfaces of the joint. Don't use so much that the glue drips out of the joint when you clamp the pieces together (a little oozing is good, though). Apply the glue and work fairly quickly because the glue will start to set in a few minutes. After you apply the glue, securely clamp the surfaces together for several hours (or preferably overnight).

When clamping a joint, apply enough pressure to pull the joint firmly together and hold the piece securely in place, but not so much that you squeeze all the glue out of the joint. If the joint starts to distort from the clamp pressure, you can be sure you're using too much pressure.

Cleaning up

You can clean up both yellow and white glue with water when they're still wet. Use a damp rag or towel and wipe down the outside of the joint immediately after you've glued it. After the glue has dried, it's a pain to remove and will ruin the finish, so take some time before the glue dries to wipe all exposed surfaces free of extra glue. Doing so will save you a lot of time and frustration later on.

If you miss some glue and it dries, you need to sand the glue off the wood or scrape it with a scraper or chisel. Unfortunately, you'll probably end up taking quite a bit of wood off in order to get all the glue because it soaks into the pores of the wood.

Choosing contact cement

Contact cement (such as Evo-Stick) is a solvent, or water-based, adhesive that must dry to tackiness before you can put the pieces together. This adhesive

Book IV

Carpentry, Woodworking, and Flooring

is great for applying plastic laminates to wood or medium-density fibreboard (MDF). Contact cement isn't all that good for wood-to-wood gluing, however.

To apply contact cement, coat both surfaces you want to glue together with a thin layer, using a rubber roller, and let them dry until tacky. Carefully position one surface over the other before letting the surfaces touch. Try putting some scraps of wood, small-diameter dowels, or cardboard between the two surfaces and then removing the cardboard after you have everything where you want it.

The main drawback with contact cement is that after the coated surfaces touch one another, they're locked in place. Ordinarily, you can't adjust them. However, some newer versions of contact cement do allow some adjustment after contact.

Solvent-based contact cement is toxic, smells unpleasant, and is very flammable. Only use this stuff with adequate ventilation, and always wear a mask. Solvent-based contact cement needs to be cleaned with a solvent-based cleaner such as paint thinner or acetone.

Relying on resin glues

Several types of resin glues are on the market, and all of them have two components that, when mixed together, chemically combine to form a strong adhesive. Always follow the manufacturer's instructions. Some come with a plastic spreader to apply the resin. The major types of resin glues are

- **Epoxy resin:** Epoxy resin adhesive consists of a two-part formula that hardens when you mix the parts together. Many formulas are available, and they vary in their set time and strength.

- **Resorcinal-formaldehyde:** This formula consists of a powdered substance that you mix with a liquid hardener. To use this adhesive, you mix the two parts together in prescribed proportions (on the manufacturer's instructions) and then apply the mixture to the workpiece. This type of adhesive is waterproof, so it's great for outdoor furniture and other projects that will be exposed to a lot of moisture. Resorcinal-formaldehyde is messier to work with, however, than waterproof yellow glue.

- **Urea-formaldehyde:** This type of epoxy has good gap-filling abilities. It comes in two parts, one powder and one liquid, and you mix the powder with water and apply it to one side of the joint. Then you apply the liquid part to the other side. This type of adhesive is water resistant, which makes it suitable for damp but not wet applications.

Knowing when to use resins

Resins aren't your everyday adhesives – they're most useful when you need gap-filling capabilities or when you need the ultimate in watertightness. The downside to these adhesives, however, is that they're

- A pain to mix
- Much more expensive than wood glue
- Toxic

You need to work in a well-ventilated area and use gloves and a suitable respirator when working with resin.

Applying resin for best results

Each brand and type of resin adhesive is a little different. Some require you to mix the two parts before applying the mixture to your joints, and others need to be applied separately. Follow the instructions that come with the adhesive.

Cleaning up

Resin adhesives are toxic; you need to clean them with a solvent-based cleaner, such as acetone. Follow the guidelines on the adhesive's packaging to find out the best way to clean the particular formula you use.

Honing in on hot glue

Hot glue, also known as *hot melt glue*, comes in sticks that you melt in a glue gun and squeeze out onto your project. You can find a variety of glue formulas made for glue guns. You can also find veneer strips coated with heat-activated glue for quick and easy edge veneering.

Knowing when to use hot glue

Hot glue is fast and easy, but not the best solution for permanent projects. However, we highly recommend it for making mock-ups of cabinets because the glue dries quickly and holds well enough for that purpose, though it's probably not strong enough to hold them together long term. Hot glue is also good for gluing small, thin pieces that are too small to nail or difficult to clamp.

The hot glue used for edge veneers is good, but we still recommend that you use a good wood glue if you want to edge veneer.

Book IV

Carpentry, Woodworking, and Flooring

Applying hot glue for best results

Using a hot glue gun is easy: Just put the glue in the gun, wait a few minutes for the glue to melt, and squeeze the trigger to apply it. The glue comes out as a thick droplet and tends to go on thick, as well, so you'll need to be careful if you're doing delicate work. See the section 'Hot glue gun' for tips on shooting glue safely and accurately.

To use hot veneer edging, put the edging where you want it and run a hot iron across it (glue side down, unless you want veneer on your iron) until it melts. Remove the iron and press the veneer down with a rubber roller until the glue hardens. Sand the edges and the joint is virtually invisible and less likely to be snagged and lifted accidentally. This step takes only a few seconds.

Cleaning up

Depending on the type of glue stick you use, you can clean up with a damp rag or a dull chisel, just like with wood glue (see the section 'Working with wood glue,' earlier in the chapter, for more information).

Guns for Pacifists

Caulk, adhesive, and glue are messy materials; whenever possible, it's best that the containers that hold them also dispense them. Many such materials are available in squeezable containers, but sometimes dispensing tools (usually called guns of one sort or another) are required.

Hot glue gun

No surprise here: A hot glue gun does what its name suggests. Insert a stick of hard-cool glue in the back end, plug in the gun, wait for it to heat up, and squeeze the trigger. The trigger action forces the hard glue past the heating element, and out the nozzle comes burning-hot, melted glue. (The section 'Honing in on hot glue' covers when and where to use this type of sticky stuff.)

The glue is not only very hot, but it also sticks to skin, so be careful! Arriving at work the next morning with a coffee table glued to your knees would be awfully embarrassing. The metal tip tends to ooze glue when the unit is hot, so protect whatever surface you rest it on. The metal tip remains very hot for a while after you unplug the tool, so use care in how and where you set it down. Use this type of glue gun when you need instant gratification or to hold something in place until you get a chance to install fasteners. It's really a lifesaver when you need to glue a very small or thin piece of wood in place that would crack if you attempted to use a fastener.

Caulking gun

A caulking gun (or 'mastic gun') dispenses caulks, mastics, and adhesives that are packaged in cardboard or plastic cartridges. The open-frame-style dispenser is easy to clean, but the most important feature to look for is a quick-release button on the back end. Press it with your thumb as you near the end of an application. If you have to fumble with an inconvenient or unreliable release system, adhesive will ooze out all over the place before you relieve the pressure.

You usually apply adhesive from a cartridge in straight ribbons, such as when you apply it to floor joists before installing plywood subfloor or to studs before hanging drywall. When using it on larger surfaces, such as on interior panelling that you're installing over existing drywall, lay down squiggly lines. Just follow the installation instructions for the product.

Cut the tip of the cartridge at a 45-degree angle with a utility knife. How much you cut off depends on how wide a bead you want, but keep in mind that you can always cut off a little more if the bead is too small. You're stuck with wider beads if you cut off too much.

Book IV

Carpentry, Woodworking, and Flooring

Chapter 3

Understanding the Carpentry Process

- -

In This Chapter

▸ Understanding woodworking plans

▸ Creating and using a cutting list

▸ Pre-milling and milling the wood for your project

▸ Examining the assembly procedure

- -

A woodworking project involves a very definite process. From choosing the wood and milling it to size to assembling the piece, you need to do each step correctly, or your project won't be successful. In fact, it may not even go together at all.

This chapter guides you through the process of building a project and shows you how the various steps along the way lead to success. You explore all the details of a project plan – the diagrams, dimensions, and procedures. You get to know the best way to choose the part of the board from which to cut each piece, and you walk through the assembly process from dry-fitting to gluing in sections.

Following Plans: Making Sense of Diagrams, Dimensions, and Procedures

Unless you wing it when you build and can visualise every step of the cutting and building process, you need plans from which to work. Plans make the construction process easy because they spell out exactly how much, what kind, and what size of wood to cut for each part of the project. In addition, plans tell you how to put those parts together. If you can accurately follow a set of plans, you can make any project for which you have the skills and tools – even assembling flat-pack furniture!

Checking out your materials list

Look through the materials list to find out how much wood, fasteners, and hardware you need to build a project. By glancing at this list, you can quickly determine what you need to buy before you get started. Figure 3-1 shows a typical materials list for a table. It runs down the parts for the project, their quantity (bordered by parentheses), and their cut size in thickness (T), width (W), and length (L).

Figure 3-1:
A typical materials list for a table.

Material list	Qty	T	W	L
1. Legs	(4)	50	50	750
2. Short rail	(2)	18	75	895
3. Long rail	(2)	18	75	1810
4. Top	(1)	25	915	1830
5. Cleats	(8)	18	38	50
6. Screws	(8)	32	#8	

Numbers, give me numbers: Measured drawings

Measured drawings are the heart and soul of a project plan. A measured drawing details every board, screw, nail, and piece of hardware that goes into a project and where each object goes. With this drawing, you should be able to build a project even without the other two sections of a project plan.

You may need some time to get used to how a measured drawing organises a project, but soon you'll be able to glance over a measured drawing and tell straight away whether or not you want to tackle the project. And with a little experience, you'll probably be able to tell how much time you need to build it.

A measured drawing shows a project from several angles to give you a better idea of how the finished project looks. However, the level of detail varies depending on who created the drawing. Some designers detail everything and include full-size drawings of joints or unusually shaped parts (the back of a chair, for instance). Other designers provide simplistic drawings that show only the overall dimensions of a part, its position in the finished product, and an overall view of the project. Figures 3-2 and 3-3 show this kind of detail.

If you don't buy project plans, we highly recommend that you make your own drawings to work from. Creating the drawings alerts you to difficult sections in the project and helps you determine how much wood you need. You don't have to be elaborate; just draw something simple. If the project includes any tricky parts (curves, unusual angles, and so on), draw those sections full size so that you can see exactly what you're up against.

We suggest that you make a template, a pattern for the part re-created in full size that you can use again and again. Templates are generally made out of 6 mm plywood or hardboard. They're really handy if you need to make more than one copy of a particular part (chairs, for example, especially if you're going to make more than one chair at a time).

Speaking of templates, we highly recommend making templates for any full-size drawings that are part of the plans you buy. Templates make milling the part to the right size much easier, and you'll always have them on hand. See the section 'Making the Cut', later in this chapter, for more information about milling.

Top

Figure 3-2:
Measured
drawings
show the
project from
several
angles and
generally
list the
dimensions
of each part.

Front

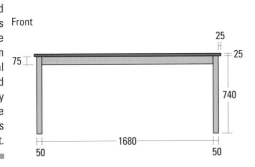

Book IV

**Carpentry,
Woodwork-
ing, and
Flooring**

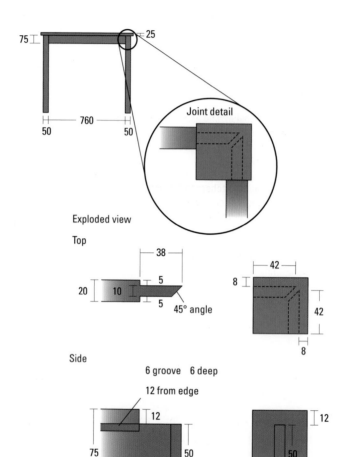

Figure 3-3:
More
detailed
drawings
for the same
project
shown in
Figure 3-2.

Putting the pieces together: Using a procedures list

A procedures list walks you through the process of assembling your project into its final form. Not all project plans include such a list because many people assume that you can figure out the best way to put a project together just by looking at the measured drawings. Procedures lists can be really helpful for beginning woodworkers, though, so we highly recommend that you find plans with detailed procedures lists when you first start out.

Figure 3-4 shows a typical procedures list. This one's pretty simple, but some plans have very detailed lists.

Procedures

1. Choose, dimension, and assemble boards for top, leaving 25 mm extra in width and length.
2. Dimension legs and stretchers.
3. Cut groove in stretchers for cleats.
4. Cut 10 mm x 50 mm x 45 mm mortises in legs.
5. Cut 10 mm x 50 mm x 42 mm tenons in stretchers.
6. Sand legs and stretchers to 150 grit.
7. Assemble short stretcher to legs.
8. Assemble glued-up leg assemblies to long stretchers and check for square.
9. Cut tabletop to its final dimensions.
10. Sand top.
11. Finish sand leg/stretcher assembly.
12. Apply stain.
13. Apply top coat.
14. Attach top to leg assembly using cleats.

Figure 3-4:
A typical procedures list.

If you buy a set of plans that doesn't include a procedures list, make your own before you start to build. Create your procedures list by carefully looking over the materials list and drawings. Then walk yourself through the construction process, writing down the steps you need to take. When you start to construct, you won't get confused and miss a joint or mill a part twice (which is really easy to do).

Creating a Cutting List

Before you start making anything, take your measured drawing, pull out the wood you have on hand, and mark where each part of the project is coming from in pencil or chalk. Doing so minimises waste and helps you plan the beauty of a project. For example, if you're making a dresser with four drawers, you want the wood you use for the drawer fronts and the face frame (if it has one) to match. You want the colour and grain patterns to create a visually pleasing arrangement. The only way to ensure that you get this aesthetic appeal is to look at each board and carefully consider where it should go. This step takes some time, and you may end up rejecting a few boards in order to find a nice composition, which is why we always recommend buying a bit more wood than you need for a given project.

Book IV

Carpentry, Woodworking, and Flooring

Check out Figure 3-5 for a look at a cutting list. The drawing on the left shows parts cut out of a solid board, and the drawing on the right shows how the parts of a carcass (the box for a cabinet) are cut out of a sheet of plywood.

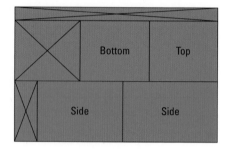

Figure 3-5: A cutting list.

Selecting the best section of the board

Not only do you need to consider the look of the wood you use for a given part of a project, but you also need to think about how that wood behaves in response to moisture changes. Figure 3-6 shows how a board expands and contracts with changes in moisture. You want to make sure that any boards that meet expand and contract in such a way that they won't tear apart a joint or weaken your project.

Generally speaking, wood moves more against the grain than with it. So, as humidity changes, you see less change along its length and more along its width. Also, because plain-sawn boards have growth rings that run at a close angle to the face of the board, you may see more movement on one side of the board than another, which can cause warping, twisting, or cupping if the change in humidity is extreme.

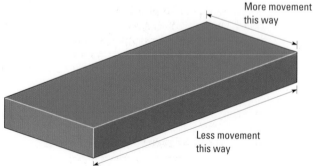

Figure 3-6: Remember that wood expands and contracts with moisture changes in the air.

More movement this way

Less movement this way

Organising your cutting list

After you've chosen the wood you'll be cutting all the parts of your project out of, your next step is to decide in what order you want to cut the boards. We usually organise our boards according to the type of cuts they need and what tool we'll use to cut them. Start with the largest pieces, cut the pieces to size, and then work on the actual joints. Proceed in stages and, if you're working on a large project, work on one section at a time.

If you don't already have the wood, take your cutting list with you to the timber merchant and mark off the parts of the cutting list as you choose your wood. Doing so helps you choose the right boards for your project and ensures that you end up with the right amount of wood. In fact, we recommend that you mark the boards that you buy while you're still at the merchant's, which saves you time when you get home. A good timber merchant will cut timber components to size if he is given a comprehensive cutting list. This can save a lot of time in the early stages of a project. He can get it to the stage referred to in the section below.

Preparing the Board for Milling

Before you cut your wood down to size, do some preliminary cutting to prepare the wood for its final milling. This cutting is called (logically enough) pre-milling. Pre-milling means cutting the board to its near-final dimensions so that the wood can acclimatise to its new size. We can't tell you how many times we've had a nice, straight board twist slightly when we cut it in half. This is the nature of wood: You can't predict what's going to happen after you change its shape. So cut the boards almost down to size and wait a day or so to see what happens.

Pre-mill a board to its final length and width plus 25 mm and to its final thickness plus 3 mm (if possible). Then let the board rest for a day or so before you do the final milling. After the board has rested, check to see that it's still flat and straight. If the board isn't, you know that you need to flatten it out and square it by using a jointer and a planer. In that case, follow these steps:

1. **Run one of the faces of the board (the wide part) through the jointer until the board is flat.**

   This step may require a few light passes. Make sure that you run the stock over the jointer in the proper grain direction to avoid tear-out (roughing-up of the surface of the wood). If you don't know which direction to feed the board into the jointer, use a scrap piece and run it through first in one direction and then the other to see which provides a cleaner cut.

2. **Turn the board on its edge and run it through the jointer with the flat face (the one you just made) against the fence.**

Book IV

Carpentry, Woodworking, and Flooring

3. **Flip the board over and do the other edge.**

   Again, make sure the freshly flattened face is against the fence.

4. **Run the board through your planer with the flat face against the bed until it's flat, too, paying attention to proper grain direction to avoid tear-out.**

   This step may take a few passes. At the end, you should have a flat, straight board.

Making the Cut

After the board is straight and flat, you can move on to the milling stage. Milling, simply an extension of the pre-milling stage, consists of doing the final cutting to the board to make the final part for your project. This process includes making all the joints, routing (like rounding over the edge of the board), and rough sanding all the parts so that they're all ready for assembly.

Follow this process when milling a board:

1. **Cut the board to width plus 1 mm.**

2. **Run the freshly cut edge through the jointer until it's at its final width.**

   Set the jointer to take off 1 mm or less and take only one or two passes off the edge to get your final width.

3. **Plane the board to its final thickness.**

4. **Crosscut a square edge on one end of the board.**

5. **Cut the board to length, measuring from the freshly squared end (the total length includes any tenons or other joints).**

6. **Cut out any mortises, tenons, or other joints.**

7. **Cut any curves or other shaping.**

   Do all shaping, such as rounding over the edge of a board, after all the joinery is done so that you don't lose any straight-line references that you need at various machines against fences, jigs, and so on.

After you mill all your parts, go over them with a random orbital sander and sand them smooth using 150-grit sandpaper. Doing so saves loads of time later on and makes getting at inside corners easy – because they aren't inside corners yet. Be careful not to sand joint parts, such as tenons; doing so changes how well your joints fit.

Putting It All Together

You can approach the assembly and milling process in several ways. Some people mill everything and then assemble, whereas others prefer to mill a section of the project, assemble it, mill the next section and assemble it, and so on. We usually combine the two and mill according to cut type. Depending on the size of the overall project, we sometimes assemble in sections. As you do more projects, you find the method that works best for you.

Preparing for assembly

After you mill all the parts (or at least those parts for the section you're working on), the next step is to lay those parts out on your workbench. Doing so helps you confirm that you have all the parts that you need and visualise the assembly process. As you lay out the parts, double-check your materials list and your measured drawing to see that you have everything and that all the parts are milled properly.

Next, get all your assembly materials ready:

- **Clamps:** Bring all the clamps you think you'll need (plus a couple extra, just in case) to your bench and put them within easy reach.

- **Damp rag and dull chisel:** You use these tools to remove any extra glue that squeezes out of the joints when you add the clamps.

- **Glue and glue brush:** You can't glue without glue! When you use wood glue (see Chapter 2), always use an acid brush (a small, metal-handled brush) to apply it. The acid brush helps you achieve an even coat, and it's small enough to get into mortises and other joints.

- **Rubber mallet:** This tool enables you to tap any joint into place and to make adjustments to the square of the piece, if necessary.

- **Straightedge:** When you glue boards edge to edge (a tabletop, for example), a straightedge enables you to see whether your assembly is flat.

- **Tape measure:** This tool enables you to check that your work is correct when it's glued.

Before you start, make sure that your work area is clean and free of clutter. Gluing a project is nerve-racking, and you don't want to trip over a tool or board while you're working. We also recommend keeping all other parts of the project away from your assembly area until you need them. Doing so eliminates any possible confusion as you work and keeps you from accidentally gluing up the wrong parts.

Book IV

Carpentry, Woodworking, and Flooring

Dry-fitting

After you apply the glue to your parts, you have only a few minutes (about five to ten with white or yellow carpenter's glue) to get everything to fit properly. Because of this time limit and the stress that you'll undoubtedly feel as a result, we highly recommend that you do a dry-fit and run through the glue-up process before you break out the glue.

Walk yourself through the process of assembling the parts in front of you by putting each of the joints together, applying the clamps, and checking for square (follow the steps in the ensuing sections). Doing so ensures that all the parts fit like they're supposed to and that you have a clear idea of what steps are involved in putting the joints together.

Time yourself as you dry-fit the parts. If it takes you more than 10 or 15 minutes, consider breaking the assembly down into several smaller assemblies that you can glue together in stages. Or at least plan on applying the glue in stages so that each joint is put together before the glue starts to set.

When you're comfortable with the process, disassemble everything, take a few breaths, and break out the glue.

Applying the glue

If you've done a dry-fit of your parts, you just need to redo the process, this time using glue as you go. You shouldn't encounter any surprises along the way. Remember that when you work with the glue, you have only a little time to get everything to fit back together again. (For more on applying adhesives, see Chapter 2.)

Here are some other hints to consider when you glue up your parts:

- **Don't use too much glue.** People often use too much when they first start out. A thin coat is all you need on each part of a joint.

- **When gluing veneers, apply glue only to the backing material and not to the veneer itself, or the veneer will curl and become difficult to work with.**

- **After you assemble a joint, push (or tap with a mallet) or clamp the joint fully in place; otherwise, the joint may lock up partway.** This step is especially important with tight-fitting mortise-and-tenon joints. When joints are wet with glue, the wood swells and the joints require more clamp pressure to assemble.

- **Don't panic.** Yes, gluing can be stressful, but if you panic, you end up with a partially assembled piece and are likely to have to start again (which is why dry-fitting is so important).

Clamping

The trick to clamping is to apply just enough pressure to pull the joints tightly together, but not so much that you squeeze all the glue out. Clamps hold the joints together until the glue has a chance to dry.

Here are some other things to consider when clamping:

- **Make sure that your clamps are perpendicular to the workpiece and not angling off one way or another.** This precaution is especially important when doing edge-to-edge joints because angled clamps can pull the boards out of alignment.
- **Don't apply so much pressure that you warp the workpiece.**
- **Make sure that your clamps are centred on the board, applying even pressure.** If your clamps aren't centred, they may warp the workpiece. Ideally, clamp pressure should be applied down the centreline of the joint.
- **If you think that you need to use an additional clamp, use it.** You can never have too many clamps (within reason, of course).

Squaring up the parts and verifying flatness

After you've glued and clamped everything properly, you need to make sure that all your parts are flat and square.

When you edge-glue a load of boards into a tabletop, you want to make sure that those boards remain flat. If you did a good job creating perfectly straight and square edges on each board, the boards will want to lay flat. The only trouble you may have is with too much clamp pressure or an uneven benchtop.

 To check for flatness, run your straightedge against the top of the boards. If you see light through the straightedge as it passes over the boards, they aren't flat. To straighten, adjust the clamps. If edges are sticking up, you may need to tap them down with a mallet.

To check that your assembled parts are square (they have 90-degree corners), you need a tape measure. This simple process involves the following steps:

1. **Measure diagonally from the upper right to the lower left corner and from the upper left to the lower right corner.**

   If these numbers match, you're square. If not, you need to square up by moving on to Step 2.

Book IV

Carpentry, Woodworking, and Flooring

2. **Gently push the upper corner of the measurement that was longer than the other towards that other corner.**

   If this manoeuvre doesn't work (it often doesn't), move on to Step 3.

3. **Take another clamp and run it diagonally from the corners that have the longer measurement and tighten the clamp until both diagonal measurements are equal.**

Cleaning up your mess

Cleaning up is our least favourite part of the assembly process – and we're sure we're not alone. After all the stress of getting everything to fit properly, all we want to do is sit back and admire our work . . . or grab a beer. But trust us when we say this: A little work now saves you loads of work later.

Glue is much easier to remove when wet. To clean up glue spills and seepage, follow these steps:

1. **Use a dull chisel or a scraper to gently scrape off the beads of glue that formed around the joints.**

   Go with the grain and be careful not to gouge the wood.

2. **Take a damp (not wet) cloth and rub around all the joints until you're down to bare wood.**

   Depending on how much glue spillage you have to deal with, you may need to rinse out your rag. We usually keep two rags available.

   Don't forget to clean up the bottoms of drawers and tabletops (or anywhere that you can't see easily).

3. **Double-check that all the joints are completely clean before you quit.**

Letting it sit

We like to assemble at the end of the day so that we're not tempted to take the clamps off too soon. We always let the assembled parts sit in the clamps overnight before we try to remove them. Doing so minimises any chance that the glue hasn't cured enough before we remove the pressure.

Chapter 4

Finishing Wood

A woodworking project isn't complete without the finish. This chapter helps you make this often-hated process (trust us, we're being nice here) of sanding and finishing into a chore that you'll love (well, maybe just tolerate). The chapter explores the frequently short-shrifted process of filling and sanding wood smooth, shows you how to add colour to your projects, and demystifies the topcoat process. You discover the best type of finish for your project and go through the steps of applying it for best results.

Filling Holes and Cracks

Even though you may have tried to use wood without any cracks, splits, holes, or gouges, sometimes you end up with imperfections you didn't notice or couldn't avoid. And sometimes these imperfections result from a misplaced chisel or other accident while making the piece. For most types of furniture, you want to get rid of any problems before you do the final sanding. This section shows you how to fill both small and large defects as well as raise dents without hassle.

Fixing small imperfections

You can fill cracks, scratches, or even slightly mismatched joints with several different products, including wood putty, wax sticks, and shellac sticks. Each of these items has its strengths and weaknesses:

- **Wood putty:** Wood putty comes as a thick paste that you spread into the hole or crack with a putty knife and then let dry and sand flush. It's available in a variety of colours, so you're sure to find one to match the wood you're working with. If you can't find a match, either add some stain to the putty while it's still soft (before you apply it) or paint on some artist's paint to match the wood's surface after you sand it.

- **Wax sticks:** Wax sticks are like crayons, only harder. They come in various colours to match different woods. You have essentially two opportunities to use a wax stick: Before you apply the final finish and afterwards. If you use it before applying the final finish, you need to seal the wood with shellac first. This step isn't necessary when you use a wax stick after applying the final finish because the finish seals the wood.

  To apply a wax stick, simply draw it on by pressing it into the defect with the tip of the wax stick, a putty knife, or your finger and then remove the excess with a putty knife or piece of plastic.

  We don't use wax sticks unless we put a wax finish on the piece, which we don't do often. Find out why in the section 'Protecting Your Work with a Topcoat', later in this chapter.

- **Shellac sticks:** Shellac sticks come in loads of colours, look good, and are easy to apply. Shellac is a natural, low-toxic product made from beetle excretions that you melt with a soldering iron and let drip into the surface imperfection. You then press it in with a putty knife or chisel and wait for it to harden. After the shellac is hard, you scrape it flush with a chisel or thin cabinet scraper and then sand it lightly with fine sandpaper.

- **Glue and sawdust:** On occasion, we've been known to use a mixture of wood glue and sawdust to fill a hole or crack in a project. Doing so allows us to match the wood we're working with exactly because we use sawdust that we created while milling the boards for the project. This low-tech solution requires just the right amount of glue and sawdust to get a filler that's both durable and stains well (not hard to do – it just takes some experimentation).

Dealing with big holes

If you have big holes – from using recycled wood or from a loose knot, for instance – you can fill them with another piece of wood, called a *dutchman*. This technique has been around as long as people have been working with wood. Some purists cringe at the thought of using wood that has a blemish large enough to require a dutchman, but in the American Southwest, where using recycled wood raises the value of furniture, dutchmen are common. Whether or not you like the rustic look, you should know how to make a dutchman. The procedure is pretty simple, and it's made even simpler with a plunge router, a 3 mm straight-cutting bit, and two collars: one 8 mm and the other 14 mm. You can buy kits that contain these parts at most woodworking tool suppliers – they're called inlay kits or inlay bushing bit with removable collar. Here's the process you follow with this setup:

1. **Make a template of the dutchman out of 6 mm plywood or hardboard.**

   Measure the size of the defect in your project and add a little extra around it – about 10 mm or so on all sides. Cut out a hole in the template material to this size. Be sure to use a large enough piece so that you can clamp this piece to the wood you want to work with and have enough room for the plunge router to move freely in the template. We recommend a piece at least 300 mm square.

2. **Attach the 8 mm collar to the base of your plunge router, followed by the 14 mm collar.**

3. **Insert the bit into the plunge router and set the depth of cut to 3 mm.**

4. **Clamp the template onto the board with the defect, making sure that the hole in the template is over the defect.**

5. **Run your plunge router clockwise along the inside edge of the template.**

6. **Carefully route or chisel out the remaining material in the centre of the template.**

7. **Remove the outer collar (the 14 mm one) and lower the depth of cut to 4 mm.**

8. **Select a piece of wood that has a similar colour and grain pattern to the wood where the defect was and clamp the template onto it.**

9. **Route around the edge of the template in a clockwise direction.**

   Be sure to keep tight to the edge of the template; otherwise, you'll cut into the dutchman itself.

10. **Remove the dutchman from the scrap wood by setting your table saw to cut 3 mm into the board.**

    If you use 18 mm stock, set the rip fence 15 mm from the side of the blade farthest from the rip fence (if your blade has a kerf of 3 mm, the rip fence is 12 mm from the side of the blade closest to the rip fence).

11. **Set the depth of cut in the table saw so that it's higher than the dutchman on the board.**

12. **With the dutchman facing out, run the board through the saw.**

    The dutchman will fall out of the board as you run it through.

13. **Apply glue to the underside of the dutchman and a little to the receiving groove and then press it into place.**

    You may need to tap it lightly with a mallet. Use a scrap piece of wood of the same species to tap against. Doing so will keep you from damaging the wood. The dutchman will stick up 0.5 mm from the surface of the wood.

14. **Sand the dutchman flush after the glue dries.**

Raising dents

If your unfinished wood has a dent, you don't need to fill it with putty or any other substance. All you have to do is place a damp cloth over the dent and cover it with a hot iron for a few seconds. The steam from the cloth will seep into the pores of the wood and lift the surface. Then all you have to do is sand the surface smooth. Pretty simple, huh?

Smoothing Out Wood

After you've removed the major defects from your wood project (see the prior 'Filling Holes and Cracks' section for instructions), you need to smooth out the fillers and get rid of the minor scratches and milling marks. Then it's time to make the surface smooth enough for the finish you want to apply. This part of the process involves using sandpaper or a scraper. We cover both approaches in this section.

Sanding

Nearly all woodworkers sand to smooth the surfaces of their projects before finishing. This process isn't rocket science – all it takes are some simple steps and lots of patience. If you don't get a finish you like, you simply didn't spend enough time sanding.

The process of sanding wood involves making progressively finer scratches in the surface. These scratches remove imperfections in the wood, such as visible scratches or uneven surfaces. Moving gradually, level by level from a coarse grit to a finer one, reduces the size of the scratches until they're so small that the wood seems smooth. Never skip a grit (see the section on grits below) of paper when sanding – doing so makes it difficult to remove scratches that the previous grade of sandpaper would've removed easily, and you spend a lot more time trying to get a smooth finish.

Sandpaper comes in a variety of types, including glass, garnet, aluminium oxide, and silicon carbide. Each type has its benefits, but we generally use aluminium oxide, which is excellent for almost all woodworking tasks. Aluminium oxide lasts a relatively long time and is able to sand all types of wood effectively. Steer clear of cheapie yellow glass paper, which breaks down too quickly. For sanding metal and for wet-sanding, an oil finish (see the section 'Protecting Your Work with a Topcoat', later in this chapter), look for black silicon carbide paper.

Getting into grits

Sandpaper comes in differing levels of abrasiveness, called grit. Grit refers to the number and size of the particles in the sandpaper. The fewer and larger the particles, the rougher the paper. Grits range from 40 to 600 – the lower numbers are for rougher papers. We generally use 80- to 320-grit papers unless we're doing wet-dry work with silicon carbide paper. In this case, we may go up to 600-grit for oil finishes.

Aside from the number rating of sandpaper grits, you have general categories:

- **Very coarse:** 40- and 60-grit papers.
- **Coarse:** 80- and 100-grit papers. This paper gets rid of scratches and other surface imperfections.
- **Medium:** 120-, 150-, and 180-grit papers. Medium is where you do most of your sanding.
- **Fine:** 220- to 280-grit papers. Fine paper is for final sanding.
- **Very fine:** From 320- to 600-grit papers. Only use this sandpaper occasionally.

Sand thoroughly with each grit of paper before moving on to the next finer grit. Determining when you've done enough sanding with one grit can be difficult until you gain some experience, so we recommend that you sand a few minutes longer than you think you need to with each grit of paper.

Trying your hand at sanding

Our regular sanding procedure consists of removing major surface defects with a belt sander, followed by smoothing with a random orbit sander, and then finishing off with a final hand sanding.

Follow these suggestions for a better and easier job of hand sanding:

- Wrap the paper around a block of wood to provide a flat, solid backing. If you hold the paper in your hand and press with your fingers, you don't get a flat, even surface, and your hand gets tired much faster.

Book IV

Carpentry, Woodworking, and Flooring

✔ When sanding irregular-shaped surfaces, such as mouldings, use a con-toured block in the same shape as the surface you're sanding. Make a block yourself by using a round dowel, for instance, on rounded sec-tions or buy sanding blocks in a variety of shapes and sizes.

✔ Tear full sheets of sandpaper into halves or quarters to make working with it easier.

✔ Clean the sandpaper when it gets clogged. Simply tapping the paper with your hand removes some of the accumulated dust. Blowing on the paper or spraying it with compressed air also does the trick.

✔ If the paper remains clogged after you try to clean it, don't hesitate to get a new sheet. Sanding with dull or clogged paper is a recipe for frustration.

✔ Follow the sanding guidelines for the type of finish you intend to apply. Some finishes, such as oils, work best with a finely sanded finish (320-grit, for example), but others, such as polyurethanes, can handle a rougher finish (150-grit). Do your homework (the section 'Protecting Your Work with a Topcoat' helps you out here) and decide what type of finish you want to use before doing any final sanding.

Scraping

Some woodworkers prefer a scraper to sandpaper. A scraper is simply a piece of metal with an edge on it that you scrape along the surface of the wood to smooth it out. When we use a scraper, we do the rough sanding work with a belt sander (if necessary) and random orbit sander up to about a 120-grit paper. From there, we use the scraper to smooth the wood.

Other people prefer to use a scraper instead of sanders. If you choose this route and your wood has major defects, you either need to use a hand plane or a thick cabinet scraper (heavy-duty scraper) to remove the defects before you move on to a regular (lighter-duty) scraper.

A scraper is a good choice for projects with oil finishes because it opens the pores of the wood and enables the oils to penetrate deeper, which gives the illusion of more depth to the final finish. A scraper isn't a good choice for fin-ishes that are designed to sit on the top of the wood, such as polyurethanes.

Adding Colour with Stains and Paints

Most people think wood looks better after it develops a patina. Patinas develop through a process called oxidation, creating a colour that's darker than the raw, freshly sanded wood that your project has right after you finish building it. Woodworkers often use stains to give the effect of an aged patina right from the start or to give less expensive wood the look of a more expensive one. Sometimes, they use stains to even out colour differences. Woodworkers use paints, on the other hand, to give colour to less-than-beautiful wood.

This section goes over the ins and outs of adding colour to your creations. From stains to paints, dyes to oxidisers, you find out how to choose the best approach for the type of wood you're working with. We also show you how to apply these different products for the best results.

Adding colouring agents such as stains, dyes, or paints requires you to sand the wood smooth and know in advance the type of topcoat you intend to use.

Wood stains come in several configurations, including pigments, dyes, and combinations of both. Likewise, you can find stains with an oil base, water base, or lacquer base. This section lays out all the options for you.

Use a knotting compound to seal any knots in timber, particularly soft woods, before the wood receives any form of treatment.

Pigment stains

Pigment stains use minerals to create colour. These stains don't actually change the colour of the wood; they simply add a colour by distributing these minerals into the wood's pores. The minerals are suspended in mineral spirit, water, or lacquer thinner (called carriers), and a component called the binder seals them into the pores.

Pigment stains are good for wood that has consistent pores, such as oak or ash, where you want to accentuate the grain patterns. They aren't the best choice when you want to even out colour changes, such as the contrast between the heartwood (the darker-coloured stuff) and sapwood (the lighter-coloured wood) in cherry. Because of this tendency, many pigment stains contain dyes to even out the distribution of colour and reduce blotchiness, making them useful for more types of wood.

Choosing stains

Pigment stains come in a large variety of colours, so you're sure to find one that fills your needs. After you pick the colour, you need to decide what delivery medium to use: water, oil, or gel:

 ✔ **Water:** We really like water-based stains because they're non-toxic, easy to clean up, compatible with a variety of topcoats, and can be layered to get just the right amount of colour.

Book IV

Carpentry, Woodworking, and Flooring

The only real disadvantage to water-based stains is that they tend to raise the grain (meaning that the grain swells slightly from the water, creating a rough texture). You need to lightly sand the stained wood after the first coat. Just make sure not to sand too much: All you want to do is take the hairs off the wood.

✔ **Oil:** Oil-based stains were the old standby, but because of their toxicity and the improvements in water-based products, the days of oil-based stains are coming to an end. Oil-based stains have only one advantage over water-based ones: Because their drying time is longer, you have more time to work with the stain, which can be helpful for beginners. Nonetheless, we don't recommend oil-based stains unless you're restoring furniture and you need to match an existing oil-based finish.

✔ **Gel:** A gel stain is really an oil-based stain, but it acts so differently that we think it merits its own category. Gel stains are handy for non-horizontal surfaces and for tricky parts like turned legs because they're thicker than other stains, reducing the amount of dripping. Gel stains also tend to lessen the blotchy appearance of some woods because they don't soak into the wood.

The main drawback with gel stains is that they're somewhat expensive and you don't find quite as many colour choices. Gel stains are oil-based, so they're smelly and messy compared to water-based varieties. Still, gel stains can be a good choice, especially for blotch-prone wood like birch.

Applying stains

You can apply stain with a brush, but we prefer to use a rag. A rag allows for better control of drips, and you get to feel the wood as you work, which helps you control the coverage. We always wear latex gloves when we use the rag approach because it can get pretty messy. Oil-based stains are toxic, so protecting your skin from contact with these finishes is important.

Before you put on a stain, seal the wood with a wood sealer or a diluted version of your topcoat. This seal keeps the stain from creating a blotchy appearance on the wood. Choose a sealer based on the stain and topcoat you intend to use. The manufacturer's recommendations are on the stain's label.

Putting stain on is pretty easy: Just wipe it on in the direction of the grain, wait a few minutes, and wipe off the excess. For a darker colour, you may need to apply additional coats (we find that two coats are generally adequate). If you use more than one coat, wait until each coat is dry before you add another. The drying time depends on humidity, temperature, and the type of stain you use. Check your stain container to see what it recommends.

Cleaning up

Clean-up procedures vary depending on the type of stain you use. Take a look at the main differences:

- **Water-based stains clean up with water.** Easy clean-up is the main reason people prefer this type of stain. Just toss the rag you used to apply the stain in the bin, wash your hands with soap and water, and wipe up any spills with a wet rag or towel.

- **Oil-based stains require more work to clean up.** You need to use white spirit to remove drips or spills and any stain that got on your hands. You need to dispose of the used rag carefully so that it doesn't become a fire hazard. We usually lay it out to dry on a brick or cement floor and then put it in a covered metal bin.

Dyes

Dyes actually change the colour of wood. One of the nice characteristics of dyes is that they go on more evenly than pigments. We really like to use dyes for cherry if we end up having to use a board with sapwood (lighter-coloured wood) in it because the dye evens out the difference in colour between the darker heartwood and the lighter sapwood.

Dyes stain whatever they touch. Soap and water don't remove dye – only time does. So we highly recommend that you wear latex gloves whenever you work with this stuff and wear clothes that you don't mind ruining. Also, some dye colours are toxic in powder or dissolved form. Read the product labels to determine what precautions you need to take.

Although dyes are available that dissolve in oil, lacquer thinner, and alcohol, we're big fans of water-soluble dyes for woodworking. You can usually buy these dyes as powder that you mix with hot water and stir until it dissolves. Water-soluble dyes come in a staggering variety of colours, and you can mix them as desired to get just the right colour. You won't find powdered dyes at your local DIY centre; get them from a speciality woodworking shop.

You apply dyes with a rag, but unlike pigment stains, you don't need to wipe off the excess. Just wipe the dye on, being careful to apply it evenly with the grain and keep a wet edge (don't apply wet dye over a portion that has dried).

Dyes benefit from having a sanding sealer applied to the wood first. Wood sealed with sanding sealer takes dye more evenly and looks much better.

Book IV

Carpentry, Woodworking, and Flooring

You can dispose of the rags you use to apply dye in the bin, and you don't have to worry about toxic smells or flammability issues. If you use a dye that dissolves in white spirit, lacquer thinner, or alcohol, you need to take the necessary precautions for these products. See the 'Pigment stains' section earlier in this chapter.

Paints

Paint is a good choice if you want to hide a less-than-beautiful wood or you want the look of a solid colour. Paints come in several varieties:

- **Oil-based:** Oil-based paints used to be the professional's choice because they go on smooth and flatten out well. Their main problem, however, is that they're toxic. Because of the vast improvements in water-based paints in the last few decades, we don't use oil-based paints any longer.

- **Water-based (latex):** For brushed-on paint, latex is our choice. Water-based latex paint goes on almost as well as oil-based paint and is non-toxic. You won't have trouble finding just the right colour.

- **Lacquer:** If you want a professional look, you can't go wrong with a lacquer. You spray lacquers on in thin coats, and they dry so fast that dust has no time to land on the wet finish. You can often spray the next coat as soon as you're done with the first.

  The main drawback to painting with lacquer is that you need special equipment, such as an air compressor and spray gun, and getting a feel for spraying the paint takes some time. After you have the stuff and figure out how to spray well, though, we're willing to bet that you won't touch a paintbrush again (at least not for putting on paint).

 The number one tip to remember when applying paint is that you need a primer coat in order to get professional-looking results. Some people skip the primer and just put on two coats of paint, but please resist this temptation. You get a much better finish if you use primer. Make sure to choose a primer that's compatible with your paint. We usually choose primer from the same company that makes the paint we're using.

After you have a good (and dry) primer coat on your wood, brush on the paint. If you use a water-based primer, lightly sand the wood with 320-grit paper to smooth the grain. When brushing, use long, smooth strokes and don't put too much paint on the brush.

 If you're using a paint sprayer, the key is to keep the sprayer moving parallel to the wood's surface and apply several thin coats rather than one thick one. Doing so reduces runs and drips.

Paint clean-up follows the same guidelines as any other finish material. Oil-based products need white spirit, lacquers need lacquer thinner, and water-based products clean up with water.

Brushes and sprayers need a good cleaning with the proper solvent followed by a soap and water wash to keep them in good condition. Make sure that you dispose of your rags properly. Oil-based products need to go into metal containers after you leave them out to dry in a safe, non-flammable place.

Protecting Your Work with a Topcoat

After all your hard work milling the wood, assembling the parts, repairing defects, smoothing the wood, and getting the colour you want, you're finally ready to put on the protective layer. A topcoat is essential to maintain the piece's beauty and structure; it also protects your work from spills and from natural seasonal moisture changes that cause wood to expand and contract. Without the protection of a topcoat, wood is more susceptible to warping and cracking. A topcoat also improves the look of the wood by adding depth and colour.

This section goes over the most common topcoat options and weighs the pros and cons of each to help you make an informed choice about what to put on your work. We also walk you through the process of preparing your wood, applying the topcoat, and cleaning up the mess when you're done.

Shellac

Shellac is one of the oldest and most loved topcoats. This product gives wood a rich, deep finish, is easy to apply and repair, and is non-toxic. Shellac is a natural product made from – get this – beetle secretions. Before you turn green, we have to tell you that you've probably encountered shellac many times before. In fact, we're sure you've probably even eaten shellac before. Shellac is used to coat pills and vegetables, among other things. We say this to let you know just how safe this stuff is. Shellac is our preferred finish for toys, for example.

Shellac's main drawback is that it doesn't hold up to liquids, heat, or scratches very well. You can minimise this problem by using a dewaxed shellac and putting a layer of varnish or wax over the top. Of course, doing so reduces your ability to repair the shellac surface easily.

You can buy shellac as flakes or premixed with alcohol. The premixed varieties have a shelf life of about six months (one company claims to make a

Book IV

Carpentry, Woodworking, and Flooring

premixed shellac that lasts years), but most flakes last indefinitely. We recommend that you buy flakes and mix it yourself. You not only get a longer shelf life, but you also can make the shellac the consistency you want.

Shellac comes in many varieties: blond, white, garnet, lemon, buttonlac, and orange, to name a few. Each has a different colour, so you can often skip the stain when using shellac.

Preparing shellac

If you buy shellac already mixed, you don't have to do anything to prepare it. If you buy flakes, you need to mix it with denatured alcohol (methylated spirit). The ratio of shellac to alcohol, called the cut, refers to how many kilograms of flakes are mixed with litres of alcohol. For most topcoats, a 1-kilo mix is good (1 kilo of shellac flakes to 5 litres of alcohol). For sealing wood, a ¼- to ½ kilo mix is good (the ¼ kilo mix goes on easier).

To prepare a wood surface for shellac, sand the project really well, going all the way up to 320-grit paper. Shellac sits on the surface of the wood and doesn't hide sanding scratches – in fact, it seems to accentuate them!

If you take your time and do a good job of sanding, you'll love the look you get from a few coats of shellac. If you skimp on the sanding, however, you're going to be disappointed with the final finish. After you finish sanding, remove all the dust from the surface by wiping with a cotton cloth dampened with white spirit and then wipe the surface with a lint-free rag dampened with alcohol.

Applying shellac

You can apply shellac in numerous ways: You can spray shellac on or apply it with a cloth, brush, or rubbing pad made up of a wad of wool wrapped in a linen cloth.

Shellac is somewhat tricky to apply because it dries so quickly. If you're new to using shellac, mix it in a ½-kilo cut (½-kilo shellac flakes to 5 litres alcohol). This cut makes the shellac easier to brush on and reduces brush marks. If your shellac dries too fast, you can add shellac retardant to slow the drying process.

To apply shellac with a brush, get the finest brush you can find. Use a natural bristle brush called a fitch brush, which is made with polecat or badger hair. Apply the finish by following these steps:

1. **Dip the brush halfway into the shellac and lightly press it into the side of the container to remove excess finish.**

2. **Start a centimetre or two from the edge of the wood and lightly drag the brush to the edge, reverse directions, and go all the way to the other edge, gently lifting your brush as you reach the edge.**

3. **Make another stroke next to this one with a small overlap of about 5 mm.**

4. **Repeat until you cover the entire surface.**

5. **Shellac the edges, repeating Steps 1 to 3.**

6. **Let the piece dry for at least an hour, and then lightly sand it with 320-grit paper.**

   Make sure to clean or change the paper when it gets clogged, which happens fairly quickly.

7. **Rub the finish with #0000 steel wool.**

8. **Wipe the surface clean with a lint-free rag.**

9. **Apply a second coat of shellac and let it dry overnight.**

10. **Start the next day by sanding this coat with 320-grit paper and follow it with the #0000 steel wool.**

11. **Wipe the piece clean with a lint-free rag.**

12. **Repeat Steps 9 to 11 until your piece has four or five coats of shellac.**

13. **Rub the piece with #0000 steel wool to get the sheen you want.**

Cleaning up

One of the great characteristics of shellac is ease of clean-up. Alcohol dissolves the shellac again, so if you find any misplaced shellac, use methylated spirit on a rag to remove it. For cleaning brushes, put alcohol in a small container and swish your brushes around in it until they're clean. Afterwards, simply wash the brush with mild soap and water.

Oil

Oil finishes, such as tung oil, Danish oil, teak oil, and linseed oil, are fast and easy to apply, but making them look really good takes time – and many coats. With the exception of Danish oil, which has some hardeners and varnishes in it, they don't protect very well against moisture.

Oils penetrate the pores of the wood. For this reason, oils don't give you the polished look that you can achieve with shellac or varnish. Also, you need to refresh oil finishes as the finish wears by adding additional coats. Oils do impart a rich, almost antiqued look to wood, though, which is why many people use them.

Because oils don't build up on the surface of wood, the wood itself must be perfect for oils to look great. This means that you need to sand meticulously with up to 320-grit sandpaper. You almost want the wood to shine on its own

Book IV

Carpentry, Woodworking, and Flooring

before you put the oil on. After you get the surface perfectly smooth, wipe it down with a rag dampened with white spirit to remove the dust and sanding residue.

Application is the easy part of oil finishes. Follow these simple steps:

1. **Put on a pair of latex gloves to protect your hands.**

2. **Using a lint-free cloth, generously wipe the oil onto the wood.**

3. **Let the piece stand for five or ten minutes.**

4. **Lightly sand with 600-grit wet/dry sandpaper.**

   This step isn't necessary for some oils, such as salad bowl oil. You need to do it only on the first one or two coats.

5. **Wipe off the excess and let it dry for 24 hours.**

6. **Buff the piece with a soft cloth.**

7. **Repeat these steps until you have four or five coats, skipping Step 4 after the second coat.**

8. **Buff the final coat with a soft cloth until you get the gloss you want.**

When using oil, watch the wood for weeping (releasing from the pores of the wood). Some woods, such as cherry, ooze out oil for a while. If you don't wipe the oil from the surface before it dries, you need to sand it off before adding another coat. This is a real pain. You may need to wipe the oozing oil a few times, so after applying the first coat, don't go anywhere until the wood has stopped weeping.

Cleaning up after using oil is as simple as disposing of the used rags and washing your hands. Use white spirit to get any oil off your hands, then wash with mild soap and water and apply hand lotion (the white spirit will dry your hands). If you spill or drip any oil, use white spirit to clean it up. Lay the rags flat until they dry completely and then put them in a metal container.

Oil-soaked rags are flammable: In fact, they're so flammable that they've been known to spontaneously combust. Don't put these rags in a bin with other stuff until they're completely dry. The only other safe way to deal with oil-soaked rags is to put them in a metal container filled with water until you can dispose of them properly.

Wax

Wax is another easy-to-use, age-old finish. Like shellac and varnish, wax lies on top of the wood, and you can build it up by applying several thin layers. Wax adds a nice patina (wood's natural oxidation process that produces a darker, rich colour) to wood and can be purchased with colouring agents to add more colour to the piece.

We don't like to use wax as a primary finish; instead, we add it to varnished or shellacked wood. Wax is very delicate – just put a glass of water on it and you get an instant ring. To us, the beauty of wax is as a final topcoat buffed to a nice gloss. Don't let our lack of enthusiasm for wax deter you from using it, though. You have many good wax products to choose from. Check out your local woodworking shop and we're sure you'll find a product that will provide the results you're looking for.

Most waxes are a blend of beeswax and carnauba wax. The more carnauba wax present, the more durable the finish – but it takes more effort to get it to shine.

Preparing for wax

Because wax is supposed to sit on the surface of the wood, we prefer to seal the wood first. Doing so protects the wood when the wax gets damaged and keeps any oils in the wax from penetrating the wood, which would make removing the wax very difficult. The wood surface under the wax doesn't need as diligent a sanding as it does if you use shellac or oil, but you do need to create a nice smooth surface. You really need to sand only to 220-grit to use wax successfully.

After sanding the wood and cleaning it with a rag dampened in white spirit, we recommend that you seal it with a ¼-kilo cut of shellac – we'd even apply two coats of shellac first. You'll get a better finish, and applying two coats doesn't take that long.

Applying wax

Applying wax is very easy – it's the same as waxing a car. Follow these steps:

1. **Put a liberal amount of wax on a cloth.**

2. **Wipe the wax on the wood using overlapping circular motions until you've covered the entire surface.**

3. **Let the wax dry until a whitish film appears.**

4. **Using a clean, dry cloth, buff the wax until the film disappears and a glossy shine replaces it.**

   Replace the cloths with clean ones as they get dirty.

5. **Keep buffing until you have a hard, shiny surface – you can't buff too much.**

   If you use a power buffer, make sure that you keep the polishing pad moving, or you may melt the wax.

Book IV

Carpentry, Woodworking, and Flooring

6. **Let the wax dry for 24 hours.**

7. **Repeat these steps at least twice, for a minimum of three coats.**

Wax is easy to clean up. A little soap and water gets wax off your hands and rags. If you use old cotton cloths to apply and buff wax, throwing them away is easier than cleaning them.

Varnish and oil-based polyurethane

Varnish, a common finish, comes in many varieties. Traditional varnishes are made of pine resins, but modern varnishes use a variety of solutions that produce a hard, durable surface. The most common type of varnish is polyurethane.

Varnish is the best topcoat for a project that will take a lot of abuse. However, varnish is toxic and hard to clean up, and because it can take a while to dry, you may end up with dust in your finish. However, these problems are becoming less of an issue as new formulas hit the market. Always wear gloves and a respirator when using an oil-based varnish.

Sanding to 150- to 220-grit works well for most varnishes. You don't need to go any smoother. Just make sure to do the best job you can, getting all the imperfections out of the wood. Varnish works best when you apply a sealer coat to the wood first. We don't recommend that you use a special wood sealer; instead, just thin the varnish down 10 or 20 per cent with white spirit and apply it as you would a regular coat.

The surface of the piece should be clear of sanding residue and dust. Clean the surface by wiping a rag dampened with white spirit over all surfaces to be varnished.

Varnish goes on just like paint. Here are the basic steps:

1. **For the first coat, thin the varnish by adding 10 to 20 per cent white spirit.**

2. **Dip the brush into the varnish about a third of the way and press the brush gently against the side of the container to remove excess finish.**

3. **Brush a thin layer on the surface.**

4. **Brush out any lap marks (overlapping brushstrokes) and drips by going over the finish with your slightly dampened brush.**

   Don't worry about getting rid of all the brush marks, only the big ones. The small brush marks will settle before the finish dries.

5. **Let the piece dry for 24 hours.**

6. **Sand the varnish out with 400-grit wet/dry sandpaper.**

   You can use white spirit as a lubricant to make the process easier and to keep the paper from clogging as quickly.

7. **Repeat Steps 2 to 6 until you have four or five coats.**

8. **After the final coat, rub the varnish out with #0000 steel wool to give it the gloss you want.**

Because varnish is solvent-based, you need to use white spirit to clean up. Swish the brush around in a bucket of white spirit to remove the finish. Follow this process up with a mild soap and water rinse and wrap the brush in plastic until you need it again.

For washing hands, white spirit is the only way to go. To avoid the mess, wear disposable gloves and throw them away after you've finished. Use a metal container with a lid on it to reduce the smell.

Water-based polyurethane

If you like the idea of varnish but don't want to put up with the smell and mess of a solvent-based product, a water-based polyurethane may be the solution. Water-based finishes are becoming very common, giving you the best attributes of varnish with the ease and low toxicity of water-based products. However, these finishes look less than sexy. (Okay, we'll admit it – they look like plastic.) Water-based finishes also raise the grain of the wood, so you have to add an extra step when using them.

You prepare for water-based polyurethanes in the same way you prepare for oil-based versions. Sand the surface well with 220-grit paper and wipe it clean. You can use a water-dampened rag to wipe off the sanding dust, but remember that it will raise the grain, which means that you have to sand it lightly again. This leaves some sanding dust, which leads to you wanting to wipe again, and so on. We usually wipe the final sanding with a tack cloth.

Because the grain is going to rise no matter what, we apply a sanding sealer and, after it dries, go over the surface with a 320-grit sandpaper to knock the grain down again. Then we wipe the surface with a dry cloth.

Apply water-based polyurethane by following the same procedure used for oil-based preparations. (See the section 'Varnish and oil-based polyurethane' earlier in this chapter.) The only difference is that some water-based products dry pretty quickly, so you need to stop messing with the finish before

Book IV

Carpentry, Woodworking, and Flooring

it starts to get tacky. Also, we usually don't sand after the first grain-raising coat unless we need to get rid of brush marks or dust specks that have got in the finish. After the final coat (three or four is usually enough), you can either leave it alone or give a rubdown with #0000 steel wool wetted with water if you want less gloss.

Because this product is water-based, clean-up is easy. Just use soap and water.

Book V
Plumbing

"I wonder if Malcolm's finished bleeding the radiators yet?"

In this book . . .

Does a chill goes down your spine when you hear the word *plumbing?* The thought of fixing problems yourself – and preventing them from happening in the first place – is probably not one you entertain often, especially when everything's working well. Plumbing doesn't usually become a priority until you're standing in puddles of murky water wondering what to do next, and then most people's first thought is, 'Where can I find a good plumber?'

This book takes the seemingly complicated world of plumbing and puts it in plain English. We make sense of the mess of pipes running into, out of, and throughout your house. And we give you the power to tackle some plumbing problems yourself – as well as the insight to know when you need a plumber.

Here are the contents of Book V at a glance:

Chapter 1

The Plumbing System in Your Home

In This Chapter

▸ Hiring a plumber vs plumbing yourself

▸ Reading up on water regulations and bylaws

▸ Understanding how water runs through your house

▸ Getting information about your water meter

▸ Figuring out your soil-and-vent pipes

▸ Knowing the importance of shutoff valves

C onsidering the range of plumbing-related replacements and repairs, a do-it-yourselfer can find plenty to do. Plumbing skills are like computer skills: After you know how to format a proposal or generate a spreadsheet, you can do it again and again, although it may have seemed difficult at first. Well, after you unclog a kitchen drain, you can use that skill (and the tools you acquire in the process) many more times. You can then confidently tackle a stopped-up bathroom drain and, before long, become the neighbourhood know-it-all for solving plumbing problems.

Figuring Out When to Do It Yourself

You can figure out how to do most plumbing jobs with a little know-how, an understanding of the rules (water regulations), and some spare time. Some of the easiest plumbing jobs to do yourself – mostly preventive maintenance – are the following:

✔ **Clearing slow-draining sinks and baths:** This task usually involves using a plunger or opening a trap to remove hair, food, or paper. You may need to use a *hand auger* (a stiff wire drain unblocker) to get the proper flow of water through the drain. Bath drains are harder to clean than sink drains, and getting a pop-up drain stopper properly adjusted may take several tries, but you can do it yourself. (Chapter 4 covers a variety of ways to unclog drains.)

✔ **Repairing or replacing leaky valves:** The steady drip-drip-drip of a tap is certainly annoying, but it's a repair that can wait until the weekend so that you have time to get your hands on the correct repair parts before you begin work. (Chapter 6 shows you how.)

If you don't already have shutoff valves (covered later in this chapter) on the water supply pipes under your sink, this is a good time to add them. Future repairs will be much easier when you can shut off the water to individual sinks or appliances. You won't have any questions, such as 'Dad, when can I wash my hair?' when the main water shutoff valve (also discussed later) is closed for plumbing repairs.

✔ **Solving toilet-cistern problems:** Whether the problem is a valve that won't shut off or a ball-float valve that won't seat properly, these repairs can wait until you have the time to work on them (see Chapter 5). But don't wait too long. A small leak can waste a lot of water.

✔ **Maintaining the washing machine:** Don't forget to check the hoses. If they've been in use for several years, change them. Purchase a set of replacement hoses that have a braided reinforced cover to prevent the hoses from bursting. The small extra cost is worth it; if a hose should burst, you'll be calling for help from more pros than just a plumber.

✔ **Preventing winter freezing:** You can prepare for winter by insulating water and drain pipes that are subject to freezing or by attaching trace heating cables Read the directions on the packet: Suggested applications for the cable and its electrical requirements should be described clearly. This prep work may save you from a huge, expensive mess after a sudden sub-zero freeze.

Knowing When to Call a Pro

Don't lull yourself into believing that you'll never need a plumber. If you have a plumbing emergency, you and your family need to know two things:

✔ The location of the main water shutoff valve (see 'Locating Shutoff Valves' later on this chapter)

✔ The name and phone number of a reliable plumbing repair company

In addition to relying on your local plumber for occasional emergencies, the following situations are best left to professionals:

- **Low water pressure throughout the house:** Several factors can cause this problem: Obstructions (rust or debris) in the water lines, which can start at the meter and run all the way to the tap aerators (small strainers on the end of the spigot); low water pressure from the mains supply ; or even poor supply-pipe design. A good plumber knows how to analyse the problem.

- **No hot water:** It's obvious what happened, but unless the hot water tank is leaking, it may take a while to find out why. If the tank is electric, it could be a failed immersion heater element, a tripped circuit breaker or blown fuse, or a faulty thermostat. On gas heaters, thermocouple burners and igniters can fail.

  No one likes to be without hot water for long. Your grandmother may have heated bath water in the kettle, but people don't do it that way today. Call a plumber for this one – he or she is likely to have loads of experience and can tell you if you need a new boiler or if the existing one can be repaired. If the boiler needs to be replaced, your plumber can hook up the new boiler, make sure that it works properly, and dispose of the old one.

  Call a Gas Safe-registered plumber to fix a malfunctioning gas boiler.

- **Waste pipe blockage:** If you've tried all the tricks you know to get your waste pipe to drain properly, yet back-ups continue, you probably have a blockage in the pipe that runs out to the main sewer. (Tree roots are sometimes the cause.) Rather than hire one of the big sewer rodding machines that you may break – or that may damage your sewer – call a plumber or drain-cleaning service. If these professionals get in trouble, they'll make the repairs.

- **Frozen pipes:** If a pipe freezes, close the main water shutoff valve (see Chapter 2) before attempting to thaw the pipe and open a tap nearby. Check carefully to see whether the pipe has already burst or cracked. If it's bad news, you may need a plumber; if it's not, hair dryers and heat guns are the safest ways to thaw a pipe. If you must use a propane torch, do so with great care – old, dry wood (which usually surrounds pipes) catches fire easily. Even if the pipe isn't burst or cracked, you still may want to call a plumber – some plumbers simply replace a section of frozen pipe rather than thaw it.

- **Extensive water pipe damage (usually caused by freezing):** Repairing the problem can take up much of your valuable time – pay a plumber so that you can earn money at your own job.

Finding a plumber at a party

We find that the best place to locate any – including a plumber – is at a neighbourhood party. Why? Because word of mouth is still the best source for a referral that you can get. Who better to work on your house than someone who has worked in your neighbourhood, where the houses are often of the same vintage? (Read that as 'similar plumbing systems'.)

Working Out a Plumbing Contract

Just as important as finding the right plumber to do the job is having a clear written agreement with the plumber before any work begins. The agreement doesn't have to be complicated, but it should contain some basic points. A contract with a plumber to repair, replace, or install a fixture should include the following:

- A description of the work to be completed
- A detailed list of the materials (brand name, style, colour, or other specifications of the exact materials) to be used
- The cost of materials and a list of all warranties that the manufacturer provides for any fixtures
- The cost of labour
- The job installation date
- The amount of deposit, if required

Understanding Building Regulations, Water Regulations, and Bylaws

Building regulations are guidelines created to ensure the safety and building standards of new and remodelled buildings. These regulations cover all the components of a building, including its plumbing pipes, by specifying the minimum standards for materials and methods used. Building regulations work hand in hand with water regulations and bylaws to guarantee that good workmanship is performed and quality materials are used.

The most important things for a do-it-yourselfer to know about building and plumbing regulations are that they exist, that they're important, and that they must be followed when repairing, remodelling, or building a home. A homeowner cannot possibly know all the interpretations of these rules, but building inspectors and qualified plumbers can provide the answers.

Book V

Plumbing

We can't possibly include all the rules in this book, so it's up to you to find out what the rules are where you live so that you don't make any errors. Before you plan any plumbing job, first check the local water regulations to make sure that you know the requirements. You can get a copy of your local water regulations from your local authority: Go to the town hall or your local council offices and find the Building Control department. You may find that this document is filled with technical jargon, so consider having a discussion with the building inspector in which you explain your project. In most cases, he or she will be able to give you the necessary advice to keep you on the right side of the regulations.

A River Runs through It

Before you begin fixing leaky taps or unblocking drains, you need to know how water gets from one place to another in your house and understand the basic plumbing system of a home, including the water meter (if you have one) and the stop valve, not to mention the soil-and-vent pipes (SVPs) – toss that acronym around among your mates and feel like a real pro!

In addition, you need to work out the location of the main shutoff valve and the many other valves that are a part of your home's plumbing system. These valves enable you to turn off the water supply to the particular fixture or appliance that you're working on or having problems with. If you want to replace a basin in the bathroom, for example, you don't have to shut off the water supply to your entire house while you do the repair. Almost all houses have a shutoff valve wherever the main water supply comes into the house, with individual shutoff valves at toilets, sinks, baths, showers, and appliances such as dishwashers and washing machines.

You can easily understand the plumbing system of your house if you keep a few basic facts straight:

- ✔ The skinny pipes bring the water in, and the fat pipes carry it out.
- ✔ Leaks in the skinny pipes or in anything attached to a skinny pipe can flood a house.
- ✔ Leaks in the fat pipes cause your house to stink.

Okay. Plumbing is a little more involved than that, but if you think of your house as having two different water systems – one that brings fresh water in (see Figure 1-1) and another that takes waste water out to a sewer or septic tank system – the maze of pipes throughout your house may start to make some sense.

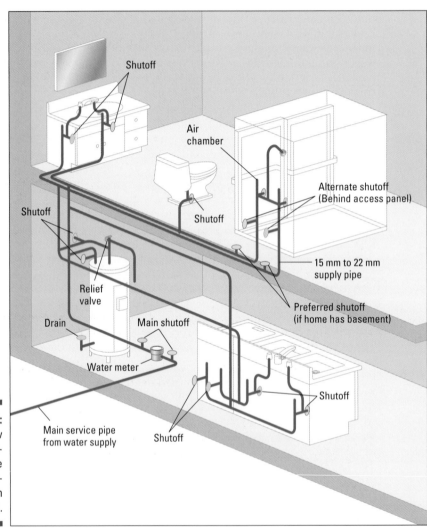

Figure 1-1: An overview of the network of the water supply pipes in a house.

Plumbing really isn't complicated, and modern plumbing materials, such as plastic pipes and fittings (elbows and unions), enable you to tackle home plumbing projects that only a decade ago would have been considered too difficult for do-it-yourselfers. Recognising the growth of the DIY market, manufacturers of plumbing tools, fixtures, and materials are constantly improving their packaging and instructions.

Homeowners are allowed to do plumbing work on their own houses. Of course, regardless of who does the work, it still must meet the local water regulations. So in the section 'Understanding Building Regulations, Water Regulations, and Bylaws', earlier in this chapter, we provide important information about how to make sure that the work that you or the plumber that you hired does passes the regulations.

Getting Water to Your House

Water running through the supplier's water main is carried to your house by a smaller supply pipe that leads underground from the water main into your house. The water typically passes through three valves and a water meter (if you have one) on its trip to your house.

The valves that help bring water into your house are the following:

- **Screw down cock:** The valve at the supplier's water main that's buried underground, usually under the street, is used to turn off the water from the main to the water company stop valve. You'd have to dig a hole in the street to get to this valve, so this valve is the water company's responsibility.

- **Water company stop valve:** A valve that's under the pavement outside the property boundary. It's buried deep in the ground (760 mm minimum) to prevent freezing – you need a special long-handled wrench to turn this valve on or off. Look around your property and find out where this valve is located (usually just outside the front garden gate, covered with a hinged plastic cover marked 'water'). If you ever face a leak in the supply pipe between the street and your house, this is the valve to turn off. You may not be able to turn it off yourself, but you can show the plumber where it is.

The main shutoff valve or stop cock

After the water passes into your house, it doesn't travel very far before meeting the main shutoff valve, which is also known as the stop cock. This valve is usually on an outside wall in a utility area of the house, or possibly in the cupboard under the kitchen sink. The main shutoff valve allows a full flow of water through the pipe when it's open. Turning off this valve (by turning it clockwise) cuts off the water supply to the entire house.

The main shutoff valve in your house probably has one of two designs (see Figure 1-2):

- **Gate valve:** Gate valves are very reliable and last for years, but they become difficult to turn after not being turned for years. If you haven't closed the main shutoff valve since you moved into your house, do it now. Better to find out that you can't turn it with your bare hands now than to wait until you're standing knee-deep in water.

- **Ball valve:** Houses with plastic or copper main water pipes leading into the house may have a full-flow ball valve. This valve is open when the handle is aligned with the pipe. To close this valve, turn the handle clockwise a ¼ turn so that it's at a right angle to the pipe.

The main valve is the one to stop most plumbing catastrophes, such as a burst pipe. Make sure that everyone in the household knows where this valve is located and knows how to turn it off. Turning the handle clockwise closes the valve. You need to turn the handle several turns to fully close the valve.

After you've closed and opened the valve, it may start to leak a bit around the valve stem. The stem of the valve is held in place with a packing nut. Tighten this nut just enough to stop the leak. Don't overtighten the nut or the valve is difficult to turn again. (If you need a cheat sheet to remember which way to turn the control, use a label or tag with the simple reminder: 'Right = off' with an arrow pointing right, for example.)

Anytime you shut off the water and allow the pipes to drain, unscrew the aerators (small screens) on the ends of all taps before you turn the water back on. Doing so keeps the small particles of scale that may shake loose from inside the pipes from clogging the small holes in these units. See Chapter 6 for more information about unclogging an aerator.

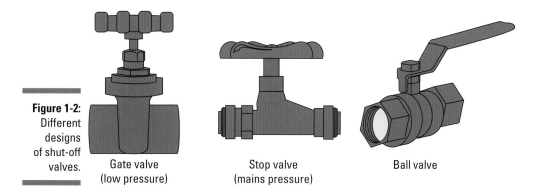

Figure 1-2:
Different
designs
of shut-off
valves.

Gate valve
(low pressure)

Stop valve
(mains pressure)

Ball valve

The water meter

If you wouldn't mind breaking any part of the water supply system, it's probably the water meter. Unfortunately, as water meters begin to fail, they usually run fast and record too much water usage, not the other way around. Besides, if your water meter stops, your local water company simply estimates your water usage to an average.

The water company owns and monitors the meter. Sometimes, the meter is buried in the ground and covered with a pop-up lid; it's usually located near the front or side of the house near the street. It's also possible that the meter may be located inside the house, but most municipal water companies have modified inside meters so that they can be read from the outside. By using plain old arithmetic, computing the difference between last month's reading and this month's reading, the water company can figure out how much water your household has consumed. Sometimes, meter readings are done on an estimated basis; other times, meter readers prowl through your neighbourhood with handheld gizmos into which they input the readings on the meters.

Reading a water meter

Most meters have a cover that opens when the hinged top is raised. The meter has a digital display or round dial that shows the number of litres that have passed through the meter. The statement for a water bill reflects the total number of litres used between the billing periods.

On the monthly or quarterly statement that comes from the water company, you can usually find an explanation of how to read the meter, so you can keep track of water usage yourself. Call your water company and ask for directions if you're not sure how to read your own meter.

By comparing the reading of the water meter over a very short time, you can spot a major leak. If you turn off all the taps (indoor and outdoor), along with any appliances that may use water (such as a dishwasher or washing machine), no water should be flowing through the meter. To check for a major leak, make sure that everything is off and then record the meter reading. Check the meter in a few minutes, and it should read the same. If the dials have moved, you have a leak.

This technique isn't good for a minor leak, such as a dripping tap. Eventually, the meter records the water used, but the amount is so small that it's difficult to notice any meter movement. Don't let the apparent lack of movement in the meter fool you, though. Over time, even a small drip, drip, drip wastes hundreds of litres of water, which is why we devote later chapters in this book to fixing leaks.

Because you pay for water that passes through the meter, any leak past the water meter can cost you big money. If water leaks from the pipes that lead to your house, it doesn't pass through the meter and therefore can't be counted by the water company. Any leak, however, can cause damage to your house.

Figuring Out Your Soil-and-Vent Pipes

The fat pipes in your house make up the soil-and-vent system (also known as the SVP), carrying wastewater to a local authority sewer pipe or your private sewer treatment facility (called a septic tank and leach field, or soakaway).

- ✔ The waste pipes collect the water from sinks, showers, baths, and appliances.
- ✔ The soil pipes remove water and material from the toilet.
- ✔ The vent pipes remove or exhaust sewer gases and allow air to enter the system so that the wastewater flows freely.

The waste pipes are usually made of cast ironor plastic. Local building bylaws that regulate the materials used in the SVP system have changed over the years, so some older homes will have a combination of materials.

A typical bathroom basin is a good example of how all these components work together. You probably haven't spent much time observing the pipes beneath your basin, but take a look and this is what you'll see:

   ✔ Water runs down the basin drain into a P-trap (so called because it's shaped like the letter), which fills up with water to prevent sewer gases and odours from getting into the house through the pipe. This water gets refreshed whenever more water runs through it.

   ✔ A waste pipe attached to the P-trap goes into an opening in the wall.

   ✔ Outside the wall (where you can't see), a waste pipe leads to a soil stack, which is the control centre of the wastewater system. Waste pipes take the wastewater to the soil stack; through the stack, sewer gases are carried up to the roof through vent pipes.

All the taps and water appliances in a house use this same system of drains, pipes, and vents. All the waste pipes have a cleanout or *rodding eye*, which is a Y-shaped fitting that's accessible so that you can clean out any serious obstructions within the system. Figure 1-3 shows a typical system, called a plumbing tree.

Locating Shutoff Valves

The shutoff valve enables you to turn the water to a particular fixture or part of your house on and off. In general, shutoff valves are below or near the source of water. But unless you know where to look, the obvious isn't always so obvious. Take a tour of all these rooms and do some serious snooping around to find the valves in your house.

Barring water from the bathroom

Most bathrooms have shutoff valves that are designed to control the water flow to the toilet, basin, and bath or shower. These fixture shutoff valves are also called isolating valves or stop valves, because they stop the water from getting to the fixture. (Hey, some plumbing terms make sense!) Knowing where each of these valves is located can save you time and energy when you're doing plumbing repairs. We tell you where to find them in the following sections.

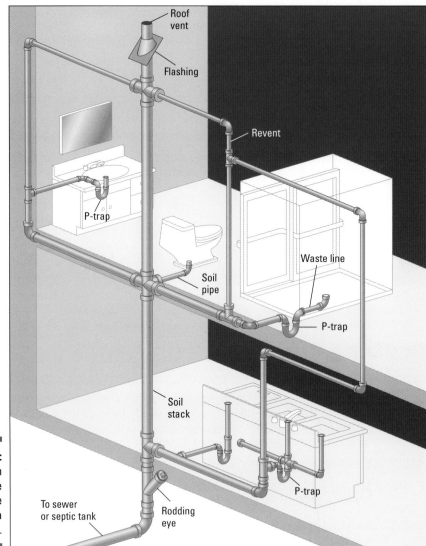

Figure 1-3:
The main parts of the drainage system in a house.

The toilet

The shutoff valve beneath the toilet is one of the more accessible valves; it comes out of the wall or floor and is clearly visible (see Figure 1-4). In fact, you've probably seen this shutoff valve many times without noticing it. Just look for a handle behind your toilet.

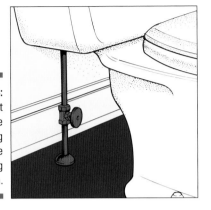

Figure 1-4:
Your toilet may have an isolating valve on the pipe feeding the cistern.

The sink or vanity basin

Your sink has two valves: One for hot water and one for cold (see Figure 1-5). A wall-hung or pedestal sink has shutoff valves that are clearly accessible, but the shutoff valves for a basin in a vanity unit aren't always easy to find or reach. So go on a cleaning binge, organise the bottles of shampoo and rolls of toilet paper in the cupboard under your sink, and find the shutoff valves. If you're lucky, the valves won't be tucked up high behind a partition. If they are, you may need to lie on your back and shine a torch to find them.

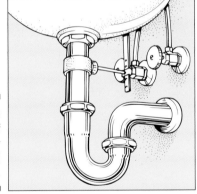

Figure 1-5:
Shutoff valves for the hot and cold water.

The bath or shower

Finding the shutoff valves for the bath or shower may take a little snooping. In most new houses, one of the walls in a bathroom contains all the plumbing pipes. So look for the bath and shower shutoff valves on the other side of the wall that contains the plumbing pipes. In older houses most of the plumbing for a first-floor bathroom comes up through the floorboards.

'How do I know which wall contains the plumbing pipes?' you may ask. The wall usually has a removable panel on the other side, which covers a recess in the wall and hides the pipes from view. The panel may be located in a cupboard, a bedroom, or a hall that's adjacent to the bathroom. So snoop around in your cupboards and look for a panel like the one shown in Figure 1-6. After you find it, remove the screws holding the panel in place, and you see the rear of the bath or shower. You may or may not find a set of shutoff valves in this wall recess.

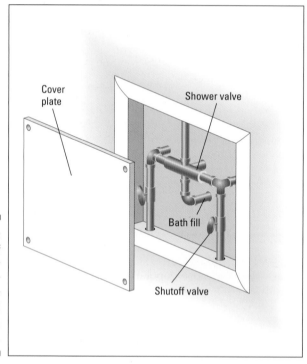

Cover plate

Shower valve

Bath fill

Shutoff valve

Figure 1-6:
Shutoff valves for a bath or shower may be located behind a panel.

If you can't find this panel, or you find the panel but then don't see any valves behind it, you haven't reached the end of your rope just yet. Many newer bathtubs and showers have shutoff valves installed behind the shower handle. Single-handle shower valves (in which you control the hot and cold water with one handle) have a cover plate sealing off a hole large enough that you can reach the shutoff valves from the bathroom side of the wall. If you remove the handle and cover, you may find shutoff valves (such as the ones shown in Figure 1-7) installed on the hot and cold pipes just before they enter the valve body. If you have a double-handled shower valve, chances are that you don't have built-in shutoff valves.

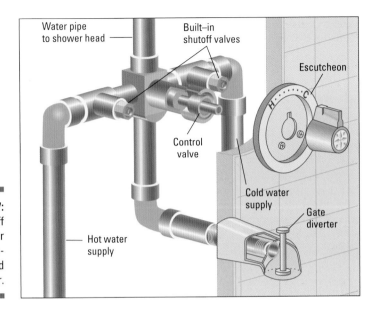

Figure 1-7:
Shut-off
valves for
a single-
handled
shower.

Labels in figure:
- Water pipe to shower head
- Built–in shutoff valves
- Escutcheon
- Control valve
- Cold water supply
- Gate diverter
- Hot water supply

Keeping water out of the kitchen

The kitchen is another big place for water usage in a home. Depending on the appliances you have installed in your kitchen, you may have water running to one or two sinks, a dishwasher, and maybe a washing machine, or an ice-maker in your freezer. The following sections give you all the help you need to find the shutoff valves for these popular kitchen features so that you can get on with the task of repairing them.

The sink

Newer houses have shutoff valves, but older ones don't always have them. The shutoff valves to the kitchen sink are located inside the base cabinet directly underneath the sink. The supply pipes may either come out of the wall or emerge from the floor.

If the supply pipes come out of the wall, you can find a shutoff valve on the hot pipe and the cold pipe. If the pipes come out of the floor and you can't find shutoff valves on these pipes, you may find a pair of valves in the basement, if you have one, under a sink.

The washing machine and dishwasher

If your washing machine and/or dishwasher are next to the sink or in the same section of base cabinets as the sink, the shutoff valves are probably under the sink. Often, when a washing machine and/or dishwasher are located near or next to the kitchen sink, the pipes leading to them are connected to the pipes that supply hot and cold water to the sink. In this case, two shutoff valves control the hot and cold water flow: One valve goes straight up to the hot or cold water connection to the tap, and the other goes off to the side of the dishwasher.

If the washing machine or dishwasher isn't located next to the sink, the water supply might come out of the wall or the floor. The shutoff valves are located under the appliance. You can get to this area by removing the kick-plate cover of the appliance, which should pull off easily. If you have trouble removing the kickplate cover, try lifting it slightly and then pulling it out. (See your owner's manual for specific instructions on how to remove this panel.) You should find the shutoff valve under the washing machine or dishwasher, usually in the front, close to the water supply pipe running into the unit, as shown in Figure 1-8.

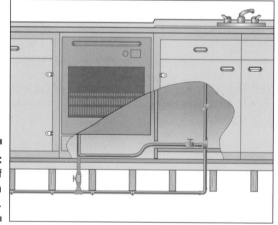

Figure 1-8:
The shutoff valve for a dishwasher.

The icemaker

Your freezer's icemaker has its own water supply, which runs through a 6 mm plastic or copper tube. In most cases, the tube leads to a larger pipe, where it's connected to a shutoff valve. Follow the tube to the larger pipe and look for the valve.

If you don't see the valve, your icemaker may work a little differently. The water supply still runs through a 6 mm tube, but that tube may lead to a larger pipe that has a clamp-on device, called a saddle, that has a shutoff valve on it to control the supply of water.

Taking it outside

If your house has an outdoor tap, called a bib tap or hose union tap, you can find the shutoff valve, called a bib valve (located in the pipe leading to the tap), in your cellar or suspended ground floor. Close the bib valve and then open the bib tap to allow the water between the bib valve and the bib tap to run out.

Letting the water run out of the pipes leading to your outdoor taps prevents your pipes from freezing in low temperatures.

A valve that's designed to make draining the water out of the exterior portion of the pipe easier controls some bib taps. This valve has a small, curled screw – called a waste screw – on its side. When you remove the screw, air can enter the pipe and speed the drainage. Turn the valve off, open the outside bib tap, and then unscrew the cap on the side of the stop and waste valve. Doing so ensures that all the water drains out of the pipe. Then simply replace the cap.

Many houses have frost-proof bib taps for which the actual shutoff valves are located well inside the house to prevent the taps from freezing in the winter months. (See Figure 1-9.) If you have frost-proof bib taps (also called *freezeless hose union taps*), you don't need to shut off the water at the valves inside the basement or suspended ground floor during the winter. Instead, these taps have a thick pipe leading into the house. If you need to turn off the water supply for repair purposes, look for the shutoff valve at the inside end of the pipe, where it connects to the water supply pipe.

Never leave a hose attached to the frost-proof bib tap during freezing weather.

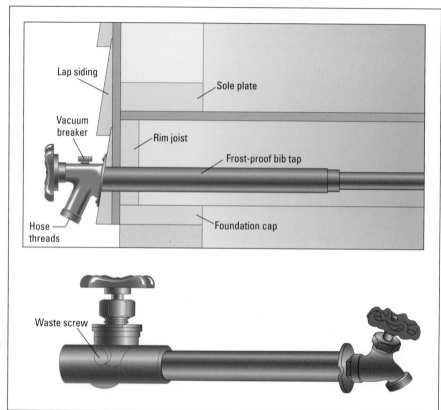

Figure 1-9:
Frost-proof
bib taps.

Lap siding

Sole plate

Vacuum
breaker

Rim joist

Frost-proof bib tap

Hose
threads

Foundation cap

Waste screw

Chapter 2

Heating, Ventilating, and Insulating Systems

. . . .

In This Chapter

▶ Keeping your boiler happy

▶ Ventilating your home from top to bottom

▶ Insulating your home from the elements

. . . .

Most grown-ups would never admit it, but their boilers frighten them. A boiler is a big, mysterious piece of machinery. Plus, as every kid knows, monsters live behind it.

We're here to tell you that a boiler is nothing to be afraid of and is less mysterious than you think. Your heating system simply heats up water and then moves that heated water around the house, through pipes and into radiators – it's really that simple. However, the technology behind this process is pretty complicated, which means that a professional must perform most of the maintenance tasks that are associated with your heating system.

The maintenance that a do-it-yourselfer can do is easy and non-threatening – we're confident that you can do it without difficulty.

Looking After Your Central Heating

Routine annual inspection and cleaning by a qualified heating engineer keep your central heating system running for many years without trouble. Don't be penny-wise and pound-foolish. A dirty, inefficient boiler costs you far more than a service call. The service-person will catch little problems before they become big trouble. And a neglected system fails years sooner than a well-maintained one.

Gauging the pressure

Most traditional central heating systems work off *indirect* pressure – meaning the pressure that comes from the weight of water in the header tank (also called the feed-and-expansion tank) at the top of the house, or in the roof space. Systems like this heat the radiators and also heat a separate tank of hot water for bathing and showering. This indirect pressure is fixed, and doesn't require any attention.

However, some newer systems have combination boilers (usually known as 'combi' boilers) and don't have a separate hot water tank. These combi boilers heat the central heating radiators just like a traditional boiler, but provide hot water to the shower and taps by 'instantly' heating water from the mains supply as it passes through the boiler. Combi systems work off *direct* pressure to provide hot water, and they also have to be pressurised in order for the central heating side of the system to function.

Sometimes the pressure drops due to tiny leaks in the system that you wouldn't otherwise notice, or after you have bled a radiator (see 'Bleeding the radiators' later in this chapter) and then the boiler refuses to fire up. If this happens, don't panic. Check the pressure gauge on the front of the boiler (it may be hidden behind a fold-down hatch or panel) – it should be reading around 1 atmosphere (check the boiler manufacturer's customer instruction booklet for the exact figure). If the pressure reading is almost down to zero, then that explains why your boiler doesn't want to fire up.

Re-pressurising the system is something you can easily do. Follow the instructions in your boilers' customer instruction booklet, which explains how to connect the *filler loop* – a flexible braided pipe that connects your boiler to the incoming mains cold water supply. You open the valve at each end of the filler loop that allows water to flow into the boiler and pressurise the system. Keep an eye on the pressure gauge, and turn the valve off when the pressure reaches 1 atmosphere (or whatever your boiler's specified pressure is). The filler loop may be hanging loose below the boiler, or the installer may have left it connected, for just such an event. Once the system has been re-pressurised, the boiler should fire up when you turn on the heating, or open a hot water outlet.

Bleeding the radiators

Bleeding a radiator is sometimes necessary in even the best of systems. If you have a radiator in your system that is cold at the top, chances are it's air-logged. Bleeding the air out of the radiator relieves the pressure and enables the system to fill normally.

To bleed the radiator, turn the *bleed valve* (a tapered screw in one top corner to let the air out) about a quarter-turn counterclockwise and keep the screwdriver or radiator key in the valve. If you hear a hissing sound, that's good – it's air escaping. As soon as the hissing stops and you see a dribble of water come out, close the valve.

Don't open the valve more than necessary; hot water will come rushing out before you can close it. At the very least, you'll make a wet mess. At worst, you could be scalded. You can help avoid this by bleeding the radiator when the heating system is off.

Ventilation: Letting You and Your House Breathe

When we talk about ventilation, we're actually talking about two different things: Interior ventilation and structural ventilation. Proper interior ventilation is vital to your family's health and comfort – it helps your home rid itself of moisture, smoke, cooking smells, and indoor pollutants. Structural ventilation controls heat levels in the loft, and moderates dampness below suspended ground floors and in the basement.

Interior ventilation

Kitchens, bathrooms, and utility rooms are the biggest sources of moisture and odours. The secret to having a non-stinky home is to have three key exhaust units: An exterior-venting cooker hood, and bathroom and utility room extractor fans.

Many kitchens have a cooker hood that doesn't actually vent anything – it just 'filters' and recycles air. To get rid of the greasy, smoky, steamy air requires ductwork to an exterior vent. If your kitchen is perpetually stinky and the walls are covered with a thin film of grease, you need to stop eating so much fried food, and you need an exterior-venting extractor fan.

Airborne grease makes extractor fans sticky, which in turn attracts dirt and dust. Clean the grill and fan blades twice a year, or whenever they start to look bad. The filters in recycling cooker hoods need cleaning every couple of months or so (depending on how and what you cook), and the fan and housing need a good cleaning every six months. If the filters have charcoal pellets inside, they need to be replaced annually. You can clean your cooker hood filter in the dishwasher. For the grill and fan blades, use a spray-on degreaser. (Test the degreaser first to make sure that it won't remove paint.) Follow with a mild soap and water wash. Finally, flush with fresh water and towel-dry.

Bathrooms generate huge amounts of moisture and some unpleasant smells. If you have incurable mildew in the shower, paint peeling off the walls, or a lingering funky smell, you need to install an extractor fan or get a bigger, higher-capacity fan. Extractor fans can vent the bad air through the wall or through the ceiling and loft. Call an electrical contractor to do the work.

Steam, hairspray, and other grooming products create a tacky surface that attracts dust, dirt, and fuzz at an alarming rate. Clean the housing, grill, and fan at least twice a year. Use the same techniques for cleaning that we suggest for cooker extractors.

Structural ventilation

To keep heat and moisture from roasting and rotting your home over time, having adequate ventilation in the loft and below the suspended ground floor (and the basement, if it's unfinished) is important.

In the loft, the idea is to create an upward flow of air. Cool air flows in through vents in the eaves and out through vent(s) nearer to, or at the peak of, the roof. Below the floor, cross-ventilation is utilised.

If insulation, crud, or dead mice block the vents, or if there aren't enough vents, the loft and subfloor area can become humid. Rot can develop. Condensed water can soak insulation, making it ineffective. Condensation from above and below can make its way into the house, ruining ceiling, floor, and wall finishes and short-circuiting electrical wiring. If you notice that your vents are clogged, clear them immediately.

Building regulations specify how much ventilation you need. As a general rule, have 1000 square centimetres of vent area for every 15 square metres of loft area or subfloor. We think more is better.

Roof ventilation

If your loft is hot and humid in the summer, you may need to install additional vents at the eaves and at the ridge of the roof. Assuming you're not a trained builder, we think it's best to leave this kind of work to a professional, someone who knows his or her way around the roof structure and knows how to install leak-free roof penetrations.

Even venting must be maintained. Make sure that each vent and screen is painted (to prevent deterioration) and that the screens are secured to the frame of the vent. Animals, tennis balls, and other common household missiles have a way of dislodging vent screens. Badly damaged vents should be replaced. Solid vent screens prevent vermin of all sorts from settling in your loft.

You can staple cardboard baffles to the rafters inside the attic adjacent to the vents. The baffles prevent loose-fill insulation from being blown into piles, leaving bare spots.

Extra vents are difficult to install and might require special tools to cut through timber, concrete block, and brick. Don't go poking holes in your walls on your own – call a builder to do the work. Professionals have the know-how, tools, and experience to do the job properly.

Underfloor ventilation

Moist air can cause rot in the subfloor space, too, attacking your home from below. Just like a loft, a subfloor area needs a good flow of fresh air. If your subfloor area is always overly damp, or if you see mildew on the walls or structure, you may need better ventilation.

Subfloor vents can be damaged in the same way as eave vents. In fact, because these vents are closer to the ground, the potential for damage is greater. Creatures that can't get into your loft will settle for the area beneath the floor. Establish a no-holes policy. Maintain subfloor vents in the same way that we suggest for eave vents.

Insulating Your Loft

One of the easiest jobs for a do-it-yourselfer is also one of the most valuable: Adding loft insulation to cut down on heating bills. Admittedly, you won't find crawling around in your loft very glamorous, and visitors won't even be able to tell that you've done anything. But you'll enjoy the benefits every month when your heating bill arrives.

Be sure to wear safety goggles, a dust mask, and protective clothing when working with insulation.

Upgrading loft insulation

The longstanding popularity of fibreglass and mineral wool insulation is based on several important features: They are excellent insulators, vermin resistant, and fireproof.

The problem with loft insulation is that handling the stuff is like hugging a hedgehog: The fibres produce an irritating itch when they contact bare skin. Plus, medical experts suspect that inhaling airborne fibres can be hazardous to the lungs. Yikes! In our experience, mineral wool insulation (such as 'Rockwool') is more irritating than fibreglass, but both should be treated with respect. This means wearing a good-quality disposable dust mask, work gloves, long trousers, and a long-sleeved shirt. If you find you are especially sensitive to the fibres, then get someone to seal the gap between your gloves and shirtsleeves with masking tape before you get to work.

To eliminate these problems, some manufacturers have developed a product called *polywrapped* or *encapsulated* insulation. The batt insulation is encapsulated in a perforated polyethylene or fabric covering that prevents airborne fibres and protects the skin from fibre contact. The product looks like a fibreglass sausage.

The perforations in the polywrap allow moisture to pass through, so the poly does not form a vapour barrier when applied over existing insulation. This feature makes the polywrapped insulation ideal for upgrading a loft insulation blanket. For areas where a vapour barrier is desired, insulation is available with the perforated polywrap on one side of the batt and a solid polyfilm on the other side. When using the vapour-barrier type of poly, you apply the vapour barrier side with the barrier facing the wall or ceiling. A vapour barrier – as its name suggests – stops moisture vapour travelling from one place to another. You usually use a vapour barrier to prevent warm, moist air finding its way from warm places (like living rooms) through to cold places (like unheated lofts) where it can cause condensation problems.

If your ceilings lack adequate insulation, choose polywrapped insulation. You can install polywrapped insulation on top of any type of existing insulation. The usual practice is to install the new polywrapped insulation at right angles to the existing insulation, as shown in Figure 2-1. You can cut the insulation with a sharp trimming knife or large scissors.

Figure 2-1:
To add insulation to a loft, install poly-wrapped insulation at right-angles to existing insulation.

Upgrading suspended timber ground floors

If your house has suspended timber ground floors, heat may be escaping downward through the floors. It's a good idea to install insulation that is as thick as the floor joists are wide.

To upgrade subfloor insulation, choose polywrapped fibreglass insulation with a perforated polyfilm on one side and a poly vapour barrier on the other. Install the insulation with the poly vapour barrier facing up.

To install the insulation, press it into the cavities between the floor joists, as shown in Figure 2-2, and staple the insulation to the joists. You can also secure it in place by nailing battens or stapling chicken wire to the joists. While installing the insulation, avoid wrinkles that can let warm air or moisture pass between the insulation and the floor joists. Make sure that the vapour retarder is in full contact with the subfloor.

If your home doesn't have a basement, or a crawlspace deep enough for you to squeeze yourself into, then insulating a suspended timber ground floor means lifting some of the floorboards first. This is fiddly work, but by no means impossible. It is best undertaken as part of decorating a room, or before fitting new carpets or hardwood flooring. With a bit of care you may be able to get away with lifting one floorboard every metre or so (about one board in six), nailing timber battens along the lower edges of the floor joists, and sliding the insulation in from the top. This is made easier if you use rigid polyurethane board insulation (such as Kingspan or Celotex), or stiff fibre-glass batts; the kind used to insulate the insides of cavity walls. All these materials are available from good builders' merchants or specialist insulation suppliers.

Figure 2-2: Pressing the insulation into cavities between the floor joists.

Chapter 3

Plumbing Materials and Tools

A hardware shop assistant can always tell when a customer has a plumbing project to tackle. The first sign is the distraught look of someone carrying a rusted pipe or an odd-shaped piece of chrome. But the glazed-over look tells it all – the homeowner is clueless about what to buy to solve his or her plumbing problem.

You can avoid being that hopeless soul by taking a look at the materials and tools that we've gathered in this chapter. With a basic understanding of what this stuff is and what it does, you can walk down the hardware-shop aisles with an air of confidence. You still may be clueless, but at least you'll be armed with the right vocabulary – and that's half the battle.

The larger the plumbing department, the more room for confusion. If you're lucky, you can find a hardware shop, DIY centre, or plumbers' merchants that has plenty of displays to demonstrate how plumbing parts and materials go together. If you're really lucky, you'll land in a shop where the assistants behind the counter or in the aisles have real-life plumbing expertise.

Finding Replacement Parts

Many times, you visit a plumbing department to find small replacement parts rather than large, new products. Take a look at these most popular replacement parts for plumbing appliances and fixtures so that, when the need arises, you know just what to ask for. This stuff may seem ho-hum, but knowing what you're looking for saves you countless return trips to the shop.

- **Washers:** A variety of washers are used in plumbing applications. They generally help seal a temporary joint. Probably the most common washer is used inside the female end (the end that screws onto the tap) of a garden hose. Washers are also used inside a tap to seal the joint between the smooth valve seat that's inside the tap and the valve stem, to prevent the flow of water. When you open a tap, the washer rises above the valve seat, which allows the water to flow.

- **Aerator:** An aerator is a small system of screens and a baffle that's screwed into the end of many kitchen and bathroom taps. Aerators introduce air into the flow of water and make it appear foamy. Aerators can become clogged with debris, so clean them regularly.

- **Valve seat:** A valve seat is present in the inside bottom of most taps. These penny-sized, doughnut-shaped brass seals are threaded on the bottom and are screwed into place with a special seat-removing tool that's similar to a large Allen key – see Figure 3-1. Because they're made of brass, which is very soft, valve seats deteriorate over time, causing taps to drip.

- **Valve stem:** A valve stem is located under the handle of both a hot- and a cold-water tap. On the bottom of every valve stem is a washer that wears out over time. If your tap is leaking, you want to replace this washer first. You can also find an o-ring or stem packing (which looks like string wrapped around the stem) designed to prevent water from leaking around the base of the handle (see Figure 3-1). Replace either the o-ring or the stem packing if water leaks from the tap stem's base.

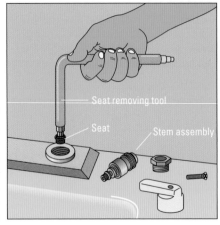

Figure 3-1:
A tap showing the valve seats and stem assembly.

Seat removing tool

Seat

Stem assembly

✔ **Washerless tap parts:** Washerless taps don't have valve seats, washers, or valve stems. Instead, they have a ball mechanism – the most common type being a kitchen tap with a single lever handle. If this type of tap starts to drip, the internal o-rings and/or ball mechanism need to be replaced. Replacement kits are widely available at DIY centres and plumbing supply shops. Some washerless taps have a cartridge-type mechanism that you can replace.

✔ **Ball float:** A ball float valve, shown in Figure 3-2, is a mechanism inside the toilet cistern that turns on the water when you flush and turns off the water after the cistern has refilled. Some toilets have a ball float – about the size of a grapefruit – on the end of a metal rod; others use a can-shaped cylinder that moves up and down according to the water level in the tank. An overflow pipe inside the tank prevents the tank from overfilling.

✔ **Toilet syphon:** A toilet syphon is located in the bottom of the toilet cistern. When you push the flush lever down, a small chain lifts a plunger inside the syphon and allows the water in the cistern to flow and flush the toilet.

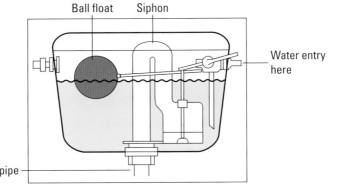

Figure 3-2:
A cistern
with a
ball-float
mechanism.

Ball float   Siphon

Water entry here

Flush pipe

Common Plumbing Supplies

Just like a good cook has a kitchen full of supplies to create new and exciting entrees, a do-it-yourself plumber needs a stash of stuff to work with pipes and fixtures. Here's a rundown of the basic materials to have on hand:

✔ **Plumber's putty:** This material looks like modelling clay and is designed to stay soft and semi-flexible for years. Use this putty to make a seal between plumbing fixtures and in areas that have no water pressure.

When you install a new tap, for example, apply plumber's putty under the tap where the tap meets the top of the sink – this putty helps prevent water from seeping under the tap and into the sink cupboard below. Other uses for plumber's putty include sealing drains in sinks, baths, and shower trays; sealing frames around sinks; and sealing other fixtures and bowls.

✔ **Pipe joint compound:** Pipe joint compound is sometimes referred to as pipe dope. It's used to seal the joint between a threaded fitting and steel pipe. Always use pipe dope when working with gas pipes; many people also use it when working with galvanised steel water pipes. Pipe joint compound is typically painted onto the threads cut into the end of the pipe that's called the male end, as shown in Figure 3-3.

Working with gas can be deadly. Get a pro to do any work involving gas.

✔ **Teflon (also called PTFE) tape:** You use this tape, a substitute for pipe joint compound, to seal the threads on steel pipe – see Figure 3-3. Use white Teflon tape for sealing pipe threads; use yellow Teflon tape, which is much thicker, for sealing pipe threads when working with gas pipes.

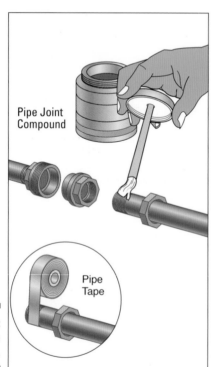

Pipe Joint Compound

Pipe Tape

Figure 3-3: Using pipe PTFE tape.

WARNING!

WARNING!

✔ **CPVC cleaner:** You use CPVC cleaner to clean CPVC pipe prior to joining it with adhesive (see 'Buying Drainage Pipes and Fittings', later in this chapter, for more on CPVC pipes). This purple liquid not only cleans CPVC pipe, but it also softens the pipe slightly and makes the adhesive work better.

Be careful when using CPVC cleaner – it stains whatever it lands on.

✔ **CPVC cement:** You use CPVC cement to fuse joints in CPVC pipe and fittings.

Never use CPVC cement on ABS pipe.

✔ **ABS cement:** You use ABS cement to fuse joints on black ABS pipe and fittings (see 'Buying Drainage Pipes and Fittings', later in this chapter, for more on ABS pipes and fittings). You don't need to use a cleaner prior to using ABS cement, but make sure that you wipe the pipe and fittings with a clean cloth.

✔ **Solder:** You use solder to seal joints when working with copper pipe. You heat the pipe and fitting with a propane torch until they're hot enough to melt the solder in a process called soldering. Solder is sold in rolls and is made from various combinations of pure lead and tin. Look for 50/50 and 60/40 for plumbing joints. (The first number represents the percentage of lead; the second, tin.) The addition of tin helps the solder stick to the copper.

✔ **Leadless solder:** You use leadless solder to join water supply pipes. Water regulations require it because standard lead-based solder leaks lead into the water standing in the pipe. Your best bet is to use leadless solder for all plumbing projects.

✔ **Flux:** Flux cleans copper pipe and helps solder adhere better. It's available in paste or liquid form, but most plumbers prefer the paste type. You must use flux when soldering copper pipe; apply it with a small brush to both the end of the pipe and the inside of the fitting – see Figure 3-4.

Figure 3-4:
Applying
flux.

Always wear inexpensive jersey gloves when working with solder and flux. The gloves eventually get eaten up (so use a cheap pair), but they protect your hands.

- ✔ **Steel wool:** You use steel wool to clean the ends of copper pipe and the insides of copper fittings prior to applying flux and soldering.

- ✔ **Emery cloth:** You use this cloth-backed sandpaper to clean the ends of copper pipe and the insides of copper fittings prior to applying flux and soldering.

- ✔ **Copper-cleaning brush:** You use this small wire brush to clean the insides of copper fittings – it cleans a fitting faster than an emery cloth does. Copper-cleaning brushes are sold in sizes to fit inside 15 mm and 22 mm fittings.

- ✔ **Propane:** Propane is a liquid petroleum product that's used in a hand-held torch, which you use to heat copper pipe and fittings and to melt solder to seal a joint.

- ✔ **Pipe thread cutting oil:** You use this light oil when threading the ends of steel pipe. Pipe thread cutting oil helps lubricate the thread cutter and wash away the steel particles that are created when the pipe threads are cut.

Finding the Right Water Supply Pipe

Water supply pipes are an important part of plumbing projects, and they're available in a variety of materials, including copper, steel, and plastic. The wide acceptance of plastic pipe has been a boon to the do-it-yourself plumbing industry because plastic pipe is easy to cut and glue together. Most homes older than 20 years have pipes made of steel or copper.

Copper pipe

Copper tube, used for water supply pipes throughout most homes, is probably the most common type in use today. Copper tube is widely available in two basic types: Rigid and flexible. This section gives you a basic rundown of copper pipe and its uses.

Rigid copper pipe

Rigid copper pipe is used extensively throughout modern homes for both hot and cold water supply lines. This pipe is widely sold in 15- and 22-mm diameters and in lengths of 2 and 3 metres.

Rigid copper pipe doesn't bend easily, so a variety of fittings are available to help you make the pipe go where you want it to go (see Figure 3-5):

- **Elbow:** Use an elbow to make copper pipe turn at an angle. Elbows (called els in the trade) come in 90-degree, 45-degree, and 22 ½-degree angles.

- **Tee:** A tee enables you to run another copper pipe off an existing pipe.

- **Straight connector or coupling:** Use these fittings when you want to continue a straight run of consecutive copper pipes.

- **Cap:** Use a copper cap to end a line of copper pipe.

Fittings for rigid copper pipe are usually soldered in place. (Refer to the section 'Common Plumbing Supplies', in this chapter, for an explanation of soldering.) Soldering involves the use of solder, flux (so that the solder sticks), and heat (usually from a propane torch).

Flexible copper pipe

Flexible (also called annealed) copper pipe is sold in coils of various lengths. Common sizes of flexible copper piping include 12 mm, 15 mm, and 22 mm diameters. The 12 mm size is commonly used for hooking up water supply pipes to dishwashers and some icemakers. Flexible copper pipe and tubing are commonly joined with compression fittings rather than by soldering.

When you buy compression fittings for either type of copper pipe and tubing, the fitting comes with a single compression ring or "olive". When you tighten a compression fitting with a spanner, the compression ring seals the joint – but not always. If the joint leaks even after you tighten it, you may have damaged the compression ring when you tightened it. Purchase a few extra olives so that you can remove the damaged one and try again.

Galvanised steel pipe

Years ago, galvanised steel pipe was the only type of pipe that was widely available for water supply lines. Today, other types of pipe, such as copper and plastic, have replaced galvanised steel because they require less labour to install. Whether you have galvanised iron pipe depends on the age of your home and the part of the country you live in. If you have galvanised steel pipe, you'll find two basic sizes in your walls: ½-inch (15 mm) diameter and ¾-inch (22 mm) diameter.

If you aren't sure whether your pipes are made of copper or steel, try to stick a magnet to the pipe. If the magnet sticks, the pipe is steel; if it doesn't, it's copper.

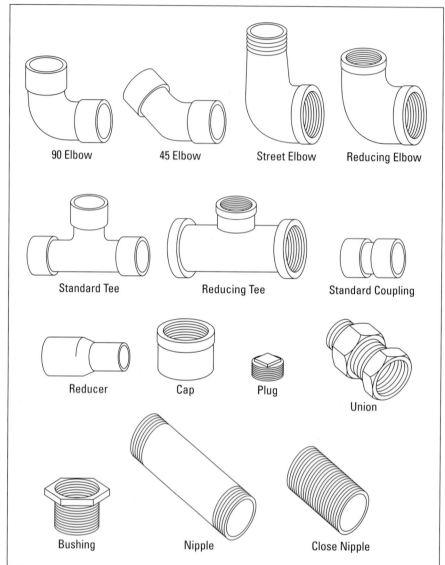

90 Elbow   45 Elbow   Street Elbow   Reducing Elbow

Standard Tee   Reducing Tee   Standard Coupling

Reducer   Cap   Plug   Union

Bushing   Nipple   Close Nipple

Figure 3-5:
Common fittings used to join iron, copper, and plastic pipe.

Black iron (really coated steel) pipe is used only for gas. Water heaters, boilers, cookers, and other appliances that use gas are plumbed with black iron pipe. This pipe is available in the same sizes and has the same fitting configurations as galvanised steel pipe.

Plastic pipe

Plastic pipe is used for water supply pipes and for waste, vent, and drain pipes.

Two types of plastic water supply pipe are commonly used today: Chlorinated polyvinyl chloride (CPVC) and polybutylene (PB) flexible tubing.

Plastic pipe is easy to work with because you can cut it to length with a fine-toothed saw. Joints for plastic pipes include elbows, tees, and caps (refer to Figure 3-5). Seal all the joints in plastic waste pipes with a liquid adhesive. Clean the joints for CPVC pipe with a special cleaner before applying a coat of adhesive.

PB tubing is joined with proprietory push-fit connectors, or standard compression-type fittings the same as those used to join copper pipe.

When you purchase any type of supply tube, always buy a longer tube than you need. You can cut copper and plastic tubes to the length you want.

Buying Drainage Pipes and Fittings

Pipes that carry water out of your home's drainage system look different from the water supply pipes that bring water into the house. Fittings designed for drainage have to make gentle turns. Standard elbows used to join pressure pipes turn abruptly at 90 degrees, but a drainage elbow has a gradual bend. Drainage tee and wye fittings have 45-degree angles.

Cast iron pipes

Cast iron pipes, commonly used for drain lines in older homes, have largely been replaced by plastic drain lines. Joining cast-iron drain lines involves molten lead and plenty of mess. If you have to fool with cast-iron drainage pipes, we strongly recommend that you call in a pro. This pipe is heavy, is difficult to work with, and requires special tools.

Plastic pipes

Plastic drainage pipes and fittings have revolutionised the plumbing industry. Plastic pipes are much lighter than cast iron and are a lot easier to work with. Two basic kinds of drainage pipe are commonly used today: Polyvinyl chloride (PVC) and acryaonitrile-butadiene-styrene (ABS). Both types of pipe are suitable for drainage. Common diameters for these pipes include 32 mm, 40 mm, and 100 mm. You can also find corresponding plastic fittings and adaptors to match the pipes produced in cast iron, which are helpful if you want to replace iron with plastic in your home. (See Figure 3-6.)

When you're buying adhesive for ABS or PVC plastic pipe, always purchase the type of adhesive recommended by the pipe manufacturer.

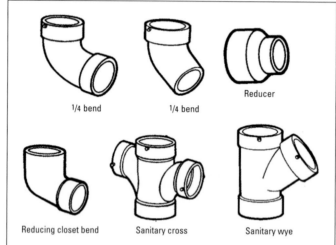

Figure 3-6: Common plastic drainage fittings.

1/4 bend   1/4 bend   Reducer

Reducing closet bend   Sanitary cross   Sanitary wye

Stocking Up on Valves

Valves control the flow of water in pipes. Your home has a valve on the incoming water pipe so that you can stop the inflow of water (see Chapter 1).

Some valves have a round knob on top that you turn to open or close the valve, but others have a single lever that you push or pull to open or close the valve. Valves are used for all types of plumbing pipe and are available with threaded ends (for use with galvanised steel pipe) and smooth ends (for use with soldered copper joints). You can also find valves with plastic bodies for use with adhesive in a plastic pipe application.

When you're buying valves, make sure that you buy the right type. Some valves have threaded female ends that accept the threaded end of a pipe. Valves are also available to attach to copper and plastic piping – this kind features unthreaded female ends designed to be soldered or solvent-welded to the pipe. Still others have a compression-type female end that clamps down on the pipe when you tighten the compression nut.

Many different varieties of valves exist. In the following list, we introduce the kinds of valves that you're most likely to encounter. See Figure 3-7 for examples.

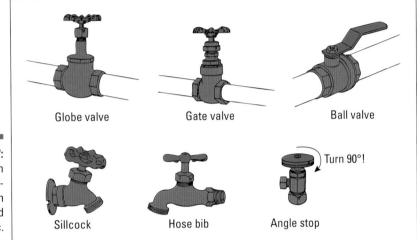

Figure 3-7:
Common valves available in both brass and plastic.

Globe valve · Gate valve · Ball valve · Sillcock · Hose bib · Angle stop · Turn 90°!

✔ **Gate valve:** A gate valve allows the full flow of water through the valve and is the best kind of valve to use at the main shutoff and in pipes supplying cold water to a water heater or other device where water flow is important. Gate valves don't have rubber compression gaskets; instead, they rely on the close fit of the parts to stop the water. Turning the handle counter-clockwise raises the wedge-shaped gate, allowing the water to flow.

✔ **Ball valve:** Ball valves can provide a full flow of water. A lever opens and closes them. Inside the valve is a ball with a hole through it. When the hole in the ball is aligned parallel with the pipe, water flows through the valve. When the ball is turned with the hole across the pipe, the water is blocked. The lever is aligned with the hole in the ball. To close a ball valve, push the lever perpendicular to the pipe; to open it, push the lever parallel with the pipe.

✔ **Globe valve:** Globe valves, which are less expensive than gate valves, are a good choice for general water control where full flow is not necessary. These valves have a rubber compression washer that's pushed against a seat to squeeze the water flow.

✔ **Stop valve:** Stop valves are a variation of globe valves. They're designed to control water running to sinks and toilets. Stop valves come in two main varieties: Angle and straight stops. Angle stops are designed to control the water flow and change the direction of the flow 90 degrees.

They're mounted on the ends of pipes under sinks and toilets when the supply pipes come out of the wall. Straight stops are designed to be mounted on pipes that come out of the floor.

Choose a valve with the right kind of outlet. A valve is designed to attach to a pipe coming out of the wall or floor and to a riser tube going to the fixture. If, for example, you want a stop valve to attach to a ½-inch (15 mm) galvanised pipe and a 12 mm riser tube, purchase a valve with a ½-inch (15 mm) female threaded end and a 12 mm outlet to accept the tubing.

✓ **Hose bib:** A hose bib looks like a miniature tap. It has a male-threaded end that's screwed into a coupling threaded to the end of a pipe. Hose bibs are commonly used to control water running to washing machines.

✓ **Sillcock valves (also called *hose union taps*):** Sillcock valves are used outside the house, on the taps that you probably use with a garden hose (called a bib tap). For houses located in cold climates, a freeze-proof version is available.

Using Plumbing Tools

When you're embarking on a new plumbing project, you have the upper hand if that hand is holding the tool designed for the job. Sure, a plain old screwdriver can tackle many of the jobs you need to do. We're not talking about pouring hundreds of pounds into outfitting your toolbox with tools. We do suggest that you begin to acquire tools as you need them, based on the suggestions we offer in this section. That way, you acquire the tools you need over time rather than forking over all your cash at once, and you have them for a lifetime.

Basic woodworking tools

As with any repair work you do around the house, you need a set of basic tools. Woodworking tools are a good place to start, because if you decide to replace a kitchen sink, for example, you'll be cutting and drilling holes in wood, driving screws, tightening bolts, and doing all kinds of jobs that at first glance seem unrelated to plumbing.

You should have these common woodworking tools in your toolbox:

✓ **Adjustable (crescent) spanner:** This spanner has a long steel handle and parallel jaws that open and close by adjusting a screw gear.

✓ **Allen keys:** A set will do.

✓ **Assorted screwdrivers.**

- ✔ **Spirit level.**

- ✔ **Claw hammer.**

- ✔ **Hacksaw.**

- ✔ **Locking pliers (also known as *vise-grips or mole grips*):** Pliers with short jaws that you can open and set to a specific size by turning a jaw-adjustment screw in the handle. When you squeeze the handles, the jaws clamp together.

- ✔ **Metal files:** You want to have both a flat and a half-round type with shallow grooves that form teeth.

- ✔ **Power drill:** 13 mm variable-speed, reversible drill with a variety of drill bits.

- ✔ **Retractable tape measure.**

- ✔ **Slip-joint pliers:** A tool with curved-toothed jaws and a hinge that adjusts or 'slips', making the jaw opening wide or narrow.

- ✔ **Staple gun.**

- ✔ **Torpedo level:** This tool is a short spirit level. A torpedo level is useful for plumbing applications because it fits into restricted areas.

- ✔ **Utility knife.**

Tools for measuring

Accurate measuring is essential when you're installing new water or drain pipes. As we point out in 'Finding the Right Water Supply Pipe', earlier in this chapter, you need to know the diameter and length of the pipe you need. A retractable tape measure can do most of the measuring – the hook on the end of the retractable tape measure catches on the end of the pipe, making it easy for you to mark a cutting point.

For more precise measurements, use a measuring device called a steel rule, which has both Imperial and metric graduations. Steel rules come in lengths of 12 to 48 inches (300 to 1200 mm), the most common being 910 mm. (The shorter length is easier to use for measuring plumbing-related pieces.) Place one end of the rule against an inside edge of the pipe and read the size at the opposite edge. This measurement may have little relationship to the pipe's nominal size, or outside diameter.

Wrenches, spanners, and pliers

A number of tools have been designed to help you work efficiently with different kinds of pipe. Other special tools make it easier to remove and install plumbing fixtures and associated components, such as water supply pipes and drain pipes.

Some of these tools, like a pipe wrench, monkey wrench, basin wrench, and groove-joint pliers, are the minimum you need for basic plumbing repairs. If you have these tools on hand, you're ready if you ever experience a plumbing failure. Have these tools on hand even if you don't plan any big plumbing projects in the near future. Besides, you can use many of them for other jobs around the house. Here's a basic rundown of these handy-dandy tools:

- **Pipe wrench:** This wrench, shown in Figure 3-8, has serrated teeth on the jaws, which are designed to grip and turn metal pipe. One jaw is adjustable, with a knurled knob. This jaw is spring-loaded and angled slightly, which enables you to release the grip and reposition the wrench without changing the adjustment. Pulling the handle against the open side of the jaws causes them to tighten against the pipe. Pipe wrenches come in different sizes, with 8-inch, 10-inch, and 14-inch being the most useful.

  Don't use pipe wrenches on copper or plastic pipe. You don't have to turn a copper or plastic pipe because it's soldered or solvent-welded (respectively) to the fitting. A pipe wrench can also crush the pipe if you apply a lot of pressure to the pipe with the wrench.

- **Monkey wrench:** The jaws of a monkey wrench are parallel to each other and set 90 degrees to the handle.

- **Spud or trap wrench:** This wrench is an adjustable one that's designed for handling drain trap and sink strainer fittings. The jaws are parallel and have a wide adjustment so they can grip the large-diameter lock ring that holds a sink strainer assembly in place. You set the jaws to size and then lock them in place by tightening a wing nut on the body of the wrench.

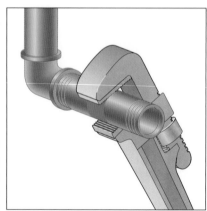

Figure 3-8:
A pipe
wrench.

✔ **Strap wrench:** This tool has canvas webbing that wraps around pipes or plumbing fittings and enables you to tighten or loosen them without marring the finish.

✔ **Plastic nut basin wrench:** Many taps have easy-to-tighten plastic mounting nuts, but they're still hard to reach. A plastic nut basin wrench (see Figure 3-9) is about 300 mm long and is designed to reach and tighten these nuts. This metal tool has notched ends that self-centre on 2-, 3-, 4-, and 6-tab nuts and fit metal hex nuts.

✔ **Groove-joint pliers:** In larger sizes, these pliers are used for holding pipes. With the pliers' long-reaching parallel jaws, you can also tighten drains and use them for a multitude of other jobs.

✔ **Tap spanner:** A tap spanner is a flat wrench, usually stamped from heavy metal, used for installing taps. You may get one when you buy a new tap. These wrenches have a variety of hex or square holes punched in them, sized specifically to fit packing nuts and other fittings on taps.

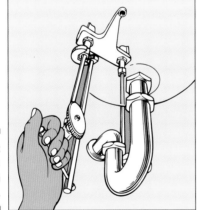

Figure 3-9:
A plastic
nut basin
wrench.

Pipe clamps

Pipe clamps come in a variety of shapes and sizes. You use these clamps to make temporary emergency repairs on a pipe that may have frozen and burst or sprung a pinhole leak due to corrosion. Place a rubber or plastic pad over the leak and then install the clamp over the pad and tighten – see Figure 3-10. Make sure that the clamp extends at least 25 mm beyond the leak.

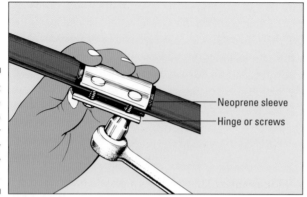

Figure 3-10:
A pipe clamp used for temporary emergency repairs.

Neoprene sleeve
Hinge or screws

Pipe cutting and bending tools

Some tools are made specifically to bend pipes, cut pipes, and dress the cut end. When you need one of these tools, no substitution will do. Consider hiring these tools if your pipe cutting project is a small one. But if you'll be involved in more than one pipe cutting job, consider investing in the tools. You'll enjoy a smug satisfaction when you can talk authoritatively to friends and co-workers about your pipe reamer, knowing that they don't have a clue about what you're saying. These tools include the following:

- **Tubing cutter:** Tube cutters come in sizes to fit tubing of different diameters. The most convenient size for homeowners is a model that cuts tubing from 12 mm to 35 mm in diameter. Some models are fitted with a built-in reamer to remove burrs inside the pipe after cutting. A midget tube cutter is designed for use in tight, tiny spaces – it doesn't have a handle, but large, knurled feed-screw knobs make it fairly easy to use.

- **Pipe cutter:** This large, heavy-duty cutter cuts steel pipe. It works similarly to a tubing cutter but has long handles for greater leverage.

- **Plastic tubing cutter:** This tool is designed for quick, clean cuts through plastic pipe and tubing. It features a compound leverage ratchet mechanism and a hardened steel blade and makes cutting pipe a one-handed operation.

- **Plastic-cutting saw:** This inexpensive saw is designed for cutting plastic pipe, plywood, and veneers. It has an aluminium or plastic handle and a 250 mm blade with replacements of either 300 or 450 mm long available.

- **Pipe reamer:** After cutting metal pipe, you find burrs or small ridges called flanges on the inside of the pipe. If you don't remove the burrs or flanges, they disrupt water flow, which leads to calcium build-up. Some cutters have built-in reamers, or you can use a half-round file. But a pipe reamer with a self-feeding spiral design, shown in Figure 3-11, makes the job fast and easy.

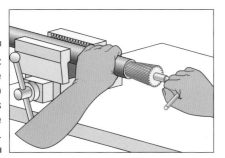

Figure 3-11:
A pipe
reamer to
file off burrs
from inside
pipes.

- **Inside/outside reamer:** This tool has a plastic housing with steel blades on the inside, which makes it handy for quick, clean, and easy inside reaming and outside bevelling on plastic, copper, or brass pipe. This tool isn't for use on iron pipe, however.

- **Spring-type tube bender:** This tool is a tightly coiled spring that aids in bending soft copper and aluminium tubing without crimping or flattening it. The benders come in sizes to fit the tubing. To use the tool, slip the bender inside the tubing with a twisting motion and then place it over your knee and bend it slowly.

- **Flaring tool:** This tool is used for flaring soft copper pipe when used with flare nuts. You find this kind of pipe on icemakers and humidifiers. Place the flare nut on the pipe and then clamp the pipe in the proper size hole in the vice bar. Tighten the clamp to close the two halves of the vice bar tightly around the tubing. Slide the C-shaped die clamp over the vice bar and position the cone-shaped die over the mouth of the tubing. Tighten the large screw to which the die is attached, which pushes the die into the tubing and forces the edges of the tubing outwards, thus creating the flare.

Plungers and augers

A true tool geek wouldn't be without the special-use tools in this category. They give power to the weak when dislodging clogs in drains, drilling large holes, providing the oomph for bending pipes, and much more.

- **Toilet plunger:** Similar to old-fashioned sink plungers, the rubber cup on this type of plunger has an extension that fits tightly into the toilet bowl. You can fold back the extension when using the plunger for sinks. For the plunger to work properly, seat the ball in the bottom of the toilet, push down gently, and then pull up quickly.

✔ **Toilet auger:** When a plunger doesn't work, a toilet auger, shown in Figure 3-12, is the next option. This tool is designed to fit a toilet bowl and clean out the trap. Fit the handle into the bowl and turn the crank while slowly pushing the flexible shaft through the hollow rod until it hits the blockage. (Chapter 5 offers more hints for unclogging a toilet.)

✔ **Powered toilet auger:** Before you call a plumber, hire this tool to make sure that the toilet is really clean. Instead of cranking by hand, a drill-like driver powers the shaft.

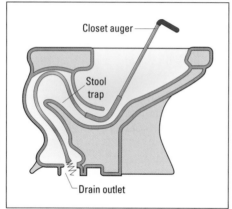

Closet auger

Stool trap

Figure 3-12:
A toilet auger for unblocking a toilet.

Drain outlet

Chapter 4

Unblocking a Sink or Bath Waste Pipe

Knowing how to unblock a sink waste pipe is one of those life skills that no one teaches in any school or university. If you're lucky, when you were young and formidable, you watched your parent or a plumber perform this unpleasant task and paid close attention. If not, well, start reading. This chapter contains the best advice that we can give to help you dislodge the most stubborn blockages and get your sink drain flowing again. This chapter also includes tips for responding to the cry 'My ring just went down the drain!' and other drain dilemmas.

Unblocking a Sink or Bath Waste Pipe

With all the different kinds of food scraps, soap, and hair that find their way down sink drains, it's not surprising that these drains get blocked up from time to time.

Symptoms of a blockage can range from water in the sink draining slower and slower to a stagnant pond in your sink or bath.

The easiest solution for drain blockages (but not necessarily the environmentally safest) is to use any of a wide range of chemical drain unblockers, available in solid and liquid forms at supermarkets, hardware shops, and plumbing-supply dealers. You pour the product in, wait for it to dissolve the blockage, and then flush the drain with running water. Chemicals are especially effective for clearing bath drains, because they contain protein-dissolving elements that can work wonders on the most common cause of bath blockages: Masses of accumulated hair.

Some chemicals can damage the plastic or rubber parts of a waste disposal unit and can cause injury if the cleaner splashes into your eyes or onto your skin. If you decide to use chemicals, read the package directions and precautions carefully and follow them precisely; the directions vary by product. If the blockage doesn't clear after a couple of tries, you're ready for a more hands-on approach.

Pouring a kettle full of boiling water down the drain is a non-toxic alternative to chemicals that often eliminates blockages.

Removing the sink trap

To unblock your sink drain, remove and clean the trap (the U-shaped or bottle shaped pipe located under the sink), as shown in Figure 4-1. Removing and cleaning the trap is easy. Wear rubber gloves.

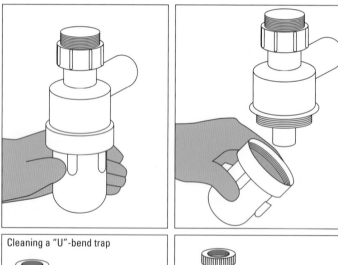

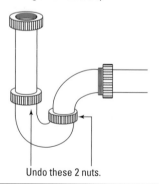

Cleaning a "U"-bend trap

Undo these 2 nuts.

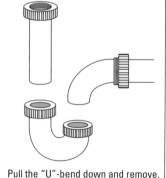

Pull the "U"-bend down and remove.

Figure 4-1: Cleaning a bottle trap (left) or a U-bend trap.

1. **Place a bucket under the trap (before taking it apart).**

   This way, you catch any debris or water that falls out when the trap is removed.

2. **Use a wrench or slip-joint pliers to unscrew the metal or plastic slip nuts a half turn or so, so that you can loosen them by hand.**

   Some traps (mainly older lead ones) have a clean-out plug instead of slip nuts. Simply remove the plug and allow the blockage to spill out.

   To protect the chrome finish on metal slip nuts, wrap tape around the jaws of your wrench or pliers. Plastic traps have slip nuts that you can usually turn by hand.

3. **Scrape out any blockage from the trap.**

4. **Tighten the slip nuts with your hands to ensure that they're threaded on the trap correctly, and then tighten with a wrench or pliers.**

   Half a turn is usually all that's necessary to stop the trap from leaking; don't overtighten.

Some people may advise you to try unblocking the sink drain with a plunger (covered in the following section, 'Taking the plunge with a bath or sink drain') before you resort to removing the trap. We believe that cleaning the trap first is a better approach, because using a plunger can push the blockaged material from the trap into the drainpipe, where it's more difficult to remove.

Taking the plunge with a bath or sink drain

A common plunger is capable of unblocking a drain that even the toughest chemicals can't budge. Unlike chemicals, a plunger uses suction to alternately push and pull the blockage within the pipe until the force dislodges the blockage. If cleaning the trap doesn't clear the blockage, try plunging the offending blockage.

Finding lost treasure

It's happened to everyone: A treasured ring goes sailing down the drain, and you're desperate to retrieve it. The best rescue tactic is to remove the trap, hoping that the object is heavy enough to settle in the lower part of the trap. Don't run any water through the drain – water may flush the object farther away.

Get a bucket and a wrench, and then follow the directions in the 'Removing the sink trap' section. Keep the bucket under the trap to catch what's inside it when you remove it from the drainpipe.

Don't confuse a common plunger that's used for drains with a *toilet plunger*, which has two cups, one inside the other. A common plunger has a wooden broomstick-like handle that attaches to a cup-shaped piece of rubber.

Before you use a plunger, remove any standing water that may contain chemicals. Splashing diluted chemicals into your eyes can cause severe damage.

Here's the plunger procedure:

1. **If the sink or bath has a pop-up stopper, remove the stopper first to give you a wider opening to the drain.**

2. **Pour a full kettle's worth of boiling water down the drain to break up the blockage.** For the chemical approach, use caustic soda.

3. **Fill the sink or bath with enough tap water to cover the rubber portion of a plunger, thus assuring good suction.**

4. **Place the plunger over the drain and vigorously push down and pull up several times.**

    If you're successful, you'll notice a sudden emptying of the sink or bath.

Putting a bit of petroleum jelly on the lip of the plunger helps form a tight seal, making the plunger more efficient.

Charming the drain with a snake

If neither cleaning the trap nor plunging clears the blockage, your final weapon is a *drain auger* (also known as a snake). This tool, a coiled spiral snake that's usually about 5 mm thick, with a handle on one end, works the opposite way to a plunger: You push the snake into the blockage and crank it to drive the snake farther into the obstruction, as shown in Figure 4-2. While parts of the blockage break up and flush through the drain, the snake helps you gain access to the blockage so that you can pull it out. Some snakes can fit as an attachment on an electric drill, giving it more power to force it through the blockage. Snakes are especially handy because they're long enough to reach blockages that are deep within a drainpipe.

You can hire a manually operated or an electric drain auger from a tool hire shop. The equipment is easy to use, but ask the assistant for operating instructions.

The basic process is as follows:

1. **Push the end of the snake into the drain opening and turn the handle on the drum that contains the coiled-up snake.**

   The auger begins its smelly journey down the drain.

2. **Keep pushing more of the snake into the drain until you feel resistance.**

   You may have to apply pressure when cranking the handle to get it to bend around the tight curve in the trap under the sink. After turning the curve, the snake usually slides through easily until you hit the blockage.

3. **Rotate the snake against the blockage until you feel it feed freely into the pipe.**

   The rotating action enables the tip of the snake to attach to the blockage and spin it away or chop it up. If the blockage is a solid object, the auger head entangles the object. If you don't feel the auger breaking through and twisting getting easier, pull the auger out of the drain – you'll likely pull the blockage out with it.

4. **Run water full force for a few minutes to be sure that the drain is unblocked.**

   Sometimes, the blockage flushes down the drain; at other times, the blockage comes out attached to the snake.

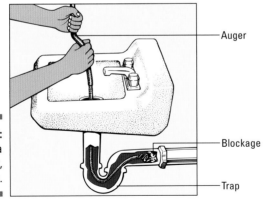

Figure 4-2:
Using a
drain auger,
or snake.

Auger

Blockage

Trap

TIP

If the snake doesn't fit down the drain or gets held up in the trap, you need to open the trap beneath the sink. Follow the instructions in the 'Removing the sink trap' section, earlier in this chapter. Avoid contact with the water that comes out of the trap, because it may contain chemical drain opener. From the trap, insert the snake in either direction until you reach and clean out the blockage.

An ounce of prevention . . .

We may be too late with this information, but your best defence against blockages is to avoid them in the first place. The following are some common-sense practices to use:

- Use a sink strainer. A blocked kitchen sink is usually the result of vegetable peelings or foreign objects entering the drain. Use a sink strainer to prevent solid items from entering the drainpipe.

- Take care of your waste disposal unit. When using a waste disposal unit, run cold water at full volume while the machine is chopping up the scraps; leave the water running for a full minute after you shut off

the unit. This precaution flushes the waste completely out of the small-diameter sink drainpipe and into the larger main drainpipe, where it's less likely to cause a blockage.

- Don't dump materials down your drain. Do-it-yourselfers often flush building materials down the drain. The most common offender is plaster or filler, which seems innocent enough going down but can harden in the drainpipes and blockage them. To prevent these blockages, never dispose of leftover building materials in sink drains. Put them in the dustbin instead.

Unblocking a Tap Aerator

If a tap seems to be running slower than usual, the aerator may be blocked with a build-up of mineral deposits. An *aerator* is a simple insert that fits inside a tap spout's chrome cap – most taps come with them – to conserve water and keep it from splashing all over the place, while still providing a steady stream and enough water pressure. Tiny holes in the aerator restrict water flow by mixing air bubbles into the water stream. The minuscule holes eventually become blocked by small mineral particles in the water.

Follow these steps to clean and unblock an aerator:

1. **Place a towel or rag over the tap cap or cover it with a bit of masking tape.**

   This protective barrier keeps the surface from being marred when you strong-arm the cap off.

2. **Using a spanner or pliers, turn the cap in a counter-clockwise motion until it separates from the tap.**

3. **When the cap is off, remove the screen and water restrictor (shown in Figure 4-3).**

   Pay attention to the way these small internal parts are arranged. When the time comes to put the aerator back in place, you have to replace these parts in the same sequence and position. See Figure 4-3.

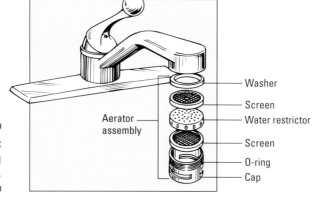

Figure 4-3:
Assembling
an aerator.

Washer
Screen
Aerator
assembly
Water restrictor
Screen
O-ring
Cap

4. **Clean the screen by flushing it with water or using a brush.** Push through the tiny holes with a needle or pin to unblock them.

5. **Soak the aerator in a cup of vinegar overnight to clean out the small holes and flush it with clear water before reinstalling it.**

6. **Reassemble the aerator in the reverse order.**

You should notice a big difference in the water flow after cleaning the aerator – not gushing water but a nice, steady stream.

Unblocking a Waste Disposal Unit

Even a waste disposal unit in a sink can be finicky, so don't expect it to devour and digest everything. For example, don't throw artichokes, fruit stones, or bones down a waste disposal and expect it to continue working without a hitch.

Never use chemical drain cleaners in a waste disposal unit. The chemicals are highly corrosive and may damage rubber or plastic parts.

Use Mother Nature's cure for your disposal: Every few months, throw half a lemon down the disposal, turn on the unit, and let it run for a minute or two. The lemon removes the build-up of residue on the interior of the disposal and deodorises the unit. You know the process is working by the fresh lemony smell.

If the instructions in your user's manual are no help, follow these steps to unblock a waste disposal unit:

1. **Turn off the electrical power switch.**

   This switch is located under the cabinet, near the disposal, or on a wall nearby. If you don't find a switch, go to the main power panel and turn off the breaker or remove the fuse that powers the disposal.

WARNING!

Never put your hand in the disposal. Remember that the switch may be defective, so keep your hand out of the disposal even when power to the machine is turned off.

2. **Take a look in the disposal.**

   Use a torch to shed some light on the problem – you may see a large object caught in the disposal.

3. **If an object caused the blockage, use a pair of pliers to reach into the disposal and remove it.**

4. **Wait 15 minutes for the disposal motor to cool.**

5. **Turn on the power and push the reset or overload protector button.**

   This button is located on the bottom side of the disposal.

If the disposal is still blocked, follow these steps:

1. **Turn off the power and insert a long dowel, the handle of a wooden spoon, or a broom handle – never your hand – into the drain opening.**

2. **Push the bottom end of the wooden probe against the blades in the unit, as shown in Figure 4-4, and rock it back and forth to free it.**

3. **When the blades move freely, wait 15 minutes for the motor to cool, turn on the power, and push the reset button.**

Some disposal models come with a large L-shaped hex wrench. If you have such a model, turn off the power, insert the hex wrench into the opening in the centre of the disposal's bottom, and turn the wrench back and forth until the blades are freed. Again, wait until the motor has cooled, press the reset button, and then try operating the disposal.

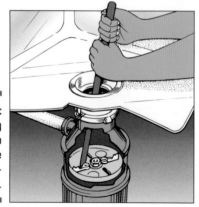

Figure 4-4:
Inserting a wooden dowel in the waste disposal unit.

Preventing bath and shower blockages

Bath and shower drains block up with soap scum and hair – not a pleasant sight. As a defensive measure, fit a strainer over the plughole to catch debris before it can enter and block the drain. Keep the strainer in place and clean it after each bath or shower. If you get into this habit (and teach your kids to do the same), the nasty build-up just can't occur.

You can find strainers in the plumbing section of your DIY centre. Measure the diameter of the drain to find one that fits and then simply place it in the plughole.

Cleaning and Adjusting a Drain Stopper

Older baths and basins have rubber plugs or stoppers to hold back the water. More modern ones might have a pop-up drain mechanism. Bathtubs have either the same type of pop-up stopper or a trip-lever (plunger-type) drain closure. When you're faced with a drain that won't hold water, you have to adjust the stopper. This section shows you how.

Trip-lever drain

A trip-lever drain system has a strainer over the drain opening and an internal plunger mechanism that closes the drain. The plug is operated by a lever located in the overflow plate at the front of the bath. Raise the lever and it lowers a plug into the pipe at the base of the bathtub, blocking the flow of water out of the bath. This plug may have a rubber seal on its base that can become old and cracked. Also, debris can get into the seat where the plunger rests, causing a slow leak.

Removing the plug, cleaning it, and adjusting the control mechanism cures most problems. Here's how:

1. **Remove the overflow cover plate.**

   The plate is held in place by a couple of screws. Remove the screws and pull out the linkage assembly, which is made up of the striker rod, middle link, and plug (see Figure 4-5).

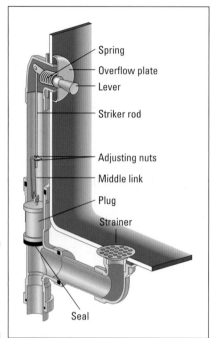

Figure 4-5:
The internal
parts of a
trip lever
drain.

Spring

Overflow plate

Lever

Striker rod

Adjusting nuts

Middle link

Plug

Strainer

Seal

2. **Clean any loose hair or build-up of soap scum from the linkage assembly.**

   The drain in your bath may not be exactly like the one illustrated in Figure 4-5, but it'll be similar.

3. **Before you reinstall the plug, inspect the rubber seal (if there is one) at the bottom of the plug. If the seal is cracked or broken, get a replacement from a DIY shop or plumber's merchant.**

4. **Replace the linkage assembly.**

   You may have to wiggle the plunger a bit to get it to fall back into the drain.

5. **Run some water into the bath.**

   If the bathtub drains but doesn't hold water, adjust the plug so that it falls deeper into the overflow passage. Remove the assembly, loosen the adjustment nuts, and lengthen the linkage controls. A little adjustment – 2 mm or so – is all that's needed.

6. **Reassemble the assembly and test again.**

   Additional adjustments may be necessary.

Pop-up drain

The pop-up drain assembly has a drain stopper in the opening. A slow-running drain can be the result of a pop-up that isn't opening fully. A leaky drain may be the result of a bad rubber seal on the pop-up assembly or incorrect adjustment of the control mechanism that connects the pop-up to the lever at the end of your bathtub, which prevents the pop-up from closing fully.

Removing the pop-up assembly, cleaning it, and adjusting the control mechanism cures most problems. Here's how:

1. **Remove the pop-up drain assembly by pulling it out of the drain (see Figure 4-6).**

   Grasp the stopper and wiggle it around a bit to get it out. The stopper and the rocker arm it's attached to will come completely out of the drain. If you see a blockage of hair or debris on the rocker arm, you may have to remove it before the stopper comes out of the drain.

2. **Remove the bath overflow cover plate by removing the screws and pulling out the assembly.**

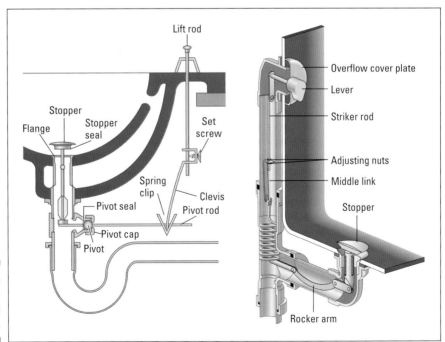

Figure 4-6:
A pop-up drain assembly.

3. **Clean the linkage assembly of any loose hair or build-up of soap scum.**

   This assembly is composed of the crank lever in the overflow cover plate, striker rod, middle link, and striker spring. The spring at the bottom of the control linkage is a magnet for hair build-up. Ugh!

4. **Inspect the rubber seal (if there is one) on the pop-up.** If the seal's cracked or broken, take the pop-up assembly to your local plumbing centre and purchase a replacement.

5. **Put the assembly back in its place.**

   You may have to wiggle the spring a bit to get it to fall back into the drain.

6. **Run some water into the bath.**

   If the bath doesn't hold water, adjust the pop-up so that it completely closes in the drain outlet. Remove the assembly, loosen the adjustment screw, and shorten the linkage controls. A little adjustment – 2 mm or so – is all that's needed.

7. **Reassemble the pop-up assembly and test again.**

   Additional adjustments may be necessary.

Chapter 5

Unblocking and Fixing a Toilet

. . . .

In This Chapter

▶ Diagnosing the cause of a toilet blockage

▶ Unclogging your toilet in a variety of ways

▶ Tackling a sticky siphon

▶ Fixing ball float valve problems

. . . .

*A*lthough clearing a blocked toilet isn't the most pleasant plumbing chore around the house, no utility is used more often than la toilette. Getting it flushing – fast – is a top priority.

Diagnosing the Problem (Yuck!)

Sometimes, you can see what's clogging the toilet, but sometimes, the source of the clog remains a mystery. In either case, the chore at hand is getting the toilet flowing freely again, and for that, you need to do a bit of detective work.

When you flush the toilet, which of these results do you see?

✔ **The water isn't swirling down as usual.** Consider yourself lucky; this is a sign of an easy-to-fix problem. The mechanism inside the toilet cistern may be clogged or stuck, so the cistern isn't filling with water. See the section 'Clearing the Main Pipe', later in this chapter, for a quick fix.

✔ **The water level goes down slowly and only weakly flushes the bowl.** This result usually indicates a partial block. Your toilet will probably clog completely the next time it's used, so get out the plunger.

✔ **The water level barely drops (if at all) and then begins to rise past the normal full bowl level.** This result is also an indicator of a partial block – one that may be located beyond the toilet.

✔ **The water continues to rise past the normal full bowl level until it overflows onto your bathroom floor.** Your toilet is blocked. Follow the instructions in the next section to clear the blockage.

Don't flush again if the bowl level rises past the normal height. You don't want to invite an overflow.

Clearing a Blocked Toilet

If your toilet plays any of the tricks mentioned in the preceding section, you have a blocked or partially blocked toilet bowl. Often, the clog is caused by a blockage in the trap – the curved passage inside the toilet bowl.

Don't attempt to unblock the toilet with a chemical drain cleaner. This process usually doesn't work and you end up having to plunge or auger through water that contains a strong chemical. Even if you don't use a chemical drain cleaner, be careful when you handle toilet water and waste – it's laced with bacteria. Wash the area, your hands, and your clothing thoroughly with a disinfectant soap.

Partial or total blockage of a toilet requires one of three solutions, covered in the following three sections.

Using a plunger

A ball or cup-type plunger is designed specifically for unblocking toilets. The rounded lower surface nests tightly in the bowl, giving the plunger great suction action to dislodge the blockage. With the plunger in place, push down gently and then pull it up quickly to create suction that pulls the blockage back a bit and dislodges it (see Figure 5-1).

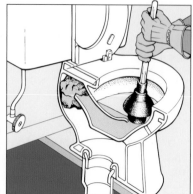

Figure 5-1:
Positioning the plunger.

Using a toilet plunger (as opposed to a sink-type plunger) keeps you from splashing as much water around, because the ball of the plunger covers the entire hole. If all you have on hand is a small, sink-type plunger, try using it – it can't hurt.

Using a toilet auger

If using a plunger doesn't work, try using a toilet auger, which is different from a snake or hand auger (see the following section, 'Using a snake'). A toilet auger is a short, hollow clean-out rod with a spring coil snake inside that has a hooked end. Attached to the coil is a crank handle that you turn – it's designed to fit into a toilet bowl and clean out a clogged toilet trap. See Figure 5-2.

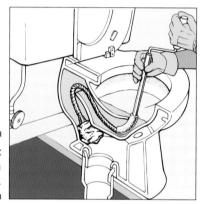

Figure 5-2:
Using a
toilet auger.

Follow these instructions:

1. **Pull the spring coil through the hollow handle until about a foot protrudes.**

2. **Insert the auger all the way in the bowl and push the spring coil back through the handle until it rounds the sharp bend in the base of the toilet trap.**

3. **Turn the crank while slowly pushing the flexible coil shaft through the hollow rod until it hits the blockage and pushes it through.**

Although the thought of hiring or buying a toilet auger may not thrill you, the idea seems amazingly wise when you're faced with a blocked-up toilet. Toilet augers are inexpensive, and they're particularly handy, because most toilet blockages occur in the trap – exactly where this tool delivers its punch. Buy one before you experience a problem and have to explain to your dinner guests that the bathroom's temporarily closed for repairs.

WARNING! If you can't get the toilet running freely with a toilet auger, don't flush the toilet, even if it seems to run a little. The water may be backing up in the soil pipe, which is the large-diameter pipe leading to the sewer or septic system (see the following section, 'Using a snake', to find out how to handle this). If the water backs up there, it can start running out of some of the ground-floor fixtures. Not a pretty picture.

Using a snake

If the toilet auger doesn't do the trick, you probably have a blockage somewhere farther down the line – past the toilet trap and beyond the reach of the toilet auger's coil. It's time to hire a snake. (See Chapter 4 for details on this tool.)

TIP Rent a snake that has a flexible shaft to bend past the tight curve in the toilet trap. The only thing worse than a clogged toilet is a clogged toilet with an auger stuck in the bowl; it's hard to explain to the blokes at the tool hire shop why your toilet is stuck on the end of their snake.

Follow these steps:

1. **Feed the flexible snake into the toilet until you feel it hit the blockage.**

2. **Pull the snake back a bit to dislodge the blockage.**

   The water level should go down, signalling that the clog is loose.

3. **Flush the toilet to push the blockage down the drain line and, hopefully, out to the sewer or septic system.**

   If the blockage is a nappy, you may have to pull the offending item all the way out of the toilet to clear the pipe.

REMEMBER The snake is a powerful tool – use it cautiously so that you don't damage the toilet or drainpipe by using too much force. If the coil becomes really hard to turn, back off a bit and pull it out of the toilet a few centimetres before attacking again. If you turn the auger too hard, you can kink the wire coil.

Singing the hard-water blues

Your toilet may flush slowly from a build-up of scale due to hard water in the high-pressure jet opening (hole) that's built into the trap of the bowl. This jet starts the siphoning action and swirling of water in the bowl, drawing waste down and out of the toilet. You can sometimes use a coat hanger to clear the hole, but if the toilet is too scaled or limed up, use spirit of salts (available at plumbers' merchants) in a very well ventilated room.

Clearing the Main Pipe

The main pipe, or sewer pipe, is the passageway for the waste that comes from the toilet and from the entire sink and bath traps. The pipe leads outside the house to the sewer or septic system. This section tells you how to clear a clog in that main pipe.

When the blockage is beyond the fixture

Sometimes, the clog is so far from the toilet or sink drain that you can't reach it with a snake. If you've fed the snake through the toilet or sink drain to its full length and still haven't reached the clog, your last resort before calling in the pros is to feed the snake through the main rodding eye in the sewer pipe that leads out of your house.

Removing the rodding eye cover

Although it sounds like an insult, the *sewer rodding eye* is a fitting with a removable cover usually located at the base of the main soil pipe (a large-diameter cast-iron, copper, or plastic pipe) where it enters the floor of the basement or takes a 90-degree turn to pass through the foundation wall. The rodding eye may also be located in the basement floor.

Plastic rodding eye covers usually come out easily, but removing a rodding eye cover from a cast-iron plumbing system can be a challenge.

To remove the rodding eye cover, gather up the following tools:

- Large pipe wrench
- Small can of penetrating oil, such as WD-40
- Hammer
- Cold chisel (a thick, short, hexagonal, steel bar tool)
- Bucket
- Work gloves
- Goggles

After you assemble your tools, follow these steps:

1. **Locate the rodding eye cover.**

   Look for a round cover with a square plug on it.

2. **With your work gloves on, try to open the rodding eye cover with a pipe wrench.**

   Place the wrench in the square tab located in the centre of the rodding eye cover and turn it counter-clockwise.

3. **If using a pipe wrench doesn't work, apply oil to the joint between the soil pipe and plug.**

   Allow the oil to work its way into the joint for 10 or 15 minutes and then give the pipe wrench another try. Doing so usually loosens a brass plug.

   If the plug isn't brass, it's probably rusted into place. To get the rodding eye cover open, you have to break it into pieces. This is standard practice with plumbers, but may seem a bit extreme. If you're not comfortable doing this, call a pro.

If you're up to the challenge of breaking up the rodding eye cover, follow these steps:

1. **Purchase a new plastic cover so that you can close up the opening after you break up the old cover.**

2. **With your goggles on, place the point of a chisel on the outer edge of the rodding eye cover and use a hammer to tap the chisel in a counter-clockwise direction (see Figure 5-3).**

   Doing so usually loosens the cover. If it doesn't, proceed to Step 3.

3. **Break off the square tab in the centre and then smash the cover into smaller parts with your hammer.**

   Keep in mind that water may be standing in the pipe, just waiting to come gushing out when you crack the plug. Use a bucket to catch any draining water.

Figure 5-3:
Removing the rodding eye cover with a hammer and chisel.

Using a snake to clear the main pipe

After you get the rodding eye open, you can push a snake into the pipe. Follow these steps:

1. **Push the snake into the rodding eye and push it down into the pipe as far as it will go.**

2. **When you reach the blockage, keep turning the snake, working it back and forth to loosen the clog (see Figure 5-4).**

3. **Run some water through the pipe from a nearby sink.**

   If the water doesn't back up from the rodding eye, you've cleared the blockage. If the clog isn't clear, see the following section.

4. **Replace the rodding eye cover and run hot water into the pipe from a nearby sink for several minutes.**

   When you flush the toilet, everything should run okay.

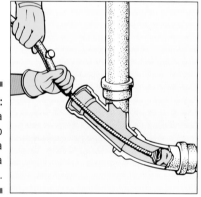

Figure 5-4:
Using a snake to loosen a clog in a pipe.

Still blocked? Call a plumber

Some blockages are so far down the pipe that your snake can't reach them. If a tree root or some other tough object has caused the blockage, your little snake won't make a dent. In either case, you could rent a power auger from a tool hire centre, but we don't recommend it. Power augers are difficult to operate and can be dangerous if the end of the steel coil gets lodged in the sewer. This type of machine has changeable cutter heads that are designed to cut roots or auger through tough clogs. If these heads jam and the steel coil kinks or breaks, you can get seriously hurt. You've done the hard part by removing the rodding eye cover and identifying the problem, but it's time for you to call for help.

Nice to Meet Loo: Fixing Your Toilet's Parts

If each flush doesn't end with a gurgle but instead continues with a hissing sound, with water running into the toilet bowl, you have a *run-on toilet*. You can fix this plumbing problem yourself. The mechanism inside the cistern may look complicated, but it really isn't.

The first thing that you need to do is take the top off the toilet cistern and familiarise yourself with the major parts. As with almost every plumbing fixture, someone is always coming up with a better design, so, over time, many different types of valves and flushing mechanisms have developed. They all accomplish the same tasks, though.

Here's a rundown of what happens when you push that flush lever:

1. **The flush handle lifts a piston inside the siphon that's located in the centre of the toilet cistern.**

   When the piston lifts, it starts water flowing through the siphon, and the contents of the cistern flow into the toilet.

2. **As the cistern empties, the large ball attached to the end of a long rod, called a *ball float*, falls with the water level in the tank.**

3. **At the other end of the ball float rod is the valve (often called the *ballcock*), which opens as the ball float moves down.**

   Water begins to flow into the cistern as the valve opens.

4. **When the cistern is almost empty, the piston falls back down the siphon, stopping the flow of water out of the tank.**

5. **When the flow has stopped, the cistern begins to fill.**

   In some models of toilet, the ballcock also directs water into an overflow tube that drains into the toilet bowl to ensure that the bowl fills with water.

6. **As the cistern fills, the ball float rises with the water level until it gets to a predetermined position and closes the ballcock, stopping the inflow of water.**

   The toilet is now ready for another flush. As long as nothing is leaking, no more water is used until the flush lever is pushed again.

An overflowing toilet is usually caused by a problem with the siphon or the ball float valve. To find the source of the trouble, remove the toilet cistern top and place it in a safe location. Then push the flush lever and watch what happens. Don't worry about the water in the toilet cistern – it's clean. You should be able to see what the problem is.

Solving Ball Float Valve Problems

A ball float valve that doesn't close completely is another possible cause of a leaking toilet. A misadjusted or damaged ball float valve is usually the cause of water dribbling into the toilet cistern, running out the overflow tube into the toilet bowl, and then going down the drain. Older toilet cisterns have overflow pipes that poke through an outside wall, so when the ball float valve doesn't shut off properly, water from the overflow will drip onto the ground outside the house.

To determine whether your problem is with the ball float or valve, look into the cistern and note whether the ball float is actually floating. If the ball float is partially submerged, you should replace it. If the ball float is floating, reach into the cistern and lift it up. The water should stop. If the water does stop, follow the ball float adjustment instructions in the following section. If the water continues to flow even though you're pulling up on the ball float, the problem is in the ballcock valve (see the next section, 'Addressing Ballcock Problems').

Work through these steps to see how to replace and adjust the ball float:

1. **Unscrew the damaged ball float from the rod by turning it counter-clockwise.**

2. **Take it to your DIY or hardware shop and purchase a replacement ball float.**

3. **Replace the ball float by threading it onto the end of the rod.**

   Turn it clockwise as you tighten it.

4. **If the water in the tank continues to run but the ball float is floating, lift up on the ball until the water stops.**

   Note the position and bend the metal rod down, lowering the ball float slightly and creating more pressure to close the valve as the water rises (see Figure 5-5). More modern ball float mechanisms have a plastic rod, which should not be bent. With these mechanisms, the adjustment is made by turning a plastic screw at the valve end of the rod to raise or lower the ball float. After bending the arm slightly, or tightening the plastic screw, release the ball and check for running water. Repeat the process, lowering the ball float, until the flow stops. Flush the toilet and check for leaking.

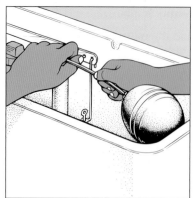

Figure 5-5:
To adjust the ball float, grasp the rod close to the ballcock valve with one hand and bend the end with the floatball down.

Addressing Ballcock Problems

No sniggering at the back there. A ballcock that keeps on leaking even after you adjust the ball float probably has some sediment in the valve body or is just worn out. Fixing a clogged ballcock isn't a project that you should undertake. With many designs that all require special parts, you may spend the rest of your life in a plumbing suppliers. A plumber can tackle this job and probably has or can get the parts, but he or she will most likely recommend that you replace the ballcock.

Now, swapping an old ballcock for a new one is definitely a project that you can tackle. Here are the general steps you take to replace a ballcock:

1. **Turn the water off below the toilet.**

   Flush the unit to drain the tank and then sponge out the remaining water from the bottom of the tank.

2. **Loosen the nuts securing the riser tube and remove it.**

   The *riser tube* is located under the toilet tank. It leads from the angle stop coming out of the wall up to the base of the ballcock valve coming out of the bottom of the toilet tank. Turn off the water before you try to remove this tube, or you'll get wet!

3. **Loosen the setscrew that holds the floatball rod in place on the top of the ballcock valve and then remove the ball float rod from the ballcock assembly and set it aside.**

4. **Loosen the large nut on the underside (or side) of the toilet cistern that holds the ballcock assembly in place.**

   You may need a helper to hold the ballcock inside the cistern to keep it from turning as you loosen this nut.

5. **Pull the ballcock out of the toilet, take it with you to a DIY centre, and purchase a replacement.**

   Also purchase a new flexible plastic riser tube in case the distance between the bottom of the new ballcock assembly and the stop valve has changed.

6. **Insert the replacement ballcock in the opening on the bottom of the toilet cistern. Thread on the retaining nut from underneath the tank, as shown in Figure 5-6.**

   Follow the manufacturer's installation instructions. Don't overtighten.

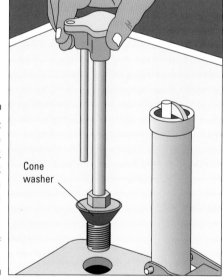

Figure 5-6: Insert the ballcock into the tank and then thread on the retaining nut from the underside of the tank.

Cone washer

7. **Reinstall the riser tube between the stop valve and the new ballcock.**

8. **Reinstall the floatball arm if the ballcock you purchased requires one.**

   You'll probably need to clip the bowl refill tube onto the overflow tube so that the refill tube is inside the overflow tube.

9. **Turn on the water and adjust the floatball so that the water fills to about 40 mm below the top of the overflow pipe.**

   If the water level in the tank gets too high, the excess water runs out of the tube and into the toilet bowl.

10. **Flush the toilet to test your handiwork.**

    You may have to make some slight adjustments to the ball float to get the tank to fill.

Chapter 6

Fixing a Dripping Tap

. . . .

In This Chapter

▶ Putting an end to a compression tap or washerless tap leak

▶ Repairing a ball-type, cartridge-type, or ceramic disk-type tap

▶ Fixing a leaky sink sprayer

. . . .

*S*topping a leaking tap is easy to do. The challenge is to determine what type of tap you have. After you know that detail and have a replacement or the material to stop the leak, there isn't much to it.

Before you begin to repair a leak for any type of tap, turn off the hot- and cold-water shutoff valves under the sink by turning them clockwise.

Stopping a Compression Tap Leak

A compression tap is so called because a rubber washer, actually made from *neoprene* (a form of synthetic rubber), is forced against a metal seat to choke off the water flow. As you turn the handle, the washer is compressed against the valve seat. If the washer or valve seat becomes damaged, a seal isn't made, and the tap leaks.

If your compression tap is dripping, the rubber washer has most likely worn away. Less common is a worn valve seat that the washer presses against when it's closed. The metal (usually brass) valve seat can become damaged if you don't change the washer before it's too worn – metal then grinds against metal and damages the seat. Hard foreign matter can also become trapped between the valve seat and the washer. If this happens, closing and opening the tap grinds the particles inside, damaging it beyond a simple washer replacement.

Replacing a worn washer

To replace a worn washer, follow these steps, using Figure 6-1 as a guide:

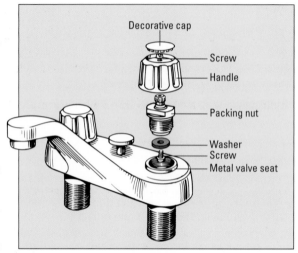

Decorative cap

Screw

Handle

Packing nut

Washer
Screw
Metal valve seat

Figure 6-1:
The major
parts of
a tap.

1. **Turn off the water to the tap.**

2. **Remove the decorative cap, if there is one, on top of the tap handle.**

   Depending on its design, you pull it up or unscrew it.

3. **Unscrew or pull off the handle and remove it.**

   If the handle sticks, gently nudge it up with a screwdriver. Wrap the screwdriver edge with a rag to prevent marring the finish.

4. **Remove the cover over the valve, called an *escutcheon*, if there is one.**

   Some types unscrew, while others are held in place by setscrews. Inspect the escutcheon to figure out how to remove it.

5. **Unscrew the packing nut that holds the body of the valve in place, turning it counter-clockwise.**

   The valve stem should come out of the base of the valve. You may have to twist the valve-stem body several turns after you loosen the packing nut and the valve stem. If it's hard to unscrew, put the handle back on the stem and give it a twist. The stem then comes out of the valve.

6. **Unscrew the retaining screw and remove the washer.**

On the other end of the stem is a rubber washer that's held in place by a screw. These valve washers come in many shapes and sizes, so take the valve stem to the plumbing department of your local hardware shop or DIY centre and get a washer that matches the old one. This task may be more difficult than it sounds, because the old washer is usually damaged and deformed. The best clue to the original shape of the washer is to peer into the valve body and take a look at the metal opening that the washer presses against – the *valve seat*. If the side of the valve seat is angled, replace the washer with a cone shape; if the valve seat is flat, get a replacement washer that's flat.

7. **Replace the old washer with the new one and reassemble the tap.**

Replacing the valve seat

If the tap still leaks after reassembly, the seat may be damaged. To replace a damaged valve seat, follow these steps:

1. **Disassemble the unit.**

See the preceding 'Replacing a worn washer' section for instructions.

2. **While the stem is out, look into the valve body and inspect the tap seat.**

Look for a brass insert inside the valve body that the rubber washer presses against to stop the flow of water. If this seat is rough, it will tear up the new washer and the valve will begin to leak again. You should replace a rough valve seat. If the tap doesn't have replaceable valve seats, you can grind the seat smooth with a valve seat grinder.

3. **If the valve has a removable seat, remove it.**

If the seat has a hexagonal or grooved opening in its centre, remove the seat with a screwdriver or an Allen key.

If the seat isn't removable (it will have a round hole), you have a really old tap. You can grind it smooth with a seat-grinding tool, found in the plumbing departments of hardware shops and DIY centres and shown in Figure 6-2. The tool, also known as a *tap seat reamer*, comes with instructions and is easy to use. The tool fits over the valve seat (where the washer usually rests) and grinds the seat. The idea is to reshape the damaged seat to accept the new washer. When using this tool, take care to keep it perfectly aligned.

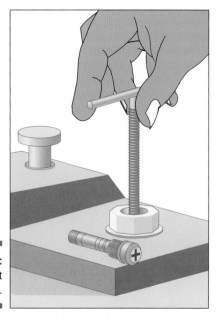

Figure 6-2:
A tap seat
reamer.

4. **Take your old tap to a well-stocked plumbing department or supplier, along with the tap stem, and purchase the correct replacement.**

   Tap seats come in many sizes and with many different thread patterns – a perfect match is critical.

5. **Replace the valve seat, being careful not to cross-thread the connection.**

6. **Coat the washer and all moving parts – including the handle stem – with heatproof grease.**

   This type of grease doesn't break down in hot water and keeps the stem and tap working smoothly for a long time.

7. **Replace the stem washer and packing as necessary.**

8. **Reassemble the tap in the reverse order that you removed it.**

Stopping a leak from a tap handle

If you have a leaky handle rather than a drippy tap, the water is leaking past the stem packing – see Figure 6-3 – or the washer. Older taps have a string-like substance wrapped around the handle stem to hold the water back. The packing eventually wears, and water can sneak between the stem and the packing. Newer taps stop the water leak with an o-ring or a washer.

Figure 6-3:
Replace the packing around the valve stem and retighten the packing washer.

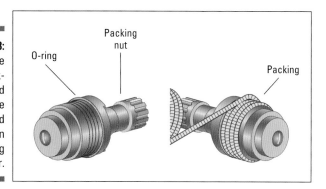

Older taps with packing are more likely to leak. Here's how to fix them:

1. **Turn off the water to the tap.**

2. **Remove the handle from the shaft.**

3. **Tighten the packing nut.**

   Turn it clockwise about ½ turn. This may be all that's necessary to stop the leak.

4. **If tightening the packing nut doesn't work, loosen the packing nut with slip-joint pliers or a wrench and then unscrew the nut by hand and remove it.**

5. **Remove the old packing from around the stem.**

6. **Replace the old packing with new packing.**

   You can find new packing in the plumbing departments of hardware shops and DIY centres.

7. **Reassemble the tap.**

Keep a supply of various sized o-rings, packing washers, packing rope, and washers handy to save you a trip to the shop at the first sign of a leak.

Stopping a Washerless Tap Leak

The new variety of washerless tap is easier to fix than a compression tap. The hardest part of this project is figuring out what type of washerless tap you have. The three sections that follow explain how to fix the three most common types of washerless taps currently on the market.

The best tip-off as to what type of tap you have is how the handle that controls the water moves:

- ✔ If the control handle moves all around in an arc (generally up and down to control the water flow and sideways to control temperature), is attached to a domelike top of the tap, and has a small setscrew in the base of the control handle, you have a **ball-type tap**.

- ✔ If the handle moves directly up and down to control the water flow and directly right or left to control the temperature (but not in an arc like the ball-type), you have either a **cartridge-type tap** or a **ceramic disk-type tap**.

If you can find the user's manual that came with the tap (a small miracle!), you may find the manufacturer's name and model number. Most manufacturers sell repair kits, which DIY centres and large hardware shops usually stock. These kits have all the necessary parts, including any special tools needed to take the tap apart and repair it.

Ball-type tap

Follow these steps to fix a single-handle ball-type tap, shown in Figure 6-4.

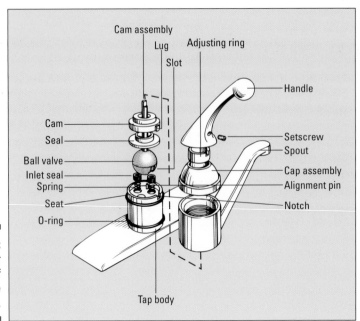

Figure 6-4:
The inner workings of a ball-type tap.

1. **Turn off the water to the tap (see Chapter 1).**

2. **Remove the handle.**

   Loosen the setscrew that secures the handle to the shaft coming out of the ball valve. The screw head is on the underside of the lever. This setscrew requires an *Allen key* (an L-shaped hex wrench that fits into the recessed socket in the head of the setscrew) to loosen.

3. **Remove the ball valve and spout.**

   Wrap tape around the jaws of your wrench or slip-joint pliers to protect the valve parts. Loosen the cap assembly (the dome-shaped ring at the top of the tap) by turning the adjusting screw counter-clockwise. Grab the shaft to which the handle was attached, move it back and forth to loosen the ball valve assembly, and then pull it straight up and out of the tap body.

4. **Replace the valve seats and o-rings.**

   When you look inside the tap body, you see the valve seats and rubber o-rings. Behind them are springs. Remove the seats, o-rings, and springs from the tap body and take them to a hardware shop or DIY centre to get the correct repair kit.

5. **Replace the parts and reassemble the tap in the reverse order that you took it apart (or follow the directions in the repair kit).**

   Make sure to reinstall the ball in the same position from which you removed it.

6. **Turn the water back on to test the tap.**

7. **If the tap leaks around the handle or the spout when the water is running, turn off the water and tighten the adjusting ring.**

   Under the handle is an adjusting ring that screws into the valve body. Slots in the top edge of the ring enable you to insert the adjusting tool into the ring and turn it. If you can't find the adjusting tool, use a large screwdriver or slip-joint pliers to turn the ring clockwise to tighten it. Unless the ring is very loose, tighten it only about ⅛ turn.

8. **Turn on the water and slip the handle back onto the control ball's shaft.**

   Adjust the ring so that the leak around the ball shaft stops but the ball can be easily adjusted.

   If you can't get the leak to stop, the seal under the adjusting ring is bad and you should replace it.

9. **Tighten the setscrew to secure the handle.**

Cartridge-type tap

Follow these steps to fix a single-handle cartridge-type tap, shown in Figure 6-5:

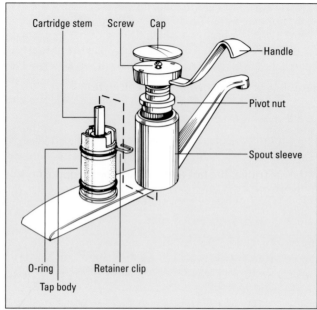

Figure 6-5:
The main
parts of a
cartridge-
type tap.

1. **Turn off the water to the tap (see Chapter 1).**

2. **Remove the handle.**

   Remove the cover on the top of the handle to expose the screw that
   holds the handle to the valve stem. Pop off the cover by placing the
   tip of a screwdriver between the cover and the handle housing and
   prying up. To remove the handle, turn the screw in the centre of the
   cap counter-clockwise; remove it and then pull the handle up and off
   the valve assembly. These actions expose the valve stem coming out
   of the valve cartridge.

3. **If your tap has a movable spout, remove the pivot nut.**

   Use an adjustable wrench or slip-joint pliers to loosen (turning counter-
   clockwise) to remove the pivot nut at the top of the tap body. This nut
   holds the spout sleeve in place and prevents water from coming out the
   top of the tap.

4. **Remove the spout assembly by twisting it back and forth as you pull up.**

5. **Remove the cartridge clip and replace the cartridge.**

   To remove the cartridge, you have to pull out the small U-shaped clip
   that holds the valve cartridge in the tap body. Pry the clip loose by placing the tip of your screwdriver between the tap body and the U-section
   of the clip.

Twist the screwdriver, and the clip comes out. Grab the clip with your pliers and remove it. Pull up on the cartridge stem with a twisting motion. If it doesn't twist out easily, reinstall the handle so that you can get a good grip on the shaft to pull the cartridge out. Take the old cartridge to your hardware shop or DIY centre and purchase a replacement kit.

6. **Reassemble the tap according to the directions.**

Make sure you replace the cartridge in the correct position – the valve body may have a notch that the cartridge fits into. How the cartridge is inserted into the valve body determines which side the hot and cold water is on. Usually you move the lever right for cold and left for hot. If you reverse the position of the cartridge, the hot and cold will be on opposite sides. If this reversal happens, take the tap apart and reverse the cartridge position.

Ceramic disk-type tap

A ceramic disk-type tap is reliable and usually doesn't require much maintenance. If you do need to repair one, however, these taps can be a bit tricky to take apart. Older models are held together by screws underneath the tap, so if you can't figure out how to get the handle off, look under the sink, and you should see a couple of brass screws. Loosen these screws and the whole cover and handle will come off the tap, revealing the valve cartridge – see Figure 6-6.

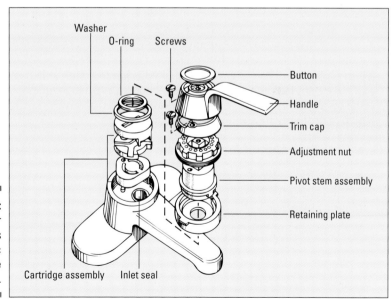

Figure 6-6:
The inner mechanics of a ceramic disk-type tap.

1. **Turn off the water to the tap.**

2. **Remove the handle.**

   Lift the handle to its highest position to expose the setscrew holding it in place. Use an Allen key or a screwdriver to turn the setscrew counter-clockwise and then lift off the handle.

3. **With the handle off, pull the decorative trim cap up and off the cartridge body.**

4. **Remove the valve seals and cartridge assembly.**

   Loosen the two screws on the top of the valve cartridge and lift the assembly off the tap body.

5. **Replace the rubber seals.**

   You can find several rubber seals under the cartridge – replacing them stops most leaks. If you replace these seals and the tap still leaks, the valve cartridge, which contains the ceramic disks, is worn and must be replaced.

6. **Take the cartridge assembly to your local hardware shop or DIY centre and purchase a replacement kit.**

7. **Install the new cartridge according to the instructions in the kit.**

   The kit will contain new o-rings to seal around the tap body. It's worth replacing these o-rings even if the old ones look like they're in good shape.

Fixing a Dish Sprayer

If you notice that the water flow out of your kitchen sink's dish sprayer (if you have one) isn't what it used to be, you can't use it as an excuse not to wash up any more! Fixing it is easy. Here's how to clean the spray head, which is probably blocked up (see Figure 6-7):

1. **Turn the water off from under the sink.**

2. **Remove the spray head.**

   Untwisting the head disassembles some models; a screw holds other types together.

3. **Clean out any blockage in the small holes of the spray head.**

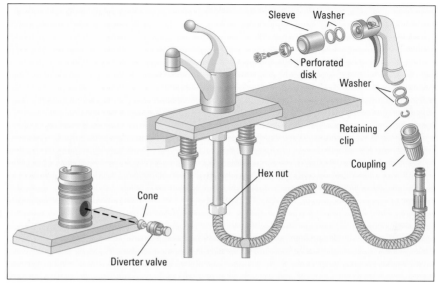

Figure 6-7:
A dish
sprayer.

4. **Check the spray hose for kinks.**

   Look under the sink and check the condition of the spray hose. It may become entangled with objects stored under the sink, restricting the water flow. Replace a badly kinked hose. You can purchase replacement sprayer assemblies at most DIY centres, but take the hose and spray head with you when you shop for a replacement: Turn off the water supply and then unscrew the hose from the base of the tap.

5. **Check the diverter valve.**

   If the spray head and hose look okay, a malfunctioning diverter valve may be the problem. A *diverter valve* is a simple device that's activated by water pressure. When the sprayer is off, the water is diverted to the spout. When you press the sprayer trigger, the water pressure in the hose drops, and the valve closes off the water flow to the spout and directs water to the sprayer. To do so, it must move freely. A sure sign of a bad diverter valve is that water flows from both the tap and the dish sprayer at the same time. This valve is located in the base of the tap behind the swivel spout, if one exists. Refer to Figure 6-7 for the location of this part. To service it, make sure that the valve moves freely and that all the rubber parts are in good shape. Replacement parts are available, including the entire spray head.

6. **Reassemble the sprayer.**

Index

FOR DUMMIES®

Making Everything Easier! ™

UK editions

BUSINESS

978-0-470-74490-1

978-0-470-74381-2

978-0-470-71382-2

Anger Management For Dummies
978-0-470-68216-6

Boosting Self-Esteem For Dummies
978-0-470-74193-1

British Sign Language
For Dummies
978-0-470-69477-0

Business NLP For Dummies
978-0-470-69757-3

Cricket For Dummies
978-0-470-03454-5

CVs For Dummies, 2nd Edition
978-0-470-74491-8

Divorce For Dummies, 2nd Edition
978-0-470-74128-3

Emotional Freedom Technique
For Dummies
978-0-470-75876-2

Emotional Healing For Dummies
978-0-470-74764-3

English Grammar For Dummies
978-0-470-05752-0

Flirting For Dummies
978-0-470-74259-4

IBS For Dummies
978-0-470-51737-6

Improving Your Relationship For
Dummies
978-0-470-68472-6

Lean Six Sigma For Dummies
978-0-470-75626-3

Life Coaching For Dummies,
2nd Edition
978-0-470-66554-1

REFERENCE

978-0-470-68637-9

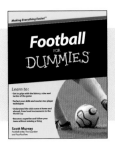
978-0-470-68837-3

978-0-470-74535-9

HOBBIES

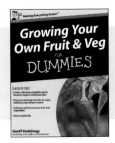
978-0-470-69960-7

978-0-470-68641-6

978-0-470-68178-7

**Available wherever books are sold. For more information or to order direct go to
www.wiley.com or call +44 (0) 1243 843291**

FOR DUMMIES®

A world of resources to help you grow

UK editions

SELF-HELP

978-0-470-66541-1

978-0-470-66543-5

978-0-470-66086-7

STUDENTS

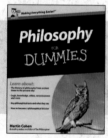
978-0-470-68820-5

978-0-470-74711-7

978-0-470-74290-7

HISTORY

978-0-470-99468-9

978-0-470-74783-4

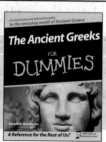
978-0-470-98787-2

Origami Kit For Dummies
978-0-470-75857-1

Overcoming Depression For Dummies
978-0-470-69430-5

Positive Psychology For Dummies
978-0-470-72136-0

PRINCE2 For Dummies, 2009 Edition
978-0-470-71025-8

Psychometric Tests For Dummies
978-0-470-75366-8

Raising Happy Children
For Dummies
978-0-470-05978-4

Reading the Financial Pages
For Dummies
978-0-470-71432-4

Sage 50 Accounts For Dummies
978-0-470-71558-1

Self-Hypnosis For Dummies
978-0-470-66073-7

Starting a Business For Dummies,
2nd Edition
978-0-470-51806-9

Study Skills For Dummies
978-0-470-74047-7

Teaching English as a Foreign
Language For Dummies
978-0-470-74576-2

Teaching Skills For Dummies
978-0-470-74084-2

Time Management For Dummies
978-0-470-77765-7

Work-Life Balance For Dummies
978-0-470-71380-8

**Available wherever books are sold. For more information or to order direct go to www.wiley.com
or call +44 (0) 1243 843291**

FOR DUMMIES®

The easy way to get more done and have more fun

LANGUAGES

978-0-470-68815-1
UK Edition

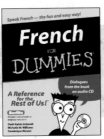

978-0-7645-5193-2

978-0-471-77270-5

MUSIC

978-0-470-48133-2

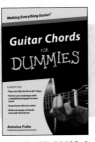

978-0-470-66603-6
Lay-flat, UK Edition

978-0-470-66372-1
UK Edition

SCIENCE & MATHS

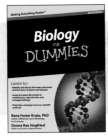

978-0-470-59875-7

978-0-470-55964-2

978-0-470-55174-5

Art For Dummies
978-0-7645-5104-8

Bass Guitar For Dummies, 2nd Edition
978-0-470-53961-3

Christianity For Dummies
978-0-7645-4482-8

Criminology For Dummies
978-0-470-39696-4

Forensics For Dummies
978-0-7645-5580-0

German For Dummies
978-0-7645-5195-6

Hobby Farming For Dummies
978-0-470-28172-7

Index Investing For Dummies
978-0-470-29406-2

Knitting For Dummies, 2nd Edition
978-0-470-28747-7

Music Theory For Dummies
978-0-7645-7838-0

Piano For Dummies, 2nd Edition
978-0-470-49644-2

Physics For Dummies
978-0-7645-5433-9

Schizophrenia For Dummies
978-0-470-25927-6

Sex For Dummies, 3rd Edition
978-0-470-04523-7

Sherlock Holmes For Dummies
978-0-470-48444-9

Solar Power Your Home
For Dummies, 2nd Edition
978-0-470-59678-4

The Koran For Dummies
978-0-7645-5581-7

Wine All-in-One For Dummies
978-0-470-47626-0

Yoga For Dummies, 2nd Edition
978-0-470-50202-0

**Available wherever books are sold. For more information or to order direct go to www.wiley.com
or call +44 (0) 1243 843291**

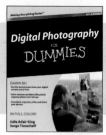

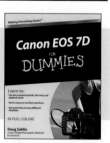

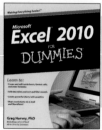